American Women Writers and the Work of History

American Women Writers and the Work of History, 1790–1860

NINA BAYM

Rutgers University Press
NEW BRUNSWICK, NEW JERSEY

Library of Congress Cataloging-in-Publication Data

Baym, Nina.
     American women writers and the work of history, 1790–1860 / by
Nina Baym
        p.   cm.
     Includes bibliographical references (p.   ) and index.
     ISBN 0-8135-2142-4 (cloth)—ISBN 0-8135-2143-2 (pbk.)
     1. Historical fiction, American—Women authors—History and
criticism.   2. American prose literature—Women authors—History and
criticism.   3. American prose literature—19th century—History and
criticism.   4. Women and literature—United States—History—19th
century.   5. Historiography—United States—History—19th century.
6. Women historians—United States.   I. Title.
PS374.H5B39   1995
813'.081099287—dc20
                                                                94-11283
                                                                CIP

British Cataloging-in-Publication information available

Copyright © 1995 by Nina Baym
Published by Rutgers University Press, New Brunswick, New Jersey
Manufactured in the United States of America

To Jack, a friend for all seasons

Contents

Acknowledgments

I received an associateship in the Center for Advanced Study at the University of Illinois at Urbana when I began the research on this project, and an Arnold O. Beckmann Scholar's award from the campus Research Board when I began to draft the book. These provided released time at crucial points, and I am grateful. The Research Board also supported a research assistant to compile the book's biographical appendix.

I could not have done this work without the University of Illinois's superb library, including its stacks, rare-book room, newspaper, and microform collections; I profited from help by research librarians and the unfailingly patient interlibrary loan staff.

Many libraries around the country graciously loaned books or provided photocopies of rare materials, and I thank them all: the Buffalo and Erie County Public Library; Cleveland Public Library; Library of Congress; Illinois Consortium of Research Libraries; Illinois State Historical Library; New York State Library; St. Louis Public Library; the State Historical Library of Wisconsin; also the libraries of Antioch College; the Art Institute of Chicago; Auburn University; Ball State University; Benedictine College; Brown University; University of California, Berkeley; Calvin College; Case Western Reserve University; Cornell University; Dartmouth College; University of Denver; University of Detroit; Dickinson College; Earlham College; East Tennessee State University; Eastern Illinois University; Emory University; Fort Hays State University; Garrett Theological Seminary; University of Georgia; Hamilton College; Harvard University; Haverford College; Hillsdale College; University of Illinois, Chicago; Illinois State University; University of Iowa; Kent State University; University of Kentucky; University of Michigan; Michigan State University; Middlebury College; University of Minnesota; State University of New York, Buffalo; State University of New York, Stonybrook; University of North Carolina, Chapel Hill; Northeastern University (Illinois); Northern Illinois University; University of Notre Dame; Oberlin

College; The Ohio State University; University of Pennsylvania; The Pennsylvania State University; Pittsburgh Theological Seminary; University of Pittsburgh; Princeton University; Quincy College; Sangamon State College; Southern Illinois University, Carbondale; Southern Illinois University, Edwardsville; Stanford University; University of Toledo; Tulane University; University of Virginia; Wabash College; University of Washington; Western Illinois University; University of Wisconsin, Parkside. Staff at the American Antiquarian Society, the Maine Historical Association, and the New York Public Library also responded to inquiries.

Friends, colleagues, and family (parents, spouse, grown-up children) have listened to my ideas and helped me clarify them. For responses to specific queries and for suggestions about particular writers I thank Liz Bohls, Lawrence Buell, Scott Casper, Cyndy Conger, Mary De Jong, Eric Gardner, Anthony Harding, Carol Farley Kessler, Janet Lyon, Ruth Perry, and Sandra Zagarell. The cordial interest of members of the Belt family, direct descendants of Emma Willard, is also gratefully acknowledged. Audiences at the American Antiquarian Society, Amherst College, Harvard University, Texas A&M University, Western Illinois University, and various panels at conventions of the Modern Language Association and American Studies Association helped me better understand and formulate some of the implications of my own work.

Thanks to Patricia Okker, who worked through several decades of *Godey's Lady's Book* and *Peterson's* for references to history. And I note with special appreciation Eric Gardner's patience and skill in piecing together the brief biographical notes from a range of diverse sources.

x

American Women Writers and the Work of History

Introduction

THE SUBJECT OF THIS BOOK is the extensive writing about history published by many American women between the founding of the nation and the onset of the Civil War. Such writing appeared in various genres and contexts, aiming at various audiences, serving diverse purposes, and driven by multiple motives. Always, however, the authors were demolishing whatever imaginative and intellectual boundaries their culture may have been trying to maintain between domestic and public worlds. They were claiming on behalf of all women the rights to know and opine on the world outside the home, as well as to circulate their knowledge and opinions among the public. Their work both registered and significantly shaped the enormous general interest in history characteristic of the antebellum period. It contributed to the vital intellectual tasks of forging and publicizing national identity by placing the new nation in world history and giving it a history of its own.

Although history is my general subject, I approach it as a literary scholar and critic interested in the genesis and cultural meanings of writing, especially published writing, and especially as connected to gender. Because feminist-inspired searches for earlier women's writing have focused until recently on woman-centered domestic fictions and on expressions of the hidden life, much of the material I consider here is unfamiliar even to scholars. The work of one or another of the better-known writers—Catharine Sedgwick, Lydia Maria Child, Harriet Beecher Stowe—may be known to specialists, but the material overall has never been brought together for systematic canvass, and since there is so much more of it than one could have imagined, its significance as an accepted kind of woman's work has not been—could not have been—recognized. Even my most knowledgeable colleagues supposed that I would find at most a few dozen women writing history before the Civil War; instead, I have turned up more than 150 women who produced historical writing in over 350 different works (with "work" usually defined as a book, making a poetry collection equal

1

to one "work" even when several poems in it are historical). I have tried at least to name most of them in the following pages, and I provide a full list of primary works along with biographical notes to facilitate further exploration.

Scholars are increasingly calling attention to writings by antebellum women that do not fit a conventional understanding of their domestic role. (Whether that role contained a reservoir of countercultural force or was necessarily cooperative with the larger culture is a different matter.) As early as 1970 Michael Davitt Bell discussed several historical novels by women in *Hawthorne and the Historical Romance of New England*. Emily Watts, although clearly preferring antebellum women's domestic and personal lyrics to their public poetry, noted many examples of the latter in her 1977 *Poetry of American Women from 1632 to 1945*. In 1981 Jane Tompkins's essay on *Uncle Tom's Cabin* (reprinted in her 1985 *Sensational Designs*) argued influentially that this wildly popular novel offered domestic ideology as serious public policy; I had suggested something similar for the novelistic subgenre that I called "woman's fiction" in my 1978 book of that name. Lawrence Buell's 1986 *New England Literary Culture* named many women writers who wrote nondomestically; he especially noted Harriet Beecher Stowe's *The Minister's Wooing* and Eliza Buckminster Lee's joint memoir of her father and brother. Buell also reported that more women than men in nineteenth-century New England defined themselves as literary professionals. Carolyn Karcher's 1986 introduction to Lydia Maria Child's historical novel *Hobomok*, and Mary Kelley's 1987 introduction to Catharine Maria Sedgwick's historical novel *Hope Leslie*, view these texts as commentaries on current events and as informed challenges to received historiography.

In her 1989 *Women and Sisters: The Antislavery Feminists in American Culture*, Jean Fagan Yellin points to women's polemical abolitionist writings, especially those by Child. As the title of their 1990 book indicates, *Declarations of Independence: Women and Political Power in Nineteenth-Century American Fiction* by Barbara Bardes and Suzanne Gossett interprets a number of women's novels as documents agitating for women's increased public presence. Sandra Zagarell has argued that women's sketches of community forward a counterpolitical ideal to Jacksonian individualism; Nancy Walker has described women's humorous writings; Joyce Warren's biography of Fanny Fern calls attention to women's journalism. Louisa May Alcott's anonymous gothic thrillers have been located and reprinted; Mercy Otis Warren's thousand-page history of the American Revolution has been reissued. Margaret Fuller's writings from transcendental theorizing to overseas reportage have been celebrated by Robert N. Hudspeth, Christina Zwarg, Larry Reynolds, Elaine Showalter, and Charles Capper, among others. My 1992 collection *Feminism and American Liter-*

ary History has essays on the nondomestic writings of Emma Willard, Sarah Hale, Lydia Sigourney, and Elizabeth Peabody; it also looks briefly at history written by Mercy Otis Warren, Hannah Adams, and Deborah Norris Logan.

It becomes ever more evident, then, that the literary profession, which opened to women early in the nation's history—indeed, it might be more accurate to say that the profession was opened *by* them—supported a very wide range of female endeavor. The profession of course was not a fixed, prior institution or a single kind of practice, but a dynamic and unstable collection of activities affected by numerous developments in literacy and leisure; in technologies of print, paper, transportation, and home furnishings; in aggregations of population and capital; and so on. These developments, which collectively fueled the circulation of print, also expelled ever more women from the previously life-engrossing routines of local subsistence economies (routines whose loss is regretted only by those never forced to submit to them), replacing such routines with activities to which writing and reading were central. Increasingly, print replaced oral tradition and apprenticeship as the main source for knowledge and entertainment in the population at large.

Within the space opened by print, many hundreds of better- and worse-educated American women, virtually all of them Anglo-Protestants from the middle or upper-middle classes and a majority of them New Englanders or of New England origin, published a huge quantity of diverse writing. This includes didactic novels and short stories about male vocation, female character formation, and middle-class etiquette; polemical novels advocating and debating a range of positions on social, religious, and political topics like slavery, Indian removal, territorial expansion, responses to European Revolution, immigration, Catholic conspiracies, temperance, water cures, dress reform, baptism by complete immersion, woman suffrage, party politics, and veterans' pensions; long and short historical fiction, orientalist fantasy, and sensation melodrama.

Beyond fiction, women published religious tracts and conversion narratives; children's books; local-color stories; village chronicles and character sketches; plays; lyric and dramatic poetry on subjects from the progress of philosophic thought through the ages to sewing; ambitious translations of a range of works written in French, Italian, German, and other European languages; biographies and biographical compendia; family memoirs; speculative epistles; histories and travel books; textbooks on subjects from ancient history to arithmetic to botany; cookbooks and other works on domestic economy; advice books for girls, boys, young women, brides, and mothers; occasional essays; humorous sketches; editorials; and manifestoes. They kept family archives, edited newspapers and magazines, organized literary salons and literary competitions, and won literary prizes.

Whatever else this work may demonstrate, whatever degree of talent or artistic ambition it discloses, it testifies powerfully to the inadequacy of current gender-based distinctions between the public and private spheres, of belief that cults of true womanhood or ideologies of domesticity confined female literary behavior to overtly celebrating or subtextually undermining women's domestic incarceration. We may discover in time that representations of female selves as privatized and domesticated beings are actually minority strands in nineteenth-century American women's literature, owing their prominence to present-day preoccupations. To the extent that this book, through its focus on one kind of female literary work, substantially reconfigures the overall picture of women's writing between 1790 and the Civil War, it implicitly rewrites all of early American women's literary history and also invites a different approach to the writing of modern women.

My point about present-day preoccupations may be briefly illustrated by the contemporary reputation of an important early woman writer, the Puritan poet Anne Bradstreet. Author of the first book of poetry produced in the colonies, she is celebrated today for her personal, confessional, and domestic lyrics, which uniquely open a window onto the private and family dynamics of Puritan life. But these affecting poems are a small segment of Bradstreet's output, and they did not appear in the 1650 *Tenth Muse*, wherein she was introduced to English audiences as testimony to the high degree of culture in America. In this context she came forward as a composer of ambitious historical poetry; the book's lengthy centerpiece is "The Four Monarchies," a rhymed history of the kingdoms of Assyria, Persia, Greece, and Rome.

Very likely and for good reason "The Four Monarchies" will engage many fewer readers today than will the family lyrics; and it is entirely appropriate for readers to mine the past for what speaks to them in the present. Yet what speaks to the present may not be what spoke to the past, and the historical Bradstreet was a quite different figure from the one we currently take her for; this has significance for our understanding of the way past women's lives fitted into the worlds of the past. Indeed, Bradstreet's poem "The Prologue," which we do read today, and which opens by announcing that "to sing of wars, of captains, and of kings" is "too superior" for her "mean pen," takes on a very different meaning when it initiates a group of domestic lyrics in a contemporary anthology (where it implies that Bradstreet chose not to write about wars, captains, and kings) and when it initiates, as it did in *The Tenth Muse*, a long poem on these very subjects.

Thus, without denying that rhetorics of domestic ideology and of true womanhood existed and exerted force on women in the antebellum cultural landscape, I suppose that to have selected these and these only from the whole is a telling commentary on us, not a historically rich representation of them. History writing by women before the Civil War is only one element in women's general occupation of the literary field; I precipitate it from the whole because this discourse, urged on women readers and practiced by women writers from the earliest days of the new nation, is arguably public in its nature. References to reading history or planning to read it, as well as familiar allusions to historical characters and events, abound in antebellum women's letters and journals, testifying to the wide currency of history among women across a range of literacies. Historical writing by women at once involved their drenching the private sphere with newly recognized public significance (as, for example, Revolutionary and post-Revolutionary women were likened to Roman matrons or Spartan mothers), and also moving women out into the sphere already agreed on as public, constituted as Bradstreet put it, by wars, captains, and kings.

Because the phrase *public sphere* has various uneasily coexisting meanings, its use needs clarification here. Throughout the nineteenth century it figured mainly in opposition to the concept of the private sphere, sometimes called the domestic sphere or women's sphere, which separated business and political activities from the home and associated them exclusively with men. As Linda Kerber has convincingly pointed out, the phrase is metaphorical; not descriptive but a figure of rhetoric, it appeared in debates over how to divide labor at different levels of the class system between the sexes. Since all proponents of expanded opportunities for women insisted that these opportunities comported with women's proper sphere, the particular contents of the sphere varied widely from one commentator to another and, increasingly, overlapped with the public sphere.

I think, however, that even as the phrase involved a significant degree of cultural contestation, it also gestured toward two fundamentally shared cultural beliefs: first, that there was a "natural" difference between men and women consisting in differential physical strength; second, that this difference made sexual division of labor socially practical even if individuals, and particularly women, were from time to time constrained by it. It did not make good social sense, for example, for women to be soldiers when even the strongest woman was no match for an average man. Accordingly, scarcely any antebellum reformers argued against the appropriateness of an association between home and women. Rather, as many historians of women have shown, they tried to devise more intellectual maternal and household tasks, to use domestic ideology as a wedge for securing access to related work like teaching or charity, or to insist that activities that did not unfit women for their household duties should not be prohibited to them.

Whereas nineteenth-century rhetoric opposed the public to the private/domestic/women's sphere, contemporary political theory, especially as developed by Jürgen Habermas and his followers, opposes the public to the *official sphere*. The former is an imagined area outside the state apparatus where public opinion is formed, and from which it affects the workings of the state apparatus that constitutes the official sphere. In this discourse both the public and the official spheres are male; the theory contains no domestic or private or woman's sphere, it having apparently been decided in advance that women play no role in public life. Many feminist critics of Habermas have pointed out this total absence of women. Yet, since for Habermas (like all students of modernity) print is a fundamental force in forming and disseminating public opinion, and since it is precisely print that American women were claiming in the nineteenth century, the absence of women is not mandated by the theory so much as it is a typical artifact of male myopia. The concrete placement of the sphere in such locales as eighteenth-century London coffeehouses, where men read and discussed newspapers, disguises the fact that print actually circulates through all kinds of cultural space. If print formulates and consolidates public opinion, and women are printed, then they are part of the public sphere as Habermas defines it.

Moreover, the home would seem to be an obvious site for this kind of public sphere, since from the earliest years of the republic men and women progressives defined it as the place where citizens and citizenship were produced, and they expanded traditional maternal duties to encompass instruction of the young not only in basic literacy (which had been part of woman's work since the seventeenth century) but also in the rudiments of patriotism, republican values, and an understanding of civic virtue. Historians call this constellation of female duties republican motherhood, and since the republican mother was also a spouse, her conversation had an impact on her husband's civic virtue as well. At the higher social levels she was a hostess and guest who could raise the moral tone, and influence the social and political temper, of gatherings she organized and attended. In this view, home and its satellite social spaces were no havens in heartless worlds, no sites for alternative human values to those predominating in official life, but the fountainheads of civic morality and thus essentially public in their nature. Home in this sense is obviously crucial to the formation of public opinion in Habermas's sense, and women were obviously participators. If women were not yet to be legislators, judges, cabinet members, or presidents of the nation—if they were not even to demand the right to vote for these officers until around the middle of the nineteenth century—nevertheless their writing shows that they thought of themselves as part of the nonofficial public sphere and intended to make themselves influential in forming public opinion, whether as writers or mothers or spouses or all of these.

It is easy to see how history could be thought of as a source, even the best source, for the kind of knowledge women needed for their duties in the public sphere so defined. Moreover, the putative lesson of history—that never before *in* history had women been given such opportunities to affect public life—was imagined to be capable of producing women themselves as patriotically attached to the state as a matter of enlightened self-interest, guaranteeing that they would use their unprecedented historical power in the service of the polity.

Therefore, advice that women should read history emerged very early on in the republic and continued in force throughout the antebellum period. The subject was quickly installed at the center of advanced female education and urged on women as the reading of choice after they left school. Following the success of Walter Scott's *Waverley* in 1814, novels, which had been previously contrasted to history, were appropriated for historical work. Reading history produced historical writing. Women teachers prepared historical lessons, took historical notes for their classes, compiled history textbooks; schoolgirls wrote historical exercises. From this core a diverse network of female history-writing practices developed after 1790, ranging from scholarly historical narratives to patriotic poetry; encompassing textbooks, fiction, poetry, drama, biography, journalism, travel books; and dealing with every conventional historical subject. Outside the network, but clearly implying it, a wealth of historical references drop casually into women's writing in nonhistorical modes.

It would be simpleminded to reduce all this material to a single purpose or offer one analytic key to its rhetoric. Topics, concerns, circumstances, and preferred genres changed. But this material nevertheless overwhelmingly subscribes to a particular world view, commits itself to promulgating a specific master narrative of world history. In this story nations are the agents and subjects of history, and the globe is becoming progressively more Protestant and republican. There have been Protestant nations, there have been republics; but because the United States is both, it is the world's most advanced nation, the most advanced nation the world has ever known.

This nationalist narrative had internationalist implications: the achievement of the United States was not the end of history but a step on the way to that end; the end would be the millennium, at which time the national character would be of little importance. When the United States demonstrated official indifference to the European Revolutions of 1848, or when Americans were less than enthusiastic about the Protestant missionary cause, accusations of historical backsliding could be made. Woman-suffrage advocates and, even more, abolitionists, might condemn the nation for falling short of its own ideals; compromisers, on the other hand, could insist that the country could not possibly fulfill its historical role unless it remained an undivided nation. Both sides put their arguments in a historical context.

Accordingly, to accept the master narrative, and to let it seemingly dictate the topics covered and the attitudes expressed, was not to commit to a given side of any political issue. On the contrary, women writers, like men, used history to bolster conflicting political arguments. And, since specifically partisan interventions were generally not considered appropriate for women, history often became a mask for their party politics, albeit a mask that kept on slipping. Proponents and opponents of women's rights; advocates and opponents of abolition; those who were pro- or anti-immigration, pro- or anti-Irish, pro- or anti-Indian removal, pro- or anti-Catholic (mostly the latter), pro- or anti-Mormon (again mostly the latter)—all invoked the same historical record to justify their positions. But if women's historical writing frequently advanced political views, it seldom offered a radical revision of the historical narrative it depended on. In the main an affiliative, not an alienated, activity, historical writing involved a sense of opportunity and potential that made it at most reformist, not radical, where its own subject matter was concerned.

My concentration on works discoverable through national compendia, as well as my Civil War stopping point, explain in part why almost all the authors were Anglo-Protestant women, mostly from New England, where the historical impulse was so much more pronounced than elsewhere, or of New England origin. (New England origin is also a trait of the small number of African American women I have found who wrote history.) This predominance, however, is not simply an artifact of my research; throughout the period Anglo New Englanders and their westward-moving descendants were in the numerical majority and as a group had the highest rate of literacy. Regional and local archives must contain large numbers of additional works, both published and unpublished, by many more women from this cohort: family and local histories, school lessons by teachers and students, patriotic poems composed for holiday observances, scripts for amateur theatricals, and the like. Within this group is a range of social status, literary prominence, and professional commitments. Some who wrote history were the most important women of letters of the antebellum era, others were thoroughly obscure. Some wrote history along with many other kinds of writing, others wrote history exclusively. Some women wrote prolifically, others produced a single book; some wrote for a living, others did not.

Answers to the questions of what history did for these women, and what they did for it, will be offered in the following chapters, which are organized mainly through genre. Chapter 2 expatiates on the reformist programs that made the study of history central to progressive early national ideas of female character and kept history central to women even as female ideology modulated from an Enlightenment belief in intellectual equality to Victorian ideas of spiritual superiority. Chapter 3 considers the specific issue of women as purveyors of history, treating a few texts that explicitly characterize the writer or narrator of history as a woman. Chapter 4 outlines the master narrative of history as it was implied in virtually all these works, drawing most of its examples from woman-authored textbooks; it also considers occasional deviations from this narrative. Chapters 5 through 9 consider poetry, eyewitness contemporary history, travel accounts, novels, and drama (closet and performed), correlating historical writing in these genres with their leading themes and tropes. Chapter 10 looks at historical writing centered on women; for although in a sense women are implicitly or explicitly the subject of all this work, writers also produced versions of what would later be called "women's history" throughout the seventy-year period I survey.

I stop around the time of the Civil War for several reasons. First, the War certainly checked the nationalistic exuberance of the historical writing that placed the United States republic in the forefront of civilized nations. Second, American history had mainly been written to that point as a great detour around sectional conflict, as well as slavery and the African-American population; the Civil War made this neglect untenable. Third, the postwar development of history as an academic profession equipped with credentialing organizations and gate-keeping strategies redefined the relations of women to historical writing, since they lacked professional access to the academy. Fourth, the number of historical works written by women, increasing in tandem with the print explosion of the late nineteenth century and the resurgent interest in historical romance in the 1890s, is so large that full or even representative recovery becomes virtually impossible for an individual researcher. And, fifth, the topic of the Civil War itself spawned an immense new historical industry in which women were very active. Northern heroism and the Lost Cause became new tropes, Gettysburg and Bull Run replaced Saratoga and Lake Erie. In short, the Civil War rewrote American history, forcing the writing of history in the nation to begin anew.

Notwithstanding that I have looked for and found some instances of African American women writing history before the Civil War, the work of looking specifically for history written by women from groups other than white Anglos remains to be done. What evidence I have suggests that there will be a substantial amount of this material, but that it will mostly date from after the Civil War, when the United States population became increasingly diverse and literacy became much more widely distributed. Given the coincidence of literacy programs and programs of frank "Americanization" in the public schools, it seems inevitable that this later history will be grappling in one or another way with the dominant historical discourse that is described in these pages (as, for example, is the case in Mary Antin's *The Promised Land*). But many archives, perhaps especially those in the west and southwest, must contain historical writings by non-Anglo women that ignore the mainstream. In addition, there are sure to be published and unpublished historical works by American women in languages other than English, circulated within immigrant communities or designed for overseas circulation. Even before the Civil War, Therese Albertine Robinson (Talvj) had written an extended history of New England in German, which she published in Germany; this appeared in English translation in London in 1851 but, as far as I can determine, not in the United States. When retrieved, these non-Anglo materials will certainly complicate and revise the historical approaches described in this study. But they also will necessarily confirm a view of American women participating with gusto in the work of writing history.

Women as Students
of History

HISTORICAL WRITING BY WOMEN brought them into print as shapers of public opinion and participants in the public sphere, but it by no means sundered the traditional association between women and the home—just the reverse. Such work developed from the campaign to install history as the centerpiece of female education, in order to connect domestic women to the polity, bring civic self-understanding to the home, and bridge the widening spatial gap between sites of public and private activity. In earlier periods, when most manly business had been conducted in or around the home space (in *The Scarlet Letter*, recall, the formal confrontation between Hester and the magistrates over Pearl's future takes place in the governor's mansion, not in a nonexistent state house), it was obvious that public and private spheres were metaphorical rather than actual places, that public and private were different ways of behaving in the same space. But homes vacated by men during the daylight hours were something different. And if bourgeois women, no longer required to spin and weave, milk and churn, were not to become a dangerously alienated and psychologically self-destructive population, they needed new kinds of meaningful work.

What that work might be was not at all a settled question (nor is it today). Throughout the antebellum years, three partly overlapping definitions of home with correlated views of women's work competed rhetorically. First, home was a haven in a heartless world, a protected retreat where men could rest and recover from the injuries they sustained in public; women's job was to soothe, divert, and entertain them. This view maintained that women had to be entirely innocent of the world to do their work properly. Second, home was a preserve for important human values at risk in the competitive, commercial, impersonal, public world; women's job was to advocate and exemplify an alternative repertory of nurturing, sympathetic, sentimental virtues. This approach justified a distinctly nineteenth-century kind of feminism, *domestic feminism*, in which home values underwrote women's direct entrance into public life for many benevolent and reformist causes.

In the third view, home was where the most important national product—the citizen—was manufactured; the domestic sphere was therefore a work site fully participant in public life. This public sense of *domestic* slides into the meaning that it still carries in such phrases as *domestic policy*—as *Webster's New Collegiate Dictionary* puts it, "of, relating to, or carried on within a country, especially one's own country." Here, home and country are indistinguishable. And *domestic* in this sense carried a particular purchase for early Americans because theirs was a republican form of government, which, according to eighteenth-century political theory, was an inherently domestic kind of polity, devoid of imperial ambitions and concerned only to govern itself. Also, according to republican theory, this sort of polity could survive only if all citizens understood what a republic was and what it demanded of them. In the home, then, were formed the beings whose virtue or vice, civic patriotism or self-interest, would preserve or destroy the republic.

Since citizens and patriots are made, not born, theorists of politicized domesticity needed only to insist on the importance of early childhood training to argue for the importance of women to national well-being. "The nature of our government demands our energies," Lydia Sigourney wrote in *Letters to Young Ladies* (an advice book first published in 1833 and in its 16th edition by 1849). "To a republic, whose welfare depends on the intelligence, and virtue of the people, the character and habits of every member of its family are of value. . . . Women possess an agency which the ancient republics never discovered," she continued, attributing the declines of Greece and Rome directly to their shortsighted preference for physical over moral force, and their related oppression and slighting of women. By contrast, "our country has conceded every thing; the blessings of education, the equality of companionship, the luxury of benevolence, the confidence of a culturer's office" to women. Women are reciprocally obliged to "give our hands to every cause of peace and truth, encourage temperance and purity, oppose disorder and vice, be gentle teachers of wisdom and charity" (143–145).

Sigourney was identifying American exceptionalism with its historically unique appreciation of women's intellectual and moral capabilities. It is no accident that the argument was historical—Sigourney loved history, taught it, and wrote it; over half of her published output is historical. From her point of view the republic needed women's agency and women needed understanding of the nation's need. Studying history was the route she recommended to reach this understanding.

In exactly the same vein Louisa Tuthill observed in her 1848 advice book,

The Young Lady's Home, that "Every American woman should be familiarly acquainted with the history of her own country, its constitution and form of government. She should know that the stability and permanency of a republic depends upon the intellectual, moral, and religious character of the people; upon this broad principle she must act, and endeavor to induce everybody to act, over whom she exercises influence" (268). Since the march of history had created a nation in which home was coextensive with the body politic, knowledge of history would show republican women in republican homes who they were and what their work was.

In brief, from the earliest years of the new republic, the study of history emerged as particularly appropriate for American women. By the 1830s, advice that women should learn history was thoroughly conventional, the subject itself had long since been installed in female academies, and American history was also becoming a required subject in the common schools of the northeast. In the introduction to her 1855 children's book of English history, Grace Greenwood takes her early training in history as a cultural given:

When in my childhood I read the charming stories of Mrs. Sherwood and Miss Edgeworth, and Walter Scott's Tales of a Grandfather, there sprang up in my heart a great longing to visit those noble old countries over the sea from whence our forefathers came; and when in my girlhood, at school, I read the histories of England, Ireland, Scotland, France, and ancient Rome, stronger and stronger grew that longing, and every year that passed after only added to its intensity, until I resolved that, God willing, I *would* see those foreign lands and those people about which I had thought and dreamed so long. (*Merrie England,* 7)

In Susan Warner's best-selling domestic novel of 1851, *The Wide, Wide World,* the child heroine Ellen Montgomery has to leave New York City to live on her Aunt Fortune's farm. Much of the conflict between Ellen and Fortune involves Ellen's struggle to resist enclosure in a preliterate rural economy, where women's work is entirely manual and taught by example. Ellen wants to preserve and enhance a new kind of bourgeois urban self constructed through book-learning.

In Chapter 14, she unpacks her little library:

"Here you are, my dear Numa Pompilius," said she, drawing out a little French book she had just begun to read, "and here *you* are, old grammar and dictionary,—and here is my history,—very glad to see you, Mr. Goldsmith! . . . My arithmetic, that's you!—geography and atlas—all right." . . . As soon after dinner as she could escape, from

Miss Fortune's calls upon her, Ellen, stole up to her room and her books, and began work in earnest. The whole afternoon was spent over sums and verbs and maps and pages of history. (142, 144)

Critics have noticed that in this novel Ellen's mentor advises her unironically to "read no novels" (564). Throughout the antebellum years, although with diminishing force, the value of history study for women figured in rhetorical contrast to the evils of novel reading. Benjamin Rush's 1787 "Thoughts upon Female Education, Accommodated to the Present State of Society, Manners, and Government in the United States of America" is thought to be the earliest expression of the argument that a taste for "history, travels, poetry, and moral essays" will "subdue that passion for reading novels which so generally prevails among the fair sex" (in Rudolph, 31).

At about the same time as Rush's essay, William Hill Brown's *The Power of Sympathy* (1789), which promoted itself as the first American novel and a model for nationally conscious fiction, justified its existence in part through moral exhortations to supposed women readers and placed history at the head of a series of acceptable female subjects:

A knowledge of history which exhibits to us in one view the rise, progress and decay of nations—which points out the advancement of the mind in society, and the improvements in the arts which adorn human nature—comes with propriety under the notice of a lady. To observe the origin of civilization—the gradual progress of society and the refinements of manners, policy, morality and religion—to observe the progression of mankind from simplicity to luxury, from luxury to effeminacy, and the gradual steps of the decline of empire, and the dissolution of states and kingdoms, must blend that happy union of instruction and entertainment which never fails to win our attention. (49)

Educational writings in the early national period are laced with hundreds of comments like this one.

Susanna Rowson, author of the extremely popular novel *Charlotte Temple*, ceased writing novels toward the end of the 1790s, when she opened a girls' school in Boston, instituted a history-centered curriculum, and began to write history herself. Her last completed novel, published in 1798 and composed as she was electing a teaching career, stated prefatorially that it was designed "to awaken in the mind of my young readers, a curiosity that might lead them to the attentive perusal of history" (*Reuben and Rachel*, 3). This is how she described the subject some years later:

14

Women as Students of History

History has always been considered as the light of the ages, the faithful depository of true evidence of past events. Confined without it to the age and country where we live, and to such branches of knowledge as are peculiar to it, we are strangers to the rest of the world, perfectly ignorant of all that has preceded, or even surrounds us. . . . Without it, we are liable to form false estimates of life, our ideas becoming either romantically wild or illiberally contracted; but the study of history leads us from ourselves and the objects immediately surrounding us, to the contemplation of all that is great and praise-worthy in former ages. . . . History is the common school of mankind, equally open and useful to all; every age, condition, and sex may derive advantages from its study. . . . It is a school of morality. . . . It entertains and instructs, forms the heart and understanding, enriches the memory, excites a proper curiosity, inspires a love of literature, corrects the judgment, [and] improves the taste. (*Present*, 52–54)

Since this commentary appears in a book of commencement exercises designed as a graduation gift for women—the 1811 collection is called *A Present for Young Ladies*—Rowson is not concerned with men and does not need to say what other writers on the subject made clear—that studying history has greater benefits for women than men. This is because women's access to real-life experience was so limited compared to men's; indeed, education by life was a mode of tuition expressly denied to women, since the consequences of error were so often irremediable. Women therefore actually needed print more than men did for all sorts of basic information. Novels were dangerous because they took time from learning and, even worse, misled inexperienced women about the real world. Early proponents of women's education, looking to supply women with accurate reading matter about real life, chose history because it conveyed true information in a narrative format whose structural resemblance to fiction made it an attractive substitute. The narrower the woman's own life circumstances, the greater the benefits of reading history would be.

Sarah Pierce, who founded a prestigious female academy in Litchfield, Connecticut, in the early 1790s, developed a particularly full version of this contrast between novels and history in her October 1818 commencement address:

It is still problematical whether the possession of a vivid imagination be of service and how far the light which it throws over the darkness and roughness of the path of life should be followed without hesitation. Imagination is a dangerous faculty where no control exists over its exercise and if accompanied in its unshackled efforts as it too often

15

is by warm feelings it often hurries the possessor to the very brink of imprudence. But imagination when controlled gives a gift to every situation in life and throws a moonlight radiance over every feeling. To direct this faculty in its proper course we have put Universal History into your hands. In addition to the effect which this science has upon the memory the advantage it gives to the imagination is immense, it destroys that sickly relish for fictitious writings which are so justly considered the bane of imagination; it places before the imagination the contemplation of the scenes of real life and by giving a relish for such scenes takes away that morbid restlessness for something new and interesting in life which the readers of fictitious works so constantly desire. (in Vanderpoel, *Chronicles*, 177–178)

Hannah Adams, the nation's first professional author and a writer of history exclusively, expressed the same sentiments in her posthumously published *Memoir*: "I read with avidity a variety of books, previously to my mind's being sufficiently matured, and strengthened, to make a proper selection. I was passionately fond of novels; and, as I lived in a state of seclusion, I acquired false ideas of life." Adams laments her plight as a typical female of her day "whose mind, instead of being strengthened by those studies which exercise the judgment, and give stability to the character, is debilitated by reading romances and novels, which are addressed to the fancy and imagination, and are calculated to heighten the feelings" (4, 14–15). She depicts herself as turning to history for self-discipline and self-creation in an era when formal education did not exist for women.

In a work published in 1815 Hannah Mather Crocker recalled with pride how she had organized a women's study circle in 1778 out of "desire for cultivating the mind in the most useful branches of science, and cherishing a love of literature; for at that period, female education was at a very low ebb. If women could even read and badly write their name it was thought enough for *them*, and by some were esteemed as only 'mere domestic animals.' But," she continued exultingly, "the aspiring female mind, could no longer bar a claim to genius. They roused to thought, and clearly saw they were given bar by the wise author of nature, as not only helps meet, but associates and friends, not slaves to man. I have reason to think that this institution gave the first rise to female education in this town, and our sex a relish for improving the mind" (*Letters*, n.p.).

But Crocker was not merely reminiscing; writing about "the real rights of women," she offered her society as an example of women developing themselves as responsible civic beings. "It is to be wished that some respectable ladies would join in a society, and by their presence and patronage promote science and literature. I think many hours might be redeemed that are now spent in frivolous calls, or trifling with some foolish novel to craze the brain, or contaminate the heart." History is, of course, a likely topic of study for this society: "If the society introduced history, let it be read first and explained. The history of our own country first. Make youth early acquainted with the virtues of their ancestors, as an incitement to the love of virtue. Then let such other works be read and lectured upon as will tend to enlarge the mind, refine the taste, and perfect them in all female accomplishments" (*Letters*, n.p.).

The hostility to novels expressed by critics in these early years seems to me to involve less a fear of fiction's radicalizing potential than the opposite. (But for a view of early novels as subversive radical documents, at least in potential, see Cathy Davidson's *Revolution and the Word*.) Critics saw novels as productive of a social passivity, withdrawal, and global discontent whose political implications were reactionary, not radical. Saturating women's interior worlds with fantasy, novels ruptured their connections with, loyalty to, interest in, and usefulness for, the everyday republican world. Producing a love of excess, expectations of pleasure, and attractions to rank that life in a self-denying republic could not possibly endorse or gratify, novels constructed women as imaginary monarchists quite oblivious to the truth that in a monarchy they would be serfs or servants, not royalty.

The economic implications of reading novels were also presented as dangers. In the early national period, when the government was struggling to retire the huge Revolutionary debt, women who spent time reading novels were thought of as parasites in an economy that demanded labor, self-sacrifice, and frugality from all. Not only was the reading of novels an idle activity, the content of novels saturated women's imagination with depictions of frivolous people. Novels were thus associated with idleness, waste, and—dread word in the republican lexicon—luxury.

This view of reading novels persisted into the Jacksonian years. In her 1831 *Mother's Book*, for example (dedicated to "American mothers, on whose intelligence and discretion the safety and prosperity of our republic so much depends"), Lydia Maria Child makes the reading of novels a form of illiteracy:

I think a real love of reading is the greatest blessing education can bestow, particularly upon a woman. . . . Yet I believe a real love of reading is not common among women. I know that the new novels are very generally read; but this springs from the same love of pleasing excitement, which leads people to the theatre; it does not proceed from a thirst for information. . . . To prevent an exclusive and injurious taste for fiction, it is well to encourage in them a love of History, Voyages, Travels, Biography. (86–87)

17

The prehistory, antinovel discourse, then, crucially assuming that young women are already readers, imagines two kinds of woman shaped by two kinds of reading. Appetitive metaphors—reading as eating, books as food—testify eloquently to the didacts' (quite possibly exaggerated) faith in or fear of the power of print over the body. "Of late years," says Child, "the circulating libraries have been overrun with profligate and strongly exciting works, many of them horribly exciting.... The necessity of fierce excitement in reading is a sort of intellectual intemperance; and like bodily intoxication, it produces weakness and delirium" (*Mother's Book*, 93). Child's repeated *excitement* conveys her sense of urgency. A nascent Victorianism enhances Child's republican ideals; it seems that ingesting historical materials might magically liberate women from corporeality altogether.

"The fondness of the sex for reading works of fiction," wrote Almira Hart Phelps in 1836, "is proverbial."

But are not the authors of such works laboring to prepare for the readers of them, that kind of food, which, so far from rendering the mental system strong and healthy, disorders and enfeebles it?... I would appeal to the experience of every female who has indulged herself much in this kind of reading, whether, after the excitement of feeling occasioned by the perusal of some fascinating novel, she has returned to the realities of life with a spirit calmed, and prepared to meet its realities with fortitude and resignation? or whether she has not at such times experienced a distaste, almost amounting to disgust, for the homely beings with whom reality surrounded her, and for the every day scenes of life? And has it not required a strong and painful effort to regain that mental equilibrium so necessary for prudent conduct and amiable deportment? (*Female Student*, 9)

Novels, Sigourney wrote in *Letters to Young Ladies*, "are calculated to heighten in the young mind those powers which need no excitement" (64); by contrast, "History has ever been warmly commended to the attention of the young. It imparts knowledge of human nature and supplies lofty subjects for contemplation" (65). So history helped form a private woman who was contented, fulfilled, and developed—a woman who, recognizing the limits of life, could negotiate effectively within them. At the same time, it helped form a good republican citizen. Educators might emphasize the private or the public face of this woman, but she was ultimately one person.

Emma Willard thought women's right to self-development was given by God; but as an educational propagandist she stressed the nation's needs. In her 1819 *Plan for Improving Female Education*, she observed that

In those great republics, which have fallen of themselves, the loss of republican manners and virtues, has been the invariable precursor, of their loss of the republican form of government. . . . It may be said, that the depravation of morals and manners, can be traced to the introduction of wealth, as its cause. But wealth will be introduced; even the iron laws of Lycurgus could not prevent it. Let us then inquire, if means may not be devised, to prevent its bringing with it the destruction of public virtue. (30)

Pointing out that morals and manners were traditional domains of female influence, Willard proposed to educate women in a way that would bind them to the polity, and transform them from silent, appetitive beings into vocal partisans, exemplars, and conservers of the national character. Not surprisingly, she thought that history was the best subject for effecting this transformation. (Later, she became nationally famous for her history textbooks.)

Making it clear that the study of history was no pastime, the reformers from the first insisted on the need to approach it methodically, to use it as a disciplinary instrument. It was not to be read, merely, but to be studied. Proper study required and developed order, self-discipline, and memory, qualities necessary for the self-governing citizens on whom a republic depended.

Judith Sargent Murray's 1798 miscellany *The Gleaner* dramatized a history-centered program for female education at home by describing a demanding curriculum imposed by the Vigillius parents on their foster daughter Margaretta:

To the page of the historian one hour every day was regularly devoted; a second hour, Mary conversed with her adopted daughter upon the subject which a uniform course of reading had furnished; and a third hour Margaretta was directed to employ, in committing to paper such particular facts, remarks and consequences deduced therefrom, as had, during the hours appropriated to reading, and conversing, most strikingly impressed her mind; and by these means the leading features of history were indelibly imprinted thereon. Mrs. Vigillius also composed little geographical, historical, and chronological catechisms, or dialogues. (60)

Elizabeth Peabody's 1832 *First Steps to the Study of History* noted, "We must not forget the pre-requisite to entering upon this long course of history. To know how to attend to reading, is a habit of mind which, generally speaking, must be formed with labor" (15). Sigourney's *Letters to Young Ladies* advised that "all systematic reading should be with a fixed purpose, to remember and to profit." To strengthen the memory demanded "persevering exercise"—you must read with concentrated, undivided attention, reflect on your reading, recite the content to someone in your own words, and whenever possible study formally with friends (70–75). In 1858 Sigourney was still conveying the same message; the protagonist of her quasi-autobiographical *Lucy Howard's Journal* continues to study history after leaving school, sometimes joined by her best friend. "It is delightful when she comes, for then we question each other about the substance of what we have been reading together, and sometimes I recapitulate what I have read in the interval, so that she may have the advantage of all" (87).

Eliza Farrar's 1836 *Young Lady's Friend* explained that "written extracts of what you read will not only assist your memory in recollecting dates and facts, but will aid you in arranging, comparing, and reflecting upon what you have acquired. They should be frequently referred to, and occasionally studied very thoroughly, if you would reap the full benefit of them. Whenever you are reading or studying, take care to have within reach, gazetteers, maps, biographical charts, dictionaries, encyclopaedias, &c., and never grudge the time that you spend in consulting them" (425). A "Course of Reading for Young Ladies" in *Godey's Lady's Book*, beginning in March 1847, tells the reader that properly to read history she must "read and meditate alternately," be sure she understands every sentence, review her reading at night before going to bed, and try to recollect it upon waking the next morning (34:174). In the *Young Lady's Home* Tuthill said that "to give clearness and precision to our ideas, and to methodize what we read . . . after finishing a book, an abstract of all the knowledge gained on this particular subject may be written" (50).

Note the centrality of training the memory in this advice. Although all education trains the memory, it makes especially good sense to define history as *the* subject for strengthening memory, since in some deep sense memory is what history is all about. Memory makes individuals into historical beings who live in past time as well as the present. Public history goes beyond what individuals can remember to install a group memory in the self; historically informed individuals know themselves as historical subjects by remembering a past they never experienced. Much present-day postnationalist theorizing interprets the installation of collective, officially sanctioned memory in individual consciousness as a way of indoctrinating, colonizing, and disarming the asocial self; curiously, had they heard this argument, nineteenth-century American advocates of historical study would have agreed with it. To study history was indeed to link individuals to the nation, to construct them as national subjects; but for these advocates of historical study, the nonnational self was not a utopian radical but an alienated parasite.

The dichotomy between history as a form of being public and novels as a way of being private comes clear in Susanna Rowson's amusing rhymed dialogues in *A Present for Young Ladies*. One starts as three students debate whether to read novels or history, and concludes when they decide against both to go shopping (37). Another compares history, bad novels, and good novels. "Ellen" interrupts "Lucy's" plot recital to contrast the inanities of a personal love-plot with the noble truths of history:

> Dear Lucy such nonsense can never be true
> For history holds no such scenes to our view. . . .
> When I was at home
>
> And read through the annals of Greece and of Rome,
> I found no such wonderful stories, not I,
> Nor was it so easy to faint and to die;
> To faint was disgrace, but on some dread occasion
> And none would brave death, but to profit the nation. (39)

Ellen observes that worthwhile novelists exist; through every line written by Maria Edgeworth, Fanny Burney, and Hannah More "the taste may be formed, / The heart rendered better, its piety warmed, / The judgment corrected." Lucy breaks in:

> Yes, all that may be
> But they're not exactly the novels for me.
> I love runaway marriages, castles and spectres,
> Libertine lovers, and gen'rous protectors,
> And fighting of duels
>
> [Ellen] oh! pray don't proceed
> Such novels as that must be wicked indeed. (44–45)

And in a third dialogue, "Harriet" complains that her father makes her read history during the school vacations:

> and then hapless I
>
> Must drag through long chapters so tedious and dry,
> And those who made kings, and those who dethron'd them
> And pilfer'd the sceptres from they who once own'd them.
> What is all this to me? I am sure I don't care
> Who is king or who queen, who at peace, or at war. (48)

The dialogue as a whole undercuts Harriet's complaint by swerving immediately to a discussion of the horrors of war and the good fortune of America at peace—observations both patriotic and historical, since the

21

nation's tranquillity is then interpreted as a direct result of its republican form of government.

Hannah Foster's 1797 *The Coquette* has the roué Sanford break in on (and break up) a domestic scene where Julia Granby is "entertaining" the heroine and her mother by "reading aloud in Millot's elements of history" (117). A year after publishing *The Coquette* Hannah Foster brought out *The Boarding School*. The motherly teacher at the heart of that work instructs her charges that "Novels are the favourite, and the most dangerous kind of reading, now adopted by the generality of young ladies"—dangerous, because "their romantic pictures of love, beauty, and magnificence, fill the imagination with ideas which lead to impure desires, a vanity of exterior charms, and a fondness for show and dissipation, by no means consistent with that simplicity, modesty, and chastity, which should be the constant inmates of the female breast. They often pervert the judgment, mislead the affections, and blind the understanding" (18). It is wiser to read poetry or essays; and, of course,

Among your hours devoted to reading, history must not be without a place. Here an extensive field of ages and generations, which have gone before you, is opened to your view. Here your curiosity may be gratified with a retrospection of events, which, by conducting your thoughts to remotest climes and periods, interests and enlarges the mind. Here various revolutions, the rise, fall, and dismemberment of ancient kingdoms and states may be traced to the different springs of action, in which they originated. Hence you may gain a competent acquaintance with human nature in all its modifications, from the most rude and barbarous, to the most civilized and polished stages of society. (25)

Farrar's *Young Lady's Friend* advised her readers not to abandon history after leaving school: what was done there "is but furnishing her with instruments for carrying on the work. . . . If she has there read a few abridged histories of various countries, they are to be regarded as a mere introduction to that study of history, which is to enlarge her views of human nature, and give her an insight into the policy of nations and the progress of civilization" (4–5). Tuthill's *Young Lady's Home* spends a chapter on the benefits of history for women. Willard counseled students in 1850 that

History will fit you to act your part in life, giving you a portion of that *faith in truth which alone can lead to wisdom.* Novels, on the contrary, impart delusion—that inward imperceptible faith in falsehood which is sure to work itself out, by folly in conduct. Whoever is imbued with a love of history—that is of truth, no longer has a passion for fiction. Thus, doubly important do I regard the study of history—both adding good, and taking away evil. (*Guide to the Temple of Time*, 30)

Elizabeth Peabody grounded her immensely productive intellectual and pedagogic career in the study of history; she wrote in 1832 that "as history is the department of human knowledge which is more within the sphere of woman's attainment than any other, so the study of it is the most important to women, and has the most direct influence in forming them for the duties peculiar to their relations in life" (*First Steps*, 12–13). Fifty years later she was still saying that, "as the art of life is the universal vocation of woman, history is what woman should read from youth to age, whatever else she does" ("My Experience," 737).

Given the ever-increasing popularity of novels throughout the antebellum era, it is obvious that the love of fiction withstood attacks upon it. The more pragmatic educators tried to distinguish worthwhile—usually didactic—novels from trash. But establishment hostility to the novel per se began to evaporate only with the success of Walter Scott's historical novel *Waverley* in 1814. This suggests that the novel, demonized as history's other, escaped its pariah status by becoming historical itself. Even as she insisted on the dangers of reading novels, Child allowed that historical fiction might be read "in connexion with history to great advantage. . . . Sir Walter Scott has furnished a novel for almost all the interesting reigns in English History"; their "influence is never in opposition to good; and to a thinking mind they afford abundant food for reflection, as well as an inexhaustible fund of amusement" (*Mother's Book*, 94).

Advocates of history for women frankly addressed a middle- to upper-class white audience whose size was hugely expanding between 1790 and the Civil War. But the mandating of American history in the public schools meant that in principle the entire population might be included in the historical mission. Some evidence shows the reading of history making its mark on people who lived beyond the boundaries of genteel culture:

She learned that in some towns in Massachusetts, girls make straw bonnets—that it was easy and profitable. But how should *she*, black, feeble, and poor, find anyone to teach her. But God prepares the way, when human agencies see no path. Here was found a plain, poor, simple woman, who could see merit beneath a dark skin; and when the invalid mulatto told her sorrows, she opened her door and her heart, and took the stranger in. Expert with the needle, Frado soon equalled her instructress; and she sought also to teach her the value of useful books; and while one read aloud to the other of deeds historic and names renowned, Frado experienced a new impulse. She felt herself capable of elevation; she felt that this book information supplied an undefined dissatisfaction she had long felt, but could not express. Every leisure moment was carefully applied to self-improvement. (*Our Nig*, 124–125)

Whether Harriet Wilson's account is autobiographical or not, by making her character read history for moral and intellectual enlightenment—by making this kind of work articulate what had long been felt but remained inexpressible—she testifies to the place that history had achieved in ideas of female character formation.

Equally telling are several essays enriched by historical allusions in an 1841 miscellany published by Ann Plato, a young African American schoolteacher living in Hartford. The book's introduction, by her minister, reaches for an African American readership—"our young authoress justly appeals to *us*, her own people, (though not exclusively)" (xix). In an essay called "Education" Ann Plato mentions Alexander, Philip, Aristotle, Milton, and Newton, and observes, "Egypt, that once shot over the world brilliant rays of genius, is sunk in darkness. The dust of ages sleeps on the besom [sic] of Roman warriors, poets, and orators. The glory of Greece has departed, and leaves no Demosthenes to thunder with his eloquence, or Homer to soar and sing" (30). In "Decision of Character," she mentions Columbus, Demosthenes—of whom "Cicero tells us that his success was so great that all Greece came in crowds to Athens to hear him speak" (43)—Pompey, Benjamin Franklin, and Robert Bruce. In "Employment of Time" she writes, "The poems of Homer inspired Alexander with an insatiable thirst for fame and military glory, and they were the foundation of the superstructure that covered the world. The memoirs of this conqueror stamped a like character upon Caesar; these, and similar ones, made Napoleon a second Alexander" (50).

If casual, fragmentary historical allusions like Ann Plato's are a shorthand form of writing history, if one proposes that historical allusiveness in a woman's text testifies to her knowledge of history (or at least her desire to be known as a knower of history) and is also an abbreviated instance of writing it, then the step from reading to writing history is minimal. The locution "She's up garret writing geography, and told me nothing in the world must disturb her, till she had finished an account of the city of Palmiry," said Temperance" is a moment of history in Elizabeth Stoddard's 1862 novel, *The Morgesons* (50), which both conveys history itself and establishes its ubiquity in the education of young women. We are reminded that students learned history (and geography, its synchronic sibling), by writing it. It seems more than likely, then, that many thousands of women wrote history in this sense at some time in their lives.

While presumably such schoolroom writing was not meant for publication, neither was it private work, since it was produced for school recitation and teacher perusal. Another kind of female quasi-public writing of history is presented in Hannah Foster's *Boarding School*. The second part of the book consists of letters exchanged between fictional former schoolmates, in which among other things they describe their reading to each other. These letters, meant to show women how to avoid lapsing into illiteracy after leaving school, probably reflect an epistolary ideal rather than actual practice. Still, they depict a network of intellectual writing in which history has its place:

I have been reviewing Millot's Elements of Ancient and Modern History; and recommend it to your re-perusal. It is undoubtedly the most useful compendium extant. The tedious minuteness and prolix details of sieges and battles, negotiations and treaties, which fatigue the reader and oppress the memory, in most works of the kind, are happily avoided in this; while the elegance, simplicity, conciseness and perspicuity of the style, render it intelligible to every capacity, and pleasing to every taste. To those who have a relish for history, but want leisure to give it full scope, Millot is well calculated to afford both information and entertainment. (201–202)

Another letter summarizes Jeremy Belknap's history of New Hampshire:

By this judicious and impartial historian, we are led, from its first settlement, to trace the progress of the infant colony. We accompany its inhabitants in their enterprizes, through dangers, through toils, and through successes. We take an interest in their prosperity; and we tremble at the dreadful outrages of the barbarous foe. Our imagination is again recalled to the gradual advance of population and agriculture. We behold the wilderness blooming as the rose, and the haunts of savage beasts, and more savage men, converted into fruitful fields and pleasant habitations. The arts and sciences flourish; peace and harmony are restored; and we are astonished at the amazing contrast, produced in little more than a single century! (206)

I have said that young women produced this kind of historical writing without thought of publishing it; yet, there is evidence when women did think about publishing they turned to these school compositions for material. The posthumously published works of the child-poet prodigies Lucretia and Margaret Davidson included school compositions on history, for example, and Anne Charlotte Lynch's elaborately produced book of poems (1853) specifically labels two ambitious historical works—"The

Mediterranean" and "Byron Among the Ruins of Greece"—as school compositions. "Byron" is doubly historical, since its subject is the poet in Greece
thinking about Greek history, and has lines like these:

Armed warriors too were there, their helmets gleaming
On deathless Marathon's green, sea-girt plain,
That now with Persia's choicest blood was streaming;
Thermopylae's "three hundred" fought again;
Again its pass was piled with countless slain,
From the invader's host, as on that day
When Sparta's bravest sons had vowed to drain
Their heart's best blood for her. (157)

Writers urged women not to abandon history after leaving school—
which recommendation assumes they had indeed studied it there in the
first place. We have seen Eliza Farrar insisting that history in school was
only the starting point of a lifetime commitment; Almira Phelps in *The
Female Student* made much the same point, advising "every young lady,
after leaving school, to commence a systematic course of historical reading," since "during the progress of school education, not more than an
outline of general history can be given" (187). She proposed that post-
graduate students read: the Bible (always taken as veracious history in this
discourse), Josephus's Jewish history, Rollin's *Ancient History*, Plutarch's
Lives, Abbe Barthelemy's *Travels of Anacharsis the Younger* (for Greece),
Gibbon's *Decline and Fall of the Roman Empire* ("there is little danger
that any one educated and settled in a religious faith should be otherwise
affected by his occasional sneers, than with pity" [189]), Vertot's *Roman
Revolution*, Condillac on the Middle Ages, Hume's *England*, Robertson's
Charles V, Voltaire's *Charles XII*, Millot's *France*, Raynal's *Political and
Philosophical History of the Indies*, Bigland's *View of the World*, Marshall's
Washington, and Pitkins's and Willard's *United States* (187–191).

Even more ambitious is a "Course of Reading for Young Ladies" described in nine installments in *Godey's Lady's Book* (March through November 1847). Although unsigned, it was almost certainly Sarah Hale's
own work, since it appears in the back of the magazine along with other
editorial pronouncements and reflects opinions she expressed elsewhere.
Even if Hale was not its author, the appearance of this "Course" in *Godey's
Lady's Book* says a great deal about what, besides colored fashion plates,
she had in mind for the huge audience of women who read the magazine.
Throughout the antebellum period, the journal, which noticed novels in
brief paragraphs, reviewed books of history and biography at length.
The "Course" does not specify history in its title, and it includes works
of philosophy and literature; still, history gets four-fifths of the space. Young

ladies are informed that they must continue to read history after they leave school, since school texts at best are inadequate compendiums showing "a mere skeleton, not the image of the past."

Fortunately for American ladies, there are aids within the reach of all. Inheriting, as we do, the wondrous stores of learning contained in the Anglo-Saxon language, now enlarged by translations of all the celebrated Greek and Roman writers, besides many gems from oriental literature, and the best of the modern, European works, we have such abundant sources of reading before us, that the great danger is of running over too many books. (34:174)

The April installment starts the course with Christian and United States history; besides the Old and New Testaments, Hale recommends fourteen scholarly books on religion and eight on American history. In May, proposed readings in Greek and Roman history amount to twenty ancients in translation and eleven works of modern scholarship. In June, books on English, French, and Italian history total over thirty-four primary and secondary works. The July installment, on Medieval, modern European (for the countries not covered earlier) and non-European history, names another sixteen titles. Among the books cited are: Milman's histories of the Jews and of Christianity, Prideaux on the connection of the Old and New Testaments, McIlvain on evidences of Christianity, Ramsay on the American Revolution, Marshall's life of Washington, Rollin's ancient history, Heeren's history of antiquity, Mitford on Greece, Niebuhr and Ferguson and Sismondi on Rome, Keightley and Hume on England, Strickland on the English queens (the only history written by a woman in the list), Wyatt on the kings of France, Thiers on the French Empire, Guizot on French civilization, Roscoe on Lorenzo de Medici and Leo X, Hallam on Europe in the Middle Ages, Alison on modern Europe, Florian on the Moors in Spain, Russell on Egypt, Frazer on Persia, Chrichton on Arabia. Hale assured readers who thought the list "very formidable" that "constant perseverance, allowing two hours in the twenty-four (and that time may be with advantage taken from the hours consumed over *novels*) would in a few months enable the reader to go through the list" (34:269); she insisted that the list was actually "very small" and promised that any "lady" who "carefully perused" the books would have "a good foundation laid for her guide to future improvement. Moreover, she will have acquired a considerable stock of real knowledge concerning the great events and chief actors in the ancient and modern world" (35:55).

The "Course" also tells young ladies how to use their learning and why it matters. Under the aegis of a Victorian ethos, working from the standpoint of genteel cultivation rather than republican politics, and addressing

27

young unmarried women not mothers, Hale invokes a figure we might call the national domestic daughter, who works perforce within the sphere of apparently private life, but whose judicious display of learning raises the tone of all American society and convinces her fellow citizens of the power of female intellect. The result will be an ever-widening circle of female influence. Ladies who read history, says the *Lady's Book*, will acquire knowledge "which can be used for the happiness and benefit of themselves and others, rather than to become learned for display or renown" (34:315). Display and renown are aristocratic motives, construing knowledge as a product to be consumed and wasted; putting knowledge to use for others' happiness is a genteel value. This course, then, not only insists on the appropriateness of historical study for women, it also insists on its centrality in the formation of a genteel, middle-class national style and identifies women as the advance guard of this national development. A careful display of learning in a bourgeois "lady" publicizes the cultural benefits of study through personal example. Hale admits that "Learning is not *all* that is necessary, the course of reading and self-training that we have recommended are not the only qualifications required to constitute a charming woman"; but still, she insists, such a course *is* necessary (35:270).

Hale promises each reader that "In exhibiting her knowledge, or rather not exhibiting it, only allowing it, like a pure atmosphere, to brighten and beautify all around her . . . a young lady can become most attractive and draw minds less cultivated to her shrine. . . . Our good, sensible American citizens have always appreciated female intelligence" (35:270). The word *shrine* assures youthful readers that although they must put personal vanity aside to do this important cultural work, vanity will be more than satisfied by the outcome. The idea of intellectual charm set out here is not new with Hale, although it reaches a kind of apotheosis in her work. Foster had written in *The Boarding School* almost fifty years earlier of history as "a species of knowledge, which will not only be of . . . use to you, in the government of your own temper and manners, but highly ornamental in your intercourse with the polite and learned world" (25–26). Throughout this discourse, for more than half a century, and from different ideological perspectives, educational reformers labored to unite charm with intellect in the ideal of an educated woman. As she contributed to the well-being of her social circle, her sex, and her country, this ideal woman also enjoyed the personal sense of achievement and the gratifying approbation of her associates. And to all this, history was the passkey, for history was what she knew.

3

Maternal Historians, Didactic Mothers

FOR WOMEN, to study history was to write it; and from a very early moment in the national life, for women to write in any quantity and on any topic was to think about publishing. In 1798 Hannah Foster reminded students how lucky they were to live in a country "where the female mind is unshackled by the restraints of tyrannical custom," where "the widely extended fields of literature court attention" and "the American fair are invited to cull the flowers, and cultivate the expanding laurel" (*Boarding School*, 31). Emma Willard's 1819 *Plan for Improving Female Education* observed that rigorous education would make women better contributors to the literary field that had "heretofore" been their "only honorable way to distinction" (34). Suffrage arguments from Margaret Fuller onward assumed that women already had access to publication and insisted that this access was no longer a satisfactory substitute for more direct kinds of political activity. Numerous single and widowed women, as well as women with feckless husbands, turned to writing throughout these decades as a respectable way to earn a living. Young girls tried their luck at prize tale competitions in local newspapers. No doubt women then, like women now, suffered personal anxieties of authorship, but these were individual crises; the sex had no need to apologize for doing literary work.

The sex did, however, have to insist that writing comported with domestic duties; no more than educational reformers did literary women question the association between women and the home. "The delicate texture of the female form," wrote Sarah Hall (not to be confused with Sarah Hale, and to be discussed in more detail below), "so inferior in size and strength to that of the man, is a plain indication that Providence has not allotted to both the same theatre of action. Her inferiority in this particular has, from the beginning of time, very naturally assigned to her employments of social and domestic life" (*Selections*, 1). Throughout the period encomiums on literary women emphasized their competence in, and even their enhanced performance of, traditional womanly tasks.

The upper-class Sarah Wentworth Morton addressed her nonliterary friends on this issue in the preface to her 1797 epic *Beacon Hill*: "I know, my fair friends, that with many, who do not write, application to literature in a female is imagined to imply a neglect of proper duties," but "it is only amid the leisure and retirement, to which the sultry season is devoted, that I permit myself to hold converse with the Muses; nor does their enchantment ever allure me from one personal occupation, which my station renders obligatory; but those hours, which might otherwise be lost in dissipation, or sunk in languor, are alone resigned to the unoffending charms of Poetry and Science" (ix). Far down the social scale, Jane Ermina Locke, who published in the 1840s, described writing as the outlet that kept her sane: her poems "have for the most part been written . . . to relieve the soul of what would cumber it unuttered, or hush the clamors of a native gift" (*Poems*, 3).

But their allotted occupation of domestic ground became precisely women's justification for professional authorship. With men increasingly invested in work outside of the home site, women made an argument for the utility of a system allotting their own sex intellectual and belletristic labor that could done at home. To be sure, the argument required one to grant that women were the intellectual equals of men—a point which, thanks to the Enlightenment dictum that mind had no sex, figured importantly in all early claims for expanded education for women. Thomas Prentiss's preface to the third (1801) edition of Hannah Adams's *View of Religions* insists that "if an invidious comparison between the sexes is in any respect justifiable, it cannot be grounded upon a defect of natural ability, but upon the different, and perhaps faulty mode of female education; for under similar culture, and with equal advantages, it is far from being certain, that the female mind would not admit a measure of improvement, which would at least equal, and perhaps in many instances eclipse, the boasted glory of the other sex" (v). Whereas early literary women and their male supporters attributed all differences between male and female minds to differences in education, Victorian women were attracted to an idea of innate mental sexual differences. But these differences, they believed, made women intellectually, morally, and spiritually superior to men, and thus better suited than the other sex to conduct the nation's important cultural work.

The print medium had the inestimable advantage for women of allowing them to circulate outside of their bodies; still, rules of sexual decorum suggested that women ought to write differently from men. These rules pushed women toward the production of edifying and moral works, as they strove to rescue themselves from earlier images of women as (in Hannah Mather Crocker's words quoted in Chapter 2) "mere domestic animals." Female didacticism and moral seriousness counterbalanced men's erudition. These views of writing as a female activity converged with the advocacy of history for women's reading to make the writing of history a "natural" field for literary women. Women could also argue that, if home was their province, then whatever in the world affected the home was their province also. And every important historical event had an impact on the home, as Mercy Otis Warren made clear in the introduction to her history of the American Revolution:

At a period when every manly arm was occupied, and every trait of talent or activity engaged, either in the cabinet or the field, apprehensive, that amidst the sudden convulsions, crowded scenes, and rapid changes, that flowed in quick succession, many circumstances might escape the more busy and active members of society, I have been induced to improve the leisure Providence had lent, to record as they passed, in the following pages, the new and unexperienced events exhibited in a land previously blessed with peace, liberty, simplicity, and virtue. . . . The solemnity that covered every countenance, when contemplating the sword uplifted, and the horrors of civil war rushing to habitations not inured to scenes of rapine and misery; even to the quiet cottage, where only concord and affection had reigned; stimulated to observation a mind that had not yielded to the assertion, that all political attentions lay out of the road of female life. (*1*:xli)

Not for a moment does Warren deny her gender; on the contrary, it figures in her text from the beginning, since the three-volume work, published in 1805, had her name on the title page. In fact, although much women's historical writing, like other writing, was published anonymously (men also published anonymously in this period for many reasons), women's anonymous history was typically gender-identified through locutions like "by a lady of Massachusetts," "by a lady of New York," "by an American lady," "by a lady"; or through pronominal references to "her" or "she"; or through other strategies. "By a lady" conceals the woman's personal identity but insists on her gender. Many of the several hundred examples of historical writing I consider in this study came out anonymously, but many did not, and all without exception identify their authors as women. Women must also have published historical writing under male or gender-neutral pennames, but it is hard to believe that such work could equal in quantity that which is gender-identified. To the extent that historical writing by women was designed to show that women could and should write history, it would have had to be identified by gender to be effective.

In short, American women's literary practices absorbed the writing of history from the start. Just about every active literary woman in the first two generations—including Hannah Adams, Judith Sargent Murray, Mercy Otis Warren, Sarah Wentworth Morton, Sarah Keating Wood, Anne Eliza Bleecker, Margaretta Bleecker Faugeres, Hannah Foster, Susanna Rowson, Sarah Pierce, and Emma Willard—wrote history without apology. Adams wrote it exclusively, and she was the first woman—the first author—in the United States to make a living from writing. The real question then was whether history as written by women would be different from history as written by men. The answer was both yes and no. To the extent that the writing of history was meant to destabilize or obliterate boundaries between the domestic and the public, women would not be likely to perform in some kind of specifically female voice; history and its authoritative voice were a single package. Elizabeth Peabody (mother of the better-known writer of the same name) identified herself on the title page of her 1813 *Sabbath Lessons; or, An Abstract of Sacred History*, described herself as preceptress of a young ladies' academy in Salem, and merged her gender with the universal in her preface; "In this age of doubt and infidelity, every friend to the interest of human kind will, the Author flatters herself, view with favourable eye her attempt to disseminate among the young the knowledge of sacred history. Friends of religion must be armed for attacks against it" (7). In the sense that the authoritative voice of universal reason, when channeled through a man, could always be mistaken for the merely male, it would actually be women alone who could demonstrate that reason was really and truly universal.

But even though women adopted history's authoritative voice in their writing, few had access to great libraries and fewer still could hope to devote their lives to scholarly inquiry. Limited in the main to synthesizing or summarizing the relatively accessible published sources, their authority was in the strictest sense derivative, as they readily conceded. Their work of publicity was facilitated by the remarkable increase in the number of historical works to draw on; to a much larger extent than has been recognized, the development of publishing in the United States before the Civil War was supported by reissues of historical writings. For some examples: Edward Gibbon's *History of the Decline and Fall of the Roman Empire*, originally published in England between 1776 and 1788, came out in the United States in Philadelphia between 1804 and 1805, and later in Philadelphia and New York in 1816, 1820, 1822, 1826, 1829-31, and many times thereafter. David Hume's six-volume history of England (he was better known for this in his own day than his philosophic writings) appeared first in London in 1754 to 1762, had a first American edition in New York (1776), and was reissued in Baltimore (1810), Philadelphia (1810, 1821, 1828, 1832, 1836, 1840, 1841, 1844, 1846, 1848, 1859), Boston (1849, 1852, 1854), Albany (1816), and elsewhere. William Robertson's 1777 history of America came out in the United States in 1798 and had gone through more than twenty editions by 1860 in New York, Philadelphia, and Albany. A translation of Charles Rollin's multivolume ancient history appeared in New York as early as 1729 and was republished in New York alone six more time by 1830; in 1834 Harper brought out the first of what would become almost annual reissues; it appeared also in Hartford (1815, 1833, 1836, 1837, 1838, 1846), Baltimore (1820, 1832), Boston (1823), Cincinnati (1832), and Philadelphia (1805, 1829, 1845).

In elite schools, these costly multivolume histories were sometimes part of the school library. Lydia Sigourney fondly remembered teaching upper-class girls in her Hartford school, which she conducted in Daniel Wadsworth's residence, where she had access to his books:

How much did I enjoy unfolding with them the broad annals of History. Seated in a circle, like a band of sisters, we traced in the afternoon, by the guidance of Rollin, the progress of ancient times, or the fall of buried empires. Each one read an allotted portion of those octavo pages with a slow, distinct enunciation, that all might without effort comprehend. At the completion of the reading the book was closed, and each related in her own language the substance of what she had read, questions were asked on the most important parts, pains taken to impress on the memory the dates of prominent facts, and encouragement given to express their own opinions of heroes, or other distinguished personages. (*Letters of Life*, 203–204)

But for less-privileged schools, or for student-owned texts, or for history books in average homes, a different kind of book was needed: portable, inexpensive, pithier. Early women teachers, who prepared classroom compilations and commentary for their students, quickly saw the possibilities for wider circulation of this kind of work. Sarah Pierce justified publishing her (eventually) four small volumes of *Universal History* as follows:

Having from long experience found that children and youth imbibe ideas most easily, when placed in the form of question and answer, and not finding any historical work of that kind, of sufficient length to interest the mind, I have compiled these Sketches for the use of Schools, endeavoring to intermix moral with historical instruction, and to obviate those objections which arise in the minds of youth against the justice of God, when they read the wars of the Israelites.—I have attempted also to give them a general notion of the government of God, and the truth of the Scripture, by a partial account of the fulfilment of prophecy. I am sensible that all this has been done by many able writers; but as their works are too expensive to be put into the hands of children, and of greater magnitude than they have time or patience to study, I have compiled this abridgement for their benefit. This history may also be useful in private families; which are not able to purchase the larger works from which it is selected. (*Universal* 1:4)

Pierce's conflation of school and home as identical sites of instruction corresponds, to some extent, with the reality that most private schools were in fact run in people's homes. And it also displays a crucial move in antebellum educational reform efforts with import for women's historical writing and for the imagined role of the mother—a move that defined book-based instruction as required work in all homes. Another instance of this can be seen in Sigourney's preface to her 1833 *Evening Readings in History*:

History is useful to the young mind, by enriching it with knowledge, and furnishing it with subjects of thought. By judicious instruction, it may convey those lessons to the heart, which confirm goodness, and stamp vice with abhorrence. Yet these good effects are often frustrated, by presenting the study to children in a style beyond their comprehension. In the following pages, the substance has been divided into short portions, that the memory may be exercised without weariness, and the understanding strengthened, without being disgusted at its nourishment. They have been written with a desire of aiding a laudable custom, established by some of my particular friends, of devoting an hour in the evening to a course of reading with the younger members of their families, and examination into their proficiency in the several departments of Education. This habit . . . while it silently and securely aids the progress of improvement, it serves to strengthen the bond of mutual attachment, by creating new sources of interest, intimacy, and obligation. (v)

And again in Sigourney's 1836 *History of Marcus Aurelius*:

This book was commenced as an assistant to parents, in domestic education. Its highest ambition is to be in the hand of the mother, who seeks to aid in that most delightful of all departments, the instruction of her little ones. The daily perusal of a chapter with them, the patient use of the annexed questions, and the repetition of this process, until the contents of the volume are impressed on the memory of the learner, will, it is trusted, confer both intellectual and moral benefit.

Though the original destination of this work was for the family circle, yet in its progress, more of collateral history, interwove itself, than had been at first anticipated. It may, therefore, be also adapted to primary schools, not merely by the knowledge it imparts, but by the love of historical research which it is calculated to cherish, and the mental discipline to which it may be rendered subservient. (iii)

In 1857 Caroline Kirkland apologized for yet another biography of George Washington on the grounds that it was especially adapted to the needs of "the older pupils in our schools, and some learners who have done with schools." For these, she went on, "the very fulness of the best lives of Washington renders them unsuitable. Details of battles and states-manship, the cruelties of war and politics, are not particularly interesting or instructive to the young. It seemed not undesirable to offer them some simple memoirs of our great benefactor and friend, in which the space usu-ally occupied by public affairs should be filled with what relates more par-ticularly to Washington himself" (v).

Between 1790 and 1860 at least twenty women published history text-books designed for school and/or home use. Most active were the younger Elizabeth Peabody, who published six history textbooks; Eliza Robbins, who published five; Augusta Berard, who published two—United States and English—with frequent editions and wide sales; and Emma Willard, who published five and made a fortune through continually updated edi-tions of her American history textbook, which was published in a com-prehensive, well-bound, durable version for private libraries and elite schools, and in a cheap abridgment for common schools.

As well as textbooks designed for adoption in various kinds of class-rooms, women also wrote historical texts for family reading. Among these are a number of works that specifically delineate women as conveyers of historical information. These often take a dialogue or conversational form, depicting the provider of history as a teacher of girls or a mother teaching her children of assorted ages (and both sexes) at home. Among the aims of this subgenre would be: to interest readers by presenting the material dy-namically, to make children feel at home with history by funneling it through the maternal voice, to model an interactive mode of pedagogy, and to make history a natural subject for women by showing a woman articulating it.

Most important, this type of text represents the mother as learned and didactic. Although any history published by a woman implicitly demon-strated that women could be historians, here the demonstration is explicit. Its outcome is an identification of mothers and teachers that works on behalf of both terms. The homelike institutional space in which the teacher narrates history makes teaching seem women's natural work. The home, when used for the mother's teaching, becomes a classroom. To the extent that married women feel confined in the home's physical space, this move precipitates them into boundless intellectual space and makes home more livable. Perhaps this representation was especially congenial to the many women in New England who had been schoolteachers before marriage. (It is estimated that by the 1840s nearly half of all New England common-school teachers were women.)

Finally, history books written in dialogue form not only gave the mother historical information but also showed her a model of motherhood in which her role is intellectual, authoritative, and associated inextricably with the printed word. These books did not erase the traditional emotional resonance of the mother's voice; on the contrary, they figured the affective strength of the maternal as an instructional advantage over the paternal, whose specialty is fear. But, reciting history in the mother's words, these books did make mothers less traditionally female insofar as the female implied the unlettered, the waywardly emotive, and the mentally limited. The depiction vigorously counters the idea that feeling precluded intellectuality. Obviously the idealized figure in these works is a version of republican motherhood; as Sigourney wrote in *Letters to Mothers* (1838), "Woman is surely more deeply indebted to the government that protects her, than man, who bears within his own person, the elements of self-defence. But how shall her gratitude be best made an operative principle? . . . Patriotism is a virtue in our sex, and there is an office where it may be called into action. . . . This office is that of maternal teacher" (13–14).

I have already noted two early representations of the maternal teacher, Hannah Foster's *The Boarding School* and Judith Sargent Murray's compendium *The Gleaner*, both from 1798. In Foster's work, Mrs. Williams is the director of Harmony Grove, a girls' boarding school run in her home. The book's first part contains Mrs. Williams's general lectures to her departing students, and the second includes a variety of letters purportedly written by these graduates to her and to each other. Mrs. Williams reminds the students that though they cannot all expect to win literary fame, a "species of writing, which is open to every capacity, ornamental to every station, is the epistolary" (31). Writing to each other, the girls learn to reproduce the voice of their maternal teacher.

If *The Boarding School* features a motherly teacher, *The Gleaner* features a teacherly mother. In letters 44–53, Mary Vigillius teaches history to her adopted daughter Margaretta by writing it. The sequence begins when she asks Margaretta to write answers to four historical questions: which hero in Plutarch she prefers; whom she esteems most among British monarchs; what her sentiments are of Mary Stuart, Henry IV of France, Charles I of England, and Peter the Great; and, "although I do not enjoin you to weigh with accuracy the *murders of a Cortez*, although I expect you will pass rapidly over the pages in which a Montezuma bled, and in which are registered the massacre of an innocent and defenceless people; yet, my dear, I am solicitous to know whom you characterize as the most amiable of all those adventurers, who quitting the chalky cliffs of your native land, crossed the broad Atlantic, to obtain establishments in North-America?" (364–365). (The right answer to this last question is William Penn.) The dutiful Margaretta responds and asks her mother "to point out my mistakes, and tell me how I ought to think of persons and things, and I request you to write me a separate letter upon each of the subjects you have proposed" (369).

Mary's response amounts to a moralized crash course in secular world history from ancient times to the settlement of America, making history the field for emotional and evaluative responses. We weep, we shudder, we thrill, and we also judge, praise, absolve, and condemn. Though Margaretta has no further speaking part, the sequence is studded with maternal endearments: "*Is not the character of Aristides perfect?*' This is the present question. Let us, my love, proceed to a careful investigation thereof, and our answer will follow" (377). "I am sufficiently acquainted with the mind of my daughter, to feel a conviction that her sentiments of Alfred the Great, will be perfectly in unison with those of her tenderly affectionate Mary Vigillius" (386). "Humanity, my dear girl, must lament Elizabeth's depraved politics, as they related to the Queen of Scots" (405). "That you may, from every delineation, deduce a salutary lesson, is the ardent wish of your affectionate Mary Vigillius" (411). No Victorian mother could have been more concerned to fill the spaces of her daughters' psyche with disciplinary love than the eighteenth-century Mary Vigillius. *The Gleaner's* educational program involves as full a development, and as thorough an advocacy, of a maternal regimen of loving surveillance and emotional blackmail, as any mid-nineteenth-century work. As the affective note identifies—one might say overidentifies—the teacher's maternalism, the subject matter identifies the teacher.

Several works of history in dialogue form elaborate on the relation of mothers and their children, including Sarah Hall's *Conversations on the Bible* (1818), Lydia Maria Child's *The First Settlers of New-England* (1828), and Anne Tuttle Bullard's *The Reformation* (1832), this last a publication of the Massachusetts Sabbath School Society. These works also go well beyond the dual purposes of conveying historical information and representing a scene of maternal instruction, to use the mother or woman teacher as mouthpiece for tendentious political or religious views.

Sarah Hall (1761–1830) was a conservative Philadelphian who contributed to and helped her son edit *The Port Folio* after Joseph Dennie relinquished control. Hall's father, provost of the University of Pennsylvania, regularly invited students into his home for study and conversation from which Hall herself was excluded. According to her son's filiopietistic preface to her posthumous selected writings (1833), she had no formal schooling; as a girl she read history and belles lettres mostly "by stealth" and in later life "was accustomed, after all her family had retired, to remain several hours engaged in study" (*Selections*, xiii, xv).

A devout Christian rationalist with intense interest in the millennium, Hall delighted above all in Biblical study. *Conversations on the Bible* (which had four editions) retells and comments on the Old Testament through the device of a learned and opinionated mother, who responds at length to questions from her three children. The historical veracity and the divine inspiration of the Biblical account are defended at every point. The mother refers to scholarly books and commentaries as she discourses; there is a parenthetical chronology; there are footnotes. The work is clearly meant to be a useful compendium of the most advanced thinking on its subject, an example of pedagogy, and a celebration of the mother. Its teaching reverses the catechismic tradition of rote recitation; the children ask questions and the mother answers them. She does not hesitate to assess, choose, or dispute authority. When Charles, a college student, says, "I have heard one of our professors say, that Ham became black in consequence of the curse pronounced upon him by his father, and thus he accounts for the colour of the Africans, his posterity," she responds bluntly, "Your professor, my dear, has no authority for his opinion" (28).

In this model of learning within the family, childish curiosity is encouraged and maternal expertise is displayed, creating a harmonious, benevolent intellectual interchange that binds the family in enlightened affection. This is maternal rather than paternal didacticism. So Fanny, the youngest, says, "But you, mother, can tell us, how long Noah remained in the ark," and Mother answers, "I am always pleased with the expression of your curiosity; I will gratify it by relating some particulars respecting the flood, which I have gathered from Brown's dictionary of the Bible" (24). When Catherine poses a question "with diffidence," Mother assures her, "You do right to inquire when you do not fully comprehend my meaning; and especially every suspicion of the nature you now intimate, should be cleared up. Every act of the Deity can be vindicated" (110). When Charles exclaims, "Dear mother! do not tell us that Jephthah sacrificed his only child!" Mother answers, "Alas, my son!—there is the difficulty which I am not able to solve to my own perfect satisfaction" (169).

Through Mother's moralizing, Hall talks past the represented family to her audience, especially her audience of mothers: "Many of our duties are repugnant to our natural feelings. The Great Supreme, however, although he has a right to implicit compliance, is pleased to conciliate our reason"; "The judicious conduct of Abigail in this instance may be a lesson to all women. In every station to which Providence has called them, they may find opportunities of mediating between violent men"; "The very natural propensity of children to imitate their parents, should be a solemn and unceasing admonition to the latter, and especially to mothers, who are observed to have a more immediate influence on their characters. From such a monster of iniquity as Jezebel, no other than an impious successor to the crown could be expected" (129, 205–206, 255–256).

Lydia Maria Child's historiographical iconoclasm is known to readers of her 1824 novel *Hobomok*, which attacked the narrow sectarianism of the founders of the Plymouth Colony. Her *First Settlers of New-England* further dismantles received Puritan history to argue against the policy of Indian removal and continue her quarrel with Calvinism. Its format has a mother reading New England history to her daughters Caroline and Eliza, soliciting their questions and objections as springboards for digressions from, or challenges to, the various precursor authorities, who are thereby discredited in the act of transmission. For example, Caroline's exclamation, "Is it possible that a belief so monstrous can be embraced by rational beings?" elicits the maternal response:

I wonder not at your incredulity or surprise; but I can assure you, that notwithstanding many metaphysical subtleties . . . [t]he first settlers of this country had been bred up in the school of controversy, and their feelings were of course adverse to the doctrines of peace and mercy which form the basis of Christianity, from having been accustomed to defend the crude notions with which they were infected by a constant reference to some detached passages or expressions of Scripture, (without any regard to their connection,) which favoured their opinions, and frequently by obscure and spurious texts; but an evil of still greater magnitude was the vain belief of their being a chosen people, and, like the Israelites, authorized by God to destroy or drive out the heathens, as they styled the Indians. (31–32)

When Eliza exclaims, "Dear mother, I cannot bear to think of the many instances of barbarity, which the records of our country exhibit," Mother answers: "You will not find consolation in perusing the details of [King Philip's] war, which are replete with scenes revolting to humanity; and will experience no relief from the most painful sensations, except in the heroism of the Indians" (155).

The First Settlers of New-England participates in the project of redefining motherhood as an intellectual and civic function; assigning historical and doctrinal expertise to the mother confirms her domestic mission while greatly extending her intellectual reach. Child's model, although it insists conservatively on an exclusive domestic function for women, offers a radical argument for married women's property rights: "If it be granted, that the moral character is formed at the early period when children receive their most important impressions from the mother, it is certainly essential that woman should not only receive an enlightened education, but that they should possess a degree of independence, which will secure to them respect and attention" (242). *The First Settlers's* representation of maternal expertise in the mother's voice extends beyond providing historical knowledge to demonstrating forensic disputational skills; amusingly perhaps, since she attacks the Puritans especially for their sectarian pugnacity, Child defines the mother as a powerful controversialist.

Yet Child, whose iconoclasm delights, whose exertions on behalf of African Americans and Native Americans inspire, finally turns out not to be a feminist dream-woman. The book's chief objection to Calvinism is that it is Jewish not Christian. "I have had frequent occasions to remark on the injury done to Christianity, by the pernicious practice of associating with it the historical transactions and institutions of the Jews. It is by nourishing this root of iniquity . . . that ample scope has been afforded for the commission of those countless crimes which have been perpetrated under the sanction of religion" (107–108); "The main prop of Calvinism is found in the election of the Jews, with all their vices, to be the peculiar favourites of Heaven" (110). Child's admiration of Native Americans rests on the fantasy that they are really uncorrupted (that is, Unitarian) Christians: "In the character and principles of Jesus, we recognize him as a teacher inspired by God to illustrate and confirm those divine impressions, which He hath graciously written on the heart. In the minds of our Aborigines this law hath not been darkened or corrupted by superstition, and they are guided by the pure lustre of that light, which is from above" (253–254).

Child's approval of Indian-white intermarriage is piquantly provocative, albeit presented as a lost opportunity rather than a present-day possibility; but not only does it derive from the same belief that Indians are primitive Christians who would in effect convert their spouses, it is also class-ridden, since it situates intermarriage exclusively on the frontier between Native Americans and the white lower class. Finally—to conclude an argument advanced only to demonstrate that it is probably unwise to try to judge women of the past by present-day standards—the title's "First Settlers" does not refer, as logic would seem to demand, to Native Americans, but to the English Puritans. Child is not to blame if some twentieth-century scholars have romanticized her. The point for all these women is not whether their beliefs are more or less conventional, more or less conservative, more or less acceptable to a later age. The point is that they insist on their rights to formulate and express political and public opinions, and use the power of the press to circulate them.

As Hall produces Bible history to defend the Old Testament against rationalist attacks on its divine inspiration and historical veracity, as Child narrates New England history to discredit Calvinism and skewer Indian removal policies, so Bullard in her history of the Reformation recounts Protestant history for anti-Catholic ends. The book is structured as a series of informal lectures delivered by a preceptress to eighteen student-boarders: five "little girls" and thirteen "young ladies." An introductory description establishes the maternal character of the well-off widow Mrs. Athearn, who had opened her school in response to the request of some mothers in her neighborhood:

Could she forgo her ease, her delightful, quiet seclusion, and assume a task at once so self-denying? . . . She saw, as she had not seen it before, that her present life was comparatively useless to her fellow men, that the ease and freedom from care she had hitherto sought, were inconsistent with the professions of religious attachment she had made to Him, who went about ever doing good.

    She saw a wide field of usefulness before her in the culture of these young, pliant minds . . . and she dared not, in the light of eternity, refuse a work so evidently an answer to her prayers for more extensive usefulness. . . . Her house was at length thrown open and filled. (*Reformation*, 11)

No doubt Bullard aims this description toward idle widows. In a passage probably directed to parents and teachers, she shows Mrs. Athearn passing "the two hours allotted to needlework, in the long winter evenings, in the room appropriated to the young ladies," where she either reads aloud "some interesting and instructive communication," or herself relates "something calculated to amuse and improve. She was anxious not a moment of the precious time of her pupils should be lost, in which they might be treasuring up knowledge; besides, she knew well the folly and idleness to which young, giddy girls are prone, when collected together without the restraining presence of an elder" (6–7).

    This scene of harmony and surveillance frames Mrs. Athearn's narrative of the Reformation in Germany, which is preceded by a general account of "the state of religion throughout Europe about that period" (13). Having inherited a fine library from her father, Mrs. Athearn is herself notably learned. At one point she has a student fetch "an old French royal quarto,—the 'Histoire du Concile de Trente,' a French translation of the History of the Council of Trent, from the Italian, by Father Paul," which she then reads to her students—in English (166–167, 168). Here is another implicit lesson for adult women: acquiring advanced knowledge is admirable, but erudition should be, and can be, put to social use.

    Typical maternal interchanges occur throughout *The Reformation*: the question, "May I interrupt your reading, Mrs. Athearn, to inquire what holy water is?" elicits the response, "Certainly; I wish you all to feel liberty in asking questions" (25). Students are encouraged to learn actively, as when a little girl asks the meaning of a word. "'Johnson, Walker, and Webster are all near at hand,' said her teacher, smiling; 'all ready to answer any such inquiry, and you know, my dear, you are far more apt to retain the knowledge you acquire by your own researches, than what you obtain by the simple, careless loan of a listening ear'" (143). Some of the narration is delivered by the older students who are studying history in class. The trope of motherhood surfaces frequently, as when Mrs. Athearn speaks about Martin Luther's mother: "Oh! how little do mothers generally feel their awful responsibility," she exclaims, and "a tear, gushing from the depth of her feelings, glistened in her eye, perhaps at the thought of her *own* responsibility as teacher and guide of so many youthful immortals" (121).

The ultimate point of this recitation, however, goes beyond providing historical information, to mobilize sentiment against the growing Catholic presence in American life. "I hope you will not rest satisfied with the brief relation I have given you, in the last few evenings, of the events connected with the memorable withdrawal from the superstitions and corruptions of the Roman Catholic Church. Search for yourselves; you will find a vast field for investigation, and a fund of information, which you may improve to the best good of many perishing souls. Even o'er the very shores of your own native country, my dear girls, the 'Man of Sin' is striding" (245–246).

Although studies of the linked movements of the Sunday School, the Bible societies, and the tract societies recognize the significance of the books produced by and for these movements, there has been almost no research into the authorship of these texts. Most likely, such research would disclose a very large number of women authors as well as a significant quantity of tendentious historical writing in this extensive material, of which Bullard's work is exemplary. *The Reformation* was her second Sunday School publication, at least; *The Stanwood Family*, a dialogue text about the American Tract Society, had appeared in 1830. "Family" here means mother and children: "Susan: 'I wish, mother, I knew more about Tract Societies.' 'Do tell us *all* about Tracts,' said Charles; '*do*,' said little Ann, as she crept into her mother's lap, hardly knowing why or what she wanted to hear. Helen seconded the children's motion, while William, who had been for some time listening, closed his Virgil, and seated himself by the fire. Mrs. Stanwood promised to comply with their unanimous request" (15–16).

These dialogue texts appear in a milieu where cultural radicalism could hardly be the order of the day; it follows that they are not initiating a maternalist ethos but dramatizing one already familiar to readers. They realize a female-dominated scene of communication and reception that their authors thought corresponded either to reality or to a widely accepted cultural ideal. The hallmarks of the maternalist voice are its frequent endearments, its endorsement of affective reactions to information, its attunement to student response, and its receptiveness to audience questions. But questions are always answered, and the answers are always firm; the voice of love is the voice of authority. "A number of such facts, presented under the double allurement of stories and of rewards, and riveted by the mother's care, will serve as stepping stones, when the broad stream of History, flowing from Eden onward, shall be forded by the wandering traveller" (Sigourney, *Letters to Mothers*, 105–106).

Like Sarah Hall's *Conversations*, Susanna Rowson's two-volume *Biblical Dialogues* (1822) defends the Old Testament by reciting its facts and affirming its divine authorship. But this, the only woman-authored dialogue text I have found with a father present, has a very different family dynamic from the others. The children ask questions and the father answers them; the discourse has its emotive side, but the pedagogic rhetoric invokes fear, anger, and punishment. "Father, will you permit me to ask you a question, and will you not be angry with me?" (1:16); "Oh what a good father God is, and you, my own papa, are so like him, for you love us and forgive us, when we are very, very naughty" (1:32); "Sir, I am ashamed of having asked so foolish a question, and I wish all children were as fortunate as we are, in having an indulgent parent, who allows us to mention our own simple ideas, and who condescends to inform us, and explain what we do not understand" (1:40).

The mother's work in this setting is to instill even more awe and respect for the father than the children already feel, and also to express the group's sentimental emotionality: "I am pleased to find that you pay so much attention to what is read, it will encourage your father to support the fatigue, of the long recitations he makes of an evening; for there is nothing so grateful to the feelings of a parent, or teacher, as the assurance that their instruction is not thrown away, but we interrupt the narrative" (1:148).

"I never read that part of the sacred history, but my heart melts with tenderness. I can so easily conceive the distraction of a mother, with her own hands committing her infant to the watery element. . . . Oh, my dear children, a mother only can comprehend, the agony of the moment when she abandoned it, or the rapture of that, of its restoration." *Here the tender mother clasped the little Amy to her heart, and burst into tears, while the other children pressed round her, kissing her hands and cheeks, as a token that they comprehended the affection which occasioned her emotions.* (1:149–150)

Scenes like this hearken back to the overflowing tearfulness of eighteenth-

43

century sentimental femininity, in whose school Rowson had written her earlier novels. They suggest by contrast that the power of the nineteenth-century maternal historian depends on, perhaps even rises from, the absence of the father from the domestic circle. Standing for the father, she has absorbed his authority while feminizing it. Rowson herself is the father's surrogate here; her name is on the title page and the book has an autobiographical preface.

The strong-minded mother we meet in these dialogues is also featured in numerous advice manuals of the time, and she contrasts strikingly with the cultic true woman, whose passive submissiveness would have totally unfitted her for energetic maternity. The didactic mother is, of course, largely missing from popular nineteenth-century *woman's fiction*, which, being about the development of independence in younger women, would have had difficulty staging its story with such a mother present. Louisa May Alcott's *Little Women* is virtually unique in plotting a strong mother into a chronicle of youthful female self-development. But woman's fiction frequently fills the mother's place with one or more surrogates, who nurture and instruct the protagonist, enacting therefore versions of the didactic mother. The same maternal place is also occupied by the narrator herself.

Maternal historians are often the implied narrators of nondialogue textbooks by women. Eliza Robbins directs her *Tales from American History* to her nephews, referring often to the "dear boys" and presenting information in light of the supposed state of their knowledge: "You know what is meant by the *civilized* and *savage states of society*. You have been taught from your little books that men who have comfortable habitations and clothing, who possess books and the arts of reading and writing, and whose business is carried on by means of coined money, are *civilized*; while those who subsist by the chase of wild animals, who live in rude huts, dress in the skins of beasts, and who have no letters, are savages" (1:13-14). "I mention this that you may understand how much better it is for you that you are born under a *free government*, than if you were the subject of an arbitrary one. In our country the government never can take a man's property without his consent" (1:97).

Again, Augusta Berard's often reprinted textbook of American history incorporates reader response in a maternal way: "Such a belief, strange and awful as it seems to us, was held, not only by the ignorant, but by the good, the great, and wise. . . . Can we wonder then, that the forest homes of America, surrounded by savage Indians, and saddened by poverty, should be filled with the same belief and dread of the evil one's power? Or is it strange that the Mathers and Sewalls of America should err in judgment?" (35). "Dreadfully cruel as this seems to us, we must remember that the Judges really believed that these people were in league with the devil, although they would not confess it, and that if allowed to live, they would do a great deal of harm. Let us then be slow to condemn, but thank God we live in better days" (36).

Yet again, Susan Fenimore Cooper's 1859 *Mount Vernon: A Letter to the Children of America*, campaigning to preserve the site as a historical monument, insists on a child readership (and incidentally says a great deal about what a literate American child supposedly knew about American history). "Dear Children: You have been taught from your cradles to honor the name of George Washington" (9); "You know already by heart, my children, the course of George Washington through that war" (13); "Children of America! brief and imperfect as this rapid sketch of a great life must appear to you, it may serve in some degree to warm anew your young hearts towards one of the greatest Christian patriots the world has ever seen" (67).

These works participated in a protracted, ongoing cultural project that may or may not have coincided with the actual state of families and the role of women at any point in the antebellum era. Textbooks featuring a maternal historian who at once conveys historical information and models a way of being motherly must, however, have helped familiarize an image of women comfortable with book-learning and a range of public discourses. They show what motherhood and teaching ought to be in a world where education is identified with books and education seems increasingly necessary for a successful life. Their maternal image merges a new kind of mother with a new kind of authority.

4

History from the
Divine Point of View

A THRILLING SPECTACLE of exciting events that really happened and extraordinary personages who really lived; an unparalleled resource for training and stocking the memory; an invaluable encyclopedia of human types
and situations—to its devotees history was all these things. And more: it
was the fragmentary record of a divine narrative progressing inexorably
toward a known end, the millennium that would mark history's closure.
From the standpoint of this finality, narrators of world or national or even
local history could assign true meaning to every event. Students of history
saw God's work; historians played God, momentarily escaping the temporal, finite sphere.

Where the Transcendental mind found epiphany in union with nature,
the historical mind found it by merging with history. Elizabeth Peabody,
the most theoretical of the women historians, spoke for many in express-
ing a preference for history, the domain of the social, over nature, the domain of unfettered ego. "To deliver the mind from the thraldom of the
present, and to prepare it to comprehend the future, the most obvious course
is to open upon it the past, which is an assured gift of God to the race.
Hence the importance of history" (*First Steps*, 1); "All history should be
studied with reverence, as a *sacred* illustration of the Providence of God"
(*Hebrews*, 3); "The events of history are God's conversations with man
upon his nature, duties, and destiny" (*Polish-American*, 117); "The chronological relation is God's disposition of events, every one of which is a
word proceeding out of his mouth. Let us read *these words* as they lie in
time, giving significance to each other" (*Universal*, IV).

Until the millennium released individuals from history, historical memory
placed them in the flow of world drama and gave their lives universal significance. Women yearning to be part of the pageant joyfully assumed the
burden of learning to remember what was not to be forgotten until the
end of time, especially joyfully because the story placed them—Protestant
American women—at the very vanguard of historical progress. The amal-

46

gam of Protestant Christianity, historicism, and national patriotism in women's historical writing is commonplace for the age, shared by men and women, visible in popular and scholarly texts alike. Although their works are variously inflected and have different emphases, the women who wrote history usually affirmed mainstream assumptions; even the occasional dissenter worked well within the dominant paradigm.

At the heart of antebellum history is the Bible. "Sacred History," that is, study of the Bible, was the main subject in Sarah Pierce's Litchfield Academy and most other serious academic women's schools throughout the era. Susanna Rowson's 1811 *Present for Young Ladies* asserted, "The Bible is the most authentic history, and should precede the study of all others; it is termed sacred history. It is different from all other history whatever. It is the history of God himself" (54–55). Forty-nine years later Sarah R. Hanna's *Bible History: A Text-Book for Seminaries, Schools, and Families* (1860) took exactly the same tack. Hanna, a principal of female seminaries in Pennsylvania, Virginia, and Ohio, claimed to have "labored over many years in the cause of education, and the greater portion of this period has taught the Scriptures, principally the historical part." Her *Bible History* proposed "to advance the glory of God and the best interests of Man" (3, 4). Science and the higher criticism had not undermined biblical authority: "still it is seen that the Bible is true; and the record stands unshaken in the war of theories, strengthened by the very facts which once seemed to threaten its overthrow;—a pillar of central truth, to which all these facts gravitate, and by the measure of their adhesion to which, their worth is tested" (51).

Once the biblical focus of history is grasped, it becomes clear that the women's main aim in teaching and writing it was to further the advance of Protestantism, an aim which brought together religious, national, and gender loyalties in one surpassing commitment. This intention controls their work from the start, as in the 1801 edition of Hannah Adams's *View of Religions*, which introduces its encyclopedic presentation with a quick overview of the state of the world at A.D. 1:

When Jesus Christ made his appearance on earth, a great part of the world was subjected to the Roman Empire. . . . By enslaving the world, they civilized it; and whilst they oppressed mankind, they united them together . . . [in a] . . . remarkable peace, . . . [which] . . . after so many ages of tumult and war, was a fit prelude to the ushering of the glorious Prince of Peace into the world. The tranquility, which then reigned, was necessary to enable the ministers of Christ to execute with success their sublime commission to the human race. In that situation, into which the providence of God brought the world, the gospel in a few years reached those remote corners of the earth, in which it could not otherwise have penetrated for many ages. All the heathen nations, at the time of Christ's appearance on earth, worshipped a multiplicity of gods and demons, whose favor they courted by obscene and ridiculous ceremonies, and whose anger they endeavoured to appease by the most abominable cruelties. (ix–xi)

At the end of the book Adams recapitulates: "The wretched state of the world at the time of our Saviour's appearance, which is exhibited in the Introduction to this work, evinces the necessity of the Christian dispensation. The gross superstition of the Pagans, the degeneracy of the Jewish nation, and the inconsistency of the ancient philosophers, and their uncertainty respecting a future state, elucidate the apostle's declaration, that 'life and immortality are brought to light by the gospel'" (502–503).

Susanna Rowson's 1822 *Exercises in History, Chronology, and Biography*, derived from her years of teaching, quizzes: "What is the first great event recorded in history? The creation of the world. The second? The fall of man from his state of innocence and happiness by disobedience to the commands of his Creator"; "What great event took place about 14 years before the death of Augustus? 4709 years from the creation of the world, in the 4th year of the 193d Olympiad, when Rome had flourished 749 years, *JESUS CHRIST the SAVIOUR* of the world was born" (6, 35). For Elizabeth Peabody in 1859 the life of Jesus Christ constituted the "turning-point of the history of the world," when "a new era for the human race began" (*Universal*, 113). For these women the record of history displayed Christian truth, and the historian's task was to make sure that the story emerged clearly from the mass of detail that sometimes blurred the narrative.

Because Christ's appearance on earth set the millennial apparatus in motion, it gave history its narrative structure and so in a sense invented history itself. Chronology, which made the temporal record possible, sliced the time it created into before and after. From this narrative perspective, God had selected the Jews to receive the Word not arbitrarily, but specifically, because from the beginning they had a sense of history—that is, a self-consciousness awareness of themselves as a people, a nation, collectively undergoing a temporal sequence of significant events. Jewish historical self-consciousness explained why the only document in the world with a record of the creation was the Hebrew Testament. It was reasonable, too, for God to give Revelation to such a self-consciously historical people, for only such a people could understand what it meant for humankind.

For all its religiosity, this historical narrative also held that the life, death, and resurrection of Christ marked the last instance of direct divine historical intervention prior to the millennium. Thenceforth God would work through natural causes. (This explains the theological horror with which Islam and Mormonism were regarded, since the founders of both religions claimed to have experienced revelations of their own.) History from the Christian resurrection onward was thought to be a progression of tangible secular events caused and motivated by human agency, though all the while directed by a hidden divinity whose purposes frequently overrode human plans.

Nations—groups of people consolidated by common origins, territorial boundaries, and particularized governments—were God's chosen historical agents in the interval between Christ's resurrection and the millennium. Nations in turn were exemplified by their rulers, who expressed the national character and directed the people's force. Over time, two interactive plot lines emerged from the flux of successive nations and national dynasties. One involved the progressive spiritualization of religion—that is, the supplanting of polytheistic material practices (idol-worship) by disembodied monotheism. The other involved the progressive access of the people to direct political power.

These narratives coalesced in the emergence of Protestant republics. The two fundamental principles of Protestantism, as for, example, Hannah Conant elucidated them in her history of the Bible in English—"the word of God the sole guide in matters of religion; individual inquiry and conviction the right and duty of all men" (46)—coincided exactly with the foundations of republican government. The premillennial narrative anticipated the progressive Protestantizing of the world through the formation of ever more republics; to tell that narrative was to take part in the action. Scarcely a paragraph in the thousands of historical pages published by women before the Civil War fails to reflect, if not purposefully feature, the Protestant dispensation under whose influence it had been produced and to whose future it was dedicated.

Most versions of this narrative relegated nations outside the Christian purview to ahistorical darkness. In her history of the American Revolution, Mercy Otis Warren explained how "It soon became apparent, that unless a timely and bold resistance prevented, the colonists must in a few years sink into the same wretched thraldom, that marks the miserable Asiatic" (1:25). Elizabeth Peabody's United States history text asked rhetorically, "Who but the free may develop the historical genius, or have any use for history?" (8), and her *Universal History* observed that "It is only peoples, free peoples, that write history" (vi). Contrariwise, the human race "is stultified, and put into a sort of catalepsy in China; in India it runs rank, like the vegetation of the climate; in Egypt, it petrifies into the stone, which seems to be the only plastic material it finds, and to which it at last yields" (*Polish-American*, 114). Students also encountered this Eurocentric view of Asia and Africa when they studied geography.

49

Anne Charlotte Lynch's *Hand-Book of Universal Literature* (1860) shows what Protestant historiography could do with the term "universal." The first chapter is on Hebrew literature, specifically the Old Testament, which "expresses the national character of that ancient people, who were selected by God as the conservators of His revelation. . . . It is the book of all centuries, countries and conditions, and affords the best solution of the most mysterious problems concerning God and the world. It cultivates the taste, it elevates the mind, it nurses the soul with the word of life, and it has inspired the best productions of human genius" (9, 12). One sees here how literary history is identified with religious history, religious history with national history. Chinese literature then reveals "the history of the religious and philosophical progress of China," where "religion at length degenerated into that mingled idolatry and indifference, which still characterizes the people" (52); in Egypt "the immaterial was soon lost sight of in the material, and this worship sunk into a degrading idolatry" (63).

Virtually alone among women history writers, Lydia Maria Child (in her *Appeal, in Favor of that class of Americans Called Africans*) gave black Africa a history:

Ethiopia held a conspicuous place among the nations. Her princes were wealthy and powerful, and her people distinguished for integrity and wisdom. Even the proud Grecians evinced respect for Ethiopia, almost amounting to reverence, and derived thence the sublimest portions of their mythology. . . . Why did the ancients represent Minerva as born in Africa,—and why are we told that Atlas there sustained the heavens and the earth, unless they meant to imply that Africa was the centre, from which religious and scientific light had been diffused? . . . It is well known that Egypt was the great school of knowledge in the ancient world. . . . Herodotus, the earliest of the Greek historians, informs us that the Egyptians were negroes. This fact has been much doubted, and often contradicted. But Herodotus certainly had the best means of knowing the truth. (149–150)

This courageous nineteenth-century Afrocentrism, however, values Africa for what it contributed to the evolution of the Protestant character. Child's three-volume *Progress of Religious Ideas* has occasional pluralist moments—"I consider the religious sentiment as always and everywhere sacred. In all its forms, I find much that is beautiful and true" (2:183)—but its core is profoundly Christocentric. "If we strive to divest ourselves of the habitual predilection for Christianity, which education imparts to us, and endeavour to approach the Gospels in the same spirit that we should examine the Sacred Books of Hindostan or Persia, it appears to me that even in that state of mind, we cannot fail to be struck with their great superiority over all the other religious teaching" (3:315). "If any one is disposed to doubt that Christianity contains within itself a vital element of progress, superior to any other spiritual influence by which God has yet guided the world, I think he will be convinced by comparing the practical results of different religious systems"; only in Christianity "do we find sympathy, benevolence, and active exertion for the improvement of all mankind" (3:433).

Within the Christian dispensation, the historical narrative began with the Creation and recounted antediluvian events from the Old Testament. It dwelled on the history of the Jews, as the people chosen both to disclose God's ultimate gift of Jesus Christ to the world and also to demonstrate in their disastrous after-history how God's prophecies were invariably fulfilled. This second point animated Hannah Adams's two weighty volumes of Jewish history:

The exact accomplishment of our Saviour's prediction respecting the destruction of their city and temple, and the calamities they have endured since their dispersion, have furnished every age with the strongest arguments for the truth of the christian religion. One of the great designs of their being preserved and continued a distinct people appears to be, that their singular destiny might confirm the divine authority of the gospel, which they reject; and that they might strengthen the faith of others in those sacred truths, to which they refuse to yield their assent. (2:330–331)

Allusions in the histories of ancient nations associated with the Jews corroborated Old Testament history and clarified its chronology, while spectacles of pagan excess threw the purity of monotheism into prominent relief. For a people whose God had now willed himself into invisibility, the displays of idolatrous nations were thrillingly horrific. One can begin to imagine how the Protestant heartbeat must have raced in the actual presence of Native American fetishes, Catholic painted images, and—for the fortunate missionaries—processions of idols like Juggernaut. Sarah Pierce explained that

After making an early and rapid progress in the arts and sciences, [the Egyptians] stopped in the middle of their career, and having been the instructors of the greater part of the world, became the slaves of their own customs. Their religion degenerated into the grossest superstition, their love of peace into cowardice, their patriotism into foolish pride. Their false ideas of grandeur produced nothing but the gigantic and the useless. (1:89)

Also, the Phoenicians "were infected with those vices, which great riches and prosperity are apt to induce, pride, avarice, and a depravity of manners. . . . They were idolaters, and sacrificed human victims to their Gods, and had beside many absurd and abominable customs. In proportion as true religion exalts human nature, superstition debases it" (1:91).

The study of Athenian Greece involved a critique of esthetics and estheticism. Nobody doubted that under the guise of their many divinities the Greeks worshipped beauty, and sternly moralistic historians read the record to show the inadequacies of even this most idealistic of earthly religions. The student would learn from the Greek story that love of the beautiful was not the same as love of the good, and that through Christianity God has, "in his own time and way, afforded the great remedy for the ignorance and sin which stood in need of this light from Heaven," as Eliza Robbins explained in her *Grecian History* (4); "the political history of nations shows that natural humanity needs the teaching of religion, and the wrath of man can only be brought under the discipline of universal justice and mercy, by the law of God, clearly inculcated"; Greek savagery in war proves "that philosophy and literature will not make men virtuous" (203).

Emma Willard's often-reissued *Universal History* explained that Greek mythology, "although it furnished a splendid imagery to the poet, yet as it taught the worship of divinities, who according to popular belief were murderers, thieves, and adulterers, it therefore exercised an injurious effect on the public morals" (1850, 75). Only Socrates escaped censure, because he, "in his doctrines of the unity and perfections of the Deity, and the immortality of the soul, comes the nearest to Christianity" (ibid.). Elizabeth Peabody argued likewise that Socrates's doctrine and death were "as much a foreshadowing and prophecy of Christianity as the inspired songs of the Hebrew prophets" (*Universal*, 22); arrayed against this great precursor, the Sophists stood for the "fatal art" of "showing that nothing is true, because every proposition may be proved false" (21–22). Child, too, despised the Sophists, accusing them in her historical novel *Philothea* of forgetting the eternal nature of truth and striving "to change it into arbitrary forms of their own making" (109).

Sparta, never confused with Athens, told a very different story: here was no democracy of esthetes, but a rigid dictatorship irradiated by a martial valor and a self-sacrificing patriotism that the Revolutionary generation had found admirable and inspiring. Sarah Pierce struggled with Sparta's ambiguities:

Spartan austerity, carried to excess, presents to our faith some objects shocking to humanity. It stifled pity and the natural affections, those valuable sentiments which are the sweetest bonds of social life. Had they tempered their severe virtues with gentleness, modesty, and humanity, they would have been entitled to higher encomiums. Their contempt of riches, their love of glory, and of their country; their obedience to the laws, and their heroic courage, have ranked them above all other heathen nations. . . They were less superstitious than their neighbors. (2:163).

But the real lesson of Sparta for the 1820s and after was that untrammeled wealth could destroy even the most disciplined society: "the constitution and laws of Lycurgus, under which [Sparta] had risen to consequence, had become subverted by Persian gold and other causes of corruption; and the self-sacrificing spirit of public virtue had passed from a degenerate people" (Willard, *Universal*, 1850, 80).

The history of Rome overshadowed all other nations, in part because the empire engrossed all the other nations. Explaining how to use color to chart national histories, Elizabeth Peabody, choosing red for Rome, instructed students to take each nation separately "in order to get the individuality of each" and weave them together "as they were in fact woven together, till at last the whole web is red with Rome" (*Polish-American*, 12). Roman history circulated in hundred of books designed for every level of expertise, from trots of chronology through Oliver Goldsmith's textbooks to scholarly tomes. Works by the Roman historians circulated in numerous translations, and were studied in the original by boys preparing for college, and again by boys in college; Gibbon was widely cited; Plutarch's Roman lives were in numerous home libraries. The thoughts and lives of the great Romans "were my daily food during those plastic years," Margaret Fuller wrote in her "Autobiographical Fragment"; "ROME! it stands by itself, a clear Word" (in Steele, 28, 29).

In some deep sense Rome stood for history itself—history as hope, history as horror and obstacle. In another deep sense, Rome the "worldly wise" (Peabody, *Universal*, 114) was the antithesis of and obstacle to the millennial, spiritual history that these Protestants were trying to discern in the turbulent murk of historical waters. The supplanting of republican Rome by the Roman Empire provided a storehouse of data for understanding the dynamics of history. Imperial Rome was at once the true God's powerful enemy and, willy-nilly, his instrument, destined to produce a networked "Europe" through which true religion would eventually be disseminated.

In subduing Greece, the Romans acquired the philosophy and arts which the Greeks imparted to the nations they had conquered; and then the Romans, in wider conquests—as far as Britain and Gaul, disseminated gradually the literature and science which they had acquired from the Greeks.

Thus, under the merciful laws of God, *war*, the lamentable and detestable means which misguided men employed to aggrandize themselves, became the cause of humanizing and improving savage, unregenerate nations; and when the unhappy effects of these wars ceased, and vanished from the earth, better results grew out of them, and to this hour exalt the condition of mankind. (Robbins, *Grecian*, 366)

But Rome resurfaced as antichrist in the great and dangerous delusion of Roman Catholicism, whose theology was ultimately Roman paganism in masquerade and whose papal structure was ultimately a secular Empire dressed up as spirituality. During the long centuries of the Dark and Middle Ages, only chivalry hoarded some small spiritual spark in its unworldly commitment to something beyond the visible, tangible, material.

The beginning of the end of this lamentable era was not the Renaissance but the Reformation—the emergence of Martin Luther and the printing press, the one to demand popular access to the Bible and the other to make that access possible. That the Reformation took off from the beliefs and teachings of a poor monk who carried the day by the sheer force of his ideas pointed to a shift in the nature of historical causation from the material to the literally ideal. Luther's example also promised obscure individuals that they could now influence the historical process as decisively as temporal rulers:

While sincere and earnest individuals raise the standard of their own times, the age, improved by their efforts, educates other individuals, who, being thus raised to a higher point of view, can command a more extended vision than their predecessors. By obedience to a law within themselves, above the existing laws of society, such individuals help to raise the moral standard of succeeding ages to a plane still more elevated. By this mutual action and reaction between the public and private conscience, the world is slowly rolled onward toward its long-promised Golden Age. . . . Every one of us can aid in the great work, if we always look inward for our guide, and follow the voice of conscience, which to each one of us is truly the law of God. (Child, *Progress of Religious Ideas*, 3:460–461)

Yet even for Child, this progress was always mediated by nations: "If only one nation would conscientiously obey [Christ's] laws, in her internal and external regulations, she would be lifted up, and draw all the nations unto her. War and slavery, the gallows and prisons, would disappear from the earth" (*Progress*, 3:459). From Luther on, modern history was the story of the mutually reinforcing development of Protestantism and republicanism against the variously combining forces of Catholic despotisms.

For all their underlying optimism, recitals of modern history could not ignore entrenched resistance to Protestant republicanism in Europe. History had somehow to escape the grip of the Old World. Hannah F. S. Lee's three books of Reformation history, focused on Luther for Germany, Cranmer for England, and the Huguenots for France, made especially clear how necessary the American continent was to God's reformist plans. Until such time as Protestant republics covered the face of the earth, the United States stood as the only nation whose existence guaranteed the validity of the entire scheme. The rapid mutation of the French Revolution through the Terror into Napoleon's Empire left the Protestant version of progressive history in undisputed possession of the American field, because the sequence of events could be explained as a function of Jacobin atheism, which in turn was the antithesis to French Catholic absolutism. Having lost its Huguenot population, France had, in effect, no republican character left in the nation on which to construct a republic. In her 1856 United States history, Elizabeth Peabody contrasted the American constitutional convention to the French, where "a despotism which had corrupted social life for ages, was to be destroyed . . . and republicanism to be created out of its ruins, by human will and wit. In America, on the contrary, two hundred years of the growth of social virtue and happiness, in their turn growing out of liberty to worship God with individual integrity, that had been all the time struggled for, was to be conserved" (183–184).

As Peabody's Burkean metaphors of abstract artifice and organic growth might suggest, the French disaster was also used to argue for the United States's English origins, to make English history and English literature part of the narrative of the United States, to make "us" a part of the English people even as our right to independence from them was insisted on. Susanna Rowson's *Exercises* asked and answered:

What great political event took place during the reign of George 3d? The American Colonies, considering themselves aggrieved, by having taxes levied by the British parliament, when they were not allowed to send representatives to sit in that house, and having vainly remonstrated, took up arms to defend and assert their rights, and after a long and glorious struggle, established themselves as free and independent States in 1783. . . . What other great revolution took place about this time? The sanguinary revolution in France, which from the year 1789 to 1815, cost Europe more lives and caused more individual suffering, than had ever been experienced before in the same period of time. . . . Every christian power in turn opposed the tide of tyranny, slaughter and infidelity, but Great Britain was the only one that steadily maintained an undeviating course. (103–104)

But the English prehistory of the American nation, and the consanguinity of the English and American people, did not change the fact that as a nation the United States was unique:

The Old World is covered with bad institutions which men have created, very often with positively good intentions, but on false notions, or at least, without large or profound ideas. These institutions have done infinite mischiefs, and are perpetuated and reproduced by the activity of the wicked and the passivity of the good. Whether the new world shall estimate and sift out these evils, or repeat these mistakes, depends on young Americans, who are now sitting in school rooms all over the country. (Peabody, *United States*, 7)

Thus it was a sense of extraordinary historical mission, not Adamic belief in the nation's exemption from history, that formed the core of the American exceptionalism expressed in antebellum textbooks of American history by both women and men. A diffuse longing to escape the demands of history may be sensed in the anticipation of the near arrival of the millennium in the early national and antebellum decades. Hannah Adams wrote her history of the Jews in the United States in part because she believed that the gathering of the Jews in the United States signified the imminent coming of the final days and also showed that the millennium would occur in the United States.

The American Revolution, or War of Independence, as it was more commonly called, resulting as it did in the formation of a republic—this republic, the only republic—became, accordingly, the most important event in world history since the Reformation, an event to be interpreted as the carrying forward of the Reformation's aims. Peabody defined the vital principle of the American nation: "the liberty to discover and obey . . . those laws of society which legitimately grow out of the destiny God has given to humanity"; this destiny was articulated "in the first sentence of the Declaration" of Independence (*United States*, 179). The centrality of the American Revolution to all representations of United States and, indeed, world history, cannot be overstated; the Constitution, in turn, acquired the aura of a second sacred book; while George Washington, so unlike any other temporal ruler the world had ever known, became the holy incarnation of republican leadership.

The New Englanders who chiefly produced the national history presented the Puritans, not as nation-builders, but as faulty ground-layers whose work was used by Providence for purposes that the pilgrim fathers never could have imagined. The separatists of Plymouth became the historiographical icon of settlement rather than the Puritans of Massachusetts Bay because, notwithstanding their residual medieval intolerance, they opposed the established church, as the Puritans did not. "To trace our history from the little band of pilgrims who first landed on Plymouth rock, through the trials of our forefathers by savage cruelty, famine, and pestilence, and to follow the patriots of the revolution through their struggle for independence, are employments which have warmed the heart and engaged the pen of many a gifted American": thus Almira Phelps assured her students in phrases that might have been taken from any of several hundred works of history (*Female Student*, 183). From this perspective one could see that the Revolution was only apparently fought for political rather than religious freedom; in fact, it was fought to preserve the Bible-reading home and the national character that such a home produced. In the picture of a polity where citizen patriots defended their homes against an imperial enemy bent on pillage and rapine (and not coincidentally using "savages" as part of his army), the protections and possibilities of the Revolution were displayed: the home-centered, female-empowering, and profoundly pacific Protestant republic emerged as a private scene with immense public import.

The post-Revolutionary vantage point gave American citizens—even schoolgirls—as much enlightenment as human beings had ever enjoyed. Sarah Hale wrote in her "Course of Reading,"

Next to our religion comes our own country; the better we understand the history of these the better we shall be prepared to read and rightly appreciate the history and literature of the Old World. Without a standard of comparison how shall we rightly compare what may be presented to us? If we are acquainted with the Bible and the history and literature of its religion, we are then prepared to read the history and literature of heathendom and judge of the spirit and influence of these dissimilar institutions. And when we know our own country, not merely as we learn it on the maps or in the geographies at school, but by studying and reading the best productions of its writers, then we shall be able to compare the past with the present and judge of the improvements of the world since days when woman was a born serf to her "lore," [sic] and the father could put his children to death at his own pleasure, and war was the common pursuit of man, and to be a "foreigner" was to be an enemy. (*Lady's Book*, 34:220)

In the early republic, as is well known, the chief problem that politically minded Americans recognized involved maintaining a republic within the existing national boundaries in the context of a hostile world, whose strifes were replicated internally by the immediate post-Constitution division of the electorate into two parties philosophically allied with either

England or France. To the Anglophiles, the partisans of France were dema-gogues threatening the new nation with anarchy; to the Francophiles, the partisans of England were closet monarchists. The nation also had to deal with threats on its borders, indeed had to establish its borders. France was pacified in the Louisiana Purchase; a second war with England stabilized the border with Canada. Not until after the Mexican War was the south-ern border secured; and, of course, notwithstanding U.S. claims to the con-tinent west of the Mississippi, the Native Americans had a different view. Over time, the problem of managing immigration emerged as signifi-cant to the future of the republic, and more than ever the teaching of Ameri-can history itself was invoked as a way to save the nation from falling apart. Emma Willard wrote in the 1852 edition of her abridged United States history:

There are those, who rashly speak, as if in despair of the fortunes of our republic; because, they say, political virtue has declined. If so, then is there the more need to infuse patriotism into the breasts of the coming generation. And what is so likely to effect this national self-preservation, as to give our children, for their daily reading, and study, such a record of the sublime virtues of our worthies of our earliest day,—and of Washington and his compatriots, as shall leave its due impress? And what but the study of their dangers and toils,—their devotion of life and fortune, can make our posterity know, what our country, and our liberties have cost? (vi)

The main problem with immigration was that so many new arrivals were Catholic. Early Federalist rhetoric about whether the republic could sur-vive its own centrifugal tendencies—including territorial expansion, parti-san strife, slave versus free states, and Catholic immigration—reminded people that the Roman Empire fell not only because it grew too rich but, even more, because it grew too big to administer centrally and too diverse in its population. While conceivably any kind of Protestant person could be brought into the republican synthesis, Catholicism seemed to under-mine the very reason for being of a Protestant republic. An enormous amount of female historicizing and pedagogic energy went into anti-Catholic period therefore went into anti-Catholic polemic and purposes. Zilpah Grant, Mary Lyons, and Catharine Beecher trained women teachers as "home missionaries"—that is, teachers who went west specifically to ad-vocate and preserve Protestantism on the frontier. Tract societies targeted their wares for urban Catholic enclaves. Bible societies tried to distribute Bibles to Catholics, who, it was assumed, were denied access to them by priests but would, if only they could read God's word for themselves, im-mediately see the light.

The Divine Point of View

In 1852, a high point of know-nothing anti-Catholicism, Emma Willard added this exhortation to her United States history:

There is a great emigration.... Some are of the bone and sinew of Europe, attracted hither by our republican institutions; while another portion is sent to our shores from jails and poor-houses; and as we have reason to believe, for the purposes of hastening on that ruin by anarchy, which European foes to freedom predict and desire. Crime accordingly increases.... If the enemies of our country operate to drive us into anarchy by overwhelming us with an unsound population, let our people the more strenuously UPHOLD LAW AND ORDER.... Then will God bring to naught the counsels of our enemies, and more and more make us his own exalted and favored people. (401–403)

Because territorial expansion throughout the period meant continual Indian warfare, the image of a heroic Protestant population overcoming savage native resistance was recurrent in the historical narrative. This was indeed no virgin land, but an occupied territory that had to be wrested from a diabolic enemy. Only a few textbook writers deviated from the insistently hostile representation of Native Americans. Sarah Sprague Jacobs memorialized the Christian Indian towns of seventeenth-century Massachusetts in *The White Oak, and Its Neighbors* (1853). Elizabeth Peabody's United States history proposed giving the (undifferentiated) Indians their own state in the Union, arguing that the Constitution guaranteed, to those bound by laws, the right to take part in making them (236). She called Cherokee removal "the most flagrant instance of a wrong, which has been suffered by multitudes of these hapless tribes, who might have been made an important element of the United States nationality, had they been treated as men, whose equal rights to life, liberty, and the pursuit of happiness were self-evident" (251). Child's *First Settlers of New-England* portrayed Native Americans as uncorrupted Christians (see Chapter 3). These were exceptions. Hannah Adams's school history of New England depicted the Native Americans as opponents to everything that Christianity stood for; if they were no longer literal demons as in Puritan captivity narratives, they were still purely evil in their benightedness.

The ignorance and darkness of the natives of New England, and the savage ferocity of their character teach us duly to appreciate the inestimable advantage of being educated and early instructed in the Christian religion. The spirit of revenge, which education and habit conspire to strengthen in the savage state, is productive of the most pernicious effects in society; and exhibits, in a striking manner, the inconceivable degree of barbarity of which human nature is capable, when destitute of the refinements of polished society, and the restrains of reason and civilization. Christianity has civilized the world, exalted the human intellect, softened the ferocity of war, taught us compassion towards our enemies, and strengthened every social tie. Such are its advantages with respect to this state, which, however great, are small when compared with those which regard futurity. (64–65)

Edition after edition of Emma Willard's United States history textbook weighed in against the Indians with sensational accounts of Indian atrocities:

Dreadful beyond description was the condition of the colonists. The object of the Indians, was totally to exterminate them, and aimed equally at the lives of the armed and the defenceless. They were withheld by no laws of religion, and their customs of war, instead of restraining, led them to the most shocking barbarities. . . . They ambushed the private path; they rushed with the dreadful war-whoop upon the worshipping assembly; and, during the silence of midnight, set fire to the lonely dwelling, and butchered its inhabitants. When the father of the family was to go forth in the morning, he knew he might meet his death-shot as he opened his door, from some foe concealed behind his fences, or in his barn: or he might go, and return to find his family murdered during his absence. When the mother lay down at night, with her infant cradled on her arm, she knew that, before morning, it might be plucked from her bosom, and its brains dashed out before her eyes. Such were at all times, the consequences of savage warfare; but, at no time during the settlement of the country, were they so extensively felt, as during the year through which this war continued. (*United States*, 1831, 67–68)

Augusta Berard was similarly impassioned:

The details of Indian warfare need not be dwelt upon. They are very horrible: but it is useful sometimes to think of the sufferings of others; and mothers in the pleasant homes of Providence, Springfield, Deerfield, and Hadley, may do well to remember the "heavy hours" of the New England women of a former generation.

The mother retired to rest, to be awakened at midnight by the dreadful Indian war whoop, to see her children cut down before her by the tomahawk, or it may be, carried away into captivity. The family on the Sabbath, on their way to church, are startled by the bullets shot by a hidden foe from behind thickets and fences. The farmer gathering his harvests, the shepherd tending his flocks, and laborer in the fields, were alike exposed to the attacks of a cunning and cruel enemy. (30)

Christopher Columbus appeared in American historiography as an exemplary hero; Ferdinand and Isabella (the latter especially) won praise; but the Spanish incursion was mainly narrated to contrast Spanish cruelty with English fairness and altruism in Indian dealings; and to contrast the peaceful, friendly South American native population with the warlike, treacherous tribes of North America. This narrative says that "we" behaved much better to "our" Indians than "they" did, even though ours were dangerous and wicked Indians and theirs were not.

"They," of course, were Catholics. Columbus's eventual disgrace made this story easier to tell; as Eliza Robbins observed in the first volume of *Tales from American History* (1829), "the character of Columbus, so grand and elevated among men, is interesting enough to requite one for all the painful feelings excited by the cruel, selfish, ignorant Spaniards, with whom he was associated" (108). In the second volume (1832) she continued the narrative with the Spanish conquests of Mexico and Peru, insisting that

we cannot honour the deliverers and benefactors of society as they deserve, unless we can oppose to them the crimes of the abusers of power—we cannot see how God brings good out of evil, unless we know what the evil is—we cannot understand that plan of Providence, unless we know what misery grows out of all guilt, and what happiness arises from peace on earth, and generosity and good will to men. Those who have read the history of William Penn and his colony, and who read that of Cortez, and of all that followed the conquest, will know what I mean. (134–135)

She had earlier confessed, however, although obliquely, that the good results of Columbus's discovery were not easily understood, and projected historical study as an exercise in cultural sophistry:

This is a short sketch of the religion and the customs of . . . a people now vanished from the earth. Where they enjoyed the luxuries of nature, a delicious climate, and a productive soil, in ease and repose, the white man has set his foot, and raised his habitation, and the toil and bondage of the slave have succeeded to the indolence and liberty of the savage. Still industry and civilization are better than sloth, ignorance, and barbarism. If you do not understand me now you will when you are older, and have learned to think, and are become acquainted with the history of many nations. (1:121)

In contrast to the obsession with Indians, African Americans are virtually absent from these histories; slavery, when it appeared, was wrapped in circumlocution and euphemism. Robbins brings slavery into her account as an evil, but only to demonstrate through historical examples that it can only be ended gradually:

> In the Bible, we read of bondmen and bondwomen among the Hebrews; and, in all Asia, the state of slavery still exists. In ancient Greece and Rome, a large part of the population were slaves, and, in modern Europe, the vassalage of the lower orders, much resembled the bondage of patriarchal times. Slavery, in any country of Europe, has never been annihilated by acts of sudden emancipation, but by a gradual change in the opinion of the people—who, by degrees, educated the lower orders, gave them trades, and enabled them to acquire property; and, at length, political regulations gave personal liberty, and certain independent rights to all people. (1:150–151)

Elizabeth Peabody simply declined to address slavery in her *United States history*: "A book intended for the public schools of all the United States, is not the place for discussion of a subject so vital to the interests of the Union as the slavery question" (308).

For many, perhaps most, writers, the evils of slavery were recognized but overridden by the need to preserve the Union. In the 1831 version of her *United States history* Emma Willard used the history of the Constitution—a document regarded, "by the friends of the rights of man, in both hemispheres, as the palladium of the civil liberty of the world" (278)—to advocate the necessity of compromise:

> That these great difficulties were compromised, holds up this convention, as an example to future times, of the triumph of strong patriotism and honest zeal for the public welfare, over party feeling and sectional prejudice. If the time shall ever come, when any American congress, or convention, shall fail to compromise amicably, disputes, which conflicting interests must produce in this extensive republic; then will the day of its degeneracy have arrived, and its downfall be at hand; then will be experienced the triumph of party feeling and sectional interest, over patriotism and public zeal. The finger of history would point with scorn at such a body of men, while she contrasted them with the wise and honest patriots, who framed the constitution. (277–278)

Child's *Appeal*, the only example of abolitionist counterhistory in all this writing, saw the Union as fatally flawed by the constitutional compromise that brought it into being, while adroitly avoiding an attack on the Constitution itself:

The strongest and best reason that can be given for our supineness on the subject of slavery, is the fear of dissolving the Union. The Constitution of the United States demands our highest reverence. Those who approve, and those who disapprove of particular portions, are equally bound to yield implicit obedience to its authority. But we must not forget that the Constitution provides for any change that may be required for the general good. The great machine is constructed with a safety-valve, by which any rapidly increasing evil may be expelled whenever the people desire it.

If the Southern politicians are determined to make a Siamese question of this also—if they insist that the Union shall not exist without slavery—it can only be said that they join two things, which have no affinity with each other, and which cannot permanently exist together. (212)

Sarah Hale, to whom preserving the Union was a life principle, published a colonization argument in the form of a historical novel, *Liberia*, in 1853. Her protagonists, a group of free Christian blacks headed by Keziah, an exemplar of republican womanhood, are likened to pilgrims (145) facing conditions similar to those of the New England settlers, even including being attacked by savages (162–163). In a typical move for advocates of colonization, Hale historicized slavery in the United States as God's way of making Christians out of the Africans, and sentimentalized the nation as nobly suffering world abuse to fulfill this divine mandate:

In 1620 the first African slaves were brought to Virginia. In 1820 the first emancipated Africans were sent from the United States to Liberia.

If a superior intelligence . . . had observed that one little ship taking its solitary way across the ocean, laden with emigrants returning, civilized and Christianized, to the land which, two centuries previous, their fathers had left degraded and idolatrous savages, would he not have thought that, of all the enterprises then absorbing the energies and hopes of man, this . . . was the one which promised to the human race the largest portion of ultimate good? And who can doubt that, in thus providing a home of refuge for "the stranger within her gates," our beloved Union was nobly, though silently, justifying herself from the aspersions of oppression and wrong so often thrown out against her? (iii–iv)

63

Such historical writing as there was by southern women concerned itself with the Revolution and the formation of the republic; the coded meaning of these events for the contemporary situation was that the South stood for republicanism and the North for imperial aggression. As the war came on, the southern historical approach was to see it as the American Revolution being fought all over again. As a male character in Augusta Evans's Civil War novel *Macaria* (1864) puts it, "When every sacred constitutional barrier had been swept away by Lincoln—when the *habeas corpus* was abolished, and freedom of speech and press denied—when the Washington conclave essayed to coerce freemen, to 'crush Secession' through the agency of the sword and cannon—then I swore allegiance to the 'Seven States' where all of republican liberty remained" (437).

The expansionist ideology of American Manifest Destiny transformed republicanism into imperialism and strained the shape of republic rhetoric. The idea that the United States republic was to inspire the formation of many more republics began to transmute into the idea that the United States itself was destined to incorporate the entire continent and, eventually, the entire world, under its own republican flag. Many women were expansionists on religious grounds; but from the start, most who wrote history offered a somewhat conservative answer to the question of how much alien population could be absorbed by the national body before it ceased to be itself. Trying to understand why they among the world's peoples had been selected to lead the historical procession, these women, along with most native-born white Americans, increasingly settled on a racial answer. Delia Bacon was reported as saying in one of her historical lectures that "only one race has any part in the world's drama. It is the Caucasian. The other races may perhaps hereafter have their history" (*New York Herald*, 1 December 1852). Bacon associated Caucasian "superiority of intellect" with head shape; the more common signifier, of course, was skin color. Whiteness might have been taken as an accidental trait, but it almost never was. A great deal of the rhetoric of whiteness and fairness in all antebellum discourse, whether historical or domestic, codes the superiority of white bodies and hence deals implicitly with slavery, Indians, and immigrants all at once.

The third volume of Eliza Robbins's *Tales from American History* (1833) gave the textbook answer to the question of Anglo-Saxon success:

Why these nations became superior to the other inhabitants of the earth is not known. God is good to all, and his tender mercies are over all; but in his wisdom he has not distributed his gifts equally. Upon this Caucasian race,—upon the men of Western Asia, of Europe, and the descendants of Europeans in every part of the world, he has bestowed superior understanding and greater blessings than to the rest of mankind.

The superiority of the Caucasian race appears in this: they have more enterprise than other men. They undertake discoveries, and distribute themselves all over the world. They have more perfect sciences, and more useful arts. Their ships traverse every sea; their books are carried abroad into every nation; their pictures and statues resemble nature herself; and they have better governments and a purer religion than other races of men. (51)

Since history was the story of nations, it was almost impossible to abandon the national concept; but from time to time somebody escaped nationalist chauvinism, although almost always (as is still the case today) on behalf of an ideal America. "My friends write to urge my return," Fuller observed in a dispatch from Rome dated 19 April 1848; "they talk of our country as the land of the Future. It is so, but that spirit which made it all it is of value in my eyes, which gave all of hope with which I can sympathize for that Future, is more alive here at present than in America. . . . I hear earnest words of pure faith and love. I see deeds of brotherhood. This is what makes *my America*" (*Sad but Glorious*, 230). Sara Tappan Robinson's militant history of Kansas depicted the United States as an enemy of the abolitionist Utopia being established in the territory by free-soil settlers—abolitionist, but also without a black population. Surprisingly, perhaps, the most truly internationalist people were the missionaries, who thought of themselves as conscripted for God's cause directly rather than through the tediously indirect route of national citizenship.

This multiply determined, flexible religiopolitical narrative demonstrated remarkable sustaining and shaping power; one finds it everywhere. The avidity with which women recycled its premises indicates that it was central to history's appeal for them. The most obvious answer to the question why women accepted this narrative of history from the divine point of view is that the historian who relayed this narrative was assuming the mantle of divinity herself. To inhabit the persona of the historian provided an enormous sense of imaginative liberation, projecting a woman into the full range of space and time as a kind of counterforce to the restrictions of her daily life.

Beyond the imagined liberation into power lies something more important still, the narrative promise that women's historical day is close at hand. They read the Protestant script as especially significant for their sex: "As the principle of liberty is better understood and more nobly interpreted, a broader protest is made in behalf of woman," Margaret Fuller wrote in "The Great Lawsuit." They saw in Protestant Christianity the only ideology that, by valuing intellect and spirituality over physical strength, opened at least some kinds of public and political space to women, and promised to protect the weak members of society from the strong. As they saw it, Protestant Bible-based respect for the printed word and insistence on every person's right to literacy had underwritten their own participation in the print sphere, as the lack of such participation by women in non-Protestant parts of the world made clear. White, Protestant, Anglo-Saxon United States women felt fully authorized by their culture to speak for history because they felt so fully that the end result of the historical narrative was, precisely, themselves.

Whatever else women thought they were doing when they wrote history, then, they thought they were combating infidelity and advancing the cause of true religion. This was Hannah Adams's mission in the eighteenth century, when she canvassed all the Christian sects to precipitate the essential Christianity from the hubbub of doctrinal controversy. In 1813, Elizabeth Peabody (mother) offered her textbook of sacred history as armor against attacks on religion. Sarah Pierce explained that her *Universal History* tried "to intermix moral with historical instruction, and to obviate those objections which arise in the minds of youth against the justice of God, when they read the wars of the Israelites.—I have attempted also to give them a general notion of the government of God, and the truth of the Scripture" (1:4). Nothing had changed along these lines when Sarah Hanna published her Bible history in 1860.

Thus, the women were one in resisting secular history. In their homogeneity they differed from the more diverse group of male historians, most of whom, to be sure, adopted the providential perspective, but others of whom were more materialist and secular. Even before the war, and certainly afterward, there were distinctions between levels of history, whereby pietistic didactic history was allotted to women and children, while a more secular historicism was associated with men. But, as we see, women before the Civil War thought this distinction told in their favor. If the United States was in the historical vanguard, Christian Protestant women were the elite corps. If they were telling the same Protestant republican story that controlled most historical writing by men, they were telling it with a sense of its gendered significance, and consequently with more fervor, than men could possibly feel.

5

Poetic Demonstrations of Learning and Patriotism

WHEN WOMEN DEFINED THEMSELVES either as students or transmitters of the millennial historical narrative, they assumed one of two distinct yet connected identities. The student, charming her social circle by her display of knowledge, is just as evidently a daughter as the didactic matron is a mother. These figures are connected because each is a stage in an idealized female life course, and also because each is developed in relation to an idealized family that is simultaneously a particular kinship network and the nation at large. In this image of family, all space or distinction between the domestic and the national disappears. Home, where the educated daughter shines and the learned mother instructs, is the designated structure for producing republican citizens aware of the historical significance of their lives; the nation is the designated structure for producing homes in which women do this progressive work. The symbol system is so thoroughly interactive and interpenetrating that locutions like "daughters of the republic" and "mothers of the republic" cease to be recognized as metaphors by those who use them. At the hub of the system, the female subjectivity absorbing these messages experiences them as part of her identity.

From this standpoint, insofar as print is a technology through which citizens are guided into the national family, women who published for patriotic and public purposes need not have been seen as breaching feminine decorum or challenging the boundaries of home space, and this point was insisted on by women activists and their supporters. Indeed, and perhaps not surprisingly, it turned out to be much easier to justify women who published for admirable civic purposes than those who published to display their supposedly inmost sensibilities. Yet, understanding the full cultural dynamics of women's literary production in the nineteenth century (and after) requires recognition that print, which can market women's writing as high-mindedly civic, can also market it as female self-display.

A variety of forms of female confessional writing emerged throughout the antebellum era to represent the personal subjectivity of women. The more contradictions and tensions there were in such a project, the more interesting was the subjectivity emerging from it. Why women should have felt impelled to represent their subjectivities; why there should have been an audience avid for such representations; whether the depictions were such as daringly to resist or lamentably to confirm cultural stereotypes; what and whose interests were served by representations of women as essentially and irremediably subjective—these questions were raised throughout the era. Indeed, they continue to be the focus today in the publication niche called feminist theory. What matters for my purpose here, however, is that even the most self-engrossed presentations of female selfhood in the antebellum era were likely to genuflect toward history and patriotism, indicating either that at the core the woman knew herself as a member of the national family and product of the nation's history, or that she found it expedient to present herself in that way. So, for example, in Fanny Fern's sensational confessional novel, *Ruth Hall* (1854), the protagonist's phrenological reading, given at great length in Chapter 76, includes: "You are strongly attached to place, and are intensely patriotic. You believe in Plymouth Rock and Bunker Hill."

Ruth's phrenological report lists without reconciling or organizing a variety of competing images, indicating the multifaceted, ever-changing, endlessly fascinating character that she is. Self-displaying presentations of female subjectivities abound in antebellum women's writing; but poetry above all was the genre to which the diverging aspects and multifarious layers of female selfhood were thematically central. The curious place that poetry occupied in antebellum women's writing is partly a function of the range of types within the genre. At one end of the scale is the dignified epic, which at least until the 1840s loomed as the most demanding, rulebound, ambitious, and admirable type of literary production. Early manifestations of United States literary nationalism always centered on a call for a truly American epic. At the scale's other end, the brief occasional lyric—despite the critics' expectation that even the shortest poem would display strict meter and true rhyme—figured as the most informal, spontaneous, ephemeral, and easiest kind of writing. Rhyme and meter appeared (as they still do appear) to have helped people invent and memorize brief poems that could be written down in spare moments. Nothing comparable was possible for any length of prose. The exigencies of household life pushed women toward the composition of brief lyrics, and, to some extent, identified the lyric as a female form in antebellum America.

It was not difficult for women to publish short poems in these years. A proliferating array of newspapers, weeklies, monthlies, quarterlies, and annuals solicited poetry for their poetry pages, poetry departments, and for scattered page filler. Daily, weekly, monthly: poems by women beyond counting appeared. Most of these short lyrics never got collected into books, since there was no substantial market in the United States for single-authored books of poetry and since few women wrote enough poems to fill out a volume. Almost none of the volumes published had more than one edition. Still, by the Civil War (the estimate is Emily Watts's) some eighty women had published at least one volume of poetry. A few of these volumes contained just a single long poem; most were miscellanies, sometimes padded out by prose. These collections embody women's attempts to prove themselves as poets by demonstrating range and skill in a variety of forms, while representing the women herself as various, fluid, and interestingly complicated.

As a genre, the women's miscellany typically contains poems of varying lengths in many moods and modes, in diverse stanzaic forms, frequently featuring one ambitious philosophical, romantic, or visionary poem that gives its name to the collection. Sometimes a long dramatic poem is part of the mix, although more typically such poems would be thought of as plays (and it is in this aspect that I will discuss them in Chapter 9). The miscellany may include songs, occasional verse, album inscriptions, satirical and light verse, narrative romances and stories and legends, poems marking milestones in a woman's domestic life (love, marriage, births and deaths of children), paeans to women's long-suffering and self-sacrificing love, poems of female friendship, poems to parents, nature poems, poems of place, patriotic poems (some composed for public recitation), political poems, poems about current events, pious and doctrinal religious poems, philosophical poems, visionary poems, elegies, eulogies, historical poems, poems of parting and greeting, poems inspired by painting and plays and statues and books and other poets (especially women poets), poems about poetry, poems about the poet writing her poems.

Each miscellany exhibits an identity specific to the writer that, given the events through which she defines herself, is ineluctably female. The mix of poetic types differs from one miscellany to the next; but yet, if biblical poetry is considered historical, as the age would have considered it, then historical, political, and patriotic poetry appear significantly in most of the miscellanies I have examined. Even when biblical poetry is ignored, as this discussion will ignore it, more than half of the books I have looked at contain historical material. Historical topics are multiply associated; a poem about the American Revolution may refer in passing to ancient Rome or Greece or the Hebrews or the Puritans or Queen Elizabeth or the Poles; a fantasy romance set in Florence may begin with stanzas on the history of that city, or Italy, or Christendom.

The anthologies of American women poets that began to appear around the end of the 1840s also included biblical, historical, philosophical and patriotic poems, indicating conclusively that such material was not thought of as inconsistent with any ideal of true womanhood. Rufus Griswold's 1848 anthology, *The Female Poets of America*, praises the female ambition manifest in long historical works. Griswold preserves Eliza Townsend's otherwise uncollected "Occasional Ode" denouncing Napoleon ("Is't not enough, thou spoiler, tell! / That, subject to thy stern behest, / The might of ancient empire fell, / And sunk to dread and endless rest? / Fallen is the Roman Eagle's flight, / The Grecian glory sunk in night" [39]); he gives a segment from and summary of Harriet Whipple Green's uncompleted six-canto epic of early Native American history, "Nanuntenoo"; and he anthologizes Sarah Hale's patriotic lesson in history and geography, "The Mississippi," which declares the river superior to the Nile, Ganges, and all Europe's rivers put together. "Our Mississippi," she proclaims, "rolling proudly on, / Would sweep them from its path, or swallow up, / Like Aaron's rod, these streams of fame and song" (59).

Extracting history from this composite distorts the genre as a whole; but for my argument the point is that even when the focus is subjective and the intention to provide a complete inventory of a self complexly relating to numerous areas of experience, history is still there with all its public implications. In some poets, of course, it is much more there than in others. Mercy Otis Warren's 1790 *Poems, Dramatic and Miscellaneous*—probably the third book of poetry published by an American woman, preceded by Anne Bradstreet's and Phillis Wheatley's books—is much more scripted to portray a historically aware and historically motivated republican mother than the typical later collection, which appeared in decades when republican motherhood was a fading ideal. Warren's poems like "A Political Reverie," dated 1774, place her appeals to patriotism in the context of an allegory of progressive world history, while parading the poet's store of hard-won historical knowledge. The poem envisions the future nation as freedom's historically destined home:

> Long she's forsook her Asiatic throne,
> And leaving Afric's barb'rous burning zone,
> On the broad ruins of Rome's haughty power
> Erected ramparts round fair Europe's shore;
> But in those blasted climes no more presides,
> She, o'er the vast Atlantic surges rides,
> Visits Columbia's distant fertile plains,
> Where liberty, a happy goddess, reigns. (189)

"To a Young Gentleman Residing in France," dated 1782, pressures the addressee to return and participate in the Revolution, assuring him that not

Poetic Demonstrations

From Hector's days to haughty Caesar's time,
When sinking Rome, ingulph'd in every crime,
When ravag'd Gaul had swell'd the tyrant's pride,
And crimson torrents wash'd the Danube's side;
Nor yet when Charles, and his more bloody son,
On carnage fed, till Europe was undone; . . .
Yet history has never mark'd a page,
With feats more glorious than the present age;
No smitten plains, or reeking fields afford,
A fairer cause to draw an hero's sword,
Than does thy country, ravag'd and distress'd,
While war's hoarse clarion roars from east to west. (225)

Her 1779 "Simplicity" deploys world history for a conventional republican argument about the threat of luxury to citizen virtue and national survival:

Rome, the proud mistress of the world, displays
A lasting proof of what my pen essays;
High wrought refinement—usher'd in replete,
With all the ills that sink a virtuous state . . .
What blotted out the Carthaginian fame,
And left no traces but an empty name! . . .
From age to age, since Hannibal's hard fate,
From Caesar's annals to the modern date, . . .
When taste's improv'd by luxury high wrought,
And fancy craves what nature never taught;
Affronted virtue mounts her native skies,
And freedom's genius lifts her bloated eyes. (232–233)

Missing from Warren's collection, however, are the two types of historical poetry that—always excluding Bible poetry—came increasingly to dominate women's writing: topographical poetry and poems of social protest. But like Warren's work, both of these types are expressions of patriotism; the subjective experience of history transmitted throughout all these poems is a passionately affiliative love of country. In the topographical poem, or poem of place, which its practitioners called the *local* poem, a local site is made historically significant through the work of a poetic imagination that revivifies some important event of the past that took place there. Typically, the event is a Revolutionary battle, which means that historical material is developed in relation to sanctifying blood sacrifice. In the poem of social protest, citizens are made aware of some national shame—almost always, Indian removal policies or African slavery—by appeals to the national past and lamentations over the central administration's abandonment of the nation's historically destined mission.

In the local poem, the poet's imaginative work reminds readers of their national origins in patriot blood, performs an act of daughterly homage, and represents a rite through which national identity is renewed. Margaretta Faugeres's "The Hudson," published in 1793, is the earliest example of this type I have found. In about 450 lines it describes the river in its progress south from Canada to New York City, saturating the scenery with Revolutionary associations. In the opening lines, Faugeres identifies herself as a woman uplifted into epic eloquence by the sublimity of her theme:

Nile's beauteous waves, and Tiber's swelling tide
Have been recorded by the hand of fame....
Whilst oh! her Genius of old Hudson's stream,
Thy mighty River never hath been sung:
Say, shall a *Female* string her trembling lyre,
And to thy praise devote th'advent'rous song?
Fir'd with the theme, her genius shall aspire,
And the notes sweeten as they float along. (358)

Along with invocations of male patriot blood, Faugeres recounts (for Fort Edward) the death of Jane McCrea, murdered and scalped by Indians attached to General Burgoyne's army when they were escoring her to her Tory fiancé. Burgoyne's memoirs asserted that propaganda based on this event had aroused an apathetic citizenry against the British. That McCrea had been attached to a Tory—that the savage allies of the British did not even respect the women on their own side—made the story that much more compelling an argument for the superiority of republicans to monarchists. Faugeres's narration exactly conveys the sensationalism:

This flood, which should have borne the nuptial throng,
Found her warm blood deep tincturing its stream!
These woods, which should have heard her bridal song,
Wildly responded all her hopeless screams!
Cruel in mercy, barbarous Burgoyne!
Ah! see an aged sire, with silver hairs,
(Whose goodness trusted much, too much to thine)
Bathing his mangled daughter with his tears!
Hear a distracted lover's frightful voice.
See, as he bends to kiss the clotted gore
Senseless he sinks! (362)

At Saratoga, Faugeres invokes General Gates, "the hero who / Rescued Columbia from a cruel foe" (363); the sight of Esopus "calls to mind when Britain's lawless bands / Wag'd impious war with consecrated fanes" (366); West Point brings in consideration of Benedict Arnold, Major André, General Wayne, and others. The conclusion invokes a future when American grandeur will have eclipsed all the other nations in history:

> And thou, O River! whose majestic stream
> Hath rous'd a feeble hand to sweep the lyre,
> Thy charms some loftier poet shall inspire
> And Clio's self shall patronize the theme;
> To hail thee shall admiring realms agree,
> Sing to thy praise, and bless our happy lot;
> And Danube's roaring flood shall be forgot,
> And Nile and Tiber, when they speak of Thee! (374–375)

In poetry like this, the female persona, merging with a site that has been saturated with history (history that her poem tries to bring to life) rises out of her everyday rounds into mystic communion with the sacred body of the nation. Caroline Gilman's "Washington's Elm at Cambridge" (dated 1836) is a later and briefer epitome of the process:

> And does not every leaf
> Stir with the strong remembrances of *one*,
> The immortal—the unconquerable chief—
> Thine own—thy Washington? . . . .

> Why, 'tis a hallowed spot!
> Here for my country a new pulse beats high,
> And woman's feeble nature all forgot,
> Here too even I could die. (*Verses of a Life Time*, 158–159)

Sarah Wentworth Morton's *Beacon Hill* (1797) is another local historical epic poem of the 1790s. This first canto of a projected epic about the American Revolution, running to about 820 lines of annotated heroic couplets, is dedicated "to the citizen-soldiers who fought, conquered, and retired, under the banners of Washington and Freedom." An "Analysis" sets out the contents and gives a hint of Morton's ambition:

Allusion to the surrounding Prospect—Invocation to the River and sylvan Deities—to the Historic Muse—Fiction discarded—Dedication to Washington—Action opens on the retreat of the Columbians from Bunker's Hill—General Howe—The Memory of his Brother—Death of Warren—Personification of Fortune and Fame—Washington at

73

Mount Vernon—Called to the Chief Command—Formation of the
Columbian Camp at Cambridge—Natural, Moral, or Political His-
tory of the Several States—Their Commanding Officers—Siege of
Boston—Its Sufferings—Negociation for the Safe Retreat of the Brit-
ish Army—Its Departure—Appointment of Congress—DECLARA-
TION OF INDEPENDENCE—Character of the Columbian
Soldier—The Poet's Prophetic Apostrophe to the Progress of Free-
dom Throughout the World. (10)

Identifying herself as a woman, conceding that she possesses nothing
resembling Homer's genius, the poet (like Faugeres) justifies her epic ex-
cursion by the significance of her subject, whose transcendent importance
and patriotic motive raise the singer above gender.

What though no Genius, with enchanting power,
Charm the coy Muses from their classic bower,
To wake with graceful art the slumbering line,
And round Columbia's native minstrel twine
One laurel wreath—yet shall her daring hand
Sketch the bold trait, the living scene command,
Till patriot glory all the scene inspire,
And with the ray of truth the coldest fancy fire. (13–14)

The canto—all she wrote of the poem—closes with a visionary procession
of freedom, headed by Columbia, parading from the Ganges to La Plata,
"Till the full ray of equal freedom shine, / And like the sun this genial globe
entwine" (52).

According to Morton's preface, she meant to include several women's
stories in later books of *Beacon Hill*, including Jane McCrea and Harriet
Ackland, to "diversify the scene, and awaken at least in the female breast,
sympathy and condolence" (ix). The English aristocrat Harriet Ackland
had successfully appealed to General Gates for permission to live with her
prisoner husband; the story routinely appeared in Revolutionary propaganda along with Jane McCrea's story to distinguish barbarous English
monarchists from gallant American republicans in terms of their treatment
of women. Rather than completing *Beacon Hill*, Morton brought out *The
Virtues of Society* (1799), a narrative poem of about 600 lines devoted
entirely to the Ackland story and making its republican point. As General
Gates responds with appropriate chivalry to Ackland's plight, one sees that
American republicans, not monarchists, are the true aristocrats. Much later
in life Morton published a miscellany of prose and verse, *My Mind and Its
Thoughts, in Sketches, Fragments, and Essays* (1823), containing short
pieces composed over many years, most of them religious and moral, some

74

of them historical and political. There are poems to George Washington; Henry Lee ("Hero and Orator, in the Annals of His Country; Victim of Persecution Through the Violence of Her Party Politics" [138]); John Jay ("What though a party's fraudful sway / Would rend thy civic crown away, / To thee a nobler hope extends, / For thee, the patriot prayer ascends" [139]); Major General Lincoln; and Aaron Burr.

The antipartisanship expressed in Morton's poems to Lee and Jay is a common tactic by which women opined on politics throughout the era. Where men were bound by party loyalties, women took up a competing version of patriotism that, because it ignored party, could be designated as the true standard of love of country. Hence, antiparty political statements appear in many women's verse and prose collections. One example is Sally Hastings's meditation poem "A Landscape" in her 1808 *Poems on Different Subjects*. The poem addresses the country's rulers, urging them to "let no Party-zeal / E'er interrupt the Happiness you feel!" and closing with the admonition: "Then do not meanly, for your private gains, / Dissolve the Union, which our peace maintains" (120–121).

In fact, exhortations to rise above party often have a clear party bias—it is no accident that Morton's victims, for example, are all from one party. Her "Ode to Time" for John Adams makes no secret of her political affiliations; the poem, embellished by historical annotation, casts all previous kingdoms from ancient Egypt through Palmyra, Greece, and Rome, onto the scrap heap, to welcome young Columbia and Adams "her chosen chief," for whom time is preparing "A crown, uncankered by the rust of years."

While withering millions on far Europe's shore
Gaze on thy rights, and all their wrongs deplore;
From thee shall time the lettered precept give,
Instruction flow—*they* drink the stream and live. (107)

In *Beacon Hill* Morton had provided a compassionate aside on the death of King Philip in the New England Indian wars; and in *My Mind and Its Thoughts* there is a "Monody," over the deaths of "young heroes" killed in the battle of the Miami, which reminds readers that "Who the wrong'd Indian's scanty gatherings spoil, / Wrest his sole hope, and strip his subject soil / . . . *They* must atone— . . . / *Their* cruel hands these desolations spread" (250). Also in *My Mind and Its Thoughts* is "The African Chief," an occasionally anthologized antislavery poem that recalls resistance to tyranny by Spartans, Romans, Greeks, William of Orange, and Washington, and urges readers to recognize these parallels to contemporary oppression of the Africans: "If these exalt thy sacred zeal, / To hate oppression's mad controul, / For bleeding *Afric* learn to feel, / Whose Chieftain claimed a kindred soul" (202).

75

Morton's poems on Africans and Native Americans belong to the second and major strand of American women's historical poetry—poems of social protest. This poetry is historical because it invariably situates opposition to Indian policy and, even more frequently, to slavery, within a patriotically historicized view of national destiny. An 1805 miscellany, *Poems on Various Subjects*, by a Pennsylvania poet named Isabella Oliver (later Sharp) has a poem "On Slavery," which gives a capsule history of the United States focused on the Revolution to contrast freedom's ideal with slavery's reality:

AMERICA! wipe out this dire disgrace,
Which stains the brightest glories of they face.
'Twas thine against oppressive power to raise
A noble standard, and attract the gaze
Of the surrounding nations, who approve
Thy arduous struggle, rising from a love
Of liberty. . . .
Oh, slavery! thou hell-engender'd crime!
Why spoil this beauteous country in her prime. . . .
Some plead the precedent of former times,
And bring examples in, to sanction crimes:
Greece had her Helots, Gibeonites the Jew;
Must then Columbia have her Negroes too! (139, 143, 144)

Similar tropes characterize Elizabeth Margaret Chandler's protest poetry, collected and published posthumously in an 1836 miscellany by Benjamin Lundy, Philadelphia editor of the *Genius of Universal Emancipation*, for which Chandler had begun writing in 1829 at the age of twenty-two. The introductory memoir eulogized Chandler as "the first American female editor that ever made this subject the principal theme of her active exertions," asserting, "it may safely be affirmed, without the least disparagement to others, that no one of her sex, in America, has hitherto contributed as much to the enlightenment of the public mind, relative to this momentous question, as she has done" (12–13).

Most of Chandler's protest poems work by transforming an initial trope of historical patriotic affiliation into antislavery commentary, establishing that her criticism of the nation derives from her love for it, sometimes even suggesting that national honor matters more to her than the condition of the slaves.

My country! . . .
Oh! I do fondly love thee! I would wind
Thy weal and woe with every thought of mind,

Rejoice to see thee crown'd with glory's wreath,
Or cling to thee in wretchedness and death. . . .
Oh! I could lay me in the very dust,
And weep in sadness o'er the cankering rust
That sheds its blighting influence o'er thy fame,
And sinks thee down to infamy and shame.
My guilty Country! these loud triumphs hush,
Think on this foul dishonouring blot, and blush! (14–15)

Effusions of nationalism and pietism accompanies every abolitionist statement. "Think of our country's glory, / All dimm'd with Afric's tears—/
Her broad flag stain'd and gory / With the hoarded guilt of years!" (64);

Oh ye! who still in cruel bondage, worse
Than e'en the Egyptian, hold the ill-starr'd slave,
Do ye not dread that God's long slumbering wrath
At length will pour its terror upon you?
Are slavery and oppression aught more just
Than in the days of Moses?—and if not,
With how much deeper hue does the dark stain
Attach itself to you, who proudly bear
The name of Christians. (90)

"The Cherokee," mobilizes love of country to oppose Indian removal:

Shall lawless force, with rude, remorseless hand,
Drive out the Indian from his father's land,
Burst all the ties that bind the heart to home,
And thrust him forth 'mid distant wilds to roam?
Oh no! . . .
Stain not with broken faith our country's name,
Nor weight her tresses to the dust with shame! (163–164)

Another antislavery writer, Eliza Lee Cabot Follen, whose poems were
collected in 1839, similarly criticizes the nation for betraying its past, in,
for example, a song "For the Fourth of July":

My country, that nobly could dare
The hand of oppression to brave,
O, how the foul stain canst thou bear,
Of being the land of the slave? . . .

The dead whom the white man has slain,

They cry from the ground and the waves:
They once cried for mercy in vain,
They plead for their brothers the slaves.

The work of Hannah Flagg Gould, whose two-volume *Poems* came out
in 1839, and her *New Poems* in 1850, also merges patriotic evocations of
early American history with antislavery and pro-Indian sentiment. In "The
Dying Revolutionary Soldier," an old soldier says that slavery is not what
he fought for:

O! let them my country be heard!
Be the land of the free and the brave!
And send forth the glorious word,
This is not the land of the slave! (173–174)

Close by the Temple of thy Liberty—
Beneath its very droppings—groans the slave;
And thousands, held in bondage by the free,
Go fettered from the cradle to the grave.
Within the echo of thy Congress halls,
Where freedom towers, and right sounds loud and bold,
God's image, when the auction-hammer falls,
The soul of man, is bidden for, and sold! . . . .

This, dear Columbia, is the fearful thing
That keeps thee under Heaven's impending rod,
And, not relinquished, on thy head must bring
Sure retribution from a righteous God. (*New Poems*, 89–90)

"The Old Elm of Boston," combines topographical patriotism with indict-
ment of national Indian policy:

I come before thee, old majestic Tree,
Not for inquiry into thy long story;
But for my eye to drink delight from thee—
To feast upon thy venerable glory. . . .

Look round! Inquire at yonder lofty dome,
How from these grounds their first possessor vanished.
Ask Justice, there in her terrestrial home,
If 't was by her the red man hence was banished. . . .

Ask the calm, meditative, upright Man—

Poetic Demonstrations

And let him not the crying answer smother,
How we have used, since here our rule began,
  Our unenlightened, helpless, tawny brother! . . .

I have not spoken yet, sublime old Tree,
  Of thine acquaintance with the *Whig* and *Tory*;
And with my fathers' battles to be free,
  That left thee mantled in Columbia's glory. (*Poems*, 2:236–239)

The incorporation of this attack on government policy in a patriotic poem shows that it is conceived as an expression of the highest form of patriotism; this poem appears alongside other local poems unproblematically extolling Lexington, Washington, the Mayflower, and similar monumentalized sites of standard American history. Patriotic songs in *New Poems* include a Fourth of July ode, a "national ode" called "The Liberty Tree," a song commemorating the Boston Tea Party, and one on the Battle of Lexington with a familiar allusion to patriot blood:

Yet are the sounds of this sad day
A mighty Prophet's word,—
These fearful sights, the dread array,
In which he may be heard!
Through battle and storms, and blood like rain,
Our march henceforth must be,
From wrong, oppression, and the chain,
To right and liberty! (84)

It is clear in context (as, for example, by provision of the name of the song to which the lyrics were sung) that these songs were performed at celebrations commemorating the events they describe, and this invites us to imagine a scene in which women wrote a good deal of thumping, tuneful verse for purposes of public recitation rather than private delectation. Public benefactor and ceremonial participant, as it were, are aspects of the woman's identity. Behind these collected hence accessible examples of the performed patriotic song must be a host of uncollected and unpublished works of the same sort produced by women for a range of local, public events in American towns and schools.

The typical compound of dismayed patriotism characterizes the historical poems in Grace Greenwood's 1850 *Poems*. Her antislavery sentiments exist along with, and are reinforced by, poems of pure passionate nationalism, as in, for example, "Putnam": "Let the haughty smile, the low defame, / The heartless worldling mock; / I thank my God, *my* fathers came / Of the good old Pilgrim stock!" (*Poems*, 37). "Illumination for Victories

79

in Mexico," a poem opposing the Mexican War, however, diverges from type by virtue of its sarcasm:

> Light up thy homes, Columbia,
>   For those chivalric men
> Who bear to scenes of warlike strife
>   Thy conquering arms again,
> Where glorious victories, flash on flash,
>   Reveal their stormy way,—
> Rosaca's, Palo Alto's fields,
>   The heights of Monterey!
> They pile with thousands of thy foes
>   Buena Vista's plain;
> With maids and wives, at Vera Cruz,
>   Swell high the list of slain!
> They paint upon the Southern skies
>   The blast of burning domes,—
> Their laurels dew with blood of babes!
>   Light up, light up thy homes! (98)

The poem ends with a sentimental yet ironic address to women readers:

> O sisters, if ye have no tears
>   For fearful tales like these,
> If the banners of the victors veil
>   The victim's agonies,
> If ye lose the babe's and mother's cry
>   In the noisy roll of drums,
> If your hearts with martial pride throb high,
>   Light up, light up your homes! (100)

Not all women, of course, were social progressives (as we would use the term today). Greenwood's poem in fact might have been directly responding to Sarah A. Nowell's chauvinistic "Battle of San Jacinto" with its conclusion:

> Shout for the conqueror's arm is now victorious,
> And War's shrill clarion hath not called in vain,
> And Freedom's banners now are floating, glorious,
> Above the field where sleep the early slain. (*Poems*, 61)

Also conservative in approach is Jane Ermina Locke's "Merrimac River, at the Junction of the Concord with Its Waters," a topographical poem identifying the vanished Indians as sacrifices to the inevitable forward movement of history, and canceling out their tragedy with the Christian promise of universal salvation: "So pass we all, the red man and the white, / And sink alike in death's eternal night; / But we shall rise—bright hope—ay, one and all,— / At the same sound,—the Saviour's trumpet call" (*Miscellaneous Poems*, 148). But Locke's 1842 collection is politically heterodox; along with a poem praising John Adams—"*Patriot, Statesman, Hero bold, / Philanthropist,* and *Christian* meek, / Often as thy name is told, / Grateful tears shall bathe the cheek" (184)—are poems supporting the Polish revolution and a rare example of a pro-immigrant Irish poem—"Give place, give place, our green land o'er / To the sons of the 'sorrowing isle'; / A kind and a tender welcome pour, / And bestow a cheering smile." (185). (Anna Hanson Dorsey, a convert to Catholicism—one of two Catholics writing history that I have found—included an Irish nationalist elegy called "O'Connel's Heart" in her 1849 collection *Flowers of Love and Memory*.)

I have already noted that Lydia Sigourney, the most prolific and best-known antebellum woman poet, urged the study of history on women of all ages and conditions, and wrote it herself in every genre and on many topics. Although Sigourney has come to symbolize the overwrought emotionality of female poetasters, her work as a whole contains a strong admixture of republican severity. Her wide-ranging historical subjects fall into four main categories: ancient and sacred history; local history of the region around Hartford, Norwich, and New London, Connecticut, from white settlement through Revolution; the American Revolution; and the history of the American Indians after European settlement. The core story of Native American history after the European arrival presented in Sigourney's writings is of Indian generosity answered by European brutality. A paradigm of this narrative occurs in a short poem called "The Indian's Welcome to the Pilgrim Fathers," which appeared in *Zinzendorff* (1835), and reads in part:

When sudden from the forest wide,
　A red-brow'd chieftain came,
With towering form, and haughty stride,
　And eye like kindling flame:
No wrath he breath'd, no conflict sought,
　To no dark ambush drew,
But simply *to the Old World brought,
　The welcome of the New.*

That *welcome* was a blast and ban
　Upon thy race unborn.
Was there no seer, thou fated Man!

'Thy lavish zeal to warn?
Thou in they fearless faith didst hail
A weak, invading band,
But who shall heed thy children's wail,
Swept from their native land? (47–48)

Sigourney's narratives of the Indian disaster lead to the culminating plea that her countrymen should return to the essence of republican Christianity and stop destroying the Indians by murder and relocation. From her historical perspective, the cessation of Indian destruction in the future—though it is much to be hoped for and though her writings are designed in part to further that goal—could not justify the erasure of past massacre. Whatever happened in future, that is, it was necessary to remember what had happened in the past. Sigourney could not accept the conviction found in so many writings of the time, and implicit in several of the poems already quoted, that the destruction of the Indians is merely inevitable.

Traits of the Aborigines of America (1822) was her first work about Native Americans. Despite its bland title and its anonymous publication, this five-canto work of 4,000 blank-verse lines, with extensive scholarly annotation, is her longest and most ambitious poem, packed with classical references and historical allusion, and dense with information about Indian tribes (for which, of course, she depended on secondary sources). Remembering that for early literary nationalists the epic was the genre of choice, one has to be impressed both by Sigourney's evident ambition here to produce an American epic and, even more, by her extremely unconventional approach to the subject. For *Traits* is structured from the Indian point of view and its narrative extends beyond the territorial United States to include the continent from the Arctic Circle to South America. This story, regardless of where it transpires, is always the same: the Indians welcome the newcomers and are exterminated. In short, *Traits* is a poem of social protest in the guise of a historical epic.

Canto 1 begins with the Indians in undisturbed possession of the continent and then introduces a chronicle of incursion: "First, to their northern coast / Wander'd the Scandinavian" (1.253–254); after a while Columbus comes—the Indians thought he and his men were Gods, "nor dream'd their secret aim / Was theft and cruelty, to snatch the gold / That sparkled in their streams, and bid their blood / Stain those pure waters" (1.44–47); Portuguese, French, Irish, English—everybody comes. Christians come, too, bringing the potential benefit of their religion to the Indians. But that benefit does not develop, because the Christians do not behave like Christians.

In Canto 2, incursions become more extensive and frequent: "Almost it seemed / As if old Europe, weary of her load, / Pour'd on a younger world

82

her thousand sons / In ceaseless deluge" (2.8–11). The bulk of the canto narrates the life of John Smith, allowing the poet to provide a geography and history of most of the world through a chronicle of his travels. Pocahontas's rescue of him is compared to Pharoah's daughter rescuing Moses—and with the same ultimately disastrous effect on her people: "little thought / The Indian Monarch, that his child's weak arm / Fostered that colony, whose rising light / Should quench his own forever" (2.1093–1096). Sigourney vacillates between comic and tragic interpretations of the narrative, and simultaneously avoids and intensifies both readings by focusing on the conversion and early death of Pocahontas herself. There is some unspecified and contradictory connection between the conversion and the death—on the one hand it seems that Christianity itself is what kills Pocahontas, on the other that, thanks to her conversion, she dies regenerate. The canto ends with brief attention to the founding of Pennsylvania, Delaware, and Florida, always from the vantage point of those who are forced out by European settlement. "Pressing west / O'er the vain barrier, and retreating tide / Of Mississippi, spread our ancestors, / Taking a goodly portion, with the sword, / And with their bow" (2.1186–1190).

Canto 3 positions itself with the now outcast and understandably hostile Indians in their various forest refuges, describes many instances of savage warfare, and contains a ringing attack on whites for their instigating barbarism as well as their hypocrisy in faulting the Indians. "Who are these, / Red from the bloody wine-press, with its stains / Dark'ning their raiment? Yet I dare not ask / Their clime and lineage, lest the accusing blasts, / Waking the angry echoes, should reply / 'Thy Countrymen!'" (3.905–910). Rejecting the truism that Indians were naturally vengeful, she shows them as inherently generous and reveals the truism as a white construction, part material—the Indians are responding self-defensively to white brutality—and part rhetorical—the Indians are often misrepresented as vengeful when their behavior is anything but.

The brief Canto 4 begins by praising the few missionaries—Eliot, Heckewelder—who went among the Indians to preach Christianity, but gives most of its lines to Tuscarora, who mocks those of his tribe who want to convert:

Behold! what glorious gifts
Ye owe to white men. What good-will and peace
They shed upon you! Exile and the sword!
Poisons and rifled sepulchres! and see!
They fain would fill the measure of their guilt
With the dark cheat of that accursed faith
Whose precepts justify *their* nameless crimes,
Your countless woes. (4.348–355)

Sigourney's point is that white behavior not only justifies Indian hostility to them as a group, but also makes understandable their hostility to the Christianity these whites claim to represent. The necessary millennial task of joining with the Indians in brotherly love has been made infinitely more difficult by the whites' betrayal of their own religion.

Canto 5 then departs from the historical record to urge on Christian Americans the true obligations of their Christianity. The narrator acknowledges that most living Indians are already demoralized and degraded; she sees the possibility—albeit at some horrendous bloody cost to themselves—of the whites' completely exterminating the Indians. But she insists that "our God hath made / All of one blood, who dwell upon the earth" (5.406–407); the only important difference between red and white people is that whites are (supposedly) Christian. "Make these foes your friends," she urges (5.541–547). Their very religion requires whites to approach the Indians in friendship in order to bring them to Christianity; and when the Indians become Christians, their justified desire for revenge will give way to religious principle. They will then become an integral part of the American republic, and that republic, though no longer purely white, will be purely Christian.

Traits continually uses references from world history to heroicize the Native Americans and deheroicize the Europeans. At various points in the poem, for example, the Indians are likened to "stern Regulus" (1.60); "the warlike Earl, stern Steward" (1.208); "the Scythian tribes" (1.224–225); "sublime Demosthenes" (2.143); "the impetuous Hannibal" (3.535); "the stern, Spartan lords" (3.656). Sometimes Sigourney accompanies these comparisons with the lament that the Indians—equally valiant, noble, eloquent as these historical figures—are doomed to extinction *without a history*. Sometimes she interrupts the Native American narrative for accounts of historical carnage far exceeding anything that the Indians have perpetrated: "O'er the tow'rs / Of lofty Ilion, wreck'd by Grecian wiles, / Why does the dazzled eye prolong its gaze / In breathless interest, yet averts its glance / Disgusted, and indignant, at the scenes / Of Indian stratagem?" (3.721–726).

Sigourney's missionary perspective, of course, depends on an idea of the Indians' likeness to whites rather than of their dignity in difference; it also assumes that Indian culture is inferior to white because it is not Christian. But she is much more critical of white culture for falling short of its Christian ideals than of Indian culture with no such ideals to guide it. In her autobiography, written forty years later, Sigourney dryly observes that the poem "was singularly unpopular, there existing in the community no reciprocity with the subject"; but the intervening years had not changed her mind: "our injustice and hard-hearted policy with regard to the original owners of the soil has ever seemed to me one of our greatest national sins" (*Letters of Life*, 327).

The title poem in *Zinzendorff* is also about Christians and Indians. The 584-line annotated poem in blank verse makes a hero of Count Zinzendorff, founder of the radical Christian Moravian sect, who proselytized among the Native Americans of the Wyoming Valley in 1742. Sigourney begins this poem with a brief mention of a much-written-about incident of the Revolution, the Wyoming Valley massacre of 1778, when an alliance of Tory Pennsylvanians and Indians slaughtered emigrant patriot settlers from Connecticut. She maintains that the massacre was actually caused by justified Native American resentment over earlier white appropriation of Indian land. Zinzendorff, unlike the land-hungry emigrants, had only Christian designs on the indigenous population. The Indians' grief over Zinzendorff's return to Europe is interpreted by the poet as prophetic of their future at the hands of people who are Christians in name only (lines 495–505). The poem closes with an appeal to Christians to desist from sectarian controversy and unite in peaceful missionary activities among the Indians. There may still be time, the poem says, to reverse history's direction and bring Native Americans into the nation whose territory they originally occupied.

Sigourney's "Pocahontas" (in the 1841 *Pocahontas; and Other Poems*) is a 504-line poem, in fifty-six modified Spenserian stanzas, recounting the life of Pocahontas as a memorial to the Indian princess. Although by 1841 American literature was full of tributes to her, Sigourney puts a recognizable stamp on the story. She begins as she had begun *Traits*, from an assumed Indian perspective in the New World before the Europeans arrive. Apostrophizing the "clime of the West," she asks whether it was not "sweet, in cradled rest to lie, / And 'scape the ills that older regions know?" An entrance into history, long deferred, begins when the "roving hordes of savage men" look up to "behold a sail! another, and another!" She sounds her motif of Christian brotherhood: "What were thy secret thoughts, oh red-brow'd brother, / As toward the shore those white-wing'd wanderers press'd?" And when Powhatan, moved by his daughter's intercession, spares John Smith's life, Sigourney notes the ironic outcome of that event with the same comparison to Pharaoh's daughter that she had made in *Traits* (Stanza 20).

"Thou wert the saviour of the Saxon vine, / And for this deed alone our praise and love are thine" (Stanza 21) Sigourney says, once again stressing the self-destructive, ironically Christian tendency of the Indians to nurture and protect white intruders. Then, moving forward in time to the era of Indian surprise attacks on white settlements, she challenges the historians' accounts: "ye, who hold of history's scroll the pen, / Blame not too much those erring, red-brow'd men, / Though nursed in wiles, Fear is the white-lipp'd sire / Of subterfuge and treachery, 'Twere in vain / To bid the soul be true, that writhes beneath his chain" (Stanza 24). The whites, answering Indian generosity with oppression and dislocation, created the vengeful Indians whose behavior they now slander and use as a pretext for further incursions against them.

The poem then chronicles Pocahontas's capture, conversion, marriage, journey to England, and early death; but it refers beyond this personal narrative to another, larger narrative—especially when it returns at the end to the long view with which it began and addresses the Indians en masse:

I would ye were not, from your fathers' soil
Track'd like the dun wolf, ever in your breast
The coal of vengeance and the curse of toil;
I would we had not to your mad lip prest
The fiery poison-cup, nor on ye turn'd
The blood-tooth'd ban-dog, foaming, as he burn'd
To tear your flesh; but thrown in kindness bless'd
The brother's arm around ye, as ye trod,
And led ye, sad of heart, to the bless'd Lamb of God. (Stanza 54)

Sigourney's conventional memorializing of Pocahontas, savior and servant of the whites, leads to an invocation of those nameless Indian dead who heroically *resisted* white incursion—"King, stately chief, and warrior-host are dead, / Nor remnant nor memorial left behind" (Stanza 56). Sigourney's poem memorializes them as well as Pocahontas.

Mary Webster Moseby (or Mosby) of Virginia had published a long, romantic, and scrupulously footnoted poem about Pocahontas in 1840, a year before Sigourney. In the preface she proudly claims direct descent from Pocahontas and offers her poem as an effort to "raise a shrine to Pocahontas" that might be especially gratifying to "her fair countrywomen" (vii). The extensive apparatus specifies where she is using the record, who her authorities are, and where she moves from authentic history into "legend"—that is, oral tradition. Because the legend Moseby especially draws on makes Pocahontas's mother a partly white woman, daughter of a Native American princess and a Nordic seafarer, it is particularly important for the poet to insist that her imaginative treatment never oversteps the boundaries of "unvarnished truth." Therefore, she documents the poem with an apparatus of scholarly quotations and citations.

In fact, scholarly notes accompany many of women's historical poems, verifying the authenticity of the material, exhibiting the extent of the poet's reading, and making the poem learned as well as imaginative. And while on the one hand the apparatus is spatially separated from the imaginative body of the poem, the circumference of citation also centers the poetic product visibly within the historical context that inspired it. As notes sprout all around the poetic text, the poet's scholarship acquires an imaginative exuberance of its own, and the "poem" becomes an amalgam of its invented core and its documented periphery.

In Maria Gowen Brooks's six-canto fantasy *Zophiel* (1833—first canto separately published in 1825), for example—a long, complicated narrative set among the ancient Hebrews—the apparatus of footnotes and endnotes becomes almost as extensive as the poem "proper." Brooks's subject derives from a passage in the Apocrypha where a beautiful Hebrew woman is married seven times, only to have her husband killed each time by an invisible fallen angel who loves her. In Brooks's version, the heroine Egla is *almost* married six times, and each bridegroom is successively killed by Zophiel, the smitten fallen angel. Because Zophiel cannot be seen, the cause of these sudden deaths appears to be Egla herself, although the mechanism of her agency is unclear. In despair over her apparent murderousness, she is about to commit suicide; but her destined lover (whom she has seen only in a vision) arrives; Zophiel is prevented from killing him by a good spirit, who turns out to be the archangel Raphael. In effect, although certainly against his own intentions, Zophiel has been protecting Egla's virginity for the man of her dreams, and the poem develops as an unusually open sensual fantasy of having many lovers without sacrificing one's chastity. The depictions of Egla scintillate with erotic tension, since her physical sexual allure and the perils of her so magically preserved and so intensely fetishized virginity are elaborated at considerable graphic length.

Zophiel would hardly seem to qualify as a historical poem in even a very relaxed definition of the type; yet this fantastic narrative is, after all, based on what might be considered Sacred History, the Apocrypha having not yet been officially decanonized. And, making each of Egla's almost-husbands a citizen of a different ancient nation, Brooks gets a chance to expatiate on a range of ancient places and customs, with a particular focus on dress, decor, and the practices of everyday life. As the story graphically interacts with extended historical and geographical footnotes and endnotes bringing a range of biblical and ancient scholarship as well as world literature in their original languages onto the page, a distinction between its fantasy and its fact becomes untenable.

Among footnotes from the first canto of 1825 are these:

"The palm is a very common plant in this country, (Assyria,) and generally fruitful: this they cultivate like fig-trees and it produces them bread, wine and honey." See Beloc's notes to his translation of Herodotus. Mr. Gibbon adds, that the diligent natives celebrated,

> either in verse or prose, three hundred and sixty uses to which the trunk, the branches, the leaves, the juice and the fruit of this plant were applied. (29)

> Fine hair has been a subject of commendation among all people, and particularly the ancients. Cyrus, when he went to visit his uncle Astyages found him with his eyelashes coloured, and decorated with false locks; the first Caesar obtained permission to wear the laurel-wreath in order to conceal the bareness of his temples. The quantity and beauty of the hair of Absalom is commemorated in holy writ. (30–31)

> It was not unusual among the nations of the east, to imitate flowers with precious stones. The Persian kings about the time of Araxexerxes, sat, when they gave audience under a vine, the leaves of which were formed of gold and the grapes of emeralds. (54)

Along with other materials, Brooks's endnotes offer substantial untranslated quotations from Fonantelle's *Histoire des oracles*, lines of Milton, translations of the poet Hafiz, and references to Voltaire's *Essai sur les moeurs et l'esprit des nations*. In an 1879 reissue of the poem the footnotes and endnotes have been combined at the back of the book, producing an apparatus of over fifty small-print pages. Here, as the history authorizes and authenticates the fantasy, the fantasy justifies and in a sense therefore sponsors the history. The fantasy gives Brooks a chance to project herself into a variety of ancient civilizations and savor their atmosphere. The work almost seems to say it: going back in time is always a fantasy; learning and imagination are mutually constituting not discrete activities of mind, both of which are aspects of female subjectivity.

Thus, along with earnest poems of historical patriotism, one finds women writing romantic fantasies that are also elaborations of history allowing them to show the ways in which learning has entered into the construction of their imaginative worlds. Anna Cora Mowatt's *Pelayo; or, the Cavern of Covadonga* (1836), "founded directly on historical facts from Southey's Don Roderick and Don Trueba" (vii), is an example—an example that incidentally shows the interpenetration of history with other kinds of belletristic sources. Another is Margaret Miller Davidson's "Boabdil el Chico's Farewell to Granada" (posthumously published in her 1842 *Biography and Poetical Remains*), based on Washington Irving's *The Conquest of Granada*. Katharine Augusta Ware's 1842 *Power of the Passions; and Other Poems* includes historically allusive romantic travel poems on Vesuvius and Athens ("That lofty dome, which rang with loud applause / Where Solon first proclaimed Athenia's laws: / The temple raised to Theseus' mighty name, / The storied arch of Hadrian's deathless fame" [23]). Sarah Anna Lewis's romantic "Florence: An Italian Tale" in her 1844 collection *Records of the Heart* begins with a narratively superfluous evocation of the Roman republic: "The mighty arm that grasped the sword / To put to flight the savage horde, / The tongue that pleaded with applause / For liberty and God's high laws—/ Caesar and Tully, when—oh! when / Will such bright stars lume earth again?" (3).

The most scholarly and exhibitionist of all the historical poems is Caroline Crane Marsh's twelve-canto *Wolfe of the Knoll* (1860), a novel-poem whose leading incidents are "taken from a tradition contained in the first chapter of the second volume of Kohl's work" (12), as though every reader knew who Kohl was as a matter of course. Marsh, married to the linguist George Perkins Marsh—who was American minister to Turkey in 1849–1854, minister to Italy when *Wolfe of the Knoll* was published, and eventual contributor to the *New Oxford English Dictionary* —had unusual opportunities for research. The action of her geographical, historical, and philological melange alternates between meticulously drawn settings of Frisia and Tunis. "Tacitus," Marsh writes in her introduction, "speaking of Germany generally, argues that the people must have been indigenous. . . . It appears, both from his testimony and from other sources, that the Frisians of the coast and the islands have, from the earliest ages, been remarkable for their courage and independence." And then she refers the reader to Appendix 2, "for an amusing version of the story of the two ambassadors, whose appearance in the theater at Rome is commemorated by Tacitus, Annal. 13, 54" (11–12).

At the other end of the learning scale, Emma Embury's first collection of poetry, *Guido, a Tale; Sketches from History. And Other Poems*—published in 1828 under the name "Ianthe"—contains a series of historical poems each introduced by a headnote giving the source: "Jane of France" from Bayle's dictionary, "Scenes in the life of a lover" from "Miss Benger's Memoirs of Anne Boleyn," "Queen Elizabeth" and "Boscobel" from Hume's *History of England*, the "Lament of Columbus" from Irving, "Mary's Lament" from Chalmer's life. A posthumously published miscellany by the utterly obscure Eunice K. True Daniels includes classical poems on "The Burial of Pompey" and "Hannibal's Dirge" with headnotes explaining who Pompey and Hannibal were and which events in their lives the poems dramatize—clear vestiges of classroom history.

The visionary philosophic poem was yet another type that allowed for a display of history, as in Caroline Lee Hentz's *Human and Divine Philosophy* (1844) and Sarah Helen Whitman's "Hours of Life" (in *Hours of Life and Other Poems*, 1853). *Human and Divine Philosophy*, composed for the "Erosophic Society" of the University of Alabama, appeared as a pamphlet. It is a Christian poem that begins by calling on the spirit of antiquity to help the poet summon the shades of ancient philosophers: "That grove is Academus—that pale sage / Athenian Plato, glory of his age. / *Almost divine philosopher!* . . . / And who is he, around whose feet, / The polished youth of Athens meet?" " (7). On to Rome: "Shall we pursue the vision?—Shall we turn, / Where classic Tiber fills his golden urn, / Where mouldering temple, wall and pillared dome, / Proclaim the fallen majesty of Rome?" (9). The vision advances to "the great of later days," including Newton, Davy, Franklin, Milton, and others who "crowd upon the vision" (13). Then comes the United States:

> Shall we still blindly turn,
> And hang, with worship, o'er a Pagan's urn,
> When our own land, a model can supply,
> With which the ancient world in vain may vie?—
> In peace, a Christian Plato,—but in war,
> Caesar, enthroned on victory's bannered car. . . .
> Resounding echoes murmur—*Washington*—
> *Washington*—answer back each rock and hill,
> Till a whole nation's heart-chords wake and thrill. (14)

Washington is not the end, however: "A greater still than Washington is here. . . . The haloed brow / Proclaims the Son of God" (14–15). The conclusion moves beyond history to the millennial point at which history can be discarded:

> Let others linger in the Gothic aisles
> Of dim antiquity,—its marble piles
> Gleam cold upon the eye, whose glances turn,
> Where Salem's towers, in golden splendours, burn.
> For us, we ask no higher boon of fame,
> Than the pure glory of *the Christian's name*. (16)

Whitman's "Hours of Life" is a three-part allegory composed in a variety of verse forms (hudibrastic, iambic pentameter couplets, quatrains in different meters) narrating the poet's search for religious certainty. The structure of Morning, Noon, and Evening corresponds to stages of individual life history and the history of the human race. Morning is dominated by nature, representing unreflecting sensuosity and thoughtless unity with things as they are. Noon stands for sorrow and the search for a stable truth, including an examination of "the dim chronicle / Of ages gone before" (18). At evening, the poet recognizes that what she wants cannot be found by the intellect; she ends on a note of "child-like trust" (34) that is much different from the unconscious joy of morning. Like *Human and*

Divine Philosophy, the poem ends with a Christian statement. And in the second part of the poem, before she abandons her intellectual search, the poet produces a historical quest similar to Hentz's search for truth:

I paused on Grecian plains, to trace
Some remnant of a mightier race,
Serene in sorrow and in strife,
Calm conquerors of Death and Life,
Types of the god-like forms that shone
Upon the sculptured Parthenon. . . .
I heard loud Hallelujas
From Israel's golden lyre,
And I sought their great Jehovah
In the cloud and in the fire. . . .
Where the Nile pours his sullen wave
Through tombs and empires of the grave,
I sought, 'mid cenotaphs, to find
The earlier miracles of mind. . . .
I turned, and from the Brahmin's milder law
I sought truth's mystic element to draw,
Pure as it sparkled in the cup of heaven—
The bright amreeta to the immortals given. (19–20, 22, 23)

Poetry, finally, was not the chief form in which women wrote history; the historical poem did not dominate their poetic output. Rather, such poetry played its part in defining a feminine sensibility that had imaginatively appropriated historical materials and manifested itself in public displays of patriotism and learning. It was written by women of diverse political persuasions; by upper-class urban women and small-town members of the lower middle class; by women of learning and barely educated schoolgirls; by professional writers and women writing in obscurity. Historical poetry fleshes out women's self-portraiture (and bolsters their self-regard) as beings at home with books, familiar with the world's panorama, devoted patriots, and political idealists.

Eyewitness History

FEW AMERICAN WOMEN were original historians in the present-day sense of combing archives for previously unknown information about the past. Still, by selecting, arranging, emphasizing, and commenting on the record, the many women who published historical work were clearly shaping it. In addition, a great many women consciously wrote to preserve a historicized archive for the future. This work, which I shall organize and discuss geographically—from New England, down the seaboard, around the frontiers, and finally beyond the nation—emerges in the context of a vast body of contemporary reportage produced by women, from which it can be distinguished by its frequent recourse to historical narrative as the key to understanding.

Eyewitness history of this kind had audience and impact in its own day. Hannah Adams's New England synthesis laid the ground for later studies of the New England mind. Deborah Norris Logan preserved the William Penn archive. Margaret Bayard Smith helped write Jefferson into popular history as an exemplar of the pure republic he served. On the basis of her local histories of Norwich and New London, Connecticut, Frances Manwaring Caulkins became the first (and for some years was the only) woman admitted to membership in the Massachusetts Historical Society. Jane Cazneau's polemics about Texas undergirded the ideology of Manifest Destiny, and Emma Willard's widely circulated history of the Mexican War and California depicted western emigration as a sacred cause. Juliette Kinzie's accounts of the Fort Dearborn massacre and Black Hawk's war were absorbed into standard Illinois history; Harriet Bishop, whose portrait hangs in the Minnesota Historical Society, preserved the record of Minnesota's earliest white settlers. Ann and Emily Judson's narratives of the Baptist mission to Burma were the missionary movement's most successful efforts to turn their people into culture heroes. Sara Robinson's Free-Soil history of Kansas had ten editions within ten years. Mary Louise Booth's history of New York City was alone in the field for several decades. Eliza Buckminster Lee's memoir of her father and brother served from the first, and continues to serve, as a source for New England church history. Lucy Mack Smith's family history is still consulted by historians of Mormonism.

These examples of influential eyewitness historical writing are published instances of numerous family and local archives produced by women. Some of these were published in journals, and some in limited, keepsake editions; others circulated in manuscripts lovingly preserved by the author's descendants. Raise the issue at any large gathering, and somebody is sure to tell of a cherished family history written by a grandmother, a great aunt, or a mother. All across the country, women kept journals about the events going on around them and wrote letters to kin and friends about contemporary happenings. They contributed letters of a more formal nature to church and town newspapers. They smuggled eyewitness and family history into novels like *Secret History; or, The Horrors of St. Domingo* (1808) by Leonora Sansay; *A Winter in Washington* (1824) by Margaret Bayard Smith; *The British Partizan* (1839) by Mary Elizabeth Moragne (later Davis); *Inez: A Tale of the Alamo* (1855) by Augusta Evans (later Wilson); and *The Black Gauntlet: A Tale of Plantation Life in South Carolina* (1860) by Mary Howard Schoolcraft.

It will be recalled that in her *History of the American Revolution* Mercy Otis Warren justified her activities as historian by observing that men were too busy making history to keep the record also:

At a period when every manly arm was occupied, and every trait of talent or activity engaged, either in the cabinet or the field, apprehensive, that amidst the sudden convulsions, crowded scenes, and rapid changes, that flowed in quick succession, many circumstances might escape the more busy and active members of society, I have been induced to improve the leisure Providence had lent, to record as they passed, in the following pages, the new and unexperienced events exhibited in a land previously blessed with peace, liberty, simplicity, and virtue. (1:xli)

It was open to any literate woman with some leisure, not merely one with Warren's elite connections, to notice and record the local and familial. They could claim to be doing this work on account of their ancestors and families; nobody denied that such filiopietism accorded with even the most traditional views of women's duties. Thanks to the rhetoric of patriotism, one's region (and even one's nation) could be troped as family, as in this explanation by Caulkins: "A conviction of the fertility of this unexplored field of research, connected with the sentiment of veneration for a region that had been the refuge and home of her ancestors, in all their branches, led to a design, early formed and perseveringly cherished by the author, to write the history both of Norwich and of New London" (*New London*, 1860, 3).

Women could also find justification for this work in their ever-expanding didactic responsibilities. "Nor need it cause a blush to acknowledge," Warren wrote, "a detail was preserved with a view of transmitting it to the rising youth of my country" (1:xlii); Caulkins said: "It is the ardent desire of the writer to engage the present generation in this ennobling study of their past history, and to awaken a sentiment of deeper and more affectionate sympathy with our ancestors" (*New London*, 1860, 3–4).

Even as they justified their work by its usefulness, the women noted their presence at the scene and insisted on their authority as recorders. Warren: "Connected by nature, friendship, and every social tie, with many of the first patriots, and most influential characters on the continent; in the habits of confidential and epistolary intercourse with several gentlemen employed abroad in the most distinguished stations, and with others since elevated to the highest grades of rank and distinction, I had the best means of information" (*American Revolution*, 1:xli). Margaret Smith: "I was carried, like many others, to the infant metropolis of our country, at the time it became the seat of the federal government. By the same circumstances, I was placed in that circle of society, which introduced me to a personal acquaintance with most of the distinguished characters that appeared on the stage of public life" (*Winter in Washington*, 1:v). Kinzie: "I was now to visit, nay more, to become a resident of that land which had, for long years, been to me a region of romance" (*Wau-bun*, 14). Harriet Bishop, assuming that as the first white woman teacher to settle in the Minnesota territory she was a historical personage in her own right as well as an archivist, spends a whole chapter of her history answering the question "Why I Came to St. Paul", and concludes, "I came because I was more needed here than at any other spot on earth" (*Floral Home*, 54). Women's eyewitness histories, then, stressed equally that they were *there* and that *they* were there.

It is the woman's own voice, also, that brings history into her account. For the historical significance of an event does not lie on the surface, but is revealed only to one who already knows history. Part of the job of the eyewitness historian is to bring out the event's significance by welding the event to its historical meaning. There is no mistaking the gusto and passion with which women did this work. Assuming the historian's responsibility was, clearly, an exhilarating experience. It is perhaps not too much to suggest that many women went, when they could, to places where they thought history was in the making; or that those who found themselves reluctantly elsewhere from where they wanted to be, were solaced by imagining themselves as agents in history.

94

One of the earliest historical accounts produced in New England is Susanna (Willard) Johnson Hastings's partly dictated captivity narrative, an Enlightenment document published in 1796 when she was sixty-six years old, and detailing her captivity among the French and the Indians a half-century earlier. Most captivity narratives depend for impact on the currency of their events; in Hastings's account, the lapse of time between event and narration produces a uniquely self-conscious historicity:

Those, who can recollect the war that existed between France and England fifty years ago, may figure to themselves the unhappy situation of the inhabitants on the frontiers of Newhampshire; the malice of the French in Canada, and the exasperated savages that dwelt in their vicinity, rendered the tedious days and frightful nights a season of unequalled calamities. . . . Had there been an organized government, to stretch forth its protecting arm, in any case of danger, the misery might have been in a degree alleviated. But the infancy of our country did not admit of this blessing. (4–5)

One motive for writing this narrative is to rescue the reputation of Hastings's long-since dead first husband; another is to advance the theory that governments should protect their citizens from war, not expose them to it; and a third is to vilify the French, in part by contrasting them invidiously with the Indians:

As they are aptly called children of nature, those who have profited by refinement and education, ought to abate part of the prejudice, which prompts them to look with an eye of censure on this untutored race. Can it be said of civilized conquerors, that they, in the main, are willing to share with their prisoners, the last ration of food, when famine stares them in the face? Do they ever adopt an enemy, and salute him by the tender name of brother? And I am justified in doubting, whether if I had fallen into the hands of French soldiers, so much assiduity would have been shown, to preserve my life. (75–76)

The story begins with the typical sudden descent of the Indians on an unprotected settlement, but it has the atypical twist of the narrator's giving birth to a daughter on the road, only hours after being captured (the daughter was named Captive). Despite harrowing memories of this extraordinary ordeal, Hastings looks back to the few months she spent among the Indians with much more pleasure than the four grueling years she was captive to the French. And she celebrates the blessings of contemporary national prosperity while reminding her compatriots that they depend on a peace that only a strong government can guarantee—a point of no small moment in 1796 and over the next decade when her story was several times reprinted:

> Twice has my country been ravaged by war, since my remembrance; I have detailed the share I bore in the first; in the last, although the place in which I live, was not a field of bloody battle, yet its vicinity to Ticonderoga, and the savages that ravaged the Coos country, rendered it perilous and distressing. But now, no one can set a higher value on the smiles of peace, than myself. The savages are driven beyond the Lakes, and our country has no enemies. The grim wilderness, that forty years ago, secreted the Indian and the beast of prey, has vanished away; and the thrifty farm families in its stead; the Sundays, that were then employed in guarding a fort, are now quietly devoted to worship; the tomahawk and scalping knife, have given place to the sickle and ploughshares; and prosperous husbandry now thrives. (142–143)

Like Hastings's more local account, Hannah Adams's general history of New England also emerged under the aegis of conservative Enlightenment politics. The book combined existing histories with Adams's own original research on Rhode Island (Roger Williams was her hero) into the first overview of the region. Without ignoring New England's political and religious controversies, Adams insisted on the shared heritage and the common character of its people. Her celebration of the region is especially strong in the later, textbook version of her history, which abridged the factual material of the original and added didactic commentary. She insists that New Englanders espoused rational religion and other Enlightenment beliefs from the first: "An ardent love of liberty, an unshaken attachment to the rights of men, with a desire to transmit them to their latest posterity, were the principles which governed their conduct"; they were "plain, industrious, conscientious," and though their piety "was fervent, yet it was also rational, and disposed them to a strict observance of the moral and social duties" (*Abridgment*, 15). Adams made the American Revolution—"one of the most extraordinary revolutions in history, replete with the most important consequences to mankind"—into an inevitable expression of this New England character: "The flame of liberty which was first kindled in New England enlightened the continent; and to the early exertions of this part of the country the other colonies in great measure owe their liberty and independence" (*Abridgment*, 145, 144). Her interpretation of the United States as the outgrowth of New England was to dominate schoolroom history for generations.

Frances Manwaring Caulkins's big books about Norwich (1845, 1866) and New London (1852, 1860) are the most truly archival of all the women's histories. They bring together research in town records, old newspapers, court documents, and other primary sources, telling (with some humor) about bridge building, road repair, fence mending, land purchases, floods and freezes, religious controversy, quarrels over the location of churches, privateering and smuggling during the Revolution, as well as covering more conventional topics like Indian relations and Revolutionary heroism and treachery. She insisted: "The hand of God is seen in the history of towns as well as in that of nations" (*New London*, 1860, 3).

Caulkins was inspired to write history by her mentor, Lydia Sigourney, who had produced a fanciful local history early in her career, the *Sketch of Connecticut, Forty Years Since* (1824). Headed by an epigraph from Scott—"Land of my sires!—What mortal hand / Can e'er untie the filial band / That knits me to thy rugged strand?"—Sigourney's book pays tribute to the memory of Jerusha Talcot Lathrop, her childhood benefactor, and to Daniel Wadsworth, Lathrop's nephew, who helped the young writer find an audience. Evoking Norwich as the site of a "singular example of an aristocracy, less intent upon family aggrandizement, than upon becoming illustrious in virtue" (4), Sigourney praises the conservative political establishment of which Wadsworth was a prominent member. She dramatizes the politics of a community whose heterogeneity is firmly contained within a class hierarchy that is secured by Madame L——'s charities, dispensed to various representatives of the deserving poor: transients, unpensioned Revolutionary veterans, industrious widows, blacks. While thus opening a rare window onto the presence of severe and widespread poverty in the early republic, Sigourney also argues that if an "aristocracy" accepts its social responsibilities, the poor can be brought productively and contentedly into the republican fabric. Only the local Mohegan Indians cannot be integrated with the polity she describes; they choose to leave town rather than live at the bottom of the social ladder.

Less comprehensive than Caulkins's histories, Electa Jones's equally pietistic *Stockbridge, Past and Present; or, Records of an Old Mission Station* (1854) is a scrupulous work of local Massachusetts history and genealogy. Information about Dwights, Edwardses, Sedgwicks, and other prominent families are certainly of historical value today; even more useful is Jones's detailed, sympathetic history of the Christian Housatonic Indians from before the Anglo arrival to settlement in the Minnesota Territory. A chapter entitled "Indian History" reprints an eighteenth-century account of the tribe written by Hendrick Aupaumut, an early convert—a rare instance of letting the Indians tell their own stories. Jones describes the successive tribal removals as choice, not coercion; this presentation may be whitewash, but it allows some agency to Native Americans rather than taking them as pure victims.

Jones's account of the Revolution plainly states the war's significance to women and their role in it:

It is a matter of history that the women of Berkshire engaged in the cultivation of the fields, that their husbands and fathers might shoulder the musket; and in one district, at least, from which the most full returns have been obtained, it may readily be inferred that Stockbridge women must have held the plow. But, it may be asked, will woman defend the system of war, and commend those who have left the pruning-hook for the spear? . . . A thousand thanks from woman's heart, that in the season of peril and death now to be recorded, the broad shield of manly strength, and manly daring, was extended over the wife, the mother, the sister and the daughter; and in commendation of those who, under Providence, won for woman the blessings of our favored land, let her grateful voice rise first, and let it die last. (169–170)

Eliza Buckminster Lee's 1849 memoir of her father and brother, written when she was sixty, is as much eyewitness church history as family narrative. Lee looks back to the turn of the nineteenth century, and makes the conflict between Calvinist father and Unitarian brother exemplify the liberalization of New England Protestantism. In *New England Literary Culture* Lawrence Buell has written aptly that the memoir presents both men sympathetically but leaves no doubt that Lee is testifying to the historical "liberation from the dark night of Puritanism that she sees as the meaning of her family odyssey" (249). Throughout the work, Lee judges Calvinist harshness from the standpoint of an advanced Protestantism: "God was next the heart of both. But the one belonged to a particular system; he was trammelled by a theory. . . . Both possessed the same principles of inward, spiritual, life. . . . One drank it from the iron pipes in which man had bent and checked the stream, the other from the pure, freshly flowing river" (136–139).

But the memoir is not only about the men of the family; Lee becomes a character in her own narrative when she writes about children and women under Calvinism. "In the stoical homes of our Puritan childhood . . . the child was subjected to the bonds of a too strict obedience; the struggle of even innocent desires with the Puritan ideas of parental authority planted many a cypress-tree in the young heart, under whose shade perished the opening buds and beautiful flowers of joy" (69). As for women, Lee says that in her mother's time "the female mind of New England was left almost wholly without culture" (97); and she bitterly faults her father for keeping his daughters similarly ignorant:

Although he was active and instrumental in establishing better schools for girls in Portsmouth, he did not allow his daughters to go to them, nor to associate much with society of their age. Perhaps some lingering fondness for the kind of education their mother had enjoyed remained in his mind, and he might have hoped to reproduce a likeness to her in his daughters. But the cloistered retirement of her children was not peaceful, like hers. However nun-like their seclusion, it was not for the purpose of reading or praying; it was filled with domestic duties and the care of younger children. Book-learning was the last necessity; they had far other and humbler duties to learn, and to perform. With an invalid wife and a small salary, the moments for indulging a studious taste in his daughters were few and far between, and for the most part stolen. Such a family was indeed a school for learning the humble and passive virtues. (98)

Lee makes this family history represent not only New England but also universal Protestant history by allegorizing her father as a religious conservative facing the avant garde in his son: "Perhaps it may not be arrogant to say, that this father and son presented an epitome of that greater controversy which afterwards divided the Church and the community" (430). Then she assumes the prophetic stance and anticipates a time "when religion will not be wholly concerned with speculative doctrines, but with the *life of truth*; and that life not manifested by the mere externals of particular forms or even of charities, but by the beauty of holiness,—the exhibition of the beauty of the perfect law, and life of God in the soul of man" (435). Here the family metaphor extends beyond the quarrel of father and son to the neglected daughter who articulates a higher kind of Christianity than even her brother had imagined, a feminized Christianity marked by a passive display of purity. In short, Lee's religious history of New England extends to her own performance as historian.

Because New Englanders imposed their own region on the nation's history at a very early moment, histories written in other regions had to cope with New England anteriority. Toward the end of the antebellum era, and timed to coincide with the opening of Central Park, a group of merchants commissioned Mary Louise Booth (who was to play a significant role in New York City's cultural life after the Civil War as editor of *Harper's Bazar*) to write the first comprehensive history of the city. The book, published in 1859, runs to almost eight hundred pages and is dense with interesting information about the city's history and culture. Booth's preface merges filiopietism and patriotism: "if this work avail in any way to bring these records of the past before the minds of the citizens and inspire them with a love for their native or adopted city, it will answer the purpose for which it is designed" (xix). The author is eager to retrieve the national narrative from New England: "We are more remiss than our neighboring cities. Boston never forgets to commemorate the anniversary of her tea-party; few New Yorkers know even that a similar tea-party was held one night in their own harbor. Boston does not forget her "Massacre;" New York is oblivious of her battle of Golden Hill, her fierce contests around the liberty-pole, and her thousands of victims from the pestilential prison-ships" (Ibid.).

In a countermove to the New England ploy of denigrating New York City as a center of crass commercialism, Booth dedicates her history to "the merchants of the city of New York, who, cheerfully sacrificing their interest to that of their country in the revolution, were the first to propose a non-intercourse act—the last to renounce it, and the only ones to maintain it inviolate" (n.p.). Her narrative of the Revolutionary War insists on the city's claim to national leadership:

Through the whole of the eventful Stamp Act epoch, the Assembly of New York stood true to the interests of the country, and to its bold protests against the enactment of the odious Stamp Act, its determined attitude in the struggle which ensued, and most of all, its earnest advocacy of the union of the colonies, aided by the efforts of the vigilant Sons of Liberty, may be attributed much of the almost miraculous success which attended the coming struggle for independence. (436)

Beyond mere chauvinism, Booth is energized by an idea that the New York, not the New England, character is truly national, because it is truly pluralistic where New England is parochially homogenous:

The broad and liberal nature of the early settlers is still perpetuated in the cosmopolitan character of the city, in its freedom from exclusiveness, in its religious tolerance, and in its extended views of men and things.... Most of the other cities of the United States have descended in a direct line from the pioneer settlers, retaining all the types of the character which first gave them birth; in New York, this primitive type, instead of being predominant, is blended with all the races of the earth; and if it be true, as one of our most eminent philosophers asserts, that a mixture of many materials makes the best mortar, there is no reason to regret it. (173–174)

In the conclusion Booth assumes the historian's right to prophesy:

let [New York] but expend her wealth ... in fostering talent, in encouraging art, in attracting to herself by liberal patronage the intellectual power of the whole country, in endowing universities, and in developing the mental resources of her own citizens, not by a lavish expenditure of money alone, but by a judicious and efficient system of public instruction, carefully superintended in its smallest details, and the time is not far distant when she will be cordially acknowledged, both by friends and foes, as the EMPIRE CITY, not only of the UNION but also of the WORLD! (792)

Deborah Norris Logan, whose husband was a descendant of William Penn's agent, worked to create and preserve an archive affirming Pennsylvania's national priority: "Perhaps it is not going too far to call the original frame of Government designed by William Penn for his Province, and the preliminary discourse affixed to it, the fountains from which have emanated most of those streams of political wisdom which now flow through every part of united America, diffusing civil and religious liberty, and favouring the expansion of happiness and virtue" (*Correspondence,* 2: 101). Her memoir of her activist husband not only vindicated his politics but also gave its own antifederalist account of the eras of Adams and Jefferson:

The breaking out of the French Revolution caused an excitement commensurate with its importance, and was doubtless the cause of that violent effervescence in the public mind which, operating on the prejudices and passions of men not yet subdued after our own contest for independence, produced a degree of party spirit which seemed at one period to threaten the safety of the Commonwealth. . . . The dominant party scorned any longer to affect even the appearance of moderation towards their opponents. Not only the public acts of the Legislature were formed to keep them in awe, but the common offices and affairs of life were proscribed. Friendships were dissolved, tradesmen dismissed, and custom withdrawn from the Republican party, the heads of which, as objects of the most injurious suspicion, were recommended to be closely watched, and committees of Federalists were appointed for that purpose. (*Memoir,* 51, 54)

Hostile to Adams, partial to Jefferson, Logan nevertheless deplores Jefferson's embarrassing failure to rise above party; "He dismissed from public service many respectable men and excellent officers to whom no fault could be justly attributed but their political opinions, and bestowed the places which they had held upon their clamorous and exulting rivals. It was not amusing, but mortifying to us, who had indulged in a kind of chivalrous expectation of patriotism and disinterestedness, to mark the avidity with which offices of emolument were sought" (104–105).

In 1824, a more ardent admirer of Jefferson, Margaret Bayard Smith, drew on her life in Washington, D.C. (her husband, Samuel Harrison Smith, edited the *National Intelligencer*), for a didactic, circumstantial, retrospective three-volume novel, *A Winter in Washington*, which is set in the city during Jefferson's last year in office. (A selection of Smith's letters, detailing Jefferson's political and social life in the young capital, was published in 1906 and made her abilities known; but the novel has not been reprinted.) Along with its network of conventional eighteenth-century plots, and its strikingly full representation of a republican mother at her best, *A Winter in Washington* provides an enormous amount of cultural and historical material, whose inclusion is justified in the preface by appeals to patriotism:

I cannot hope to infuse into others the enthusiasm I felt on my first arrival in the metropolis of our empire. . . . It was not the contemplation of the natural beauties of this favoured spot, which most excited my enthusiasm; it was the mind's-eye view which I took of this rising metropolis of our wide-extended empire—this new capital of a new world, that warmed my feelings, and dilated my mind, with the vast scenes which lay embosomed in futurity.

Our nation, as well as our capital, claims an origin brighter and purer than that of the other nations of the globe. (viii, x)

The novel's descriptions of official and informal social events in the capital are openly partisan. Here, for example, is an extract from the description of the July Fourth celebrations:

The wide plain extending before the president's house, was covered with temporary booths and awnings, which sheltered the gay groups collected on the occasion. The different corps of militia from the city and its environs, passed in review, and paraded on this extensive common, before their civic commander-in-chief. . . . [President Jefferson] stood without his hat, and his white locks waved in the breeze. How simple, how august, and venerable, was the appearance of this good and great man! Dressed in the plain garb of republican simplicity, in the midst of a free and happy people, he stood in no need of the regalia of kings, or the pomp of courts, or the guards of despots, to secure either respect or safety. (3:216–217)

A Winter in Washington contains an extended description of a visit to Jefferson's home, Monticello, and ends with a description of his leaving office: "This was true republicanism, in all its simplicity—its sublimity; for the sight of a great man, voluntarily resigning power, is far more grand and impressive than that of the one who assumes it. Such a sight realizes the Platonic and Utopian visions of philosophers and philanthropists, and is the verification of that liberty and equality of which they only dreamed" (3:283).

All these histories, produced from the older regions of the nation, attempted to shape the developing United States by deriving a national ideology from the country's beginnings. Denizens of the more recently and thinly settled parts of the country thought they were witnessing the unfolding of a nation's historical destiny. The vanguard of history, from this point of view, was to be found on the various frontiers. A historicized rationale of frontier conflict on behalf of God's millennial plan seems to have circulated throughout American antebellum culture much more than did the ahistorical Adamic myth of virgin land. After all, the occupation of vacant wilderness would not have required divine sanction nor called out sacrifice and struggle. It was the conquest and dispossession of indigenous people that necessitated the sacred ideology of Manifest Destiny.

A strident rhetoric of historical inevitability and moral self-righteousness, often accompanied by an undertone of doubt or even dismay that God's plan really requires extirpating the native population, characterizes antebellum border history as it was produced on the spot by white women no less than by white men. A feminist scholar might be tempted to believe that white women expressed more sympathy than men did for the Native American plight, but without a great deal of comparative study of texts by both men and women it would be irresponsible to say this. What can be said on the basis of women's writing alone is that where sympathy is expressed it is cautiously advanced from an assumed position of cultural superiority. White women's criticism of the anti-Indian policies of a white patriarchy always emanated from the privileged place their culture had allotted them; they were not about to bite the hand that fed them. They accepted as a defining point of their advanced civilization precisely that they—women—are deputized to criticize its practice when it betrays its principles. Believing that Christian republican society was better than any other culture where women were concerned, believing that the state of savagery was characterized by oppression of women, these women could never cross the literal and metaphorical borders on which so much of their history writing was situated.

Whatever ethical conflict the women's border histories might have registered with respect to the Native Americans, nothing similar obtained when the adversaries were Roman Catholics or political despots, as was supposedly the case in both Texas and California. Here the march of Protestant republicanism could be played out guiltlessly. So, whereas the Mexican War is conceptualized today in terms of its extension or containment of slavery in the United States—whereas, that is, the abolitionist view of the conflict has come to prevail—that war and its preliminary skirmishes appeared in contemporary Texas border history as a crusade in which Protestant republicanism opposed Catholic despotism on behalf of history itself. Even before it was a question of annexing Texas to the United States, the land had been located within the Protestant-republican grid, in an argument that the republican United States would be best served if its territory was bounded by other republics.

The New Englander Mary Austin Holley was the first of three women to write Texas histories. As a cousin of Stephen Austin and beneficiary of a substantial grant of land from him, she was connected materially and emotionally to the region. Stephen urged her to write on the territory's (and his) behalf and provided her with much of the source material for the two different versions of her *Texas*. The first *Texas* appeared in 1833, before the Texas Revolution, and made a reasoned case for Austin's wisdom in accepting Mexican rule; the second appeared in 1836 during the war and made an emotional case for the necessity of separation. Much in the two books is the same, but the historical material is quite different. Taken together, the two books imply a narrative of Texas's fall from grace as History makes its inevitable appearance in a timeless Eden.

In both versions Texas history begins with and centers on Stephen Austin. "When, in the progress of years, the state of Texas shall take her place among the powerful empires of the American continent, her citizens will doubtless regard Col. Austin as their patriarch, and children will be taught to hold his name in reverence; for, though there have been many other respectable men engaged in the work of colonization, yet Col. Austin began the work, and was the first to open the wilderness" (1833, 108).

The 1833 book is structured as a series of journalistic letters to someone back home, over whose shoulder, as it were, anonymous readers peer. An imaginary settler is created and placed in a Texas landscape, where he or she is at once alone in a natural Eden and also part of a primitive community whose shared goals and productive harmony invite comparison with the New England pilgrims. This early Texas fulfills every legitimate need of the human spirit.

Ones [*sic*] feelings in Texas are unique and original, and very like a dream or youthful vision realized. Here, as in Eden, man feels alone with the God of nature, and seems, in a peculiar manner, to enjoy the rich bounties of heaven, in common with all created things. . . . There are no poor people here, and none rich. . . . They are bound together, by a common interest, by sameness of purpose, and hopes. As far as I could learn, they have no envyings, no jealousies, no bickerings, through politics or fanaticism. There is neither masonry, anti-masonry, nullification, nor court intrigue.

The common concerns of life are sufficiently exciting to keep the spirits buoyant, and prevent every thing like ennui. Artificial wants are entirely forgotten, in the view of real ones, and self, eternal self, does not alone, fill up the round of life. Delicate ladies find they can be useful, and need not be vain. Even privations become pleasures: people grow ingenious in overcoming difficulties. Many latent faculties are developed. They discover in themselves, powers, they did not suspect themselves of possessing. Equally surprised and delighted at the discovery, they apply to their labours with all that energy and spirit, which new hope and conscious strength, inspire. (127–129)

In the enthusiasm of her propaganda, Holley goes so far as to describe the United States as another worn-out Old World nation; she addresses equally those wishing to escape "from confinement and poverty in the northern cities of America, or from the slavery and wretchedness of the crowded and oppressed communities of Europe" (13). But even in 1833, history's shadow darkens the vision; Holley writes prophetically that were Texas to "hereafter become the victim of foreign domination, or the theatre of domestic oppression, it would not be the first instance of an Eden converted into an abode of sorrow and wretchedness by the folly of man" (84).

Although in 1833 Holley insists that she has no interest in politics, she nevertheless opines that separation from Mexico, impolitic at the moment, must always be a possibility because Texas really belongs to its settlers, not to the distant Mexican government:

Until recently, neither the Mexican government nor the Mexican people, knew any thing of this interesting country, and, whatever value it now possesses in their estimation, or in the opinion of the world, is to be attributed, entirely, to the foreign emigrants. They redeemed it from the wilderness,—they developed its resources . . . without the cost of a single cent to the Mexicans. This consideration, certainly, gives to those emigrants, a natural and just claim upon the liberality of their government, and authorises them to expect a system of colonization, of revenue and municipal law, adapted to their local situation and their infant state. (114–115)

The 1836 *Texas*, written in the midst of the Texas Revolution, represents the territory as irretrievably fallen into time. Esthetic rhapsodies on landscape are gone, replaced by an urgent political rhetoric that draws on the readers' assumed knowledge of the historical narrative of Protestant-republican progress.

Before this sketch is completed, the besom of destruction may have passed like a whirlwind over this beautiful, and once thriving and happy land, and the blood-hounds of Mexico torn up every vestige of civilization. . . . Though the flowers of May on these magnificent prairies have withered, and though the delicate mimosas which forms their carpet has shrunk from the unhallowed tread of an army, warring against Liberty, yet, sprinkled with the life-blood of freemen, and consecrated by deeds of unparalleled heroism, will they not spring again with renewed sensibility, and bloom on in redoubled lustre and perennial beauty? Texas has had her *Leonidas*, and many a *Curtius*; every man will become a *Cincinnatus*. (1–2)

Defining Texas as an extension of American Protestant republicanism, in 1836 Holley insists that the United States is morally bound to aid and support people who are in effect its own nationals. Mexicans, she writes, are ignorant, degraded, timid, irresolute, brutal, cowardly, indolent, of loose morals; many of them are infidels, and those who are not are all "involved in the grossest superstition" (128). Besides, she (disingenuously) insists, there are almost no Mexicans in Texas; most of the population is pure American. "The active and enterprising New Englander—the bold and hardy western hunter—the high-spirited southern planter—meet here upon common ground, divested of all sectional influence, to lend their combined energies to the improvement of this infant but delightful and prosperous country" (129).

Holley prints Stephen Austin's plea for help from the United States and echoes it. She promises that once Texas is emancipated, "its moral influence will not stop short of the Pacific. Such *must* be emancipated. What can resist the moral impetus already given? What stop the progress of the anglo-Saxon race? What stifle the free principles, which the sons of Texas imbibed with their mother's milk in the land of Washington—the land of the brave and the free?" (293). Her accounts of battle allude to familiar historic precedents: "The first blow was struck in the cause of Liberty on the 28th inst. at Gonzales, the Lexington of Texas" (335). "On the 6th inst., about midnight, the Alamo was attacked by the entire Mexican force, commanded by Santa Anna in person. A desperate contest ensued, in which prodigies of valor were wrought by this Spartan band" (353–354).

The second woman writing about Texas for American imaginations was Jane McManus Storms Cazneau (1807–1878), who often published under the name Cora (or C.) Montgomery. She became involved with the Austin colony in 1832, when her family secured land in Texas. Much more racist, political, and confrontational than Holley, Cazneau identified her Texas interests with the Democratic Party early on. As a journalist in New York during the 1840s, she wrote on behalf of Texas annexation for the *New*

York Sun; her jingoistic essay, "Presidents of Texas," appeared in John Louis O'Sullivan's *United States Magazine and Democratic Review* for March 1845. This piece predates O'Sullivan's coinage "manifest destiny" by four months and very likely occasioned it. Later that year Cazneau expanded her essay into a short book, *Texas and Her Presidents*, in which she defined Texas as always and already part of the United States. Her argument rests heavily on sentimental family rhetoric:

The annexation of Texas was the natural result of the attraction of republican gravitation. By political birth and every habit of thought in national pride and in family interests, Texas was the beauteous and legitimate daughter of the Union. She might have been alienated, and her two last Presidents labored unceasingly to that end, but her filial and patriotic love triumphed over their wiles, and we are now joyously celebrating her welcome home. . . . Texas, the child of her own republican faith and blood, was not to be refused her fitting place at the family altar. (iii–iv)

Like Holley, Cazneau begins Texas history with the divinely appointed Austins: "At the required moment, Divine Providence called forth a man, or rather a family, fit and ready to redeem Texas from the savage, and create a new Anglo-American state" (11). In this view, Austin's job, like the Puritans', is to clear the terrain of Indians so that "the broad prairie" could become "dotted by the homes of the white race" (15). Any thought that Texas might be part of a republican Mexico was delusory:

There was between the two races such a want of national sympathy, such a difference in language, social customs, and almost every habit of thought, that they could not understand, and knew not where or how to trust each other. With the Mexican, adhering with devout love to the faith of his fathers, not to be a Catholic was to be an outcast from all religion. . . . [The colonist] from his infancy had been taught to believe the union of church and state adulterous, demoralizing, and in no way binding on the conscience of freemen. . . . In Mexico, where nine-tenths of the populace are of mixed blood, negroes are eligible, in the eye of the law and public opinion, to the highest offices, and frequently fill them too, to the entire satisfaction of their constituents.

The inflexible determination of the colonists never to mingle in marriage, nor share the responsibilities of the ballot-box with the African race, implied, therefore, a high contempt for Mexican sentiment. (16–17)

Mexican and Anglo are two difference races; racial pride is the main explanation for colonial resistance to Mexican rule. Naturally, the higher race practices the higher religion. Far from being ashamed of this racialist rationale, Holley is proud of it.

Texas and Her Presidents anchors its history of Texas in these presumptions, beginning with Austin, moving to the Revolution of 1836—blaming Sam Houston, to whom she is unforgivingly hostile, for the losses at Goliad and the Alamo, where "the death of the last man happened while General Houston was idly lingering over the wine cup" (45)—and concluding with a tendentious account of the decade of independence, in which she judges the presidents according to their sentiments for or against annexation. Cazneau's expansionist ideology dominated much of her other historical and propagandizing work. She wrote in favor of Cuban annexation in *The Queen of Islands and the King of Rivers* (1850); she advocated the secession of all of northern Mexico preparatory to its becoming part of the union in *Eagle Pass* (1852), named for the border town where she lived for a few years. The book is antislavery and horrified by the United States's treatment of Indians, yet thoroughly devoted to the doctrine of Anglo racial superiority:

This way is open to us, and there is no other in which we can redeem the two unhappy races who are in contact with white domination on this continent. Assign them homes and give them industrial teachers—I am speaking now of the Red Race, for to the African, colonization abroad is the only resource, but on the same principle of community and patriarchal guidance—assign sufficient and permanent domains to the tribes still in existence. . . . The youth of the tribe [are] to be collected and taught letters, morals and industry, at permanent and systematic schools. As they advance in years they can till the land and man the workshops for the community, on such terms of reward as shall be just and beneficial to the general weal, but always under the joint supervision of government and their own chiefs, until civilization and the capacity of self-government shall have taken firm root. These tribes would be nurseries for such a powerful, efficient and economical border cavalry as is the especial want of this republic. (42)

Let her petition on behalf of the Indians not be distorted "into a wish to deprive the exiled African of his portion of sympathy," she writes. "We owe him—and in the march of the age it will come to him—instruction, freedom, and a home in the land of his fathers" (138).

In 1855 Augusta Evans, a twenty-year-old Alabama woman who had lived in Texas during 1845–1849, made Texas the subject of her first novel,

Inez: A Tale of the Alamo. Like most historical fiction, this historical novel about the Texas Revolution connects a private romance to events of public importance. The book recounts several battles at length and with little reference to the love plot, making sentimental centerpieces of the massacres at the Alamo and at Goliad. The novel makes these sites sacred through the blood of martyred soldiers, and it insists that annexation of the territory by the United States was the only possible response to their sacrifice.

Whatever the Texans were fighting for in 1836, to Evans twenty years later they were fighting for the United States and its Protestant republican values. She insists on this connection in her running motif of Catholic versus Protestant. Interpreting her Texas concerns through the perspective of historical progress, she allots her scholarly heroine Mary two chapters of religious monologue containing a Protestant narrative of European history for the edification of her cousin Florence (Florry), the foil, who has briefly strayed into Catholicism.

The voices of slaughtered thousands, [says Mary] borne to us across the waste of centuries, bid us remember the Duke of Alva, the Albigensian crusade, the massacre of St. Bartholemew, and the blazes of Smithfield. . . . Florry, contrast Italy and Germany, Spain and Scotland, and look at Portugal, and South America, and, oh, look at this benighted town! A fairer spot by nature the face of earth can not boast; yet mark the sloth, the penury, the degradation of its people, the misery that prevails. . . . Oh, Florry, does not your heart yearn toward benighted Italy? Italy, once so beautiful and noble—once the acknowledged mistress of the world, as she sat in royal magnificence enthroned on her seven hills; now a miserable waste. . . . Tell me, Florry, what caused the dark ages? Was it not the gradual withdrawal of light and knowledge—the crushing, withering influence exerted on the minds of men? (Chap. 18)

The recital ends with the bogey of papacy stalking across the American nation itself: we must "vigorously resist this blasting system of ignorance, superstition, and crime which, stealthily approaching from the east and from the west, will unite and crush the liberties of our glorious Republic." Since as a matter of historical accuracy Texas was not in 1836 part of the United States, one sees *Inez* in 1855 contributing its historical mite to nativism and know-nothingism. Perhaps *Inez* succeeded because of the author's novelistic talent; but something else is implied by the reviewer in *Godey's Lady's Book*, who anticipated "a good run" for the novel "during the present excited state of the public mind on the vexed questions of religious faith and observance" (April 1855).

Mary Henderson Eastman, whose proslavery novel of 1852, *Aunt Phillis'*

Cabin, was meant to counter *Uncle Tom's Cabin*, had lived at Fort Snelling, which at the time was principal U.S. military outpost in the Northwest, during the 1840s. The 1849 *Dahcotah* was the first of four books that she and her artist-husband Seth published containing, as the publisher of one of them put it, "attractive and beautiful stories of Indian Life" in an "elegantly illustrated volume" (*Romance of Indian Life*, xi). All four books combine Seth's superb engravings with Mary's written sketches. These sketches, even as they express considerable sympathy and respect for their subject, and claim to be presenting, "not the red man of the novel or drama, but the red man as he appears to himself, and to those who live with him" (*Dahcotah*, 39), are devoted to the work of transforming "him" into an esthetic and consumable object. The process is undergirded and justified by a conviction that Indians have no future, that the memorial approach is appropriate and even constitutes a kind of moral compensation.

At the same time, the earlier books in the series do have a uniquely ethnographic approach. Particularly striking is Eastman's recognition that Native American oral tradition was not merely poetic and imaginative but also historical. She realized that lack of written language did not necessarily imply lack of a historical sense. If we knew how to interpret, she suggests, we could extract Indian history from their stories. "It was from the Dahcotahs that I obtained the incident, and they believe that it really occurred. They are offended if you suggest the possibility of its being a fiction. Indeed they fix a date to it, reckoning by the occurrences of great battles, or other events worthy of notice" (*Dahcotah*, 166). She also recognizes that Native American rituals are culturally significant: "Their dances and feasts are not amusements. They all have an object and meaning, and are celebrated year after year, under a belief that neglect will be punished by the Great Spirit" (*Dahcotah*, xx).

Dahcotah gives considerable attention to Native American women as conveyers of tribal culture through ritual activities and storytelling. In view of the stereotype of women as transculturally peaceful in nature, Eastman supposes that Indian women were more attracted to Christianity than Indian men. Maneuvering between intense feelings of sympathy for the Native American plight along with guilt over white barbarism, and equally intense beliefs in Protestant Christian superiority and the inevitability of Indian disappearance, *Dahcotah* subsides in an anticlimactic call for Christianizing the remnant.

They are receding rapidly, and with feeble resistance, before the giant strides of civilization. The hunting grounds of a few savages will soon become the haunts of densely peopled, civilized settlements. We should be better reconciled to this manifest destiny of the aborigines, if the inroads of civilization were worthy of it; if the last years of these, in some respects, noble people, were lit up with the hope-in-spiring rays of Christianity.... We know the great Being of whom they are ignorant; and well will it be for them and for us, in a day that awaits us all, if yet, though late ... we so give countenance and aid to the missionary, that the light of revealed truth may cheer the remaining period of their national and individual existence. (*Dahcotah*, xvi)

Of the four Eastman Indian books, *Dahcotah* is closest to its subject and most marked by a desire to represent the Sioux around Fort Snelling in the practice of their daily lives and in their own words. *The Romance of Indian Life* and *The American Aboriginal Portfolio* (both 1853) are more distanced and romantic. The fourth, *Chicora, and other Regions of the Conquerors and the Conquered* (1854, republished in 1855 as *The American Annual: Illustrative of the Early History of North America*), is a juvenile history, starting with Columbus and narrating Native American history as a series of encounters between native tribes and white encroachers characterized either by the resistance that Indians make to, or the friendship they offer, white people. This approach centers Native American history on the perspective of the little white child supposedly reading the book: "The life of the sachem of Mount Hope may charm the youth that loves to hear of the brave, and the good, who have passed away. Well may they who now revel on his noble inheritance, bear in their hearts an admiration for the virtues he possessed, and a grateful remembrance of the kindness shown, by the great red man, to their forefathers" (39). The leading theme of *Chicora* is Indian patriotism. Rather than demonizing or sentimentalizing Native Americans, Eastman makes them subjects of a heroic chronicle, much as another historian might have treated Greece or Rome. Pontiac, who lived only for his country, Keokok, whose "remarkable courage" was "animated by a devoted love for his people" (100), and many others, come before the young reader as national heroes, like the greats of Greece and Rome. Patriotism is a virtue wherever it is displayed, and it is magnanimous to admire the courage of those one has vanquished in a fair fight. In context, the history seems designed to insist that it *was* a fair fight by which the Indians were dispossessed, and to screen the reality of contemporary hostilities by the fiction that the Indians had already vanished.

The most engagingly liberal of the frontier eyewitness histories is Juliette Magill Kinzie's 1856 *Wau-bun*, which looked back a quarter century to life on the Illinois-Wisconsin frontier when the author had spent two years with her husband, Indian agent John Kinzie, Jr., at Fort Winnebago. Kinzie, by 1856 a leading citizen of Chicago, wrote in part to produce a memorial of early Illinois for the great second wave of immigrants that she rightly saw was coming. Central to that history would be the typical installation of the writer's family as historical founders; in this case, Kinzie alleges that white survival on the frontier in the Deerfield massacre of 1812–1814 was owing entirely to the heroism and sagacity of her father-in-law, John Kinzie, Sr. Her account of this event derived from the oral testimony of her mother-in-law, and thus (in a gesture to be repeated in numerous traditions of women's writing) transported female oral narrative into the written record.

Also central to Kinzie's family purpose was vindicating Indian agents and traders (her husband had been a member of the first class, her father-in-law one of the second) from accusations that they were responsible for everything wrong with official United States Indian policy. As early as 1824, for example, the young Lydia Maria Child, in a sketch in her (anonymous) *Evenings in New England*, had a didactic aunt explaining, "the government of the United States, no doubt, intends to be just in their dealings with this unfortunate race; but the business is sometimes entrusted to agents, who are artful, dishonest men" (74). Kinzie's position was, contrariwise, that agents and traders had a real stake in Indian survival and a much better understanding of the actualities of Indian social organization than the Washington bureaucracy. Implicit in *Wau-bun* is Kinzie's belief that a multicultural society really could have flourished in the west if the government had acted in good faith. Moreover, for all that she was devoutly Episcopalian, she did not think Protestantism a prerequisite for citizenship. From its title on, *Wau-bun* is in many ways itself a multicultural performance; not only Indians, but also French-Canadians, and the interracial offspring of Indian and French-Canadian marriages, and an assortment of varied characters on the, granted, vanished frontier, speak for themselves. Evidently, Kinzie's situation as a particularly favored beneficiary of events that she deplores is not comfortable (the Kinzie property on Lake Michigan became the nucleus of downtown Chicago). But she has, nevertheless, greater awareness and range of sensibility than the more evangelistic frontier writers.

The most serious attempt by a white woman to write Indian history from the Native American point of view with a reasonably sophisticated understanding of the limitations and inevitability of the historian's own approach is *The Iroquois, or the Bright Side of Indian Character* (1855), by Anna Cummings Johnson, one of two women (confusingly) who wrote as "Minnie Myrtle." Her aim, as she explains in the preface, is to produce an accessible and accurate popular Indian history:

The Antiquarian, the Historian, and the Scholar, have been a long time studying Indian character, and have given us plenty of information concerning Indians, but it is all in ponderous tomes for State and College libraries, and quite inaccessible to the multitudes. Those who only take up such books as may be held in the hand, sitting by the fire, still remain very ignorant of the inhabitants who peopled the forests, before the Saxon set his foot upon our shore.

There is also a great deal of prejudice, the consequence of this ignorance, and the consequence of the representations of our forefathers, who were brought into contact with the Indians, under circumstances that made it impossible to judge impartially and correctly.

This ignorance and prejudice I have attempted to dispel. (11–12)

Among her printed sources Johnson lists Parkman; Charlevoix; La Hontan; Colden; Smith; Macaulay; Morse; Bancroft; William L. Stone; Schoolcraft; Lewis H. Morgan; Col. Thomas L. McKenney, administrator of Indian affairs; Alfred B. Street's "Frontenac"; Colton's "Tecumsah"; poems by Hosmer. But, seeking eyewitness immediacy, she also lived for some months in western New York with a missionary family to the Iroquois, profiting from their knowledge of the language and their willingness to introduce her to native informants, several of whom are also named—Dr. Peter Wilson; Mr. N. T. Strong; M. B. Pierce; N. W. Parker; Ely S. Parker (17).

Beginning with a survey of Iroquois government, religion, culture, legendary literature, and eloquence, Johnson continues through a sequence of historical biographies of the great Iroquois leaders: Red Jacket, Cornplanter, Logan. Not until Helen Hunt Jackson's *Century of Dishonor* would a woman writer again be so critical of white behavior. "As I read over volumes of history in order to glean the truth from the great mass of details, I cannot help being struck with the different manner in which massacre and bloodshed are represented when Indians are spoken of, and when the same things are recorded of white men," she observes. "The Indian is called a barbarian and blood-thirsty assassin—the personification of cruelty and revenge"; but when the same deed is recorded of the American army, "it is called 'gallant,' a 'brilliant achievement,' a 'glorious exploit!'" (215–216). She continues, "Instead of wondering that they hated white people, I only wonder that the wounds they received should ever have healed—that they do not rankle for ever, and produce utter detestation and unconquerable enmity to every thing with a pale skin" (216–217). "The history of Treaties is by far the darkest of all the pages of Indian history," she declares (245). But the book's conventionalism comes clear in its strong endorsement of missionary activities among the Indians, its acceptance of the social desirability of producing *civilized, Christian* Indians.

One woman who actually settled on the frontier with missionary intentions was Harriet E. Bishop, a Vermont Baptist who was the first schoolteacher and Sunday-school teacher in the Minnesota Territory.

Arriving in St. Paul in 1847, she published *Floral Home* ten years later. This, the first history of Minnesota, combined settlers' manual, promotional hype, gazetteer, historical archive, travel account, and autobiography. "In this volume the aim has been to present the reader with a truthful picture . . . of the beauties and rare advantages of this Floral Territory. And the most important object of its publication will be secured if men and women of sterling worth, are, by it, induced to identify themselves with the interests of this youthful empire, and labor to make it the first state of our glorious Union" (preface, n.p.).

Bishop's is a New England-based Providential history, connecting the founding of Minnesota with the settlement of Plymouth in the familiar narrative of historical progress: "the energy and enterprise, born and nurtured on that sterile soil, have no parallel in the world's history; and for their full development, they have pushed on towards the setting sun" (17). "For centuries, the mighty Northwest smiled in unpraised beauty. . . . The Red Man remained undisputed and undisturbed owner of the soil. . . . The reeking scalp was exhibited in the horrid war-dance, and the captive was tortured in the most cruel manner that savage malice and hate could devise. But in the great plans and purposes of Jehovah, a moral dawn appears. The march of empire is westward" (17–18).

Her chronicle moves from the establishment of Fort Snelling to the arrival of the earliest civilian settlers, including missionaries, men and women who had "taken life in hand, and entered upon the great and trying work in this vast arena, of instructing the blood-thirsty savage in the principles of the Gospel, or leading his dark mind to the fountain of life and peace" (39). She has much to say about the contributions of women—"whose unwritten lives would make many an interesting chapter in our country's history; without their cooperation the foundations of society could not have been laid" (46)—and finds them comparable to the Revolutionary foremothers in hardihood, patriotism, and bravery. The book ends with an invocation of republican motherhood appealing particularly to prospective women settlers but also to American women more generally: on them it depends "whether the individual American citizen shall be a curse or a blessing, and whether the nation shall be rent and prostrated by the feuds of corrupt men, or fulfill the mission of the great Christian republic of modern times" (340).

Bishop's assertion of white superiority coexists with her account of coming to Minnesota in response to a call for a teacher who would love the Savior, and "be entirely free from prejudice on account of color, for among her scholars she might find not only English, French, and Swiss, but Sioux and Chippewas, with some claiming kindred with the African stock" (54). *Floral Home* has chapters about the Dakota Sioux, the Winnebagos (resettled after the Sauk war), and the Chippewas; it admits, even boasts, that the author received a marriage proposal from a Sioux brave. To some extent, and in defiance of her own intentions, Bishop conveys a scene of interactive border culture in which she, personally, draws the breath of emancipated life, even as she expects and celebrates events that must bring this period of transition to an end. Territorial organization "was the glorious birthday of our territory; the great epoch in its history. Immediately the tide of emigration set in this direction" (125). "Who can doubt that she is to shine the brightest star in the galaxy of our republic" (146). "Transplant New England institutions on our soil, and we could ask no more. But we are rapidly approaching a period when the west will no longer look towards the rising sun for her educational light, nor longer shine in borrowed rays, but will illumine the entire nation with her own brightness" (316).

The narrow limits of Bishop's affection for and interest in Native Americans, the extent to which her celebration of the multicultural scene depends on the certainty of its impermanence, may be clearly seen in the hysteria of her 1863 book, *Dakota War-Whoop*, a narrative of the Sioux uprising of 1863. "I knew the Indian from an acquaintance of fifteen years, and I knew no good of him" (76). Here Indians are demonized, atrocities against whites are elaborated in graphic detail, accounts of Indian defeat offered as Providential interventions: when Little Crow, for example, supposed instigator of the uprising, becomes the first Indian to be scalped after the state introduces bounty hunting, she writes: "A more marked instance of Providential retribution, history probably does not record" (343). This book, like so many eyewitness histories, also has specific political intentions: first, to insinuate that the uprising was really initiated by the Confederate States (the Civil War was in progress by then), and second, to defend the military commander of the territorial forces: "If we look to historic facts, we find no more successful campaigns against the Indians, than have been those of Gen. Sibley. . . . The name of Henry H. Sibley will live on history's unsullied page. Posterity will laud him, when those of his calumniators will be lost in the great whirlpool of oblivion" (377).

Like other parts of the continent, California was deemed by these women writers to have been without history before Anglo settlers began to move there. In her 1849 *Last Leaves of American History*, a combined narrative of the Mexican war and a history of California, and from the vantage point of her established reputation as a historian, Emma Willard considered how best to transform "a poor anarchical territory of an ill-governed state" into "an integral part of the American Republic" under the particular historical circumstance of an emigration "such as the earth has never seen before" (110). True to her lifelong republican principles and her belief in history, she imagined the state's future as a function of how historically instructed and virtuous the settlers were:

Many of our ablest and most enterprising citizens . . . are intending to settle in that salubrious clime. God grant that nobler views than the mere love of gold, accompany them thither. May they feel, with a deep sense of responsibility, that they are going to lay the foundations of a new and an important state. Let them look back for an example to their forefathers. Like them, may they be temperate, virtuous, and public-spirited. . . . Let their faces be sternly set against anarchy, the scourge, and too often the destroyer of free governments. To this end, let them uphold law, found schools, observe the sabbath, and maintain pure Christianity. (230)

Eliza Wood Farnham also wrote about her experiences in California; like other work of its type, *California, In-Doors and Out* (mostly written in 1851, not published until 1856) merges travel narrative, geography, settler's manual, and autobiography with history. In her description of the California landscape, Farnham balances or oscillates between romanticized religious raptures in the presence of sublimely empty landscapes and equally rapturous invocations of the smiling industrious scenes that are to displace them:

The beating of the distant surf rather aids than breaks the silence. . . . I look out on a picture so filled with repose and beauty, that while I gaze, the hateful stir of the world in which I have lately been mixed up, seems to die out of the universe, and I no longer remember it. . . . I wonder, while beholding it, that religious and devout thankfulness to God does not continually ascend from the hearts of those who dwell in so fair a portion of his creation. (44–46)

Cover the bay with sails and steamers, variegate the uniform green of the fertile plain with grain-fields, orchards, gardens, farm-yards, and houses; dot the sunny slopes with vineyards, and let the church-spires be seen pointing heavenward from among occasional groups of dwellings, and I know not what would be wanting to complete the picture, and make it one on which the heart and eye could dwell with equal delight. (75)

Imagining a future California that is an imitation New England, Farnham grapples directly with two facts, one geographical and the other historical. The first is that the California climate is not congenial to New England ideology; or more precisely, the climate is too congenial for New England ideology: "Even Puritanism, tough and tenacious as it was, would have been shorter lived had the Mayflower landed her inflexibilities on this laughing coast. The rock-bound shores and inhospitable soil, the wintry skies overhanging the sterile mountains and stony vales of New England, were far more favorable to earnestness in the religious as well as the working life of man than ours will ever be" (139). This problem, she believes, can be overcome; in line with the progressive view of religious development, Farnham imagines that a "less exacting and more kindly" faith could develop in the milder climate (140).

More serious is the second, historical problem: California is already being occupied by white populations lacking in New England virtue and self-restraint. These people, not the indigenous Native Americans or Mexicans, constitute at once California's threat and its opportunity. On the one hand is the horrifying possibility of "a condition in which all the knowledge and art of civilized life shall be made to subserve the most corrupt desires, in which wealth and power shall be the servants of dishonorable motives, of frightful lust and greed, and in which any sort of merit may be driven shrinking into a corner, ashamed almost of its own character, and trembling at the restraints itself imposes" (140–141). On the other is the possibility of radical developments of democratic governance: "California will always be the nucleus and home of the extreme of democratic tendencies. . . . The moral and political elements of this state will almost surely make it the theatre of first test for the most radical questions" (276–277).

For Farnham, the conservative force that will control democracy without extirpating it is the power of pure women, a power all the more needful because of what is delicately described as the "many defections among the reputable of my sex in this state" as well as the "destroying army of another class" (386). Unlike Emma Willard, whose republican ideology trusts the stern power of a virtuous male elite, Farnham expects women to save the state by their domestic spirituality. (Notwithstanding, an appendix to the book, which updates it, strongly defended vigilantism.) She appeals to the mystique of womanly self-sacrifice; woman must settle where "she will feel herself in an enemy's country" and must "bear her trials in silence" (156–157) for the world's good. "Only in the presence of women of California will one day have an honorable place assigned them, when history shall fill her noblest office and truthfully interpret the motives that lead to noble actions. For they come regardless of the trials and dangers that await them. . . . The home, holiest and purest nursery of what is good in the heart, springs up everywhere before woman" (294–295).

Certain that the disreputable aspects of California life must eventually give way to the power of female domesticating, Farnham launches the state into a millennial future, as the incubator of history's next great age:

California is the world's nursery of freedom. The centuries that have brooded over her since the treasure was first poured into her bosom, have witnessed no event so significant to the nations as its development under a free government. It marks an era to which, in future years, the new men of nations grown hoary in despotism, will point as the time when the masses began to gather the earth's treasures and make them their own.

The lessons in political and religious freedom learned here, will be remembered and repeated beneath the palm-trees of India—in the tea-fields of China—among the frozen snows of Russia—in the saloons of the proudest cities of Europe, where doted monarchy yet hugs his shivering members together. . . . The islands and continents of the Pacific—latest conquests of man's knowledge and enterprise—last redeemed from the midnight abyss of time—shall bring their treasures to redeem the millions, and their light shall spread abroad, and the millions shall receive both the treasure and the light. (327–329)

California, In-Doors and Out supported Fremont's gubernatorial campaign, especially praising his opposition to slavery. But Farnham's tropes strongly suggest a wish to keep not just slavery but an African population out of California as well: "Slavery ties the arteries of civilization. No life and vigor can travel eastward or westward through its dark dominion. May its black shadow never come nearer to the soil of California than it is today" (507). Indeed, as one reads the repeated expressions of rejoicing at escape from the tired old eastern seaboard throughout frontier histories, it becomes depressingly clear that white people were happy to leave behind the institution of slavery, the political battles over it that affected all national politics, and the black population as well. Alongside the millennial clarion sounds the somber theme of a nation already ruined, both because it has been constitutionally forced to sanction an unholy institution as the very ground of its existence, and because it must now accept responsibility for a population so unlike the Euro-American as presumably to be outside any imaginable national future.

Elizabeth Lyon Roe opens her 1855 family history, *Aunt Leanna; or, Early Scenes in Kentucky*, by explaining that the partly fictionalized work "is mainly founded upon incidents connected with the emigration and settlement of Colonel Matthew Lyon and family to Kentucky, and their unwilling participation in the universal custom of slave holding, and of their benevolent and self-sacrificing efforts for the emancipation and improvement of their slaves" (vi). The narrative shows how her antislavery father (who left Vermont in this account because he was disgusted with local politics) colonized Lyon County with a contingent of fellow Vermonters and was unable to avoid owning slaves. All attempts to employ whites having foundered on incompetence or insolence, the family starts to hire slaves from the southern settlers, but is soon persuaded by the slaves themselves to purchase them away from their harsh masters. When Lyon institutes an accounting system to give his slaves credit toward manumission, he is besieged by even more African Americans pleading to be bought. When the father loses all his money during the War of 1812, the Lyon family is sustained by the loyalty and affection of their African American dependents. At the end of the story, the author, now an adult, leaves Kentucky with her husband to settle in Illinois, "that they might spend their days in a free state, or where African slavery was not tolerated" (230).

For all Roe's glimpse of an otherwise little-chronicled locale, her praiseworthy politics and moving descriptions of affectionate relations between black and white people, she closes with five chapters—forty-seven pages—of procolonization argument. Similarly, Sarah Hale's 1853 *Liberia*, a combined history of and novel about Liberia designed to induce free black readers to emigrate to a country where they could freely develop their own national republican future, does not so much doubt the capacities and capabilities of blacks as insist that these cannot be historically fulfilled in the United States.

And again, in Sara Tappan Robinson's history of Kansas from a Free-Soil perspective (she was wife of its Free-Soil governor), the abolitionist cause on behalf of which these New Englanders had emigrated and were risking their lives seems either utterly abstract or else concretized as an ideal of a territory inhabited by only one race. *Kansas* went through several editions in a short span of years and was, according to Eli Thayer (a prime organizer of territorial Free-Soil settlement) "a very efficient aid in our great work" (*Kansas Crusade*, 35). It is a settler's manual with a difference, offering its readers the usual inducements for emigration augmented by the chance to be active in a holy cause. Although more journalism than history, the narrative acquires meaning for United States history as that history acquires meaning through the march of millennial progress. The Kansas-Nebraska bill, seemingly "the knell for the burial of Liberty," also sounds the alarm: "the hosts of freedom must marshal their forces, and draw their lines against the lines of slavery, and each man fight courageously" (8). "In the prospect of freedom's bulwarks raised high and strong we can yet exult. . . It may cost many valued lives; but we will lay each corner of this altar of freedom with the serene, abiding strength of a holy faith; trust all to Him who maketh 'the darkness as the noonday,' and the end will be glorious" (164). Notably absent from the book are discussions of the economic motives to colonization and the removal of the Indians that had to precede settlement.

Still, *Kansas* works at the outer limits of the familiar Protestant-national synthesis. Because the United States government aids the Missourians, the "America" being fought for is an imaginary construct arrayed against the nation's real government; as Robinson's language formulates it, it is ideal "America" versus the "U.S." In a chapter historicized by its title—"The 'Reign of Terror' in Kansas"—Robinson writes that for "the first time in the history of the American people has an American town been besieged and its inhabitants robbed, by forces acting under the instructions of U.S. officers" (249). The fight finally is less against slavery than for an "America" identified with New England Puritanism; gathering for worship, the pioneers "felt that two thousand miles lay between us and the pleasant sanctuaries of our fathers," but when "the services commenced with the singing of hymns learned long ago, and we heard, in the persuasive, winning tones of the preacher, the same heavenly truths which will render one's life here as holy as elsewhere, let us so will it, we felt that New England was in our midst" (42). Presenting the move west as a restatement of the nation's New England origins and hence a recovery of New England historical purpose was a simplifying stroke of powerful imaginative import at work in many of these texts: Robinson, Farnham, Bishop, Willard. Even Hale likened the emigrating Africans to the New England pilgrims. Here, apparently, is less a desire to escape history than a wish to reclaim the United States for its betrayed historical mission.

Perhaps the most telling of these New England recoveries is Lucy Mack Smith's family history, which is also an account of the early Mormon church. *Biographical Sketches of Joseph Smith, the Prophet, and His Progenitors for Many Generations*, a partly dictated work, was composed late in 1844 after Lucy's sons Joseph and Hyram had been murdered in an Alton, Illinois, jail; suppressed by Brigham Young, it appeared in London and Liverpool in 1853. As though to insist on her nationality in the face of mainstream views of Mormons as monstrous others, Smith highlights the family's New England origins; the work begins with extracts from her father's journals about his service in the French and Indian War. Having thus established her roots, Smith develops the Mormon story as the outcome of a visionary family's quest for true religion, a quest that originates with Lucy herself. Before marriage, living at Tunbridge, Vermont, with a brother, she determined "to obtain that which I had heard spoken of so much from the pulpit—a change of heart." But

Another matter would always interpose in all my meditations—If I remain a member of no church, all religious people will say I am of the world; and if I join some one of the different denominations, all the rest will say I am in error. No church will admit that I am right, except the one with which I am associated. This makes them witnesses against each other; and how can I decide in such a case as this, seeing they are all unlike the Church of Christ as it existed in former days! (37)

She writes later,

I heard that a very devout man was to preach the next Sabbath in the Presbyterian Church; I therefore went to meeting, in the full expectation of hearing that which my soul desired—the Word of Life. When the minister commenced speaking, I fixed my mind with deep attention upon the spirit and matter of his discourse; but, after hearing him through, I returned home, convinced that he neither understood nor appreciated the subject upon which he spoke, and I said in my heart that there was not then upon earth the religion which I sought. (48)

Under Lucy's influence, her husband becomes "much excited upon the subject of religion; yet he would not subscribe to any particular system of faith, but contended for the ancient order, as established by our Lord and Saviour Jesus Christ, and his Apostles" (56–57). In distress, both he and his wife begin to have visions—that is, dreams—that make Joseph's eventual visitations seem entirely natural. Although Joseph Smith's biographer Fawn Brodie writes that "he grew up in a family with a prodigious appetite for the marvelous" (*No Man Knows My History*, 412), it seems truer to Lucy Smith's account to say that the family did not recognize the marvelous as a distinct category, and especially did not distinguish dreams from visions: "After falling asleep that night, I saw my sons in vision. They were upon the prairie travelling" (259).

Joseph's vision is accepted without question as a gift to the entire family, which then unites to preserve and publicize it, and not incidentally to write itself into world history. By the time they are on the way to Kirtland, Lucy has become "Mother Smith," a leader and prophet—"I was filled with the Spirit of God, and received the following by the gift of prophecy" (251)—and an effective proselytizer herself:

On account of brother Humphry's age, I wished him to take charge of the company, but he refused, saying, that every thing should be done, just as mother Smith said; and to this the whole company responded "yes." . . . I then called the brethren and sisters together, and reminded them that we were travelling by the commandment of the Lord, as much as father Lehi was, when he left Jerusalem; and, if faithful, we had the same reason to expect the blessings of God. (173)

Lucy Mack Smith's Mormon history, then, is controlled by the most radical—or perhaps the most reactionary—millennial framework thus far seen, wherein the Protestant insistence that individuals must interpret God's word for themselves detaches itself not only from the practices of all existing sects but also from the anchors of the Old and New Testaments as well, to create a testament of its own. This process carries to the ultimate degree both the sectarian factionalism so typical of the religious life of the northeast, and the longing such factionalism itself engenders for escape from controversy. And this is all expressed in the vision of replicating the orthodox interpretation of the Puritans settling America:

"That book," replied I, "was brought forth by the power of God, and translated by the gift of the Holy Ghost; and, if I could make my voice sound as loud as the trumpet of Michael, the Archangel, I would declare the truth from land to land, and from sea to sea, and the echo should reach to every isle, until every member of the family of Adam should be left without excuse. For I do testify that God has revealed himself to man again in these last days, and set his hand to gather his people upon a goodly land." (180)

Mainstream Americans did not share the Mormons' view of themselves. Smith's claim to have received a new revelation defied the fundamental Protestant assumption that New Testament revelation was the last supernatural intervention before the millennium. The publicity surrounding polygamy equated Smith with the other false prophet, Mohammed. For women with faith in a vision of progressive female influence under Protestant republicanism, polygamy was especially abhorrent. In several versions of her United States history, Emma Willard repeated her assertion from the 1849 *Last Leaves of American History* that Mormonism was "one of the most extraordinary impostures of the age" (*Last Leaves*, 18). She said in the 1852 edition of the U.S. text that the religion's laws "give his followers license to commit every crime" and especially "degrade and demoralize women" (332). The 1868 edition opined that making Brigham Young governor of the territory had been a bad mistake, since "the whole community was bound to their chief, either as accomplices in crime, or as fanatical dupes" (440).

A substantial sensationalist anti-Mormon literature claiming historical authenticity arose in the 1850s to warn women away from plausible, smooth-talking, handsome, diabolic Mormon suitors, including, for example, Metta Victor's melodramatic and thoroughly nonhistorical *Mormon Wives* (1856). Maria Ward's 1855 *Female Life Among the Mormons: A Narrative of Many Years' Personal Experience*, in contrast, is a historically informed and by no means politically unsophisticated novel whose author's claim to firsthand experience, whether true or not ("Maria Ward" may be a pen name, but bibliographers accept that the writer was a woman), gives it the aura of eyewitness history. The story—which focuses on a powerful female character who mistakenly believes that Mormonism opens a field for her energies—narrates the Nauvoo settlement, the trek to Salt Lake, and the establishment of the Mormon theocracy in Utah from a perspective combining bitter opposition to Mormonism with open admiration, even awe, of the energy and commitment of leaders and adherents:

The Mormon exodus, though not regarded at the time in such a light, was a missionary effort on a grand scale, and in the most effective form. The Mormon church, thus established, became the germ of a city, and planted the seed of all its evils and abominations around it. How far into the future this movement will reach, in its influence upon the destinies of the western portion of our continent, or even upon our Republic, it is impossible at this time to decide.

But it need not be supposed that all this has been accomplished without effort, and labor, too, of the most zealous and untiring description; and, in this respect, at least, other denominations of Christians might profit by their example. . . . In a few years, Utah has become the centre of the Mormon world, the basis of a powerful State, and the stronghold of a church differing from Christianity in all its essential points. (295–296)

Most eyewitness history by American women was about the United States; here most American women lived their lives, and here was history's cutting edge. Most, but not all—a few women testified differently, producing histories from an international or transnational perspective that remained, however, committed to Protestant millennialism. Indeed, the sense of United States betrayal of or indifference to its millennial obligations powerfully motivated their extranational witnessing. Some women—especially antislavery women—saw the republican uprisings of 1848 as a sign that Europe had again become the site of historical leadership; a much larger number saw the cutting edge of history at work in the foreign missionary movement.

The European continent, shadowed by the outcome of the French Revolution, seemed to be reemerging into historical daylight with the republican revolutions of the 1840s. The foremost partisan of European revolution was Margaret Fuller, whose Roman dispatches of 1848 insist that the United States was no longer historically worthy: "My friends," she wrote, "talk of our country as the land of the Future. It is so, but that spirit which made it all it is of value in my eyes, which gave all of hope with which I can sympathize for that Future, is more alive here at present than in America. . . . Here things are before my eyes worth recording, and, if I cannot help this work, I would gladly be its historian" (*Sad but Glorious Days*, 230).

Fuller imagined herself a Roman, but her letters to the *Tribune* were so suffused with the Protestant republican vision that Horace Greeley received many complaints about her ultra-Protestantism.

I have always been satisfied from the very nature of [Jesuit] institutions that the current prejudice against them must be correct. . . . Their influence is and must be always against the free progress of humanity. The more I see of its working, the more I feel how pernicious it is, and were I a European, to no object should I lend myself with more ardor than to the extirpation of this cancer. (*Sad but Glorious,* 187)

How any one can remain a Catholic—I mean who has ever been aroused to think, and is not biased by the partialities of childish years—after seeing Catholicism here in Italy I cannot conceive. (*Sad but Glorious,* 205)

Fuller's Roman Revolution was as much religious as political, its onset comparable to the advent of Christianity: "As in the time of Jesus, the multitude has been long enslaved beneath a cumbrous ritual, their minds designedly darkened by those who should have enlightened them, brutified, corrupted amid monstrous contradictions and abuses; yet the moment they heard a word correspondent to the original nature, 'Yes, it is true,' they cry" (*Sad but Glorious,* 250). Looking ahead, she does not doubt that

All Europe, including Great Britain . . . is to be under Republican Government in the next century. . . . Every struggle made by the old tyrannies, all their Jesuitical deceptions, their rapacity, their imprisonments and executions of the most generous men, only sow more Hydra teeth. . . . *The work is done; the revolution in Italy is now radical, nor can it stop till Italy become independent and united as a republic.* Protestant she already is. . . . The New Testament has been translated into Italian; copies are already dispersed far and wide; men calling themselves Christians will no longer be left entirely ignorant of the precepts and life of Jesus. (*Sad but Glorious,* 278–279)

Fuller's manuscript history of the uprising did not survive the shipwreck in which she drowned; whether the failure of the revolt led her to reimagine the United States as the center of millennial hope cannot be known. The eyewitness history of her dispatches, however, shows her fired by the typical conjunction. She finds herself present at a place and time whose intense historical importance she recognizes by virtue of the historical frame she already possesses; she claims a privileged relation to the events she is narrating by virtue of her presence on the scene; and she wants that presence to be known. If at the outset Fuller lacked the family connection that authorized so many of these women, she secured such a connection for herself through Ossoli, her Roman lover and later her husband. More generally, she was empowered to write this history because she was the Protestant republican in its most developed form—the law-giving woman.

Back at home, Lajos Kossuth's American fund-raising journey attracted numerous women idealists. When the skeptical Francis Bowen wrote in the *North American Review* (January, April 1850; January 1851) that Kossuth was misrepresenting the situation—that his "republican" Magyars were actually aristocrats with neither a popular base nor republican sentiments—Mary Lowell Putnam countered in the *Christian Examiner*, calling the Magyars

a people in whom a sense of justice and love of freedom are innate, and in whom these qualities have been kept alive and strengthened by the habit of self government. . . . The nobles of Hungary are not only of all races, but of all degrees of rank and fortune. There is a very large class of them who have nothing in their manner of living to distinguish them from the common peasant. They wear the same coarse dress, and follow the same occupations. These peasant nobles are described as a highly dignified, thoughtful, noble race of men . . . not only ardent, but intelligent patriots. They are versed in the history of their country, and understand the nature of their institutions. (May 1850: 446, 454)

In 1852, Elizabeth Peabody published her *Crimes of the House of Austria Against Mankind*, a pro-Magyar compilation drawing on Mary Putnam's work, designed in part to suggest what a "history of Europe written from the republican point of view, a history of nations and not of their governors" might look like (3). Peabody encourages the United States to intervene in European affairs when republican revolutions are at stake; she imagines the millennium as an era of international peace built on a foundation of republican nation-states: "is it not possible that this national integrity and international justice and love, is the ultimate attainment of humanity on earth; the fullest realisation in this sphere of the prophetic vision, and the poet's dream" (176).

At virtually the same time, Therese Albertine Robinson, a highly educated German immigrant who wrote under the name Talvi, brought out her *Historical View of the Languages and Literature of the Slavic Nations* (1850), a scholarly Pan-Slavist set of national and literary histories running over four hundred pages, on which she had been working for more than seventeen years. Talvi defined Pan-Slavism as "the close connection or union of all the Slavic races among themselves" and explained that "of this great family . . . Russia is the natural head, the great animating soul, into which the other parts all must naturally be absorbed at last" (86). Her survey took up "the history of mental cultivation among the Slavic nations from its earliest dawn; their intellectual development; the progress of man among them as a thinking, sentient, social being" (vi). The approach was evangelical Protestantism at its most intense. Historical and religious progress were the same.

It is to the introduction and progress of Christianity, that [these various nations] owe their written language; and to the versions of the Scriptures into their own dialects are they indebted, not only for their moral and religious culture, but also for the cultivation and, in a great degree, the existence of their national literature. The same influence Christianity is even now exerting upon the hitherto unwritten languages of the American forest, of the islands of the Pacific, of the burning coasts of Africa, of the mountains of Kurdistan; and with the prospect of results still wider and more propitious. Indeed, wherever we learn the fact, whether in earlier or more recent times, that a language, previously regarded as barbarous, and existing only as oral, has been reclaimed and reduced to writing, and made the vehicle of communicating fixed thought and permanent instruction, there it has ever been *Christianity* and *Missionary Enterprise* which have produced these results. It is greatly to the honour of Protestant Missions, that their efforts have always been directed to introduce the Scriptures and the worship of God to the masses of the people in their own native tongue. In this way they have every where contributed to awaken the intellectual, as well as the moral life of nations. (vii)

Far less scholarly than Talvi, the missionary women who produced eyewitness accounts of bringing the gospel to "perishing millions" represent themselves as fired by just that historical zeal that she identifies. The missionaries looked elsewhere than Europe for the historical events that were to bring the world closer to its appointed end. Women were active in the movement from the start. Writing in 1855 about the three wives of Adoniram Judson, who was the first American Baptist missionary to Burma, Arabella M. Willson observed:

Among the many benefits which modern missions have conferred on the world, not the least, perhaps, is the field they have afforded for the development of the highest excellence of female character. . . . The missionary enterprise opens to woman a sphere of activity, useful-ness and distinction, not, under the present constitution of society, to be found elsewhere. . . . It seems peculiarly appropriate that woman, who doubtless owes to Christianity most of the domestic consider-ation and social advantages, which in enlightened countries she re-gards as her birthright, should be the bearer of these blessing to her less favored sisters in heathen lands. If the Christian religion was a Gospel to the *poor*, it was no less emphatically so to woman, whom it redeemed from social inferiority and degradation. . . . Never until on the morning of the resurrection "she came early unto the sepul-chre," was she made one in Christ Jesus (in whom "there is neither male nor female") with him who had hitherto been her superior and her master. (iii–iv)

To Lydia Sigourney and Sarah Hale, propagandists for the missionary movement, the movement's emergence in tandem with women's increasing social influence was no coincidence. The argument that only Protestant Christianity gives woman her social due and her God-given place runs throughout missionary testimony, and women were urged to join the cause specifically to educate their heathen "sisters" and improve their lot.

All three of Judson's wives were extraordinary women, and the first and third—Ann Hasseltine and Emily Chubbuck—had literary and publicist talents that they devoted to the missionary cause. Ann in particular helped develop missionary eyewitness history as religious propaganda. Her initial epistolary accounts of the Judsons' life in Burma, written for missionary publications, were combined and expanded in *A Particular Relation of the American Baptist Mission to the Burman Empire* (1823). Her later ac-count—of the Burmese uprising against England, her husband's related imprisonment, and her own efforts to succor him in prison and secure his release—came into posthumous circulation in an 1830 memoir of her life by James D. Knowles. This narrative made her even more of a hero than her husband, and formed the basis of what the historian Joan Brumburg has called a veritable Judson industry. The image of Ann Judson's trials and martyrdom seems to have combined the allure of remote places, for-bidden spectacles, heroic exertions, and a glorious death.

In some ways the most interesting of Judson's wives was Sarah, his sec-ond; but she was not a writer. Her life story was written, at Adoniram's request, by Emily Chubbuck, a literary celebrity publishing under the name Fanny Forester. Emily's conversion and marriage to Judson were publicized in a narrative according to which a worldly but virtuous woman came to recognize women's true role in world history.

The important point about missionary history was its universalism; the movement made a supranational appeal to individuals and had little use for nationalist patriotism. "The world is now one large community, and the work of converting the nations is a great enterprise, calling for the swift and speedy action of all the Redeemer's Church on earth," Eliza J. Bridgman wrote in her missionary account of China (120). "Let us sympathize with our dear Redeemer in his interest in the conversion of the world. Let us be co-workers with each other and with God! How blessed, how dignified this work, to be co-workers with God in saving the ignorant and benighted! If we do fulfill the great object of our being in this respect, we shall not have lived in vain," Eliza Cheney Schneider echoes in her missionary account from Turkey (209). And from Africa came Mrs. E. F. Hening's missionary history, "sent forth to claim the notice of . . . all who feel an interest in the extension of the Redeemer's kingdom. May God make it instrumental in deepening that interest, and prompting to more fervent prayer and liberal effort, not only for Africa, but for all the nations who now sit in darkness" (iii).

A truism of the missionary approach was that the regions they were colonizing for the Bible lacked history. For them history began, the clock started to tick, precisely when they themselves arrived; not individuals merely, but entire continents were to be redeemed, brought by missionary visitation, into progress toward the millennium. Only occasionally, therefore, do the missionary histories recount indigenous history, and when they do it is only to emphasize the improvement brought to life by the introduction of Christianity. Mary Davis Wallis's *Life in Feejee* (1851) was based on journals kept during two long sojourns on the island in 1844 and 1848. Although Wallis was not herself involved in missionary activity—she was the wife of a merchant—she published on behalf of the missionary cause, especially to contest the romantic antimissionary view of native peoples as children of nature. Wallis's representations of oral accounts of Fiji history focus on interribal warfare accompanied by ritual cannibalism, and on the ritual strangling of widows. "The Vewa people do not need their clubs and spears now, because the time has come when they shall learn war no more. It was exceedingly affecting to see these, so late relentless cannibals, thus peacefully giving way their implements of war, and laying them at the feet of those who had brought the gospel to them" (285). Anna M. Scott's *Day Dawn in Africa; or, Progress of the Protestant Episcopal Mission at Cape Palmas, West Africa* (1858) told the same progressive story: "How encouraging the thought that on the spot, where once was heard only the groans of the dying *gidu* victim, or the shrill unearthly cries of the '*Kwiiru*,' keeping their nightly orgies, is now heard the cheerful hum of the printing press" (33).

Since so much of this missionary work was dedicated to bringing supposedly inferior peoples into the fold, the most unusual of all missionary accounts was Nancy Prince's *Narrative of the Life and Travels* (1850), published for the author in Boston. Prince was a free African American, devoutly Protestant, a native of Massachusetts who had lived in Russia for some years when her husband served in the Czar's domestic retinue. Back in the United States, she attended abolitionist meetings until their contentious factionalizing drove her away in disgust: "Were it not for the promises of God, one's heart would fail," she wrote. "God has in all ages of the world punished every nation and people for their sins. The sins of my beloved country are not hid from his notice" (47–48). In November 1840, the now-widowed Prince left the United States for the first of two long visits to Jamaica, where she had hoped to aid, "in some small degree, to raise up and encourage the emancipated inhabitants, and teach the young children to read and work, to fear God, and put their trust in the Savior" (50). But her efforts were not supported, and she returned to the States. "It is not surprising," she commented, that the Jamaicans were "full of deceit and lies, this is the fruits of slavery, it makes master and slaves knaves" (65).

Prince's eyewitness account includes a history of Jamaica and the West Indies implying an entirely different kind of Protestant historiography from one in which the progress of the world toward the millennium is registered by the spread of Christian republicanism. For Prince, progress is measured in strides toward universal emancipation. Her approach places the United States not in the forefront but at the very rear of the historical procession, since in this country slavery is both practiced and defended.

Thus, to Prince, it is her own benighted (yet still beloved) country that needs to be awakened to history. No matter how horrible the present condition of the emancipated Jamaicans, "their present state is blissful, compared with slavery" (57). In one of Prince's anecdotes, a Jamaican woman rejoices in her freedom, gained after "God spoke very loud" to white people "to let us go." Prince comments: "I would recommend this poor woman's remark to the fair sons and daughters of America, the land of the pilgrims. 'Then God spoke very loud.' May these words be engraved on the post of every door in this land of New England. God speaks very loud, and while his judgments are on the earth, may the inhabitants learn righteousness!" (69).

7

Tourists in Time

LIKE THE TOPOGRAPHICAL POETRY discussed in Chapter 5, the eyewitness historical writing discussed in Chapter 6 aims to make a mute scene reverberate with historical significance. But in eyewitness historical writing, the scene is only at that moment becoming active in the historical parade, whereas in topographical poetry, history has left the scene behind. Eyewitness authors are claiming to report on the very moment when history brings the hitherto dateless place into the march of chronology. In the opening lines of "Pocahontas," for example, Lydia Sigourney represents this moment as an awakening.

Clime of the West! that, slumbering long and deep, . . .
Heard not the cry when mighty empires died, ...
See! Europe, watching from her sea-girt shore,
Extends the sceptred hand, and bids thee dream no more.

(*Pocahontas*, 13)

Contrariwise, when the writer is on a spot redolent of ages of history that have left no visible traces, her historicizing mission requires her to vivify the present scene by re-creating the vanished past. A poem about the battlefield of the Brandywine in Pennsylvania by Elizabeth Chandler shows how this is done. The poet reminds readers that "there wild war hath pour'd his battle ranks, / And stamp'd in characters of blood and flame, / Thine annals in the chronicles of fame" while also conceding that "all is over now,—the plough hath rased / All trace of where war's wasting hand hath been" (*Poetical Works*, 48–49). She takes two "relics" from the site, a pebble and a wild rose, to keep her own memory active—"To tell that I had trod the scene of war, / When I had turn'd my footsteps homeward far" (50).

This poet, we see, is a tourist in both space and time—literally in space, imaginatively in time. The experience she records unites space and time, and merges the viewed scene with her own historically enriched imagination. The present-day view does not disappear; it oscillates complexly with another picture which, though created entirely in the poet's imagination, still takes its inspiration from the poet's presence on an actual site. These are the pleasurable and romantic mystifications of historical tourism.

Although historical societies were in process of forming throughout the earlier settled parts of the United States during the antebellum era, historical touring as such in this country (indeed, touring as such) was only in its infancy. Of course there was traveling, but the topography of marked and preserved sites, the network of convenient transportation, the roster of lodging places, the handbooks and guidebooks necessary for tourism did not exist. Anne Royall, radical Democrat and prolific journalist, was one of the few women in these early years to think about the United States in touristic terms. During the 1820s she traveled expressly to collect material for a guidebook to her native land. Her *Sketches of History, Life, and Manners, in the United States* (1826) brings together a great deal of diverse information, including history in two formats—as paragraphs of facts and as descriptions of visits to important sites.

In these visits, Royall seeks to experience—and does experience—an epiphanic merger with the past. "I sought with eagerness the ancient dwelling of the venerable Penn" (232); "I was on the famous Bunker Hill, where they risked their lives in defence of that liberty for which they forsook their native land! I was on the spot where the brave Gen. Warren died!" (328–329). In *Letters from Alabama* (1830), Royall does the same kind of work for the old southwest: "At length I have reached the state of Tennessee, the land of Heroes. I have been in the state about three hours, and already I seem to tread on sacred ground. . . . The victory of New Orleans, the battles of Tallashatches, Talladega, and Emuckfau, all passed in retrospection before me—the brave, the intrepid, the invincible JACKSON, and his brilliant achievements engrossed every faculty of my mind" (89–90).

If historic tourism was one's ambition, of course, the United States could not begin to compare with Europe. And although large-scale overseas tourism was not to develop until after the Civil War, a small number of American women did tour in Europe, a smaller number in the Near East, earlier on. England, France, and to some extent Italy were by this time well along in the process of creating national identity through monuments and historic shrines, and even in the 1830s Americans in Europe had access to an apparatus of handbooks, guides, monumentalized sites, and congenial hotels frequented by compatriots. The practices of tourism were, of course, not restricted to women, but women were largely restricted to them in their encounters with foreign lands. Almost none of them went abroad as scientists, explorers, scholars, navigators, merchants, or soldiers of fortune. Excepting the missionaries, and a few artists who settled in Italy, women were overseas as wives, as sightseers voyaging with families or friends, or as journalists intending specifically to write about their travels.

Since recently the related topics of touring and travel have become popular subjects for academic theorizing, a few points need to be stressed here. One theoretical perspective sees both traveling and touring as imperialistic appropriations of subject peoples by a dominant "gaze." Another contrasts travelers and tourists as independent, resistant selves versus manipulated objects of mass indoctrination. Where the first perspective is concerned, one must understand that American tourists in Europe were not the colonizers but the colonized; they were traveling from the outback to the cultural center. And where the second perspective is concerned—if, today, touring seems restricted and banal in comparison to individualistic travel off the beaten track—these nineteenth-century women clearly experienced tourism as intensely liberating, just as many twentieth-century people do today. Perhaps this was and is false consciousness, but who are we to say so? What oppresses one liberates another; it depends on the starting-point. For antebellum women, tourism was an adventure, precipitating them into a much larger world than they had known before, stimulating their imaginations, and filling their memories. If the "gaze" has power, touring gave women that power, much more so when the objects of that gaze were themselves powerful. Therefore, women were much more interested in developing, exploiting, expanding, and configuring the role of tourist to their own needs than in contesting or rejecting it. They stuck to the beaten track because that was where the sites they wanted to visit were located. Nor did they seek out experiences nobody had ever had before; quite the opposite, they wanted to see what others had seen, know what others had known, feel what others had felt.

It was an important part of the touristic experience to write it down in journals or letters. Published tourist accounts by women almost always take the shape of revised journals or familiar letters. These modes, however, are not to be equated with the private or confidential. Notwithstanding another current-day academic theoretical tendency, to see all published work in the journal or letter form as some kind of feminine invasion and/or subversion of the public sphere, the real origins of the published letter and journal lie in the form of print itself—in the "letters to the editor" columns of newspapers and periodicals. This genre has been a public practice from its inception, and women have always made use of it.

Even if print was not an overt issue, the travel letters that women sent home and the touring journals they kept were not really private. They were designed to circulate through the extended family and the neighborhood. But the possibility of publication was always there, as when the recipient of a particularly interesting letter sent it to the local newspaper. Unquestionably, searches through old newspapers and periodicals as well as local archives would turn up numerous instances of women's published tourist writings beyond the ones discussed here. For other women, seeing their journeys in print was a forthright intention. As soon as she returned home from her trip to France and Spain, for example, Caroline Cushing retrieved her journal-letters from her father and set to work revising them for publication. When she died before completing the task, her husband brought her book out as a memorial to her desire. Professional women of letters who went overseas on purpose to gather literary material frankly used their journals and letters as depositories of materials for future publication.

Women's tourist books cover the range of typical subjects in different proportions according to the interests of the author—paintings; sculpture; architecture and public monuments; landscape; gardens; meeting or seeing celebrities; attending social events and witnessing public ceremonies; observing the panorama of everyday life in city, town, and country; struggling with an unfamiliar language; getting through customs; food; fashion; comparative prices; the weather and climate; the condition of hotels; the state of roads. Almost always, history was one of the subjects covered. Coverage might be minor and perfunctory, or major and extensive; still, virtually all tourists produced some historical writing when they recounted their travels.

Between 1832 and 1859 at least these sixteen women published tourist accounts of Europe and the Near East that contained historical material: Caroline Cushing, *Letters, Descriptive of Public Monuments, Scenery, and Manners in France and Spain* (1832, posthumous); Emma Willard, *Journal and Letters from France and Great-Britain* (1833); Fanny W. Hall, *Rambles in Europe* (1838); Sarah Rogers Haight, *Letters from the Old World* (1840); Catharine Sedgwick, *Letters from Abroad* (1841); Lydia Sigourney, *Pleasant Memories of Pleasant Lands* (1842); an anonymous "Lady of New York," *Over the Ocean* (1846); Margaret Fuller (whose dispatches from Europe for the *Tribune* between 1846 and 1850 are collected in *These Sad but Glorious Days*); Caroline Kirkland, *Holidays Abroad* (1849); Nancy Prince, *Narrative of the Life and Travels* (1850—discussed in Chapter 6); Anne Tuttle Bullard, *Sights and Scenes in Europe* (1852); Grace Greenwood, *Haps and Mishaps of a Tour in Europe* (1854); Harriet Beecher Stowe, *Sunny Memories of Pleasant Lands* (1854—part of Volume 2 uses her brother Charles's journal); Octavia Walton Le Vert, *Souvenirs of Travel* (1857); Anna Cummings Johnson, *Peasant Life in Germany* (1858) and *The Cottages of the Alps* (1860); and Caroline Paine, *Tent and Harem: Notes of an Oriental Trip* (1859). The majority of these women, we see, were literary professionals who planned to publish accounts of their travels sooner or later; Margaret Fuller and Grace Greenwood were expressly salaried for the work. Others, however—Cushing,

Hall, Haight, Le Vert, Paine—never published anything besides their tourist accounts.

Like other forms of historical writing, historicized tourist narratives depend heavily on the written record. Almost all the tourists seem to have prepared for their trips by extensive reading in a range of literature, including earlier travel accounts, contemporary tourist guides, standard histories of the various countries they were visiting, and literary works like Madame de Staël's *Corinne; or, Italy* (1807, translated into English the same year) for Italy, Byron's *Childe Harold* (1816–1817) and *Manfred* (1817) for Italy and Spain, and Washington Irving's *Sketch-Book* (1819) for England. *Corinne* not only gave readers an extensive tourist account of Italy, but it also assured them, via the hero's experiences, that "the study of history can never act on us like the sight of that scene itself. The eye reigns all powerfully over the soul. He now believed in the Old Romans, as if he had lived amongst them" (Book 4, Chap. 2). In "The Voyage," the first essay in *The Sketch-Book*, Washington Irving provided a paradigm paragraph for the colonial American's arrival in Europe: "None but those who have experienced it can form an idea of the delicious throng of sensations which rush into an American's bosom, when he first comes in sight of Europe. There is a volume of associations with the very name. It is the land of promise, teeming with every thing of which his childhood has heard, or on which his studious years have pondered."

In most cases the tourist writers brought books with them, and they often cribbed substantial amounts of historical description from these sources, simply stating that they were incorporating such-and-such an authority or precursor tourist into the account. They did not think of this as plagiarism, but as an efficient way to convey true information. What the writers never cribbed, however, was the record of their own responses to historical sites—even when (as was usually the case) these responses were identical to those of hundreds or thousands of earlier visitors. The identical response was just what was desired, and what the audience back home wanted to hear about. The right emotion was a kind of guarantee of its authenticity. To visit a historical site and not feel what one was supposed to feel would have been a great disappointment. Indeed, tourists both female and male read assiduously in the sources to enable themselves to have the most appropriate responses—the most knowledgeable, the most complex—possible. This behavior should not be scorned; it is called education.

It is clear from several of these accounts that prior reading in history was also a great motivation for tourism. Fanny Hall begins her *Rambles in Europe* by stating that "From the time when the tales of the nursery began to be superseded by the graver studies of history and geography, and my mind opened to the perception of the wonderful fact, that beyond the broad seas there existed other lands not less fair and goodly than my own, I have felt the most ardent desire to visit those lands" (1). In the introduction to *Merrie England*, a children's book based on her travels and organized as a historical tour of prominent sites, Grace Greenwood said she had longed "to visit those noble old countries over the sea from whence our forefathers came" ever since her childhood reading of fiction by Sherwood, Edgeworth, and Scott; and that "when in my girlhood, at school, I read the histories of England, Ireland, Scotland, France, and ancient Rome, stronger and stronger grew that longing" (7). Catharine Sedgwick in *Letters from Abroad*, writing about Thrasymene, reminisced about "the days when, in our 'noon-time' at the old school house, I used to creep under my pine desk to read the story of Hannibal, and devoutly hope that he might always be victorious. Do not all children sympathize with the boy who swore eternal hatred to the Romans, and kept his oath so filially?" (2:298–299).

Except for Emma Willard and Margaret Fuller, these women were not visiting Europe to chronicle current events. Willard went abroad to study educational institutions in England and France, but was elated to find herself in France at a time when political disturbances threatened to bring down the government; she wrote about all this at length to correspondents in the United States. I have already discussed Margaret Fuller's eyewitness historical writing in Chapter 6; she was an indifferent tourist until the Roman Revolution ignited her imagination. But both women understood current events through the scrim of their knowledge of history. Willard urged her compatriots to be prepared to accept La Fayette as an emigrant to the country of which, as a participant in the American Revolution, he was in the deepest sense already a citizen. Fuller's investment in the Roman uprising could not be separated from her attachment to Roman history, as her earlier-written "Autobiographical Romance" (ca. 1840–1841) makes absolutely clear:

There is somewhat indefinite, somewhat yet unfulfilled in the thought of Greece, of Spain, of modern Italy; but Rome! it stands by itself, a clear Word. . . . Suckled by this wolf, man gains a different complexion from that which is fed by the Greek honey. . . . The history of Rome abides in mind, of course, more than the literature. . . . I steadily loved this ideal in my childhood, and this is the cause, probably, why I have always felt that man must know how to stand firm on the ground, before he can fly. In vain for me are men more, if they are less, than Romans. (in Steele, 29–30)

Caroline Kirkland, however, recorded the majority desire to avoid current European events whenever possible. She was in Europe for art and the past. As she noted upon arriving in England, "Nothing charms the American traveller more than the relics of the old times—times which seemed commonplace enough, no doubt, to the people . . . who acted in them, but which, coming to us through the golden mists of poetry and tradition, have a glory which the present, however remarkable, can never possess" (1:30). In Italy she pushed this attitude further, remarking, "I had always cared far more about Italian pictures than Italian politics, and . . . as for the 'affairs of Italy,' I had sedulously averted my eyes whenever I saw anything under that head in the newspapers" (1:182).

Kirkland wants only to *see* Europe, not to take part in its life—to make it a spectacle, an esthetic entity, the source of esthetic emotions. Insofar as the spectacle includes history, this makes history itself into something esthetic. The point needs stressing, because, again, in much present-day theoretical discussion, history and the esthetic are constructed as mutually exclusive categories, the former fully political and the latter totally devoid of political import. Or, more precisely, the category of the esthetic is viewed as a myth whose claim to refer to an apolitical reality can be unmasked, by historicist analysis, as a politically conservative ploy.

Women's historical tourist writings in these decades, however, moved in a different ideological direction. They recognized fully that they were absorbing history into the category of the esthetic, but emphatically represented the esthetic as progressively not regressively political. It took no particular political sophistication to realize that it was humanly far preferable to be able to relish the beauty of the Coliseum in the silent light of a full moon than be torn apart by lions. If anything about their esthetic enjoyment troubled these women, it was taking any pleasure at all in the horrific and bloody past; but history itself came to the rescue of those who felt morally compromised. Their pleasure was explainable by the very fact that these awful events existed in spectacle form only; to summon them up was always to remember the contrast between then and now:

We wandered over [the Coliseum's] different stages, rising one tier above the other, and through its many arcades, obtaining through the open arches beautiful views from without; and the effect of the moon-light streaming through the various openings, into the vast area within, was extremely beautiful. In the delicious stillness that reigned around, the imagination had full play, and after gazing as we had, upon the life-like images of the dying and falling gladiator, and the disc players in the various attitudes, it was not difficult to people it with the voluptuous populace that once filled the immensity of space before us; not forgetting the poor persecuted christians, who were also here made to play their part, for the amusement of the blood-thirsty multitudes, who thronged to glut their appetites with these cruel entertainments. How great the contrast now! The scene so quiet and peaceful; shrines and crucifixes line the area where the victims played their part; and where thousands once rushed in to enjoy the bloody spectacle, soldiers guard the entrance, that now visitors may enjoy the scene safely, and without interruptions from bandits or assassins. (*Over the Ocean*, 239–240)

Still, the core of the tourist's historical epiphany, as this extract shows, rises not from thoughtful pleasure over the advantages of living in the nineteenth century (epiphanies are never the product of thought), but in the thrilling mergers of the spectator with the site as it once existed in all its grandeur and horror. Writers of tourist history use three strategies to present these epiphanies. First, they refer to the activity of what they call memory, by which they mean not memory of reading or learning history, but memory of historical events themselves—as though these had already been experienced firsthand. Second, they do not try to conceal the work that has preceded the encounter of self with site, the extent to which they have already loaded their minds in advance with material that is to be called out at the appropriate moment. And third, they enunciate the presence of epiphany—the thrill of standing on historic ground—by repeated uses of the word that invokes presence: "here."

These strategies can be seen across the range of tourist texts, and I shall document them in order. Cushing found that scarcely a room in the Tuileries palace "but awakened recollections of some terrible scenes of the revolution" (1:127). "After passing the Red Sea," Paine wrote, "we come to certain landmarks, the very names of which fill one with memories of the stupendous train of transactions of which this peninsula was, for forty years, the theatre" (254–245). "I can never describe the feelings with which I walked about and finally perched myself near the top of this vast ruin [the Coliseum], and recalled to memory the scenes of its former days" (Bullard, 104); "Actually treading on the soil of Palestine . . . all my historical recollections, sacred and profane, came fresh to my memory" (Haight, 2:34); "I do not love Queen Elizabeth's memory much, but could not help feeling that the certainty of standing where she had stood, was something" (Kirkland, 1:41); "Inconceivable grandeur of thought and memories of the undying past swept over my mind, as I looked upon these majestic ruins, ever entrancing to human interest" (Le Vert, 2:104); "Historical recollections of Rome—the memories of battles, and triumphs, and sieges, and revolutions—how they stormed upon the heart! Scenes in the victorious, disastrous, splendid, and guilty reigns of her emperors, the countless tumults and insurrections of her republics, seemed to pass before me" (Greenwood, 177); "There came thronging upon the memory the thrilling recollections of the past, the remembrance of that period when Rome . . . sat enthroned in power, and gave laws to the civilized world" (Hall, 2).

Memory is connected with the processes of association, as when Haight writes: "Turn the eyes which way you will on the border of the *Nile*, listen to the numerous sounds which fall upon the ear, and a thousand associations start up at once, connected with one's earliest recollections of sacred and profane history, classic lore, and vulgar tradition. These being one's first impressions on reaching the 'River of Egypt,' they do not cool, but go on accumulating in number and interest every mile one proceeds up its noble stream" (1:99). Le Vert wrote that Rome "is truly the 'City of the Soul,' inspiring a grandeur of thought by its thousand spells of association and memories of the 'undying past.' Rome absolutely magnetized me, enchaining every emotion, and filling each hour with some precious remembrance of classic or historic interest" (2:161). Fanny Hall recorded her responses to the site where Paul landed to go up to Rome: "The associations belonging to the spot make it worth a pilgrimage to look upon it, all ruinous and dreary, and uninhabitable as it seems. What emotions may we suppose to have filled the breast of the heroic Apostle, as, a prisoner, alone, unsupported by human authority or influence, he approached the heathen capital of the powerful Roman empire!" (182).

Some of the women tourists recognized that the emotion they were feeling was an artificial product, or even an illusion requiring careful nurture to be sustained. Kirkland was particularly attuned to the possible self-deceptions entailed by this urge to travel in time. She wrote of Kenilworth that

It is absolutely necessary to the spirit of the thing, to be able to sit with the eyes shut, and recall the associated ideas, and then to have leisure and quiet to fit them to the actual scene. . . . There are just landmarks enough to serve the purpose of fancy. As everything is better conveyed or expressed by means of the inherent poetry or philosophy of it, so is the Kenilworth of Elizabeth's days more completely restored to us by these few remaining towers and walls, than it could have been if every battlement were standing unbroken. (1:42)

She said that in Italy one needed Arezzo, Childe Harold, and the Lays of Ancient Rome, to "bring the glorious past visibly before us, or rather transport us at once into its living spirit. At least these poems make us feel as if we were breathing the spirit of the past; and if it is something else that we breathe—something created by the genius of the poet—the sense of pleasure is the same" (1:247); and she complained about guides because of "the disgustingness of such a presence at a time when one would possess one's soul; the perpetual vicinity of a vulgar mind when the very zest of the moment lies in forgetting all vulgar things; the ceaseless iteration of threadbare commonplaces, while the best powers of memory are tasked to call up its most precious hoardings" (1:118).

Similarly, Bullard regretted the tardiness of their diligence in reaching Rome. "Much depends on first impressions, and we had hoped to have entered Rome by sunlight, and prepared our minds, by a glorious entrance within its walls, for a feast of enjoyment in our researches afterwards" (99–100). Paine even complained that "the enthusiasm excited by associating [the Pyramids] with remote antiquity . . . is less likely to be felt when you are surrounded by chattering Arabs, persecuting your very soul for backsheesh, than while sitting and viewing the thing calmly, with the eye of faith, by your own fireside" (227). Stowe and her party emoted over Gray's churchyard; "imagine our chagrin on being informed that we had not been to the genuine churchyard"; the group consoled itself "with the reflection that the emotion was admirable, and wanted only the right place to make it the most appropriate in the world" (2:249–50). She reported a parallel experience walking on Bothwell Bridge, "trying to recall the scenes of the battle" as described by Scott, only to be "rather mortified, after we had all our associations comfortably located upon it, to be told that it was not the same bridge—it had been newly built, widened, and otherwise made more comfortable and convenient" (1:65).

Grace Greenwood described a similar discomfiture in a mock-heroic passage:

As I walked slowly on, my thoughts went back three hundred years, when knights and ladies gay went dashing up this pass, followed by fair pages and fairer maids, dainty minstrels and jolly friars, faithful esquires and stout men-at-arms. I could almost hear the tramp of mail-clad steeds, the light curvetting of palfreys, the clang of armour, the jingle of gilded bridles, the laughter of young gallants, and the sweet voices of merry dames. I could almost see the waving of banners and plumes, the flash of shields and arms, and gorgeous vesture, as the glory of feudal power and the flush of beauty swept by. Alas for wasted sentiment! I all too soon ascertained that this rocky pass was constructed by the late earl, the castle formerly had a different approach. (16)

It is clear in Greenwood's description as in the other cited passages that the "history" the traveler summons is a highly constructed conception, perhaps an invention—and that the tourists know it. Which means that, at no very deep level, they recognized that history was imaginary. "Like the fabled wand of the magician, the very name of Rome had possessed an electric power, darting along from century to century, and calling up visions

139

from the great past, which fired the imagination while they thrilled the soul. The dream of my youth was now a reality. I was looking upon that noble city" (Le Vert, 2:170). "In imagination, I peopled those seats [of the Coliseum] with one hundred thousand spectators, said to be present at its dedication, and with them witnessed the games in honor of it, which lasted one hundred days. I saw the sacrifice of two thousand gladiators and five thousand wild beasts, which then took place" (Bullard, 104). "My imagination called back from the dead the hundred thousand people who filled this vast circuit" (Sedgwick, 2:160). "My imagination carried me back to those days when the Saviour of the world condescended to make his abode in that very place upon which my eyes were then gazing, and I almost fancied I could see him mingling with his fellow-citizens in their daily occupations" (Haight, 2:41). "I almost fancied I could see the lines of gallant triremes stretching from the Piraeus to Aegina. . . . Thence I followed them in imagination throughout that long and disastrous campaign" (Haight, 2:285).

Recognizing the seductions and deceptions of the various processes by which they summoned up the historical past did not stand in the way of these women's enjoyment. They convey their successful transcendence of time through repeated use of the word "here." "Here then was the actual scene of so many of those most affecting incidents, so pathetically described . . . which I had years since perused with almost painful interest, little dreaming that the places, which witnessed them, would ever be presented to my eyes" (Cushing, Letters, 2:176). "And oh! how many scenes of blood have been enacted here. We saw the very spot where Anna [sic] Boleyn and Catharine of Aragon, and Lady Jane Grey, and hosts of others were beheaded"; "Here was once the seat of superstition and the centre of earthly enjoyment. Here Caligula lived in splendor, power, luxury and crime" (Bullard, Sights, 39, 167). "Here in the old French revolution, stood the guillotine. . . . Of all the victims here perished, it is Marie Antoinette who is most frequently mentioned.—But it is Charlotte Corday and Madame Roland, that interest me most, particularly Madame Roland . . . and even now her dying exclamation is on my lips, as I think on these tragic scenes" (Willard, Journal and Letters, 59). Here, as it were, is Fanny Hall at the Coliseum—"Here, on this very spot, untrodden now save by the feet of strangers who come to gaze upon the magnificent ruin, have stood the most powerful potentates the world ever saw. . . . And here those holy men, who dared, in the evil of persecution, to profess the religion of a crucified Saviour, have been torn limb from limb by ferocious wild beasts" (1:193–194). "Here Louis XVI, Madame Elizabeth, and many of the nobles of France met the fate of the hapless queen. Swiftly through my mind were wafted the scenes of those terrible days" (Le Vert, 1:95). "Xenophon, with his ten thousand veterans, here consummated his famous retreat from Asia"; "It was here that [Cleopatra] entertained her noble Roman; on this spot the hardy soldier was softened into the doting lover, the general of Roman armies into a loiterer of the harem" (Haight, 1:28, 85).

Catherine Sedgwick spoke for all these women when she said, in her *Letters*, she "was not prepared for the sensations to be excited by visiting these old places of the Old World. There is nothing in our land to aid the imperfect lights of history. Here it seems suddenly verified" (1:28). In Naples she noted "a fresh and undreamed of pleasure; I know not why, unless it be from a sort of triumph over time; for here the past *is* given back, and the dead are yielded up" (2:263); "we sat down in porticoes where they once sat talking of what Caesar was doing in the provinces and Cicero was saying in the Forum" (2:264); and after several more pages in the same vein, "Here [in Baia] was the scene of Nero's parricide; here lay the elder Pliny" (2:282).

As the extracts above may have already suggested, busy tourists did not attribute historical significance equally to every European place they visited; and of course the number of places they visited was quite limited. A couple of women reported on trips to Spain, working out their historical itineraries with reference to Irving's *Conquest of Granada* and memorializing the country as the historical site where Islam was driven out of Europe by the very same Queen who financed Columbus (facts that apparently neutralized her having been a Catholic and initiating the Inquisition). At the Alhambra, Caroline Cushing looked out on "many a spot rendered forever memorable, by being associated, not only with the tales of fiction, but with the no less fascinating recitals drawn from actual history," and followed this remark up with a paragraph on Boabdil's departure from the Alhambra drawn straight from Irving (2:301). A couple of women reported trips to the Holy Land with sojourns in Egypt and other sites in Africa and Asia Minor; truly off the beaten track at this time, these women provisioned themselves and their readers with extensive historical researches in archaeological and biblical material.

Still, although no two itineraries are identical in these tourist books, the typical tour in these decades included England, France, Switzerland, and Italy. Within these four chief sites, tourists stopped where the tourist industry was already developed and worked with what the industry made available to them. There was plenty of history in Switzerland and Florence, but tourists mined these places for scenery and art, respectively. When they went to specifically historical sites, they knew what they were looking for: in England, the bad behavior of the Tudors; in France, the bad monarchical behavior that produced the Revolution followed by the even worse behavior of the Revolutionaries; in Italy, the bad behavior of the emperors. In brief, these tourists acted out just the narrative of innocent America meeting evil Europe that American literature has made so familiar to us. They acted it out, one surmises, not because they were particularly innocent in fact, but because this was the story dictated to them by their understanding of history.

Nor did many of them consider that their elated responses to history might imply some strong attraction to the many evils they found in it, or that they might have gone to Europe specifically to be on evil ground. Stowe alone among them even raised this as an issue, although she declined to pursue it:

I cannot understand nor explain the nature of that sad yearning and longing with which one visits the mouldering remains of a state of society which one's reason wholly disapproves, and which one's calm sense of right would think it the greatest misfortune to have recalled; yet when the carriage turned under the shadow of beautiful ancient oaks, and R. S. said, "There, we are in the grounds of the old Black Douglas family!" I felt every nerve shiver. (*Sunny Memories*, 1:60)

Whatever moral problems they might have felt were resolved by channeling history through the rhetoric of sentimentalism, which had always allowed one to dwell at length on the conditions of victims so long as one expressed sympathy for them. In England the primary occasion for such accounts was a visit to the Tower of London. "We saw the very spot where Anna Boleyn and Catharine of Arragon, and Lady Jane Grey, and hosts of others were beheaded; and saw the very instruments with which their heads were severed from their bodies, and the block on which so many heads have been laid" (Bullard, *Sights*, 39). "Queen Elizabeth's Armory is filled with strange weapons, battle-axes, pikes, halberds, and also with instruments of torture. My soul sickened as I looked upon them, and I thanked the good God that those dark days had vanished before the clear light of civilization.... Under the pavement of the church of St. Peter's were buried the bodies of Lady Jane Grey, of Essex, of Northumberland, of Anna Boleyn, and other victims of tyranny" (Le Vert, 1:42). Catharine Sedgwick was devastated to find the Tower closed on the day she had set aside to visit it: "Ever since in my childhood my heart ached for the hapless stateprisoners that passed its portals, I have longed to see it.... I was like a crossed child when I felt that I should never see the Black Prince's armour, nor the axe that dealt the death-blow to Anne Boleyn, nor the prison of Sir Walter Raleigh, nor any of the Tower's soul-moving treasures" (*Letters*, 1:47). Grace Greenwood, who did get to see these treasures, "stood with a sick heart by the instruments of fortune, laid my hand upon them, studied the atrocious ingenuity of their contrivance, yet could not believe the revolting truth, that in the reign of a queen, a very woman, one would say, regarding her weaknesses, human forms had writhed within them, human bones and sinews cracked under them, human hearts burst with excess of pain, true human souls grown wild and shrieked out false confessions" (*Haps and Mishaps*, 75).

The demands of sentimentalism required these women to reject Queen Elizabeth; they criticized her both for being too much like a woman (jealous of Mary Queen of Scots's beauty, as in Greenwood's comment above) and too little like one (cruel and vindictive, in imprisoning and executing Mary, whose possible complicity in the murder of her own husband disappeared from the account). After visiting Linlithgow Castle, Mary's birthplace, Fanny Hall wrote that "Three hundred years have not sufficed to wipe away the stain which is attached to Elizabeth's character from her jealousy and ill-treatment of her beauteous rival. How would that vanity, which was her grand foible, have been wounded, could she have foreseen the judgment which posterity would pronounce upon her; could she have been aware that the world would well-nigh have forgotten Mary's faults in sympathy for her misfortunes!" (2:188–189).

A sentimental obsession with queens continued into France, where these republican women were almost all Burkean in lamenting the fate of Marie Antoinette. Only the rigorous republicanism of Emma Willard enabled her to escape the lure. Versailles, she wrote,

brought back to me all the feelings of sympathy, with which I had once regarded Marie Antoinette; considering her a high-souled, persecuted, suffering woman;—which have since given place, to more painful thoughts, of gifts perverted, and crimes punished, with which I am now led to regard her fate. More hapless, it is true, than that of suffering virtue; but not like that, entitled to respect, and complacent regard. She was corrupted by her situation; and by means of her situation, she spread widely around her, the influence of vicious manners. (*Journal and Letters*, 109)

Ever the didact, she made her visit to Versailles serve for a lesson about monarchical extravagance and power:

This vast pile, with all its appurtenances, is said to have cost France between 30–40 million sterling. Like extravagance in private life, it brought pecuniary embarrassment and vain regrets in its train; and Louis XIV is said to have destroyed the records of his profusion; but its consequences remained, and his descendants to this day may reckon them, among the causes of their downfall. (69)

The world has but one Versailles, and it is to be hoped it will never have another. Men now understand too well their rights, and their strength, to allow one of their own number, again to fancy himself the state; and to use its united toil, to uphold his personal vanity, and gratify his luxurious pleasures. (73)

The other women reproduced the sentimental spectacle of Marie Antoinette that Willard declined to endorse. At Versailles, Fanny Hall wrote, she

could not refrain from reflecting with sadness upon the fate of poor Marie Antoinette.... She came from her father's court with a guileless heart, a charming simplicity of character, and a love of innocent pleasures. *Here*, surrounded by all that could add splendor to royalty, and, what to a woman is of infinitely more value, happy in her domestic relations, she had enjoyed for a few brief years all that earth can bestow; and then, meekly kneeling upon the scaffold, her life was offered up a sacrifice to atone for the only fault she had committed—that of having worn a crown. (1:50–51)

Le Vert had a similar response: "I seemed encircled by a spell of magic power, and lingered long.... The guide, perceiving the interest I manifested, showed me every relic still existing of the heroic and unfortunate queen. The spot was pointed out to us where she stood when the Revolutionists surrounded the palace, and when she showed herself to them, disarming the infuriated mob by the dignity and grace of her bearing" (1:89). The Place de la Concorde produced the same associations and emotions:

The delicious fountains of the "Rond Point" were throwing up their sparkling waters as we passed into the "Place de la Concorde." I never crossed it, and looked upon its splendor, that the thought of Marie Antoinette did not come between me and its brightness, and Charlotte Corday too, that brave enthusiast, was often in my mind. (Le Vert, 1:121)

I recollected the seas of innocent blood which had soaked the soil, and reflected upon those scenes of carnage and murder, the narration of which had so often inspired me with the deepest horror, pity, and indignation. Here the ill-fated Louis, the unfortunate Marie Antoinette, the amiable, the lovely Elizabeth, expired in ignominy, amid the taunts and reproaches of a merciless rabble. Here too the blood-thirsty Robespierre and the terrible Danton paid the just penalty of their enormous crimes, even upon the same spot, which they had so often reddened with the blood of innocent and helpless victims. (Caroline Cushing, 1:71–72)

My soul staggered under the awful thought that these peaceful streets and that quiet square were once one vast surging, raging sea of human ferocity—that near where the two ornamented fountains are playing in the pleasant sunshine, stood the guillotine, spouting blood!—that there had mad yells, and brutal howls, and low murmurs of infernal satisfaction hailed alike the murder of Louis, Marie Antoinette, the Princess Elizabeth, Charlotte Corday, and the just punishment of Danton, Robespierre, and their fiendish crew. (Greenwood, *Haps and Mishaps*, 155)

In Rome, the traveler's struggle to resist the appeal of the horrid spectacle emerged at its strongest. Le Vert viewed Rome from a balcony: "Immortal histories clustered about every object, and inconceivable grandeur of thought and memories of the undying past swept over my mind, as I looked upon these majestic ruins, ever entrancing to human interest" (2:104); she wrote again,

Never was the joy of existence greater to me than during those three hours of the young day, spent upon the Monte Pincio. It was not a bright, gay happiness, but a deep, serene, sublime feeling; a gratitude to God that I had seen Rome, whose glory even in my childhood had been as a halo around me. Like the fabled wand of the magician, the very name of Rome had possessed an electric power, darting along from century to century, and calling up visions from the great past, which fired the imagination while they thrilled the soul. The dream of my youth was now a reality. I was looking upon that noble city, once the queen of nations, and the home of heroes, patriots, poets, and philosophers. . . . In scenes like these, the past so mingles with the present, we are scarcely aware how we cross the gulf which separates them. (2:169–170)

The key tourist site in Rome was the Coliseum. The site had witnessed some of the most awful events in history, and it was beautiful. Here the reality that the tourist had made all of history into esthetic spectacle came most clear to her, and here she waged her fiercest battle against the Empire. Grace Greenwood said the Coliseum was thronged "to the eye of the spirit, with dark visions of fear and horror, of fierce fight and deadly encounter, brutal ferocity and diabolical cruelty. The blood of innumerable martyrs seems yet rising from the once trampled and gory arena, a cloud between us and the beautiful skies. What a terrible power has a place like this over the imagination!" (*Haps*, 172). Bullard, who had written anti-Catholic Sunday school history (see Chapter 3), found the Coliseum to be the most magnificent ruin I have yet seen. . . . I can never describe the feelings with which I walked about and finally perched myself near the top of this vast ruin, and recalled to memory the scenes of its former days. . . . Of what scenes of gaiety, and splendor, and cruelty, has this been the receptacle! Of what a parade of beauty, of vanity, and of folly as well as suffering, has this been the theatre! . . . In imagination . . . I saw the sacrifice of two thousand gladiators and five thousand wild beasts, which then took place. I saw Ignatius torn to pieces by wild beasts, and the many Christian martyrs who, in this arena, gave up their lives. Although I visited the Coliseum in the very noon-tide of a bright and beautiful day, it wore such a sombre and dreary aspect to me, from the associations connected with it, that I had no desire to visit it by moonlight, as most travelers do, to add to it the gloominess and silence of midnight, the company of owls and bats, or the awfulness of solitude in such a bloody circus as this has been. (*Sights*, 104)

Fanny Hall called it "The wonder and admiration of the world. Pity it is that we cannot, as we gaze upon this sublime and wondrous pile, dissever it from all its terrible associations" (1:117).

The woman who suffered most acutely from Rome was Harriet Beecher Stowe, who did not visit Italy on the voyage chronicled in *Sunny Memories of Pleasant Lands*. On that trip, Stowe's Protestant self-certainty remained unruffled. She accounted for the "woes of France," for example, by "the fact that a Jezebel de Medici succeeded in exterminating from the nation that portion of the people corresponding to the Puritans of Scotland, England, and Germany. . . . Their great difficulty has been, that the destruction of the reformed church in France took out of the country entirely that element of religious rationalism which is at once conservative and progressive" (2:408–409). But in Italy during the winter of 1859 she began to write her deeply conflicted historical novel about that country, *Agnes of Sorrento* (1862). The novel is set at the end of the fifteenth century. Like most historical novels, it braids a fictive love plot into presumably real events, in this case the struggle between Savonarola and the Borgia Pope Alexander. By moving her action from Sorrento to Florence to Milan to Rome, Stowe makes the book into a tour of Italy as well as a historical fiction. She allegorizes three regions of Italy—Sorrento as natural beauty (and the innocent feminine); Florence as art (and the noble masculine); Rome as history (and the evil masculine). The allegory interprets the quarrel between Savonarola and the Pope as a quarrel between art (or idealism) and history. In the short term, history wins; but in the long run, we know, art will claim the victory.

Standard Protestant history made Pope Alexander exemplify the worst excesses of worldly Renaissance popes, but viewed Savonarola's cruel intolerance as no less frightful and equally revealing of the nature of Catholicism. Stowe was certainly historically innovative in presenting this character as a proto-Luther, a "great reformer whose purpose seemed to meditate nothing less than the restoration of the Church of Italy to the primitive apostolic simplicity" (259). Even more surprisingly, she compares the Florence over which Savonarola temporarily held sway to Puritan New England. Writing about England in *Sunny Memories*, Stowe had deplored Puritan anti-estheticism:

Cromwell seems literally to have left his mark on his generation, for I never saw a ruin in England when I did not hear that he had something to do with it. . . . When we see how much the Puritans arrayed against themselves all the aesthetic principles of our nature, we can somewhat pardon those who did not look deeper than the surface, for the prejudice with which they regarded the whole movement; a movement, however, of which we, and all which is most precious to us, are the lineal descendants and heirs. (1:243–244)

But in *Agnes*, as commentators on the novel have observed, Puritanism is one with estheticism:

A republic, in the midst of contending elements, the history of Florence, in the Middle Ages, was a history of what shoots and blossoms the Italian nature might send forth, when rooted in the rich soil of liberty. It was a city of poets and artists. Its statesmen, its merchants, its common artisans, and the very monks in its convents, were all pervaded by one spirit. The men of Florence in its best days were men of a large, grave, earnest mould. What the Puritans of New England wrought out with severest earnestness in their reasonings and their lives, these early Puritans of Italy embodied in poetry, sculpture, and painting. (257)

The love story in *Agnes* pairs Agostino, a young aristocrat opposing the Pope, and Agnes, a commoner (though she turns out to have some aristocratic blood), a pure innocent and a devout Catholic. In the book's Roman climax, she is rescued from the Pope's clutches by Agostino's men. In Stowe's descriptions one clearly sees the author working through her own problems with Rome:

Then, as now, Rome was an enchantress of mighty and wonderful power, with her damp, and mud, and mould, her ill-fed, ill-housed populace, her ruins of old glory rising dim and ghostly amid her palaces of to-day. With all her awful secrets of rapine, cruelty, ambi-tion, injustice,—with her foul orgies of unnatural crime,—with the very corruption of the old buried Roman Empire steaming up as from a charnel-house, and permeating all modern life with its effluvium of deadly uncleanness,—still Rome had that strange, bewildering charm of melancholy grandeur and glory which made all hearts cleave to her, and eyes and feet turn longingly towards her from the ends of the earth. Great souls and pious yearned for her as for a mother, and could not be quieted till they had kissed the dust of her feet. (329–330)

Louisa C. Tuthill resisted the lure of Rome in her work of armchair tourism, a beautifully illustrated *History of Architecture, from the Earliest Times; Its Present Condition in Europe and the United States* (1848)—but, then, she did not visit the spot:

Here sat the conquerors of the world, coolly to enjoy the tortures and death of men who had never offended them. Two aqueducts were scarcely sufficient to wash off the human blood which a few hours' sport shed in these imperial shambles. . . Such reflections check our regret for its ruin. As it now stands, the Coliseum is a striking image of Rome itself; decayed, vacant, serious, yet grand. . . . After the people became vitiated by luxury, and lost their Roman dignity, and their emperors were the most monstrous examples of vice, every work that they undertook showed a want of taste and order, a departure from all simplicity and true beauty. Splendid and gigantic, but wanting in the beautiful and true proportions of the Grecian Temples, these works can never be safe models for imitation. (109)

The nontraveler Tuthill is relevant to an account of women's historical tour-ism because, as a popularizer of Ruskin, she offers a Europe constructed through Gothic architecture and Classical Greece, rather than one defined by the Reformation and Classical Rome. Gothic was the style "adapted to a new and pure religion," combining Christianity with "the purer Grecian style," which itself had combined "a love of the beautiful, for which the Greeks were remarkable," with "the lofty character, stamped upon all the works of ancient Greece by the stern dignity of republican simplicity" (149–150). Tuthill's account anticipates a completely different circuit from the one traveled by antebellum tourists, whose Gothic repertory included at most Chartres and the cathedral at Milan, and who never visited Greece at all.

Antitourist jeremiads and satire developed after the Civil War in specific response to mass tourism. The closest one comes to these among the antebellum women travelers are Anna Cummings Johnson's two books on Germany and Switzerland. Johnson, whom we saw living among the Iroquois in Chapter 6, rejected the typical historical and esthetic itinerary, lived in small towns, employed local girls for guides, and vigorously attacked the "superficial and desultory manner of observation and reflection" of most guidebooks (*Peasant Life*, 47–48).

Although Johnson had little use for the sentimental historicizing of typical tourism, both her European travel books include substantial historical sections. She alone among visitors to Switzerland went beyond cursory, obligatory references to William Tell to recount the federated nation's long struggle toward republicanism; she alone preferred the supposedly independent mountaineers nurtured by Alpine scenery to the scenery itself. As for Germany, the only other woman to visit that country with history in mind was Harriet Beecher Stowe, who had gone there specifically to visit places associated with the life of Martin Luther. Johnson by contrast pursued the histories of the various German principalities to answer the question of what kind of American citizens emigrants from these places would make. (Answer: good citizens.) Unimpressed by tourist rhetoric that made the awful past acceptable by estheticizing it, she applies her Protestant republicanism with logical rigor and rejects all monumentalizing of the horrific past.

Commerce and trade were the refining and civilizing influences which awoke Europe from barbarism, without which her nobles and knights might to this day have been the ignorant and stupid boors they were for six centuries, and yet those engaged in trade and commerce are still looked upon as beneath even the impoverished descendants of some haughty baron. . . . Wherever we look in that age or in this, we see that it is the humble and useful arts to which mankind owe all their progression, and in which we must place our hope for the permanency of civilization. The encouragement of the fine arts alone does not promote the comfort or true elevation of a people. It is proverbial that only barbarians can produce the highest kind of poetry. . . . In the cities and countries where art is in the most flourishing state, the masses of the people are in the greatest degradation. (*Peasant Life*, 109–111)

In the horrors of the French revolution, historians ascribe effects to wrong causes. The murders and atrocities of revolutionists are crowded into a small space, but the blood spilt during the reign of terror would not equal that which was shed during the long and not less terrible reign of a succession of Bourbon princes. (*Peasant Life*, 208–209)

The Cottages of the Alps praises Swiss independence and self-reliance:

The insurrections and disputes of which we read so much in Switzer-land are misunderstood and misrepresented. Monarchists quote them to prove the instability of republics, and the unfitness of the people to govern themselves; when the truth is, they prove exactly the con-trary. So long as oppression existed in any form . . . so long there was restlessness and discontent. . . . As soon as they were free, they were content. (236–237)

The staunchly antimonarchist Johnson sounds like Fuller when she wishes that "some mighty whirlwind would sweep over this great continent and scatter for ever the dust and cobwebs of centuries from their habitations, and some purifying flood wash out the dank and mould that cover with the gloom of ages their minds and hearts" (*Cottages*, 246–247). More self-consistent than Fuller, she feels no attraction for Rome—but, then, she did not visit it:

In ancient Rome there were fifty public baths where now there is not one; and in all Italy there is the same destitution of everything which modern civilization demands for the physical, and mental health of the people. . . . If half the money which has been spent on palaces and churches had been devoted to aqueducts and other means of cleanliness, thrones and steeples would not now be tottering as they are to their foundations, and dukes and princes fleeing everywhere for life. To people who are never troubled with human sympathy, these will be very revolting statements, and those who travel only to admire architecture and fine paintings, will think it unpardonable to expose what is beneath. (*Cottages*, 254–255)

That there are no immense galleries, nor so much of the artistic in architecture, is not evidence, in Switzerland or America, that art is not appreciated. The Swiss demolished the castles, not because they were beautiful, but because they were to them associated with tyr-anny, barbarity, and everything base and contemptible in humanity. This is the motive which has destroyed them in every country. Those who built them and inhabited them were the veriest boors that ever crossed a threshold. Art could not be to those who knew them, and cannot be to any one who has studied the history of nations, the rep-resentative of the highest civilization. (*Cottages*, 399)

In these and similar passages, Johnson attacks the tourist approach to history for its fundamental conservatism. Not that she was antihistorical. Far from it. But from her rigorously anti-esthetic point of view, among the most important reasons to know history was knowing when to forget about it.

Imaginary Histories

A FEW HISTORICAL NOVELS by American women appeared before the publication of *Waverley* in 1814—notably, Anne Eliza Bleecker's *History of Maria Kittle* (1793, posthumous); Susanna Rowson's *Rebecca, or The Fille de Chambre* (1792) and *Reuben and Rachel* (1798); Sarah Sayward Wood's *Julia and the Illuminated Baron* (1800) and *Ferdinand & Elmira* (1804); and Leonora Sansay's *Secret History; or, The Horrors of St. Domingo* (1808). But *Waverley*, which established a model for historical fiction and rescued the novel genre from its outcast status, made the Radcliffean gothicism, epistolarism, seduction conventions, and rhetoric of sensibility in these works look quite obsolete, and they sank from public consciousness.

While *Waverley* certainly initiated a vogue for historical fiction in the United States, the genre never dominated American reading and writing practices. Lyle Wright's bibliography of American fiction from 1774 to 1850 shows that historical novels by men and women published after 1814 never totaled more than a small and ever-decreasing fraction of published novels. Except for James Fenimore Cooper's works, few had even a second edition. By 1850, Cooper's *The Spy* (1821) had gone through nineteen editions; *The Pioneers* (1823) eighteen; *Lionel Lincoln* (1824–1825) fifteen; *The Last of the Mohicans* (1826) nineteen; *The Bravo* (1831) eight; *The Heidenmauer* (1832) ten; and *The Headsman* (1833) nine. During the same period, however, Harriet Foster Cheney's *A Peep at the Pilgrims in Sixteen Hundred Thirty-Six* (1824) had just three editions, Lydia Maria Child's *Hobomok* (1824) one and *The Rebels* (1825) two, and Catharine Maria Sedgwick's *Hope Leslie* (1827) two. Both Child and Sedgwick had more success in other modes—Child's journalistic *Letters from New York* (1841, 1843) had eleven editions and Sedgwick's fictionalized advice book *Home* (1835) had twenty. Although, as Mary Kelley and others have reminded us, reviewers compared Sedgwick's historical fiction favorably to Cooper's, Sedgwick's partisans were her friends as well as publicists of New England.

152

Cooper was a true market phenomenon, more popular than most American writers of any kind of fiction in his day, even at his least popular. Partly because his works circulated so widely, historical fiction has been made to seem more central in the development of American fiction than it actually was.

Among other reasons, it is likely that Scott's and Cooper's historical novels were popular because their emphatic masculinity helped make the novel an acceptable genre for men to write and boys to read. Most authors of historical fiction in the antebellum United States were men. But women also wrote historical fiction; and it would be a mistake to think of the type as one in which only the most intrepid woman dared to perform, and then invariably with the aims of contesting, destabilizing, or subverting the received record. As we have seen, the American women who wrote nonfictional historical prose and historical poetry were not trying to poach on forbidden ground or dismantle the record. In fact, as we have also seen, the record told a story they liked, one authorizing their performances as historians, a story wherein only Protestant Christianity accorded women their rightful place in society, and Protestant Christianity flourished only under the republican form of government they themselves enjoyed. A critic of today therefore needs to think twice about ascribing revisionary motives to the antebellum women who wrote historical novels. In context, it looks as though the project of the American women who wrote historical novels was not to challenge received history but to show that historical fiction, like other forms of historical writing, was not an exclusively masculine genre.

In defining historical novels, I exclude fictions that locate their action in the past but whose history is entirely cosmetic and confined to introductory locutions like "It was in the reign of the haughty Queen Elizabeth that" or "The sun was rising on the marble palaces of seventeenth-century Venice when," or to capsule lineages for contemporary characters like "her father fought bravely at Bunker Hill." The novels that are more thoroughly historicized bring in notable historical personages or important historical events to make a historical point, and give the imagined story a shape that is significantly determined by the time and place of its setting. Between 1792 (when Susanna Rowson plotted *The Fille de Chambre* around the American Revolution) and 1864 (when Maria Susanna Cummins published *Haunted Hearts*, a novel set during the War of 1812) upwards of fifty women published more than seventy-five such novels or novellas. Over twenty women's prose miscellanies contain historical fiction, and the number of uncollected historical stories published in the periodical press is substantial. Many well-known American women of letters gave historical fiction a try, but few of them practiced in that genre exclusively. Other women seem to have floated a single historical novel and, when it failed to attract an audience, abandoned literary work altogether.

Some of these single-novel productions, as, for example, Anna L. Snelling's pro-Harrison novel about the War of 1812, *Kabaosa; or, The Warriors of the West* (1842), seem to have been addressed to immediate political affairs. But all historical novels by women—like those by men—had contemporary agendas as well as antiquarian interests and expressed a variety of political opinions. Wood's *Julia and the Illuminated Baron* was a conservative novel exploiting the Illuminati scare of the 1790s: "The Revolution in France, and the perturbed state of Europe, have opened some scenes that would, without these amazing shocks to the political world, have lain hid in obscurity; to some of these [the author] has had recourse, and many, very many serious truths are interwoven with the story of Julia" (iv–v). Leonora Sansay's *Secret History*, like other accounts of the Haitian slave uprising, gestures toward the United States throughout its narrative, as when it says of Haitian slaveholders, "Dearly have they paid for the luxurious ease in which they revelled at the expense of these oppressed creatures" (35).

So-called "Indian novels" by women and men appeared at particular moments in the antebellum era because the topic was as central to the American present as to the American past. They flourished in the 1820s because of the impassioned debate over Cherokee removal; they reappeared in the early 1840s to support Harrison's presidential campaign—he had been in command at the victory over the great Tecumseh at the Battle of Tippecanoe in 1811; and they had another resurgence in the early 1850s, when the gold rush made it clear that there was no place on the continent where Native Americans could be safely sequestered from white intruders. In each decade, one side argued that although the Indian nations were certainly doomed, individuals might be converted to Christianity and made allies and even productive citizens of the United States; the other side countered that Indians were irremediably savage and would fight to the finish.

As for Europe, some historical novels expressed conservative fears of Jacobin atheists and insisted that only alliance with England would secure the nation's future; others poured liberal scorn on monarchists and insisted that only complete isolation would keep the nation safe; still others were anxiously anti-Catholic works written in favor of Know-Nothing nativism and against Irish immigration. In their topicality, historical novels resemble other kinds of advocacy fiction, including novels featuring sectarian, temperance, and pro- and antislavery positions. Not one of these novels, however, can be called a proletarian or socialist fiction. History had, as yet, no place for that kind of imagining.

Besides Sansay's *Secret History*, novels about slavery include Frances Hammond Pratt's *La Belle Zoa* (1854) about the Haitian Revolution; Sarah

Hale's procolonization *Liberia* (1853); Mary Howard Schoolcraft's *The Black Gauntlet* (1860), a vicious proslavery novel with a good deal of South Carolina history; and Harriet Beecher Stowe's *The Minister's Wooing* (1859), a novel set immediately after the Revolution with an antislavery subplot. African Americans play minor roles in many other historical novels by women, chiefly northerners; they are local-color types or devoted domestic servants (or both), coding the message *nothing wrong here*. Even in *The Minister's Wooing*, emancipated slaves joyfully elect to stay on as paid servants in their manumitters' employ.

About two-thirds of these historical novels or novellas are about the United States. As a whole, novels of American history imply a familiar nationalist narrative about winning independence from England and securing territory from the Indians. A substantial number of them, therefore, fall into the overlapping categories of Revolutionary and Indian fiction—there are two dozen (roughly half of the whole) of the former type, sixteen (roughly a third of the whole) of the latter. Most of the eight novels about early New England and six about the War of 1812 have prominent Native American characters or motifs. No matter what their particular focus, they aim to participate in the patriotic work of establishing and affirming national origins, characters, and values. One might hypothesize that if the reader of a historical novel was imagined as a female, the woman writer might see her cultural work as including presentation of a model of female national character. And in fact just about all the historical novels published by women before the Civil War do feature female protagonists— the exceptions are a few juveniles like Mary Gertrude's *Philip Randolph* (1845) designed for boys.

But female protagonists presented technical and imaginative problems to the writer who was trying to feminize Scott. Scott connected a love plot, centered on an ordinary couple, to ongoing events of great historical significance, centered on royal dynasties, wars, and diplomacy. One could attach an ordinary man more or less naturally to this male-dominated record by making him a subaltern, attaché, courtier, or military officer; and it was then easy to bring in an ordinary woman as his appended sweetheart. But if the woman was to be the central character herself, she had to be imagined as participating more directly in historical events than as somebody's girlfriend. How was this to be done?

The solution to this problem did not consist of introducing her as a rebel inclined to subvert the course of American history—in which case she would have been both unpatriotic and unsuccessful—but in making her act to preserve or forward some historical trend that was only embryonic in her own time. The trend that she was chosen to stand for, curiously, was the cultural refinement of America, which preserved the good aspects of aristocracy. Women's contribution to American progress—and through America, the world's progress—in historical fiction is their (not always appreciated) gift to the raw society of good manners, taste, graciousness, refinement, wit, spirit, and other values at once aristocratic and feminine. As Richard Bushman has explained in *The Refinement of America*, the general dynamic here involves the ever-widening circulation of goods and practices into ordinary American life and homes that were associated with a wealthy style of life, which women took particular responsibility for. Bushman interprets domestic novels as manuals of gentility that also identified women as custodians of the genteel. In the historical novels this dynamic gets a moral and historical aspect by equating gentility with liberal Christianity and political republicanism.

This adaptation of an ethic of aristocratic gentility can be seen in two historical novels by antebellum women that have been much written about by feminist critics in recent years—Child's *Hobomok* (1824) and Sedgwick's *Hope Leslie* (1827). Both protagonists—Mary Conant in *Hobomok* and Hope Leslie in the eponymous novel—are in fact aristocrats. Mary is an earl's granddaughter. When the book opens she has just recently come to the primitive colony, where her domestic life is dominated by an exceedingly bigoted and uncouth Puritan father. "During her stay at her grandfather's, she had become familiar with much that was beautiful in painting, and lovely in sculpture, as well as all that was elegant in the poetry of that early period; and their rich outline was deeply impressed upon her young heart. For her mother's sake, she endured the mean and laborious offices which she was obliged to perform, but she lived only in the remembrance of that fairy spot in her existence" (47). Later in the story, after her mother dies and her Church of England lover is supposedly lost at sea, Mary offers herself to the adoring Indian, Hobomok, a gesture that the narrator insists is a maddened attempt to escape from a community to which she is so far superior, and in which she is totally isolated. When Charles Brown (the Anglican) resurfaces, Hobomok obligingly departs for the western wilds; Mary's chastened father, who had earlier forbidden her to associate with Brown, now welcomes their marriage. An entire society's softening is foreshadowed in the father's change of heart, which Mary has inadvertently brought about by running away with an Indian. Mary's mother, albeit an earl's daughter, had no power at all to move her husband; she dies of self-sacrificing love and overwork in a time and place that have no use for superior cultivation.

Hope Leslie is the granddaughter of "Sir" William Fletcher; she has passed her early childhood amidst aristocratic luxury in England; her American counterpart, the male protagonist Everell Fletcher (her second cousin), is educated in England. Throughout the novel, Hope is portrayed as a much classier character than everybody who surrounds her, including even Governor and Mrs. Winthrop. Mary Conant and Hope Leslie are more theologically latitudinarian, esthetically sensitive, socially polished, and politically republican than the Calvinist hierarchs they live among in America, and as these values increasingly improve the quality of everyday life, the budding nation is pushed toward its nineteenth-century flowering.

In *New England Literary Culture*, Lawrence Buell has identified this narrative with the Unitarians, a group that produced a particularly large number of prominent New England women writers, including Child and Sedgwick. Because history is progressive, and the Unitarians its most advanced manifestation, the Puritans need not—should not—be presented as history's culmination. The long road traveled from the seventeenth to the nineteenth century is exactly what the novels are about insofar as they are historical. Child and Sedgwick, therefore, perform no culturally subversive acts when they deplore Puritan shortcomings.

But even though the novelists do indeed say harsh things about the Puritans, many passages in *Hobomok* and *Hope Leslie* imply that the authors are trying to defend the Puritans against widespread cultural denigration rather than participating in that unfilial discourse. There is no other way, for example, to interpret the early passage in *Hobomok* in which the narrator pointedly extenuates the first generation from charges that they were "a band of dark, discontented bigots," and winds up saying that "whatever might have been their defects, they certainly possessed excellencies, which peculiarly fitted them for a van-guard in the proud and rapid march of freedom" (6). Similarly, the narrator of *Hope Leslie* says that the word *pilgrim* "should be redeemed from the puritanical and ludicrous associations which have degraded it, in most men's minds, and be hallowed by the sacrifices made by those voluntary exiles" (18); she frequently reverts to Puritan virtue, sometimes at length. "We forget," she says—thus gesturing toward a hostile consensus out there in the culture—

that the noble pilgrims lived and endured for us. . . . They came not for themselves—they lived not for themselves. An exiled and suffering people, they came forth in the dignity of the chosen servants of the Lord, to open the forests to the sun-beam, and to the light of the Sun of Righteousness—to restore man—man oppressed and trampled on by his fellow; to religious and civil liberty, and equal rights. . . . What was their reward? . . . They saw, with sublime joy, a multitude of people where the solitary savage roamed the forest—the forest vanished, and pleasant villages and busy cities appeared—the tangled foot-path expanded to the thronged high-way—the consecrated church planted on the rock of heathen sacrifice.

And that we might realize this vision—enter into this promised land of faith—they endured hardship, and braved death. (72–73)

Part of what the Puritans endured was Indian savagery, and part of what they did for us was clear the ground. A white feminist reader may be tempted to believe that women authors, more than men, offered a vision of egalitarian and respectful relations between white women and indigenous people. But the enlightened Christian gentility particularly represented by the heroines can only increase the ultimate distance between Anglo civilization and Native Americans. Notwithstanding Mary's dalliance with an Indian husband and Hope's companionship with Magawisca, daughter of an Indian chief (the Indian connections in these books are always aristocratic), the outcomes of both novels show that the Indians were destined to be supplanted by a civilization that was not only stronger than, but also morally superior to, theirs.

Sedgwick is even more forthright than Child about the inevitability and morality of Indian removal. True, she allows Magawisca to describe the Puritan assault on Fort Mystic during the Pequot War from the Indian point of view; but Washington Irving had already made a much stronger case for the New England Indians and against the Puritans in his influential essay about King Philip's War, "Philip of Pokanoket," collected in the *Sketch-Book* (1819). If the "Philip" sketch is the standard, then *Hope Leslie* is only lukewarm; Sedgwick's determination to defend New England from New Yorkers like Irving constrains her expressions of sympathy for the Pequods. Whatever protofeminist or pro-Indian daring she manifests in allowing Magawisca to recite the Pequod narrative, she also neutralizes by making Magawisca the source of the most intransigent resistance to conciliatory white overtures. At her trial, Magawisca tells her accusers, "I am your enemy; the sun-beam and the shadow cannot mingle. The white man cometh—the Indian vanisheth" (292); later she rejects the pleas of Hope and Everell to live with them in similar language: "The Indian and the white man can no more mingle, and become one, than day and night" (330). The outcome is voluntary vanishing, like Hobomok's.

Had Sedgwick really cared to revise history, she might have observed that the mingling so stoutly declared impossible by Magawisca had in fact been occurring all along the frontiers, producing a substantial mixed-blood population. The preface to *Hope Leslie* defends the realism of Magawisca's depiction by likening her death-defying defense of the captive Everell to the example of the well-known Pocahontas. But Pocahontas could also have set a fictional precedent for "mingling"; her marriage to John Rolfe had produced offspring, and many distinguished Virginia families were already proudly claiming her as an ancestor. Just three years after *Hope Leslie* appeared, Sedgwick's sister-in-law Susan Sedgwick published a juvenile historical novel of the frontier, *The Young Emigrants* (1830), which—though it argues that if the greatest happiness of the greatest number is a good, it is good for a thinly settled Indian population to be replaced by the denser population of whites—still features accounts of white captives refusing to return to their natal families. The book also instructs readers that although the Indians are destined by Heaven to lose their "identity as a people," some of them no doubt "will accept the advantages of civilization" (112) and become citizens of the United States.

Regard for contextual accuracy, then, requires one to be careful about claiming that antebellum women demonstrated a multicultural sensibility. The hope that Indians might join white society, when it was expressed, always implied an assumption of white cultural superiority. Hope Leslie wants Magawisca to stay with them: "The thought that a mind so disposed to religious impressions and affections, might enjoy the brighter light of Christian revelation—a revelation so much higher, nobler, and fuller, than that which proceeds from the voice of nature—made Hope feel a more intense desire than ever to retain Magawisca; but this was a motive Magawisca could not now appreciate" (332). There are friendships, or at least companionable moments, between white women and Native Americans in antebellum women's historical novels, but they are seldom egalitarian and never resonate emotionally like the tie between Cooper's Natty Bumppo and Chingachgook. Natty, a lower-class character who operates outside the genteel system, can associate democratically with Indians without losing class; the genteel protagonists of the women's historical novels, who equate gentility with their essence, cannot cross the cultural line. Therefore a white woman who makes her home among the Indians is lost to herself and to the historical future. Mary Conant is not lost in this way, because marriage to Hobomok does not mean life among the Indians; Hobomok, whose "loves and hates had become identified with the English" (31), has left his tribe to live alone on the margins of Salem. Hope Leslie's sister Faith, who has married an Indian and joined his tribe, refuses to be repatriated; the narrator calls her "spiritless, woe-begone—a soulless body" (338).

The questions whether there are gender differences between treatments of Native Americans in antebellum fiction by women and men, and if so what these differences are, cannot be addressed persuasively without a close reading of novels by men that is not undertaken here. It does seem unlikely, however, that men's fiction would have shared the women's recurrent representation of Indians—both male and female—moved to protect, serve, and even respectfully adore the Anglos whose superiority they intuitively recognize. This, after all, is what is at stake in Hobomok's love for Mary; Child conjoins his rejection of an Indian spouse with his "reverence, which almost amounted to adoration" for Mary (33). This trope may well represent a specifically female erotic daydream (by contrast, as Natty and Chingachgook demonstrate, the male fantasy is homosocial); it would not seem to promise much satisfaction to men. Since Indian women as well as Indian men are given the work of recognizing the protagonists' superiority, the figure can be read nonerotically as a means to signify what could not be expressed, perhaps could not even be acknowledged, in a society that, along with rejecting aristocracy, has rejected the idea that people differ in intrinsic worth. Indian devotion marks the protagonist as one of nature's noblewomen. As a plot device, too, Indian recognition of white superiority accounts for the frequent help given by admiring Indians, male and female, to captive or endangered white characters.

To be sure, for every "good" Indian there is a bad one who either remains unmoved by the protagonist or resents the attention she receives from others in the tribe. Native Americans in Revolutionary fiction, which constitutes the largest group of historical novels about the United States by women writers, are always dichotomized according to whether they support the patriots or the British. It is useful to remember that, along with reactive bloodshed as whites advanced across the continent, Native Americans participated in all the major American wars, and almost always against the colonists. In the French and Indian War they mainly fought against the English; in the Revolution and War of 1812, they mainly fought with them. It is more than poetic sentiment that makes historical novels about the United States focus so centrally on the Indian trope.

The most openly romantic relationship between a white woman and a Native American man in women's historical fiction occurs in Elizabeth Oakes Smith's *The Western Captive; or, The Times of Tecumseh* (1842), whose male protagonist is Tecumseh himself. Had Tecumseh

been the foe to any other people, Americans would have been ready to do justice to his memory; but time will remove the prejudices that must always cloud the fame of a reformer, and when the name of the last Indian shall have been inscribed upon the scroll of eternity, monuments will be reared to his memory. Reflecting that Metacom, Pontiac, and Tecumseh struggled for the very boon, for which our fathers bled and died, liberty for their wives and children, their names will be inscribed with the great and good of all ages, who have sought to do good for their country. The circumstances of failure will not detract from the ability with which their plans were conceived, or the devotion with which they yielded themselves to a great mission. They will cease to be enemies, and become patriots. (38)

The female protagonist, Margaret, has been captured in youth and brought up in the tribe. She loves Tecumseh, and he her, but their chivalric love remains unconsummated. Margaret feels that the "purity" of her emotions "carried her out from the dominion of self into companionship with greatness and virtue, in whatever shape" (26); that is, because her love is nonsexual it is legitimate for its object to be an Indian. To prove her purity, she dies; Tecumseh severs just one lock of her "long, beautiful hair" before he "turned away to the solitude of the forest" (38). Margaret's adversary is an Indian woman, Ackoree, who has lost the competition for Tecumseh's affections and is abetted in her anti-Margaret machinations by Tecumseh's adversary Kumshaka, who is in love (but not chastely) with her. The division is clear: a good Indian recognizes the superiority of the white woman, a bad one does not; the white woman signifies asexual spirituality, the Indian woman physical lust.

In Ann Stephens's *Mary Derwent* (1858), Catharine Montour is the white wife of the Indian chief who leads the Native American warriors in the Wyoming Valley massacre. Catharine had run away to the Indians in desperation, marrying an Indian, not because she loved or desired him, but because he desired *her* and threatened to harm other whites if she refused him. Although in the early days of their marriage she has some influence over him, when she tries to avert the Wyoming massacre by pleading with him, she is not successful:

Never in the days of her loftiest pride had Catharine Montour appeared so touchingly lovely, so gentle and woman-like, as on that evening. She had been pleading for her people with the fierce chief— pleading that vengeance should not fall on the inhabitants of the neighboring valley in retribution for the death of a single brave. But . . . since the fierce pride of Catharine's character had passed away, her influence over him had decreased. . . . When almost as stern and unyielding as himself, Catharine might command—now she could but supplicate. . . . When moral goodness began to predominate in Catharine's character, he mistook its meek and gentle manifestations for cowardice, and she became to him almost an object of contempt. There was no longer any power in her patient perseverance and persuasive voice to win his nature to mercy; the daring spirit which had formerly awed and controlled his, had departed forever beneath the gradual deepening of repentance in her heart. (321)

Thus these representations of Native Americans keep the markers of unbridgeable cultural difference firmly in place. I will make this point one last time with the example of Susanna Rowson's 1798 *Reuben and Rachel; or, Tales of Old Times*. In the first of its two volumes, Rowson develops an intricate genealogy for the main Anglo characters, twins who are prototypes of the American citizenry. Notably, and uniquely, these Anglo characters are not wholly Anglo or wholly white. Their ancestry amalgamates Spanish (or Italian) descent from Columbus; Native American (they are at least one quarter Indian); and English aristocratic (they descend from the

Dudleys and Lady Jane Grey). A significant part of the historical material recounts the story of a heroicized Columbus, whose son marries an indigenous woman. With Robertson's history of America as her source, Rowson makes the Spanish into demons in their treatment of native peoples (a function of their cynical Catholicism and their greed) in contrast to the relative restraint of the Anglos, who buy land from the Indians, do not enslave them, and labor seriously for their conversion.

Rowson shows that seventeenth-century Indian warfare, while justified to some extent by white depredation, is extremely bloody and cruel; these are no noble savages. The Indians were

plundering and burning their habitations, and either massacring the inhabitants, or taking them prisoners and carrying them up the country, where they often exercised on them the most wanton barbarity, scalping, maiming and disfiguring them, if at least they suffered them to escape with life. But what could be expected from the untaught savage, whose territories had been invaded by strangers, and who perhaps had suffered, from the cruelty of the invaders, in the person of a father, brother, son, or some near connexion. Revenge is a principle inherent in human nature, and it is only the sublime and heavenly doctrine of Christianity that teaches us to repel the impulse, and return good for evil. (1:142)

When the action of *Reuben and Rachel* moves to the present, the novelist ignores the part-Indian genealogy she has laboriously constructed and presents the characters as purely white. A chief's daughter falls madly in love with the captive Reuben, but he does not reciprocate. She eventually kills herself, assuring Reuben's wife, "thou art a happy woman, for thy husband is a man of honour. He saw the weakness of a poor, unprotected Indian maid, he pitied her folly, but took no advantage of it" (2:360). The national identity, as it congeals, is firmly Anglo, its affective engagements solely with the mother country. At the novel's end the chief characters inherit an English estate and title; they keep the money but reject the title, since titles, according to Reuben, "are distinctions nothing worth, and should by no means be introduced into a young country, where the only distinctions between men and men should be made by virtue, genius, and education" (2:363). Even more suggestive of Rowson's affiliative intentions, she ends her story before the American Revolution begins, which means that her characters, though colonials, are still fully English.

The Native American motif in women's historical fiction, then, is used to help depict a culturally superior female protagonist. Other New England historical novels besides *Hobomok* and *Hope Leslie* represent their female protagonists as both ahead of their time and innately aristocratic.

A Peep at the Pilgrims, published in the same year as *Hobomok*, is much more scholarly and historically informed than *Hobomok* (or, for that matter, than *Hope Leslie*—a fact that Sedgwick graciously acknowledges in a narratorial aside in her novel). It is also much more filiopietistic. It covers the settlements of Plymouth, Boston, the Connecticut Valley, and western New York, stopping the action to incorporate extensive tracts of historical information and commentary, connecting the protagonists with all the important crises of early Puritan life, devoting an entire chapter to a military account of the Pequot War, and staging many debates and conversations between persons prominent in early New England history. Clearly it means to instruct its readers in New England history as well as entertain them with a good story.

The conventional historical plot of this novel is about liberalizing the Puritan polity, but at the same time the Puritans are defended vigorously and at length. Major Atherton (from whose perspective the narrative is mostly presented) is a Church of England man; Miriam Grey, beauteous daughter of a deeply orthodox Puritan and "the fairest maiden of New-England" (8), catches his eye. No transplanted aristocrat, Miriam still has an essential gentility that sets her apart from the throng; there was "something superior, Atherton thought, something more tasteful, in short indescribable, about this female" (25).

Miriam's father forbids her to marry a non-Puritan, and she therefore dutifully rejects him: "I thank God, that I have had strength to sacrifice my inclination to principle and duty" (300). Herself a staunch Puritan, Miriam informs Atherton—in language that redirects rather than eradicates aristocratic values—that she, as "daughter of a devoted, self-denying Christian, of one, who forsook fortune, kindred, and country, to plant the truth, and establish a Christian church and colony, in an unknown savage land, would not exchange her proud title, to become the jeweled empress of a world!" (75).

The book's major action details Miriam's going to aid a sick cousin in the Connecticut Valley just when hostilities break out with the Pequots; her capture and preservation through the intervention of Mioma, Chief Mononotto's wife; her restoration to Atherton; and her reunion with a grateful father, who now sanctions the marriage. "Atherton's attachment to the primitive habits of New-England daily strengthened, and familiarized to its simple mode of worship, he became eventually a sincere, but liberal Puritan" (462); the father lives to see "a new generation rising up to take the place of their fathers, and hand down to their children's children those principles of civil and religious freedom, which guided the Pilgrims to the Rock of Plymouth" (463).

Dovetailing the Pequot War to the crisis of her love plot, Cheney produces a novel replete with captures and rescues. The war, rather than Puritan bigotry, is also her historiographical focus, and the narrator endorses the official Puritan view of the colony's relations with the Native Americans—land was bought at a fair price unless it was already vacant, and the Puritans were never violent except in self-defense. By contrast the "fierce and warlike" Pequots "lay in ambush for the solitary and unsuspicious . . . burned houses and destroyed every thing within their reach . . . unhumanly murdered in cold blood, even innocent children and defenceless women," and subjected captives to "the most cruel tortures" (304). The Puritan victory over the Pequots "strikingly exhibits the firmness and courage of the early settlers of New-England. Indeed, considering the weakness of the colonies, and their limited resources, and the strength and numbers of the enemy, their success appears almost miraculous" (447). As for Puritan bigotry, Cheney acknowledges it but minimizes its historical importance; if the Puritans "exhibited a spirit of persecution, which has entailed a lasting reproach upon their memory," still "they erred with good intentions and upright hearts; and every candid mind will find a ready excuse for their failings, in the excitement of the times, and the comparative darkness of the age in which they lived" (260).

As well as exemplifying virtues that American society will increasingly value over time, the refinement and gentility of Miriam produce immediate social benefits because they win the admiration of a man whose cultural liberalism is necessary for New England's future development and help reconcile the antagonistic factions represented by father and suitor. It is the fictional daughter who creates the republican family—one from which the republican mother is notably absent.

Miriam like other female protagonists does her good work mainly, although not entirely, by being or representing herself, as in the self-referential speech rejecting Atherton's proposal. The novel attempts to maneuver Miriam into other situations that allow her to describe herself: "And should I shrink from a dangerous duty?" she says to Atherton as she departs for the Valley. "Would not that father blush for the weakness of a daughter so unworthy of parents, who dared and suffered without fear, in the cause of liberty and religion?" (326); "I have no fears for myself," she tells him later; "I am a rugged daughter of New-England, unused to the gentle nurture of your English maidens, and from childhood accustomed to fatigue, and taught to meet the unavoidable evils of life without repining" (432).

No matter that these self-representations are not wholly accurate—what matters is that insofar as speech is action, then historical novels make it the action especially fit for women. Nevertheless, Miriam cannot always be declaring herself; there are many moments when she has to do her work without, as it were, knowing that she is doing it. In church, even before he has met her, Atherton is entranced by her appearance, and he sits where he can watch her "every movement without altering his position so much as to occasion remark; and the unconscious girl little suspected with what diligence every article of her dress and every motion of her person was scanned" (25). The word *unconscious* here insists that Miriam is not exhibiting herself for Atherton's benefit, but it insists equally that women are always likely to be on exhibit and so can never stop performing. Even out on a boat on a stormy night with only one's father, somebody is looking: "as a ray of light occasionally glanced on the countenance of Miriam Grey, Atherton remarked with admiration the serenity of its expression, and the air of calmness, mingled with awe, with which she regarded the angry elements. Apparently unmoved by fear or anxiety, she gently reclined on her father's protecting arm, while she both maintained a profound and unbroken silence" (98).

Cheney's *Rivals of Acadia: An Old Story of the New World* (1827) continues the project of Puritan hagiography while presenting women in history differently from *A Peep at the Pilgrims*. Set in 1643, its historical subject is the competition between two French colonizers (D'Aulney and La Tour) for possession of Nova Scotia and for military help from Massachusetts. The love plot pairs Arthur Stanhope, the liberal Puritan Englishman who leads the Boston militia in Acadia, and Lucie, La Tour's ward. Through Stanhope's perceptions, the novelist shows how different French and English settlers are: "reminded by all around him, of this noble triumph of mind and principle over the greatest physical obstacles; and he strongly felt the contrast which it presented to the habits and opinions of the settlers, with whom he had been lately associated." La Tour and D'Aulney colonized "from interest and ambitious motives; their followers were in general actuated by a hope of gain, or the mere spirit of adventure, which characterized that age; and, if religion was at all considered, it was only from motives of policy. The purity and disinterestedness of the New-England fathers was more striking from the comparison" (254).

Impressed by the contrast, Stanhope settles in New England with Lucie, who has escaped from the form of captivity that is represented in these novels by being a despot's ward. "It was their ambition to fulfil the duties of moral and intellectual beings; and the rugged climate of New-England became the chosen home of their affections" (268). The story, then, represents original New England virtue as an attraction for people who, whatever their national origins or religious affiliation, have innate republican sympathies. Because the action takes place in a French settlement, Cheney can make it stand for Europe, thereby attacking aristocracy, Jesuitism, and other Old World vices without attacking England; in fact, the contrast between Massachusetts and Canada is explicitly England versus France. In other words, this is a strongly pro-English novel. Cheney can also contrast the position of women in the Old World with the possibilities for women in the New without making the Puritans oppressors of women.

Eliza Buckminster Lee's *Delusion* (1840) and *Naomi* (1848), however, return to the theme of early New England's antipathy to superior females. In *Delusion* a demented child lodges accusations of witchcraft against the protagonist, Edith, who is "superior to the age in which she lived" (109). In the trial that follows, the depiction of which draws on available histories of the Salem witchcraft proceedings, Edith is condemned and deserted by all her associates. She rejects the pleas of her fiancé Seymore, a cowardly divinity student, to save herself through false confession and, later, to escape from prison without trying to clear her name. *Naomi* retells this story in a much longer novel about the conflict between Puritans and Quakers. *Naomi* incorporates substantial quantities of historical material, some in footnotes, and gives a detailed, scholarly depiction of Boston in 1660 with a large cast of characters. At the novel's outset, Naomi has arrived from England to join her mother and stepfather in Boston, only to discover that her mother has died. Her stepfather, a prosperous, hypocritical merchant, affects religion, because at that time "to attain any degree of consideration, it was as requisite to be religious as it is now to be honest" (30). The Puritans, who believed themselves led into the wilderness by God "to preserve the true faith once delivered to the saints," had in fact constructed a society characterized by "religious bondage" (8).

Caught between religious bigotry and commercial hypocrisy, Naomi seems so quintessentially Protestant that her alienation in New England can only be a severe condemnation of the colony. Even in her first short interview with the ministers, she feels the "pressure of that spiritual domination over conscience, that, like an iron chain placed around a vigorous tree, checks not its upward growth, but eats into its very heart, and mars its expanding and symmetrical beauty" (76). Although she is later to be tried as a Quaker, Naomi is not drawn to Quaker religious practice, because the Quakers who came to America were of a "low order," trying "by every mean and malicious tale, by every secret and unfair practice, to injure the fair fame and impair the usefulness of the ministers"; their "efforts all tended to the subversion of civil order, and to bring anarchy into the church and into the government of the country" (171–172). Naomi's so-called crime is helping "a condemned Quaker to escape from justice," an act that, the narrator insists, "was totally different from that of being a Quaker" (387).

Naomi's purity of being is essentially quietistic: "from the refinement of her tastes, and the beautiful purity of all her thoughts, she shrank from the contact of daily intercourse with the ignorant and the vulgar. The soul of benevolence and of loving-kindness, she yet felt keenly all that offended the purity of her mind in low ideas and vulgar expressions" (336). But, as the passage shows, this kind of inner purity cannot be made visible to spectators except in a class-bound display of gentility, the rhetoric of which recurs throughout the book: "The women rushed to the open windows to express their surprise, and in some instances their contempt, that a well-dressed and beautifully mounted young lady should be hurrying to such a disgraceful spectacle. They exulted in their own superior delicacy and refinement, and thus concealed from themselves the stirrings of envy at Naomi's beautiful appearance" (232). At the bar with Quakers, Naomi's appearance "presented a strange contrast to the wild and witch-like appearance of these women. The first glance would have told the most careless observer that there could be nothing in common between them" (386). Naomi's appearance, thus, is vital to the novel's moral point:

Naomi was this day paler than usual, and her hair, which until her imprisonment she had worn curled, according to the prevailing fashion, was combed plainly around her temples, and confined in a knot at the back, giving to her head a purely Grecian form. The extreme coldness of the day obliged her to wrap herself in a cloak of crimson broadcloth, open at the throat, and lined with a dark sable fur; the collar was thrown a little back, and the white throat contrasted with the dark fur of the lining. (387)

To be sure, the extreme coldness of the day might have obliged her to wear a cloak, but not necessarily a crimson one and surely not open at the throat. Nor is the novelist unaware of the import of these descriptions, as when a few pages later the Reverend Wilson helps her remove that very cloak:

Had Naomi been bent upon conquest, she could not have attired herself more becomingly than she had done unconsciously, and without a thought except of the extreme coldness of the day. She wore a close-fitting dark-velvet dress, the sleeves and the neck (which was open) being trimmed with the fur of the silver-gray fox. A white cambric chemise, or gorget, as it was then called, was drawn closely up to the beautiful white throat, and her hair, without curl, was plain upon her temples. (405–406)

These uncomfortably duplicitous (to at least this reader) moments of female self-regard, interlocking with the discourse of fashion, are an extreme development of the strategies already noticed in *A Peep at the Pilgrims*, and emerging in historical novels by American women as early as Ann Eliza Bleecker's *The History of Maria Kittle*. In that novella about the French and Indian War, the bereaved heroine, a prisoner of the French, is housed with a sympathetic Englishwoman in Montreal while waiting to be ransomed. She receives visitors—women in similar situations—in her hostess's parlor: "She was dressed in a plain suit of mourning, and wore a small muslin cap, from which her hair fell in artless curls on her fine neck: her face was pale, though not emaciated, and her eyes streamed a soft langour over her countenance, more bewitching than the sprightliest glances of vivacity. . . . After some time spent in tears, and pleasing melancholy, tea was brought in" (68–69). This vision allots nothing for a woman in history to do but register and perform her victimized situation to the greatest esthetic advantage. It testifies, I think, to the difficulty of finding a way for Protestant republican women to act before their allotted time and place in history had come.

The difficulty is exacerbated in *Naomi* because her beautiful appearance does not win people over. She is condemned by "the ministers, as well as the magistrates," because "unconsciously to themselves" they had "allowed a strong prejudice to grow up in their hearts against this humble girl. She had dared to think for herself and to differ from those who were alone the true interpreters of the meaning of the Bible, the true ministers of the only true church" (391). "It was the taint of heresy, the sin of daring to think for herself, the unpardonable crime of daring to differ from the church in opinion, the non-submission of her own mind to the minds of her ministers and judges, that condemned Naomi" (419). Historically effective action by Protestant republican women is not possible until a Protestant republic has come into being; and this, at least according to Lee, early New England is *not*. Lee even goes so far as to resettle Naomi, the icon of a future American nation, in New Jersey. *Naomi* is the most hostile of the early New England novels; but they all view the settlement of Massachusetts as a crucial, Providentially ordained, yet at best partial break with the past.

Except for *Naomi*, however, New England historical novels do insist that the Puritans were the national progenitors. Still, these make up less than a fifth of the historical novels overall, and in the rest, the Revolution, not the landing at Plymouth Rock, constituted the originary moment. Historical novels about the Revolution make up only a tiny fraction of the Revolutionary material with which American public culture was saturated in the antebellum era. All kinds of artifacts worked the Revolution and George Washington into their rhetoric. And no matter what the topic, historical novels managed to associate it with the Revolution, as in this example from *Love's Labor Won* (1862, serialized 1857) by E.D.E.N. Southworth, a novel about the War of 1812:

This month of June, 1812, was a month big with the fate of nations as well as of individuals. The bitter disputes between the young Republic and the "Mother Country," like all family quarrels, did not tend toward reconciliation, but on the contrary, month by month, and year by year, had grown more acrid and exasperating, until at

Imaginary Histories

length a war could no longer be warded off. . . . Never had Young America before, and never has she since, taken so rash and impetuous a step. Never had an unfortunate country plunged headlong into an unequal and perilous war under more forbidding circumstances. . . . Yet no sooner had the tocsin sounded through the land, than "the spirit of '76" was aroused, and an army arose almost as miraculously as the myrmidons of Aegina. (175–176)

It seems to have been an unacknowledged convention that Revolutionary fictions would have at least one scene in which Washington figured. The main male character in Catharine Sedgwick's *The Linwoods* (1835) carries out a mission for him, and the double wedding that closes the novel is presided over by Martha Washington. In Diana Treat Kilbourn's *The Lone Dove* (1850), the Washingtons act as the protagonist's foster parents and express a desire to adopt her formally. Southworth opens *Love's Labor Won* at a ball hosted by the Washingtons, where "the beauty, talent, fashion and celebrity of the 'Republican Court' were present. . . . Through them all, but greater than all, moved the Chief, arrayed simply, as a private gentleman, but wearing on his noble brow that royalty no crown could give" (24–25).

A chronological list of Revolutionary novels by American women includes many more novels than can be described in this chapter—*The Fille de Chambre* (1792) by Susanna Rowson; *Saratoga: A Tale of the Revolution* (1824) by Eliza Lanesford Cushing; *The Rebels; or, Boston before the Revolution* (1825) by Lydia Maria Child; *Resignation: An American Novel* (1825) by Sarah Ann Evans; *Grace Seymour* (1830) by Hannah F. S. Lee; *The Linwoods; or "Sixty Years Since" in America* (1835) by Catharine Maria Sedgwick; *The British Partizan; A Tale of the Times of Old* (1839) by Mary Elizabeth Moragne Davis; *The Neutral French; or, The Exiles of Nova Scotia* (1841) by Catharine Read Williams; *Charles Morton; or, The Young Patriot* (1843) by Mary S. B. Shindler; *Philip Randolph; A Tale of Virginia* (1845) by Mary Gertrude (probably a penname); *Sir Henry's Ward; A Tale of the Revolution* (1846) by Ann Sophia Stephens; *The Lone Dove: A Legend of Revolutionary Times* (1850) by Diana Treat Kilbourn; *Evelyn: The Child of the Revolution* (1850) by Mrs. John Hovey Robinson; *Captain Ashleigh; A Tale of the Olden Time* (1854) by Eliza Ann Dupuy; *Molly; The Story of a Brave Woman* (1857) by Ellen T. H. Putnam; *Agnes* (1858) by Mary Hayden Pike; *Mary Derwent* (1858) by Ann Sophia Stephens; and more.

The male patriot characters in all these novels are military men who take part in important battles, carry out important missions, or perform crucial secret services for the great Washington himself. The novels rely on family metaphors of political life—nations as families, the Revolution as a

169

family quarrel, Washington as the father of his country—to make an organic connection between the domestic love story and history. As they develop this national romance, the novels refer constantly to the progress of the war, reciting a succession of battles that repeated the historical lessons of school textbooks and Fourth of July celebrations. The novels introduce chapters with paragraphs of pure historical narrative and include expository historical interchapters that read like the textbooks from which they were undoubtedly cribbed. This was not plagiarism; it was relaying the voice of history. The narrator's frequent patriotic interjections remind readers of their inestimable good fortune to live in a republic, and convey the author's own patriotism. The winter at Valley Forge is described over and over, and the horrors of war are detailed with a graphicness that emphasizes the sufferings and sacrifice of the Continental Army on behalf of the future. The most concrete accounts of male brutality narrate the savagery of the Indian allies and Hessian mercenaries employed by the English. This presentation simultaneously exonerates and excoriates the British; if they did not actually carry out the atrocities of the Revolution, they certainly allowed them to take place.

Revolutionary novels tended to feature variations of two plots, one of which might be understood to be offering a liberal, the other a conservative, understanding of women's place in the Revolution. In the liberal plot, best exemplified in *Saratoga* and *The Linwoods*, the protagonist first detaches herself from allegiance to the Tory side as it is personified in her father, in favor of the rebel cause as it is personified in a patriot suitor. Then, after a certain amount of spoken defiance and perhaps some secret aid to the patriots, she brings her father around to her point of view, reconciling him both to her suitor and the republic. Since this story of a daughter who reconciles a monarchical father to a republican husband also controls the plots of New England historical novels, it should be thought of as the basic narrative through which the female national identity was conveyed.

Before the daughter performs the traditional womanly role of peacemaker, she carries out acts of untraditional resistance to paternal authority. The explanation for this behavior is her nascent nationality. The plot unites the private with the public story: the truly important achievement of the republican daughter is securing her father's allegiance to the nation, an achievement obviously fraught with public significance. Whereas in the private realm the daughter insists on the right to choose her own spouse—a right of extreme importance, obviously, for women—in the public realm she defines a newly democratic relation between self and state and wins consent to this relation from the book's personification of the old autocracy. Remarkably, this republican daughter is charged with the cultural task of engendering a republican father. The absence of mothers furthers a plot in which daughters have to stand alone, and a debate between the daughter and her father (rather than her mother) makes political sense if the system being revolutionized is a patriarchy. What kind of Oedipal fantasy this might be is not clearly apparent.

Conservative plots, of which *Grace Seymour* is the most fully developed example, are not so sanguine. The paternal figure, much more villainous than in the liberal plots, undermines the Enlightenment trust in universal reason and natural benevolence on which progressivist history depended. Having no power that can move this kind of father, the daughter subsides into Old World female passivity and waits for her rebel-lover to rescue her from the clutches of Old World tyranny. Rescue means captivity, and captivity is indeed the motif of Old World women's historical fiction as it is of New World women's captivity narratives. The despotic father's authority is to be overturned only by violence, and hence only by sons.

Yet there is a way in which the politics of these conservative novels may be seen as more radical than the liberal novels, because the liberals obviously endorse a rapprochement between the United States and England, while the conservatives imply that the ideology of the republic would be fatally compromised by such a reconciliation. Liberal novels insist that England has come to terms with American independence, and urge Americans to accept their filial ties to the mother country. Conservative novels argue against the establishment of close ties to any monarchy. The possibly radical implications of a conservative plot are most clearly visible in Robinson's *Evelyn*, where the despotic father turns out not to be the protagonist's father at all, but an impostor who wants Evelyn's fortune. As the subtitle of the novel—*The Child of the Revolution*—shows, this kind of daughter cannot possibly have that kind of father. The republican daughter is a literal child of the Revolution.

It is safe to say that historical novels of the Revolution were as much about contemporary relations with England as they were about the Revolution itself. Usually, the paternal action that calls out daughterly resistance is the father's designation of some aristocratic cad (sometimes a cad posing as an aristocrat) as his daughter's future husband, disregarding her own preference for a worthy man. The convergence of the private and public is symbolized by the aristocrat's disrespect for women. He may have a known history as a seducer or, more horridly, may be secretly married; he may even be blackmailing the father. Insisting that a good American woman will always recognize the superiority of an honest republican to a deceitful aristocrat, these novels make love a matter of conjoined head and heart, politics and privacy, national and domestic spheres.

The plot devices summarized here are not unique to women's historical novels; they govern the domestic novels and novels of American manners that women wrote and read much more assiduously than historical fiction. Autocratic fathers ritually defied; snobbish, dandified foils to the all-American male regularly rejected; and paternal infidels brought into the fold—these situations recur in antebellum women's novels set in the everyday world of the present. From an ideological perspective, these genres discovered a more successful way to tell the Revolutionary daughter's story than the Revolutionary novel itself—and, not incidentally, proved the point that women's time to act lay in the present, not the past. In an important way, then, they carried an implicit historical message.

Women protagonists in Revolutionary novels are not fighters; their gentility forbids it. The heroine of *Captain Molly: The Story of a Brave Woman* is the genre's most military-minded protagonist, but all she does is carry water to her husband on the battlefield. None of the real-life cross-dressing female soldiers of the Revolution appear as protagonists in women's novels about the war. Interestingly, however, male protagonists in trouble are often rescued through efforts of decidedly ungenteel women. In *Hope Leslie*, Everell Fletcher's life is saved by Magawisca's intervention (although Everell and Hope Leslie later reciprocate by rescuing her from prison). In Dupuy's *Ashleigh*, the hero is rescued by his faithful Native American servant, who turns out to be a cross-dressed Indian woman; in Sedgwick's *The Linwoods*, a male character is rescued from prison by a middle-aged (hence de-eroticized) manumitted African American woman who changes places with him. This strategy, allotting more active roles to women who are not white and/or not genteel, stresses the middle-classness of the novels' values. There are occasional local-color scenes where lower-class or rural women (frequently the same category) make bandages, feed armies, or melt pots and pans for ammunition; but the protagonists are not part of these communal activities.

Because the upper-class protagonists of Revolutionary novels ally themselves with a middle-class republic while intransigent Tories and Loyalists depart for England or Canada, the books show the United States as a country where the upper class is an archaism; ultimately there will be no upper class at all in this nation. The novels also present relations between the genteel and working classes as an interaction between responsible leadership from the one group and voluntary deference from the other. Men from the working classes, who were, in fact, the Revolution's foot soldiers, are represented as such in the novels and praised lavishly; men and women of this class do much of the actual labor depicted in Revolutionary fictions: hewing wood, drawing water, driving coaches, cooking meals, plowing fields. Clearly, social class and physical type are associated; the more substantial bodies ascribed to lower-class people correlate with less refinement.

Working men and working women also provide choral commentary, offer comic relief, and—speaking many dialects and originating in many nations—stand for the multiform "people" whose destiny is to be governed by an Anglo meritocracy. In these representations the "people"—a group whose boundaries include African Americans but not Indians—preserve their culturally diverse folkways, apparently authorized to retain their particularity so long as they do not encroach on the work of governing or standing for abstract nationality. This is not melting-pot fiction. Its multicultural solution, one might say, is to preserve ethnic differences at the margins of the power structure.

On the whole, the genteel historical tasks of the female protagonist are not very exciting. An exception to this generalization might be Catharine Read (Arnold) Williams's *Aristocracy: or, The Holbey Family* (1832), which invents a conspiracy against President Jefferson, discovered by the protagonist, Adelaide. Even though Adelaide's guardian is centrally involved in the plot, she decides to disclose it to Jefferson. On her way alone at night to warn him, she overcomes her maidenly fear by sternly summoning up her patriotism:

Her thoughts travelled back through the long lapse of ages; she thought of other climes—of the tyranny of power—of feudal times.... "And shall these horrible scenes be renewed in our happy land?" said she mentally, "shall Liberty's last home be polluted by the footsteps of those who would introduce such horror here? Shall the savage scenes of those terrible *border wars* be acted over again in our country? Forbid it Heaven! Better that the lives of all these plotters of '*reform*' as they call it, should at once answer for their crimes, than that such a state of things should exist here." (204)

Disclosing the plot to Jefferson, she saves the nation. Williams, a radical Democrat from Rhode Island, also wrote *The Neutral French; or, The Exiles of Nova Scotia* (1841), a strongly anti-British novel in two volumes about Acadia. Her Acadian heroine, Pauline, returns to France some years after the exile and persuades Louis XVI to support the American side during the Revolution.

"Yes, Sire, I am one of the Neutral French; one of those unfortunate exiles, eighteen thousand of whom were, twenty years since, driven from the province of Nova Scotia, and scattered as paupers among the now United States, contrary to all their pledges to us, and our good treatment guaranteed to the king of France."

"Ha!" exclaimed Louis, "I begin to comprehend. Traitors and monsters of cruelty! was that the way it was done?... Give me a succinct history of this transaction." (2:91)

This Pauline does, although perhaps not succinctly since her account goes on for over four pages. She concludes, "Remember, great King, you are one of God's vicegerents here on earth. . . . By the blood shed in Canada, and now deluging the plains of fair America, be entreated to interpose an arm of power between them and their oppressors!" Louis replies: "Thou hast prevailed; the people thou hast so eloquently plead [sic] for shall be remembered" (2:95).

Both these genteel protagonists affect history via extraordinary acts of public speech whose success, however, depends on the mind-set of the man who listens to it. We have seen in *Naomi* and *Mary Derwent* that a man who cannot think of women as other than a body cannot properly hear her when she speaks. But this does not mean that women are not allowed to speak; on the contrary, they are always allowed to speak—but only so as to dramatize their futility. Eliza Cushing's *Saratoga*, for example, features an argument between the protagonist patriot Catherine Courtland and her Tory father:

"Dear father, every event of my life links me, with fond associations, to this land. . . . How then can I wish evil to her cause! How, when I speak of her afflictions, can I repress the feelings which overflow my heart!"

"Go, go, you are an enthusiast, Kate," said her father, touched by her earnest appeal, but striving to resist its influence. "Your fond, foolish sex have always some darling theme to rave about, and it is fortunate for us, that your fancies are only suffered to waste themselves in words, or the world would be kept forever in an uproar."

"Alas! dear father," said Catherine, laughing, "since it is the only way in which they are permitted to waste themselves, we may be pardoned for making a good use of our privilege; though, I think, were wc less limited, we should soon disprove the assertions of those who predict misrule and anarchy, as a necessary consequence of suffering us to exercise power." (128–129)

The phrase "suffering us to exercise power" catches exactly the dilemma of female historical agency in earlier times. The character must laugh when she says "alas," say "alas" when she laughs, because she is still in the power of a father who reflects and conveys an absolutist social structure. Unless society—that is, the powerful men who run society—is already prepared to listen, a woman's speech is mere spectacle.

The difference that history has made for women along these lines may be gauged from the different stories Stowe invented for *Agnes of Sorrento* (1862) and *The Minister's Wooing* (1859). As already noted in Chapter 7, the fifteenth-century heroine of *Agnes* incarnates female virtue and spirituality. Since these are religious qualities, and the only available religion is Roman Catholicism, Agnes is a believing Catholic. The gaze of licentious clerics transforms her moral and sexual purity into objects of lustful desire; that there is no other way to "take" an attractive woman before Protestantism makes it clear that the body is a spiritual symbol. Agnes is literally taken, kidnapped; kidnapping or captivity tropes the situation of all women in her time and place. Her rescue at this historical juncture requires a masculine force that Stowe connects to emergent Protestantism via Savonarola.

But in *The Minister's Wooing*, set in post-Revolutionary Massachusetts, history has given a similar heroine significant cultural power. Mary Scudder is as pure as Agnes, but far more dynamic. Her energetic enunciation of a pandoctrinal Protestantism effects the conversion (and presumably ensures the salvation) of her lover, James. Her theological views, written out for the benefit of her minister, Samuel Hopkins, and fully reproduced for readers, contrast with his Edwardsian Calvinism and become the novel's Gospel. Protestant republicanism has given women not just the word, which they have always had, but the power of the word as well.

In a sequence full of historical symbolism, Mary also "rescues" her married French Catholic friend, Virginie de Frontegnac, from the lustful intentions of the American would-be despot, Aaron Burr. Mary faces down Burr in a verbal contest, routing him by the ability of her woman's voice to enunciate the truth. This exchange vividly represents the way that the advance of Protestant Christianity has shifted power between the sexes, making a man like Burr at once a political anachronism and a national danger. The appealing but childlike Virginie—marooned in the backwaters of history, where women have no influence, education, or self-esteem—is brought into the historical mainstream by her friendship with Mary. She reads the Bible for herself and matures into the companionate wife that her husband deserves.

Representing public enemies as sexual predators, as in *The Minister's Wooing*, is another typical way to merge the public and private implications of a story. The image of the upper-class male hunting for female victims obviously conjoins the personal and the political, and appears across the full range of American antebellum fiction. In urban melodramas and domestic fictions alike, the womanizing dilettante is always a scion of the upper class. As we recall, aristocracies are foundationally misogynistic. Mary Scudder's immunity to Aaron Burr's sexual magnetism, her willingness to challenge him, model the proper feelings and responses of republican women to would-be despots. In historical fiction the great American villains—Aaron Burr and Benedict Arnold—are always sexual profligates. Eliza Dupuy's novel about Burr, *The Conspirator* (1850), combines his attempts to found an empire in the West with his attempts to possess the daughter of one of his supporters. Ann Stephens's novel about Arnold, serialized as *The Ruling Passion* (1860) and published in book form as *The Rejected Wife* (1863), has Arnold secretly marry a pure maiden from Connecticut, whom he cruelly abandons to seek a bigamous connection with a reigning belle.

If nonrepublican polities were thought to be unfriendly to female development, then it stands to reason that historical novels about the Old World would typically take the form of tragic melodramas in which women were basically passive, the form that, in fact, they do take. Except for two terribly written novels by Sarah M. Howe—*Eustatia: The Sybil's Prophecy* (1852) and *The Soldier's Daughter; or, The Conspirators of La Vendee* (1853)—both light-hearted swashbucklers designed for a good read, the historical novels advance sober models in which the relentless advance of Protestantism is bitterly contested by the joint forces of political and religious despotism. A huge number of stories about imaginary Protestant women martyrs in Catholic Europe appeared in the periodical press. The long shadow of Fox's *Book of Martyrs* no doubt influenced this fiction. Sedgwick, Sigourney, Child—in fact, all the well-known women of letters— seem to have produced at least one martyr story. On the other side, the only explicitly antinativist historical novel I have found is Ellen Key Blunt's *Bread to My Children* (1856), a work about early Maryland, reminding readers that Catholicism is neither new nor dangerous in American life: "And now, freeman [sic] of Maryland! Have we lived to see the day when this memorial is forgotten—this 'pledge' of the Irish peer broken in the bitter persecution which would sweep away every foothold of his countrymen?" (89).

Much more typical is Eliza Dupuy's *The Huguenot Exiles; or, The Times of Louis XIV* (1856), whose author declares herself a descendant of Huguenot refugees in the preface and expresses hope that

At this particular epoch, a work covering the whole ground of the romish persecutions which preceded the revocation of the edict of Nantes, may be acceptable to the public. My object has been to render it popular by giving to its pages all the interest of a vividly told story, while it yet possessed the merit of dealing more in fact than in fiction. . . . If the perusal of these pages induces the uninformed reader to learn anything of the tendency of the Church of Rome, my chief object will be attained. . . . No royal race, imbecile and tyrannical as they usually have been, can compare with the Pope in crime; for no one family could have produced such a series of evil men as have arrogated to themselves the authority of God on earth, and reared a vast ecclesiastical despotism which is the curse of every country in which it has ruled. (v–vi)

The story focuses on a persecuted Huguenot family from Languedoc. The protagonist Eugenia is in love with a son of this house; with a Protestant father, a Catholic mother, and a Protestant lover, she brings into focus the church's struggle to keep desirable females and their property in the fold. When argument fails to move her, the establishment resorts to force, leaving her nothing to do except enunciate a passionate but futile defiance. Imprisoned, brainwashed, hypnotized, and finally about to be forced into a convent, Eugenia is rescued at the altar by her Huguenot lover, with whom she emigrates to America in 1686.

A different approach to the Protestant subject is Sallie Rochester Ford's *Mary Bunyan; The Dreamer's Blind Daughter. A Tale of Religious Persecution* (1860). This simply written novelization of John Bunyan's life for Baptists stresses three important women: Bunyan's wife, Elizabeth; his daughter Mary (who loves William Dormer); and Elizabeth Gaunt, a woman preacher. Elizabeth Bunyan endures her husband's twelve-year imprisonment while keeping the household together; Mary Bunyan endures her father's imprisonment, takes over for her mother when the mother is overcome with grief and fatigue, and, later, endures separation from William, whose execution, however, sends her into a fatal decline; Elizabeth Gaunt, the novel's most vocal woman, is martyred.

The doubly negative impact of history on women at this historical moment—through their men, and in their own lives—could not be plainer. Each woman briefly gets the power to speak, but to no avail. The timid wife rouses in her husband's behalf—"How can she falter when her husband's life is at stake? No, no; she could face judges and justices, kings and courtiers—yea, the assembled world, to plead for her innocent husband" (123)—but the justices laugh at her. Daughter Mary tries to petition the king himself, who is momentarily stimulated by her beauty ("Her kerchief is of snow-white, and the nobleman who dashes by, turns his head to look on that symmetrical form, so plainly, yet so chastely clad, which, with modest, lady-like air, keeps pace with the rough countryman at her side" [249]) but loses interest when he realizes that she is blind. Elizabeth Gaunt dies because she preaches.

Therese Albertine Robinson produced two historical novels about lesser-known European countries showing that women in nations out of the mainstream were even worse off than women in countries where Protestantism was developing. *Heloise; or, The Unrevealed Secret* (1850) and *Life's Discipline: A Tale of the Annals of Hungary* (1851) are historical novels about Russia and Hungary, respectively; both feature beautiful heroines whose beauty only makes them men's prey, and who live to be rescued from one man by another. The staple and important point of this fiction is that female beauty does not guarantee female power.

The trope of female captivity also surfaces in classical fiction, where

Christian maidens representing the people are subject to the lustful desires of Roman aristocrats. But although women published many short stories on this model, only a few wrote novels of ancient history. Only a few men did, too: the type required more scholarship and accuracy than most writers male or female could muster. Excluding Fanny Wright's 1822 polemic against organized religion couched as a classical fantasy (*A Few Days in Athens*), I find only three woman-authored novels of classical history: Lydia Maria Child's *Philothea* (1836), Harriet Vaughan Cheney's *Confessions of an Early Martyr* (1846), and Eliza Buckminster Lee's *Parthenia; or, The Last Days of Paganism* (1858). Cheney's *Confessions* is the slightest of these productions; set in Nero's Rome, it is noteworthy only because it establishes the foundations for the aristocratic (male) narrator's conversion in the training he received from two women. His Greek mother, enlightened by "the wisdom of Socrates and Plato," taught him "to look higher than the gods of marble and the deities of earth, and in a great First Cause, though mysterious and indefinite, to discern the source of nature and the fountain of all intelligence" (7); his Jewish nurse instructed him in knowledge of "the great Being, whom she devoutly worshipped" (11).

Parthenia, set in the fourth century A.D., deals with the Emperor Julian (the Apostate, 331?–363), who renounced Christianity and tried to return the empire to paganism. Like *Naomi*, this novel is bifurcated between lengthy textbook presentations of relevant history and the plot line; the history is mainly military and the plot is romantic. Perhaps influenced by the association of classical literature with Plato, the action unfolds mainly as a series of discussions among characters. In *Parthenia*, Lee gives us a typically beautiful and sublimely virtuous protagonist, here a priestess of Athena who falls in love with Julian when he visits Athens. For his part, Julian comes as close to falling in love with her as the lack of women in the record of his life, and the lack of an ideology of love in his religion, will allow. In fact, Julian's failure or inability to love becomes the hinge between his historical plot and Parthenia's romance. When Julian asks Parthenia to marry him, she rejects him even though she loves him, because—having become a Christian while he was at war—she recognizes the inadequacy of his feeling for her. His story continues on its historically destined way, and she enters a convent.

Throughout the novel as well as in her preface, Lee attempts to exonerate Julian's apostasy for a Christian readership, attributing it in proto-Lutheran terms to his disgust with religious shams and excesses, his innately Puritan (and hence fundamentally admirable) temperament. At the same time, however, being an aristocrat, Julian cannot accept Christ's low birth or the democratic implications of his interest in the poor, weak, and mild: "he could not admit the idea of a divine nature in the humble form of a servant, with a crown of thorns" (35). *Parthenia* also looks for a Christianity different from Roman practice—specifically (and consistent with Lee's other work) a practice oblivious to the public sphere, rooted in the private, female, domain. When Julian objects that the new religion had allowed the murder of his family, his interlocutor—notably for Lee's woman-centered approach, the empress Eusebia—responds, "All those were cruel acts of state policy.... We must look to private life for reforms; the humble religion of Jesus begins there. All women should be Christians" (40). To which Julian responds like a true Roman: "Yes, the new faith is suited to women, and to men like women.... It is worthy of the abject, the cowardly" (40).

More than one woman instructs Julian in the connection between the Christian and the womanly. Christianity alone, he learns, "has given woman her true position. With you Romans, and even with the refined Athenians, we were domestic slaves;—this was not enough degradation for us, and you have added Asiatic luxury to our effeminacy, to sink us still lower. Had not Christ, with tender and beautiful regard for woman, raised her up the equal and friend of man, how hopeless had been our condition!" (304). And Parthenia herself is "won to belief in the divine origin of [the] Christian religion, when I found it admitted women to equal privileges with man,—gave her a soul, and made her the partner of man's serious occupations, rather than the slave of his passions" (235). Julian is thus right to diagnose Christianity as a woman's religion, and given his martial character he is destined to reject it. He "had never dreamed of anything sacred in woman" and is not ready to contemplate the idea. "That Christian idea had but just begun to penetrate through the sensualism of Heathenism.... The beautiful Athenian was the only woman that he would have raised to the throne, and that not altogether because he loved or esteemed her, but because she had been priestess of Pallas Athena" (359). To Parthenia Julian's offer is "a glimpse into the paradise which the Grecian and Christian maiden, in moments of joy, had alike dreamed of. Could she take the first enchanted step?" The answer is, "Alas, no! the two-edged sword of conscience barred the entrance. She turned from it,—and a momentary, but almost insupportable, pang of grief shot through her heart.... She saw that the Emperor sought her more as an ornament for the pageantry of his worship, than for herself alone. Her heart beat calmly again" (361, 364).

Parthenia's withdrawal to the convent may be thought of as a gesture of voluntary self-immolation, by which the woman ahead of her time expresses her awareness that history is not yet ready for her. The woman who tells Julian that all women should be Christian also says that "when women are really Christian in heart and in truth, they will attain their true position, and take their part in the great events of changing society.... When women are thoroughly Christian, they will be the mothers of princes "worthy to reign" (166–167). But when will the day come? It has not come at the end of *Parthenia* and, it seems safe to say, Lee did not think it had come in 1858 when she published the novel.

Child's *Philothea* begins in Periclean Athens and anachronistically combines many well-known figures from Greek political and cultural history who lived over two centuries. As the author writes in her preface, she means the book as a fantasy, not as a sober history. Philothea, protagonist of the main plot, is granddaughter of the philosopher Anaxagorus, while Eudora, protagonist of the subplot, is ward of the sculptor Phidias and object of the lustful attentions of the statesman Alcibiades. In a number of lengthy dialogues Child has historical characters enunciate her opinions on various subjects that—as reviewers noted from the first—pertain more to current affairs than to classical Greece. The theology is transcendental, the politics conservative, especially where women are concerned. The only cultural options for women in this period, according to Child, were marriage and republican goodwifery or sexual libertinage and notoriety. In this context, the goodwife is the only allowable choice—and more significantly, the brighter coming day does not seem to include any change in women's condition; they serve the polity best in lives of domestic seclusion devoted to their husbands. This position is elaborated early on in the novel when Philothea meets Aspasia and verbally chastises her.

The celebrated Aspasia was an elegant and voluptuous Ionian, who succeeded admirably in pleasing the good taste of the Athenians, while she ministered to their vanity and their vices. The wise and good lamented the universal depravity of manners, sanctioned by her influence; but a people so gay, so ardent, so intensely enamoured of the beautiful, readily acknowledged the sway of an eloquent and fascinating woman, who carefully preserved the appearance of decorum. Like the Gabrielles and Pompadours of modern times, Aspasia obtained present admiration and future fame, while hundreds of better women were neglected and forgotten. (20)

The presence of this bad woman allows the novelist to abandon, at least descriptively, the modesty and frugality she usually endorses:

A garland of golden leaves, with large drops of pearl, was interwoven among the glossy braids of her hair, and rested on her forehead.

She wore a robe of rich Milesian purple, the folds of which were confined on one shoulder within a broad ring of gold, curiously wrought; on the other they were fastened by a beautiful cameo, representing the head of Pericles. . . .

[Her] couch rested on two sphinxes of gold and ivory, over which the purple drapery fell in rich and massive folds. In one corner, a pedestal of Egyptian marble supported an alabaster vase, on the edge of which were two doves, exquisitely carved, one just raising his head, the other stooping to drink. On a similar stand, at the other side, stood a peacock, glittering with many coloured gems. The head lowered upon the breast formed the handle; while here and there, among the brilliant tail feathers, appeared a languid flame slowly burning away the perfumed oil, with which the bird was filled. (24, 27)

As Aspasia and Philothea converse, the courtesan says, "They told me I should find you pure and child-like; with a soul from which poetry sparkled, like moonlight on the waters. I did not know that wisdom and philosophy lay concealed in its depths" (28). Philothea answers with a challenge: "When men talk of Aspasia the beautiful and gifted, will they add, Aspasia the good—the happy—the innocent?" (30).

A slight quivering about Aspasia's lips betrayed emotion crowded back upon the heart.... With impressive kindness, the maiden continued ... "Beautiful and gifted one! Listen to the voice that tries to win you back to innocence and truth! Give your heart up to it, as a little child led by its mother's hand! Then shall the flowers again breathe poetry, and the stars move in music. . . . No longer seek popularity by flattering the vanity, or ministering to the passions of the Athenians. Let young men hear the praise of virtue from the lips of beauty. Let them see religion married to immortal genius. Tell them it is ignoble to barter the heart's wealth for heaps of coin—that love weaves a simple wreath of his own bright hopes, stronger than massive chains of gold. Urge Pericles to prize the good of Athens more than the applause of its populace—to value the permanence of her free institutions more than the splendour of her edifices. Oh, lady, never, never, had any mortal such power to do good!" (32–33).

After shedding a few sentimental tears over her lost virtue, Aspasia resumes her public manner, and Philothea retreats into obscurity, leaving Athens to tend first her ailing grandfather and then her ailing husband. They die, and so does she. While of course the main premise of a historical novel is that its protagonists, if they are invented figures, must have been unknown to the record—and while, therefore, Philothea's obscurity is entirely appropriate—the book nevertheless brings into view a curious general conundrum in women's historical novels. The implication of the historical narrative that they all espoused was that women were becoming increasingly influential in public affairs, which means that they had not been important in the past. In brief: there were no women in the historical record. Aspasia shows that this is not so. Although to be sure their numbers are few, women have been powerful in history. How to square these women with the historical narrative was the question whenever one of these characters came into a story. Child's answer seems to be that these women, because they sacrificed their essential womanliness for power, ceased to be women when they became influential. In terms of the progress of history, they count against themselves, because they show to what depths a woman had to stoop in order to attain the heights.

Whenever the focus of a story is directly on a powerful woman, the question demands answering, and a veritable obsession with female sovereigns and royal consorts throughout the antebellum era means that the question is raised again and again. The most frequent answer in American writing seems to be that these women were not really powerful at all, but only seemed to be so. Two women, for example, wrote about Joanna I (1326–1382), Queen of Naples from 1343 to 1381, who was imprisoned and eventually executed by her adopted son: Louisa J. Hall published *Joanna of Naples* (1838), and Elizabeth Ellet brought out *Scenes in the Life of Joanna of Sicily* (1840). Both writers used Anna Jameson's *Lives of the Female Sovereigns* (1831) as a source, and neither manifested any interest in Joanna's politics and achievements. They stressed the domestic tragedy and Joanna's sentimental imprisonment, thereby depriving her of whatever power she may have exerted in historical fact.

The novelist to grapple most fully with the problem of prominent women was Ann Sophia Stephens, who serialized several novels about the queens of England using Agnes Strickland's multivolume histories and Shakespeare's Tudor plays for her main sources. These novels include *Alice Copley* (book, 1844) about Mary Tudor; *Clara* (serial, 1844) about Elizabeth Woodbridge, widow of Henry IV, and her daughter Elizabeth, wife-to-be of Richard of Gloucester (Richard III-to-be); *Anne Boleyn* (serial, 1846) about the second wife of Henry VIII; *The King's Legacy* (serial, 1846), a novella about Lady Jane Grey, queen briefly before Mary Tudor; *The Tradesman's Boast* (serial and book, 1846) about Edward IV, Queen Elizabeth, Edward's mistress Jane Shore, the imprisoned Henry VII and his exiled wife Margaret of Anjou; *The Lady Mary* (serial, 1847) about Mary Talbot, Eleanor Howard, and Anne Boleyn; *Lost and Found* (serial, 1848) about Charles II, his Portuguese queen, and his mistress; and *The Royal Sisters* (serial, 1857) about Mary and Elizabeth Tudor. Strickland wrote about these women as people with political and religious agendas of their own that significantly affected British history. Stephens denies them all political power and conscious political motivation. For them, everything was private and erotic; the private life is decoupled from the public sphere, shown to be entirely beside the point of politics and history. These novels, in effect, take the opposite tack from the republican novel with its insistence that the personal is always political. But the insistence that celebrated women of the past were only seemingly powerful does not in the least contradict the republican narrative; rather, it approaches the story from the other side of the coin—considering not what women are finally becoming, but what they historically had been.

The queens in Stephens's novels live in constant thrall to the shallow sexual whims of their partners, whose passions are strong but transient. Sexual allure is all these royal women have to trade with, and this is a currency of little value. They dress extravagantly, adorn themselves with priceless jewels, style their hair bewitchingly—all of this described at a length that makes the term "costume drama" most appropriate—exert every feminine wile, and tear their passions to tatters in a succession of flamboyant speeches. Still, kings do what they always meant to, appropriating or discarding partners as they please. But at the same time, and usually through contrast with a pure, innocent foil, Stephens shows these victimized women as passionate and vain, victims of their own self-misunderstandings as well as kingly inconstancy. To play by these rules, she seems to say, is to die by them. This is the old seduction motif writ large.

Stephens's grandiloquent Tudor novels carefully circuit around the one indubitably powerful female monarch whose story could not be forced into this erotic pattern. *The Royal Sisters* ends with Elizabeth's ascension. Elsewhere, the pattern is ruthlessly imposed. *Alice Copley* makes Mary Tudor the aging, peevish, jealous wife of Philip of Spain (who is attempting to seduce the pure and Protestant Alice), construing Mary's anti-Protestantism as pure sexual jealousy. In *Anne Boleyn*, Stephens acknowledges that when Henry divorced Catherine to marry Anne he brought the Reformation to England, but insists that Anne had no part in this world-shaking result:

How weak and fragile a thing has sometimes instigated those great events that have stamped themselves on the history of nations, as it were, with a footprint of iron. To the lovely girl whom we left feeble and broken-hearted upon the couch of pain, may be traced that political, social, and religious convulsion that shook the church of Rome to its centre, and rescued a great kingdom from her sway centuries before it could have been accomplished by the natural progress of mind. Passion after all is sometimes stronger than intellect. (*Peterson's,* 10:206)

To be fair, one must observe that Stephens makes Henry, too, the object, not the subject, of historical force, the pawn of his own passions appropriated by an overriding Providence for its own purposes.

Stephens's melodrama mainly eschews the formal strategies of didacticism while working like most melodrama to implement a didactic point. She represents these regal women as bad or useless or miserable or weak because, in their time, history and women had not yet come into productive alignment. She simultaneously fully exploits the glamour of the nonbourgeois, nonrepublican, non-Protestant image of the female and dismantles any relation between this image and female power. Also in most of these novels, a good, pure, pious, innocent, virtuous, commoner Protestant, if not actually Protestant, woman somehow escapes the toils of the monarch and monarchical exhibition and thereby escapes capture by history. Sometimes, independent, active, resourceful, bourgeois counterexamples enter the narrative to remind readers of where history is going. *The Tradesman's Boast*, for example, portrays the merchant and working classes of London united to help Margaret of Anjou return to France after her failed attempt to rejoin and free her husband; the same novel also depicts Jane Shore, Edward IV's bourgeois married mistress, as a class traitor.

In 1857 Stephens serialized a novel about women in the French Revolution—*The Belle of Liège*, which opposes a demonized radical Theroigne de Merincourt and a sentimentalized Marie Antoinette. Unlike Stephens's regal English queens and Marie Antoinette herself, Theroigne is highly effective politically, but to awful effect, and only because she desires revenge on the count who seduced and abandoned her. Agreeing that callous aristocratic behavior toward simple rural maidens is ample justification for the uprising against them, Stephens still makes Theroigne herself apolitical. "Her genius, her beauty, everything was given up to the one grand idea of vengeance on the caste that had insulted her, on the man who had wronged her" (*Peterson's*, 32:338).

A political interpretation insinuates itself into the plot when Theroigne tells her seducer, Maury, that "the crimes of aristocracy have trampled down the bosom of France, as you have trodden on my heart" (343); the populace, feminized vis-à-vis the masculine aristocracy, is well represented by a jilted woman. But when Theroigne comes to power and exercises vengeance against her seducer by inciting the female mob against Marie Antoinette (who is loved, but chastely, by Maury), according to Stephens she and the mob cease to be women. The analysis is sexual but not political; whoever has power is male. Repeated depictions of female futility and masculine arrogance show that until history finds an appropriate public space for women and produces women who can fill that space *as women*, women will remain politically and personally undeveloped. This requires much more than a change of rulers, it requires a thorough renovation of the polity in the direction of republican egalitarianism—in the direction, that is to say, of the Christian republic currently epitomized in the United States.

This is exactly what history taught about women excluded from the Protestant-republican dispensation.

The relative scarcity of biblical novels does not mean lack of interest in Bible history. Retellings of Bible stories permeated the culture. The press published innumerable biographies of biblical characters in prose and poetry and circulated countless engravings of Bible scenes. Depictions of biblical women in various media made up an archive of important documents for female character formation, which constitutes a body of material overlapping with, and almost certainly more extensive than, the texts discussed in this study. But Bible stories were thought to be narratives or representations of true history, not fiction. Reverence for the Bible and awareness of its embattled status as literal truth kept people from writing fiction based on it. Joseph Holt Ingraham had a great success with a novel of biblical spectacle about the life of Christ, *The Prince of the House of David* (1855), which he followed with *The Pillar of Fire* (1859), about Moses; but few other antebellum writers attempted to work this lode.

The only woman writer to try, it seems, undertook the work for the prudently didactic end of familiarizing students with everyday Hebrew life. Maria Tolman Richards, a Baptist, first published biblical fiction in periodicals, and then collected it as *Life in Judea* (1854); *Life in Israel* (1857); and *The Year of the Jubilee* (1858). The preface to *Life in Israel* justified fictional treatment of the Bible on the grounds that it would make readers feel comfortable with biblical history. "It is to be feared," she wrote, "that, in the mind of the young, the various scenes and events of Scripture are too often but a series of statistical facts and isolated abstractions" (viii). She aimed "to supply parallel details of local and circumstantial character, which may serve to unfold some of the prominent eras of Biblical history, and to invest with new interest the reading of the Bible" (ix). The preface explained how carefully she dealt with sacred materials:

The characters employed are of three classes: those of sacred history, of profane history, and of imagination. With regard to the first, or Scripture characters, the writer has not presumed to use them, except so far as they are presented in the Sacred Word. . . Two or three slight deviations from this rule will be explained by notes in their appropriate places. The characters of profane history, in their natural traits and public acts, have been exhibited strictly in accordance with the records concerning them; while, in their private relations, they have been made to subserve the particular design of the writer in their introduction. The imaginary characters have been drawn with special reference to the development of the spirit of the time in which they are represented. (ix)

The preface also cites fifteen major sources besides the Bible. The result interweaves biblical event with events in contemporaneous kingdoms and with a detailed, plausible picture of everyday life in biblical lands conveying the experience of being an Israelite when scriptural events unfolded. The imaginative work here consists not in inventing terrific scenes of thrills and agony, but the reverse—creating domestic and familiar scenes of everyday Hebrew life to make readers feel at home among them. To thus bourgeoisify and domesticate the remote ordinary, Richards focuses on women and families in her two *Life* books. Along with presumably accurate details of dress, home furnishings, cookery, and the like, the values are thoroughly nineteenth century.

In general, biblical history was thought to constitute the one exception to the idea that there were no prominent good women in history. As a prophecy of the coming of Protestant republicanism, the Bible was interpreted as a storehouse of female characters who were both good and important. Richards's novella, *The Year of the Jubilee*, is a narrative retelling of the story of Deborah the lawgiver, poet, and military leader (Judges 4 and 5), a favorite character among progressive women whether they supported the franchise or not. There is no mistaking the women's rights message in this respectful and faithful rephrasing of the sacred text. But here the historical novel has reached its outermost limit, since the history recounted by the writer is no longer imaginary.

The Tyrants' Victims

WOMEN ARE NOT GENERALLY ASSOCIATED with the stage in antebellum America; yet, if the category "drama" covers works written for production that were never commercially performed and poetic dramas meant only for reading, one finds a substantial number of historical plays published by women before the Civil War. Including a few sacred dramas, I have found about thirty, by perhaps two dozen women, on topics ranging through biblical, classical, European, and American history. These plays, though composed in the context of an emergent professional theater, also reflected the habits of an extensive parlor culture dependent on recitations and amateur theatricals. As early as the 1790s schoolteachers began to compose dramatic pieces for student performances. Susanna Rowson's *Present for Young Ladies*, we recall, printed several student dialogues, and the records of Sarah Pierce's Litchfield Academy include manuscripts of two "sacred dramas"—a didactic genre invented by the Englishwoman Hannah More—about Ruth and Jephtha's Daughter.

If only a small fraction of this dramatic material got into print, a smaller fraction still was performed commercially, and some of what was performed has been lost, including Annie Kemble Hatton's *Tammany* (the first "Indian" play), staged in 1794, and Elizabeth Oakes Smith's *The Roman Tribute; or, Attila the Hun*, of which extensive quotation and plot summary in Rufus Griswold's *Poetry of American Women* provide the best record. Among the small number of American women who devoted themselves to the professional theater there is a faint trail of historical and political production. Louisa Medina, the most active of these women, adapted and staged at least eleven novels including Bulwer Lytton's historical *Last Days of Pompeii* in 1835. Anna Cora Mowatt (whose comedy of manners *Fashion* made a splash in the 1840s) wrote, staged, and starred in *Armand; or The Peer and the Peasant*, set in Louis XV's France, which played in England and the United States in 1847, and was published in 1855. Charlotte Barnes Connor's *Octavia Brigaldi*, whose fifteenth-century Milan setting masked its treatment of the Beauchamp scandal that rocked Frankfort, Kentucky, in 1825, was produced in New York in 1837 and in England a few years later. An extremely up-to-date play about John Brown by a Mrs. J. C. Swayze was staged in New York in 1859.

Some of the extant published but unperformed plays seem to have been designed for commercial production. *The Fair Americans*, about the War of 1812, by the Philadelphian Mary Carr (later Clarke)—the play is also known to theater historians by its subtitle, *Return from the Camp*—interpolates songs and stage business and prints detailed stage directions; Caroline Keteltas's *Last of the Plantagenets* (about Richard III) signals its ambitions through a prologue for the lead actor. According to Delia Bacon's biographer, her *The Bride of Fort Edward* (about Jane McCrea) was originally composed for a specific actress. Other historical plays by women professionals like Mercy Otis Warren, Elizabeth Ellet, Caroline Gilman, Sarah Hale, and Louisa McCord, as well as by occasional writers like Margaretta Faugères, Charlotte Barnes Connor, Maria Henrietta Pinckney, Sarah Pogson, and Harriette Fanning Read, were designed as closet verse from the first. Like historical novels, these plays connect fictional characters to important historical events and notable personages. But whereas fictional characters in novels are usually everyday people who make a temporary, fortuitous connection with the historically significant, fictional characters in plays are usually members of a ruling family—especially wives and daughters—whose lives are tragically ruled by history.

Because obligatory patriotism characterized the American theater throughout the antebellum decades, there is a quasi-historical overlay in some of these plays that blurs the line between the cosmetic and the structural in historical drama. Take, for example, Frances Wright's *Altorf*, staged in New York in 1819 and published in Philadelphia the same year. This play is set in the Alps during the wars between Swiss mountaineers and the Austrian Empire; according to Wright's preface, it cannot be fully understood unless one is familiar with "the insurrection of the Swiss cantons in the fourteenth century; the violent and wanton tyranny exercised by Austria and her Deputies over that intrepid race of Mountaineers; and the spirit of heroic firmness with which they rose against that tyranny" (v). Wright also attributes the play's New York success to American ideology and history: "America is the land of liberty. Here is the country where Truth may lift her voice without fear;—where the words of Freedom may not only be read in the closet, but heard from the stage. England pretends to be an unshackled press; but there is not a stage in England from which the dramatist might breathe the sentiments of enlightened patriotism and republican liberty" (iv). The prologue specifically interprets the play's story as an analog to the history of the United States:

The Tyrants' Victims

No royal pageantry this night displayed
Crowds your Columbian stage with vain parade. . . .
A nobler inspiration wakes the lyre
'Tis liberty's unconquerable fire,
That liberty for which our fathers bled
When Washington their free battalions led.
Like them, Helvetia's sons, a hardy race,
Toiled at the plow, or laboured in the chace:
Obscure but blest, until a tyrant's hand
Stretched its unhallowed grasp over their rugged land . . .
And shall the tale of liberty be told
To ears unwilling and to bosoms cold? . . .
Freedom, that roused the poet's kindling art,
Will touch the springs of each Columbian heart,
And will associate with magic spell
The name of Washington with that of Tell. (2)

But in fact, Tell's name is not spoken in the play, which develops a psycho-
logical romance about an emotionally unstable Byronic hero, whose er-
ratic behavior has fatal consequences for the two women who love him.
Since this at best ambiguous hero is a republican, the play cannot really be
doing the political work the author claims for it. More likely, she was wrap-
ping it in the national banner to win audience approval and using the Swiss
setting for its romantic, rather than historical, resonance.

If *Altorf* falls just outside the classification "historical," Caroline Lee
Hentz's Swiss play, *Constance of Werdenberg; or, The Heroes of Switzerland*, falls just within it. According to Quinn, this play was performed in
1832; the (Macon) *Georgia Citizen* published it in five installments in April
and May of 1850, after Hentz had scored a big literary success with her
domestic novel *Linda*. In *Constance*, real historical figures appear and others are talked about—Gessler, Landenberg, Melchtal. Real battles are
fought. "The tyrant's fallen! Gessler, the haughty, lies / Powerless, trans-
fixed by Tell's avenging hand." Hentz's political sentiments and her praise
of Swiss republican intrepdity are virtually identical to Wright's:

Thou know'st how long Helvetia's freeborn sons,
Have groaned beneath imperial Albert's yoke
How long his haughty delegates have scourged
Our lofty peasants, monarchs of the soul,
Bold dwellers of the hills, with spirits high
And tameless as the eagles of the cliffs;
They spurn the hand, that presses bondage on them.
(*Georgia Citizen*, 4 Apr. 1850)

189

Most of these historical plays are formally similar. Their five-act structures, blank verse, soliloquies, asides to the audience, eavesdropping, expository openings, reports of offstage action, and occasional prose-speaking comic characters funnel Shakespeare through eighteenth-century neoclassicism and echo Joseph Addison's *Cato* (1713). Recombinations of Shakespeare's plot devices are ubiquitous, as are rewritings of his lines, and echoes of his tragic characters. The plot of Elizabeth Eller's *Teresa Contarini*, for example, blends *King Lear* with *Julius Caesar* and *Romeo and Juliet*; Margaretta Faugeres's *Belisarius* makes the blinded Roman hero into a philosophic King Lear and models his adversary, the Empress Theodora, on Lear's wicked daughters. *Belisarius* opens with a melancholy soliloquy by the Emperor Justinian adapting the language of Henry V on the eve of Agincourt to Justinian's situation as a ruler always threatened by treachery:

> The precious *gale*, that through the lattice blows
> On the tir'd body of some sleeping slave,
> (When weary day hath sunk beneath the main)
> Cools the high ferment of his feverous blood,
> And gives *him* slumbers sweeter; but to *me*
> Its gentle whisperings seem like sounds of death—
> From dreams of *mutiny*, and *schemes*, and *murder*,
> I start. (7–8)

Since Shakespeare had long been recognized as the greatest writer in English, this allusive network may be thought of either as signaling extraordinary cultural presumption on the part of women writers or, on the contrary, as suggesting that the trail he had blazed was now open to all. Either way, the publication of these historical dramatic poems points to the highest level of literary aspiration (though not necessarily of literary achievement) among antebellum women. Writing about Elizabeth Oakes Smith's verse tragedy, *The Roman Tribute*, approving her ambition and achievement, Rufus Griswold called dramatic poetry "the field which next to the epic is highest in the domain of literary art" (179).

For a late-twentieth-century reader these verse plays often seem to have all the melodramatic bombast of Shakespeare's plays and none of their poetry; yet perhaps the programmatic refusal of ordinary language, the florid grandiosity, is just what literate antebellum Americans might have thought of when they thought of high literary art. Clearly, writing of this kind liberates the writer from the mundanity of the lyric domestic forms that are so much more typical of women poets. Indeed, if women's lives were more embedded in concrete particulars than men's, if therefore a domestic vernacular literature supposedly suited their constricted experience and intellectual range, the very showiness of these plays might make a counterstatement. What was repressed or suppressed elsewhere could come out safely here, all the more since—as in the historical novels discussed in Chapter 8—the dramatic outbursts of female rhetoric were cordoned into earlier historical eras and shown as futile anyway.

For, obsessively, these plays represent, not the silencing of women, but the futility of their speech. As we have already seen in Chapter 8, whatever power a speaking woman may have depends on the state of the society in which she talks. Scenes of lengthy but futile female vocality in historical novels show that women were allotted the power of speech in earlier historical epochs precisely because such epochs valued brute force, not the word. The word, the pen, Christ, republics, women: all come to power together; and though they are together changing the world, the world must already have changed if they are capable of exerting power.

If historical novels show earlier women as ineffectively noisy, historical plays do so even more. The chief scenes in historical dramas featuring women involve pleading with or defying tyrants. The women's voices match or overmatch the men's, but words count for nothing when their bodies are all they have to back up their words. In many plays the woman arrays herself in her most attractive garb for these scenes of entreaty, hoping to make her femininity work for her. But the strategy, which parades her body before the despot, only reminds him that she is both attractive and weak, therefore available as a possession and negligible as an adversary. If she lacks physical allure, she is unable to gain a hearing from the tyrant in the first place. She must be beautiful to catch his eye; having caught his eye, she cannot make him take her words seriously. She is negated in advance. Negated, she talks more; the more sound, the less power. In one historical tragedy after another, quantities of female sound and fury fill the scene in order to signify nothing; the representation of that nullity is the point of the scene.

Thematically, too, as the plays exhibit the historical inefficacy of the female voice at some length, dramatic excursions allow the woman writer herself (paradoxically, perhaps) to venture far beyond the boundaries of the futile female voice in history. For the rocks against which women's voices shatter and foam are the figures of powerful males, and more than any other genre in which historical writing is conducted, drama lets women write for and in this very voice of masculine power. Here is not the voice of Reason that, though previously available only to men, was adjudged a universal property in Enlightenment thought and triumphantly claimed by women. Here is rather something truly and exclusively male—man at his uniquely worst, man the tyrant, man the repository and expression of deadly godless force. In historical plays, women writers could play at being such a man and enunciate tyrannical bombast of the deepest dye. The most extreme instance here is Maria Henrietta Pinckney's representation of Agathocles (361?–289 B.C.), tyrant of Syracuse, the subject of *A Tyrant's Victims*, published in her anonymous *Essays, Religious, Moral, Dramatic, and Poetical; Addressed to Youth; and Published for a Benevolent Purpose* (1818), "by a Lady."

The book is dedicated to Edward Pinckney, "youthful son of a genuine patriot," whom the author hopes will prove himself "like his father, an ornament to his country, name, and profession"; the play's introduction explains:

The character of Agathocles must create in every mind detestation of tyrannical power; and at the same time impress it with a strong conviction, that such monsters are permitted to rule with unlimited sway, for a while, that mankind may abhor their enormities, and by contrasting the illustrious qualities of a Scipio, a Paulus Aemelius, an Alfred, a Washington, with an Agathocles, a Nero, or a Napoleon Buonoparte, love true virtue and magnanimity.... To present to youth pictures of imperfect virtue, because uncertain of immortality; or the consequences of vicious passions, unrestrained by pure religion and morality, either in examples from the ancient or modern world—I conceive to be the best motive for dramatic exhibitions. It has governed my humble endeavors. (114)

Agathocles is center stage for most of the production with lines like: "How many citizens were massacred / To gratify my soaring ambition? / More—yet more sacrifice it demands" (119); and, "Tools of my power, when useless, they're destroyed / Friend, foe or child, ambition only knows / As they may serve its mighty purpose" (154).

The tyrannical rant of men is not empty words, however. Behind it lies the fact of tyrannical brute force. The tyrant's language is authentic testimony to his power. If female rhetoric in these plays is more strenuous, it is because it points to nothing beyond itself. The signifiers of the victim's rhetoric are ungrounded; the rhetoric turns inward. The woman raves, the tyrant speaks all too truly. In a world run by tyrants, women go insane. This is the political and historical meaning of conventional female madness in these antebellum dramatic representations. At the same time—and this point must not be overlooked—these plays offered splendid opportunities for actresses to exhibit themselves and their histrionic talents. As citizens of a later historical epoch, the actresses always conveyed a historical contrast between the historical women in the plays and the contemporary women speaking for them.

Dramatic writing by American women begins with Mercy Otis Warren's pre-Revolutionary political satires, *The Adulateur*, *The Defeat*, and *The*

Group, published in Massachusetts newspapers between 1772 and 1775. These plays, exposing the malfeasance of royal appointees, were designed to win public opinion over to the patriot cause. Not meant for the stage but for the press, they helped forge a vital link between print and resistance in the Revolutionary period. In the turmoil after the Revolution, Warren wrote two historical verse tragedies, *The Ladies of Castile* and *The Sack of Rome*, published in her *Poems, Dramatic and Miscellaneous* (1790). Although neither play had American subject matter, both were suffused with Warren's anxiety about the future of the republic.

According to her preface to *The Sack of Rome*, the play was meant to teach readers to "shun the luxurious vices, or the absurd systems of policy, which have frequently corrupted, distracted, and ruined the best constituted republics" (10). She writes in the preface to *The Ladies of Castile* that its events "will ever be interesting to an American ear, so long as they triumph in their independence, pride themselves in the principles that instigated their patriots, and glory in the characters of their heroes, whose valour completed a revolution that will be the wonder of ages" (100). The approach implies that the American Revolution was fought not only for living Americans and their posterity, but for all who have struggled for independence throughout history. The American Revolution is the redemptive moment of all secular history, and to preserve its fruit—the United States—is the vital obligation of every son and daughter of the republic.

Published in a book rather than the newspapers, these didactic plays address an elite audience of the politically powerful (and their spouses), not the people at large. Exemplifying early American republican ideology to perfection, both insist that the survival of any form of government depends on the virtue of its leaders—their self-discipline, their ability to put the welfare of the polity ahead of their own passions. More precisely, the ruling passion of leaders should be the welfare of the state. Both plays show what happens to a state whose governors cannot govern themselves. It is not that a vicious public official will, sooner or later, cross the line between private and public and harm the state. Rather, every act of a public official is already public; there is no line to cross.

In *The Sack of Rome*, when the emperor Valentinian rapes the virtuous matron Ardelia (who then commits suicide, as a virtuous Roman wife must do), he is killed in reprisal by Ardelia's husband, Petronius Maximus. Maximus, becoming emperor himself, attempts to force Valentinian's widow Edoxia into marriage; in outraged fury, she opens the city of Rome to Genseric, king of the Vandals, bringing about both the city's downfall and her own. Not the barbarian invader himself, but a prior series of self-indulgent acts, Edoxia's included, destroys the city. These acts exemplify a widespread loss of civic virtue in fifth-century Rome. When Genseric states, toward the end of the play, that "'Tis time to rase her from the list of nations, / And blast the world no more by Roman crimes" (83), he is right.

The Sack of Rome has a complement of virtuous Romans who enunciate a counterethic to that prevailing in the emperor's house, of whom the most important is Gaudentius. Rome, he says,

> Might yet emerge and more illustrious shine,
> If party rage and luxury should cease,
> And peace give time to make a just reform
> Through each corrupted channel of the law;
> Or if simplicity again returns,
> And government more energy assumes. (16)

The play has only two women characters (Ardelia's rape and suicide occur offstage, and she never appears): the Empress Eudoxia and her daughter Eudocia, the latter a passive ingenue but the former an agent in her own right. Before opening the city's gates to Genseric she listens to, but rejects, Gaudentius's argument:

> Though great thy wrongs, much greater must thou fear,
> If Genseric's rapacious brutal hosts
> Should enter Italy—my sovereign forbear,
> And like the gods, benignantly forgive;
> Nor let resentment kindle up anew
> The flames of war. (75)

Gaudentius reads the Vandals correctly, for Genseric parcels out the young Roman women (Eudocia included) among his officers and exiles Edoxia, leaving her nothing to do but voice an impotent rage:

> Hah! traitor, is it thus thou meet'sr Edoxia? . . .
> Oh! burst my heart—and let my eye strings break,
> Let furious billows swallow up his fleet,
> And darkness cover nature in the wreck,
> Ere I obey, and see my household train,
> Lag at the feet of his triumphal car. (80)

When Genseric suggests that "A milder tone becomes a captive queen" (ibid.) and announces "I now forbid a murmur, or a sigh" (81), she counters

> Thou may'st forbid the morning sun to rise;
> Bid ocean cease to lave the pebbled shore,
> Or Roman souls to mix with Vandal slaves,
> And be obey'd—ere sighs are hush'd,
> Or execrations cease. (Ibid.)

Sighs and execrations, however, have no real force; Genseric sends Edoxia away in golden chains and levels the city. The dramatist shows that women in high places are public figures whose supposed private actions have public consequences even as their power is always subject to men's greater force.

The American implications of *The Ladies of Castile*—which is about the sixteenth-century struggle of the united Spanish municipalities against the imperial invader, Charles V—are fairly evident. The play's villains are turncoats: Velasco, regent in Charles's absence, and Pedro, a lout who sells out for the chance to marry Louisa, Velasco's daughter. Velasco is like an American Tory, mistakenly believing that he owes loyalty to Charles; Warren makes him tyrannical and intemperate, insinuating that those attracted to despotism, however they justify themselves in terms of honor and loyalty, are fundamentally despots themselves. As Charles's regent, Velasco stands for the principle of political parasitism in contrast to independence and self-governing localism.

The contrasting women in *The Ladies of Castile* are more virtuous than Edoxia but not more fortunate—Maria, wife of the patriot leader Padilla, and Louisa, daughter of Velasco. Maria is as patriotic as her husband, with a fortitude and self-transcendence that set her apart from most women. After Padilla's death, she successfully urges the citizens and soldiers on, proposing to lead them to battle personally, comparing herself to Semiramis and Zenobia (164). The fight is lost, but not before readers encounter a woman's voice with real power.

Louisa is timid and overemotional: "I . . . weep Spain's happier days. . . . I yield to grief / 'Till floods of tears relieve my tortur'd soul" (118), she laments. Too self-absorbed to feel the polity's anguish personally—"this little self obtrudes; / I cannot boast disinterested grief" (119)—she is nonetheless thoroughly implicated in political life, since she loves Maria's patriot brother Francis, who is anathema to her father. Her key scene of futile vocality—which plays off against Maria's effective public utterance—involves pleading with her father for Francis's life after he has been captured. Her words have no effect, and when Velasco learns that she has secretly married Francis, he repudiates her, even suggesting that she ought to kill herself to redeem the family honor. Which she does, in a gesture that is interpreted as Velasco's murder of his own child—another sign of the depths to which a tyrant will stoop.

With Pedro putting lust ahead of civic loyalty, and Velasco trying to sell his daughter for a military advantage and then denouncing her (rather than himself) as a whore, the connections between the corruptions of despotism and personal vice are clear. Yet the play's final prayer, asking God to "bend the wayward mind of man" to virtue (178), suggests that virtue is unavailable to human beings without God's special intervention, and it will be made available to them, therefore, in God's own good time. And, in God's good time, the American Revolution came to pass; this is the play's subtext. "The nations have now resheathed the sword," Warren writes in her preface; "the European world is hushed in peace; America stands alone:—May she long stand, superiour to the spirit of intrigue, or the corrupt principles of usurpation that may spring from the successful exertions of her own sons:—May their conduct never contradict the professions of the patriots who have asserted the rights of human nature; nor cause a blush to pervade the cheek of the children of the martyrs who have fallen in defence of the liberties of their country" (101).

Belisarius, eponymous hero of Margaretta Faugeres's 1795 play, was a general under Justinian I unfairly imprisoned by the emperor in A.D. 562. The play opens when Belisarius is released from prison, and after a series of episodes designed to exhibit his character as a model republican—a soldier averse to war who fights "to purchase *peace*, not to extend dominion" (32), who acts from "*principle* and not for hire" (10), who seeks "his country's welfare, not its riches" (24)—the plot reunites him with a contrite Justinian through the agency of the emperor's nephew Tiberias. Along with two good domestic women—one of whom goes mad from grief—the play has two very bad women. One is the Empress Theodora, who is responsible for Belisarius's imprisonment. The second is Julia, who loves Belisarius and uses her influence with Justinian's enemies to get him appointed commander of anti-Justinian forces—an offer that the noble Belisarius loyally rejects. As in Warren's plays, high-status women inevitably have public power; they could not be merely domestic even if they wanted to. Like high-status men, therefore, they must control their passions and think of the state. At the end, Julia is reduced to futile rant:

Avaunt, nor til I've told the hideous tale
That weeping *Truth* pour'd in my startled ear,
Think to decoy me hence. Thou, Justinian,
Hast from my heart torn every bleeding nerve
Sacred to *love* or *pity*. The stern *mandate*
That bore me *mad* from my deluded lover,
Stamp'd on its seal the horrors of my fate,
And doom'd me to a life of ceaseless woe.
And thou, vile woman, impious Theodora,
Who dar'd to break the ligaments of affection,
What though thou now mayest steep thine hands in blood,
Yet think, oh! think, remorseless, fiend-like woman,
The day of retribution is at hand. (38)

Soon after this speech she is "seiz'd with horrible convulsions" and dies.

The Tyrants' Victims

Belisarius's virtuous wife also dies a maniac; as Tiberius reports,

> when her sight glanc'd on his alter'd visage,
> With violent fury springing from her bed,
> She shriek'd so awfully, and form'd such curses,
> As shook my soul with horror; then she wept,
> And strain'd her husband to her beating bosom,
> And pitied him awhile—then rag'd again,
> And tore her hair, and mangled her poor flesh,
> Till wasted quite with the tremendous combat,
> She sunk upon her consort's breast, and died. (39)

Belisarius, then, has two madwomen, one woman monster—"Devil incarnate, scourge of this wide empire" (36)—and one good republican daughter who presages the future. Eudoxa, instructed in stoic virtue by her father Belisarius, will marry Tiberias and become an empress who will neither destroy nor be destroyed herself.

A strikingly different configuration occurs in Sarah Pogson's *The Female Enthusiast: A Tragedy in Five Acts* (1807), whose heroine, Charlotte Corday, speaks some of the strongest lines of any women in early American literature. But unlike the women in Warren's and Faugeres's plays, Corday approaches the tyrant Marat to kill him, not to plead with him. Charlotte is no unsexed woman; her act of enthusiasm is carried out on behalf of the domestic sphere. When public duty calls her fiancé to the front and disrupts family life, Charlotte starts asking questions:

> Had duty never call'd De Verneuil hence
> Here had I stayed in peaceful ignorance—
> That duty, which led me first, to ask of wars,
> And Government, and other scenes, than those
> Infolding sweet domestic harmony.
> Then to a wider field my views were opened. (7)

Over time, the questions produce an answer: she concludes that duty requires her to murder the tyrant. Nothing less will restore domestic peace. She has to stifle her womanly nature to carry out this act that the future of womanhood requires:

> Strong are thy claims, O, nature! now do I
> Feel them with an iron force. . . .
> Let me then, whisper that foul name, Marat,
> And the last conflict end. The monster's name
> Steels ev'ry thought—and female weakness flies.

197

Marat's tyrannical bluster in Act 3 justifies Charlotte's deed, while conveying Pogson's horror over the outcome of the French Revolution:

> With strength I am arm'd—and mighty energy,
> To crush the murd'rer, and defy the scaffold.
> Let but the deed be done—for it, *I'll die.*
> For it, I sacrifice—I quit myself,
> And all the softness of a woman's name. (14)

Citizens! Patriots! spill your bravest blood;
Raise high the pile of slaughtered sycophants!—
Exterminate all those—who dare presume
To check this radiant dawn of liberty.
. . . Well ye know
Whose blood to spill—And whose to
    spare—without
The tedious mockeries of courts and judges,
Judge for yourself—and quickly execute. (23–24)

Asked why she killed Marat, Charlotte replies: "The cause of virtue. . . . My soul is satisfied— / A woman's arm, when nerved in such a cause, / Is, as the arm of the avenging angel. / Think not I am a foe to liberty" (27). She calls herself a patriot whose memory will eventually be venerated by the country that now condemns her. And she concludes in lines of intriguing allusiveness:

Should the demon of carnage present—
Another fiend, as murd'rous as Marat,
May he soon share that horrid monster's fate
And the true patriot who dares cut him off,
Find in his country's gratitude—reward.
Delusion now blinds the rude multitude,
And the worst enemy is called a friend—
While their best friend must meet a *traitor's* doom. (43–44)

After Corday's fiancé kills himself in grief, the rest of the family decide to emigrate to the United States, where

Domestic ease securely reposes;
There, we may yet enjoy tranquillity
And 'midst the scenes of true born liberty,
Taste the pure blessings that from freedom flow. (50–51)

The Tyrants' Victims

In this tragedy, the successful American Revolution is distinguished from the failed French one; the hackneyed phrase "true born liberty" contrasts the organic growth of an inherent trait to a dictatorial imposition of "liberty," that can only reproduce a new form of tyranny.

Since Charlotte knifes Marat without bothering to plead with him, her case proves the rule that when women's only weapon is language, they are bound to be the tyrants' victims. In Hentz's *Constance of Werdenberg*, when the protagonist is wrongly accused of murdering her husband by a despot, she defends herself at length even while conceding that "In vain / Were all appeal before a bar like this" (*Georgia Citizen*, 2 May 1850). The villain responds: "I know thy tongue / Is gifted with most marvellous persuasion. . . . Before to-morrow's sun shall gild the Alps, / The night of death shall wrap thee." The decree produces more talk from Constance:

Not yet, ye ministers of death! My voice
Shall leave an echo in these storied walls.
Hear me, thou man of blood, thou heart of stone;
Thou, who enthron'd upon thy judgment seat,
Hurl'st down thy bolts, upon a suffering land,
Thy doom is seal'd. (Ibid.)

Her prophecy has no effect on the villain. This play has a happy ending; Constance and her husband (not dead after all) are rescued by Swiss patriot-peasants, who, being true republicans, appreciate women.

Elizabeth Ellet's *Teresa Contarini* is set in fourteenth-century Venice, where political life was tightly supervised and controlled. In this polity no woman has a chance, and Ellet gives Teresa several different pleading scenes—with the authorities not to imprison her father, with her father not to force her to marry the hateful Contarini (now her husband) pleas fail, with the authorities again after Contarini (now her husband) falsely incriminates her former lover. None of these have any impact on the auditors. "Come—come—displease me not" responds her father (158). "Nay—lady; / This cannot aught avail. . . . Go thy way, and hope the best," say the authorities (167). "So lovely in disdain! / She shall be mine, despite her scorn and hate!" vows Contarini, if anything moved the wrong way by Teresa's eloquence (169). "Off! I'll no more / Of clinging and of honied words!" says her father (174). Near the end of the play, to be sure, a distracted Teresa interrupts the Council of Ten to expose her husband's perfidy and save her lover, and catches its attention: "If my words are wild and wayward, / They are truth!" (223). But it is not her accusations so much as her father's corroboration and a goodly amount of documentary evidence introduced by a subsidiary character that persuade the councilors.

199

In the meantime the lover has been put to death, and Teresa ends the play dead in the arms of her contrite father.

According to Rufus Griswold's elaborate plot summary of Elizabeth Oakes Smith's lost *The Roman Tribute*, this play develops another version of the plot of ineffectual female pleading and insanity. Griswold says the play was set in "a familiar period in the history of Constantinople when Theodosius saved the city from being sacked by paying its price to the victorious Attila" (179). The drama features one woman—Eudocia, wife of Theodosius—destroyed by another—Pulcheria, Theodosius's sister. Pulcheria's motives are personal, not political—thwarted love for the prime minister, Anthemius, "a soldier, a statesman, and a patriot" (Ibid.), whom she wrongly believes to be Eudocia's lover. Griswold says Pulcheria is "haughty, revengeful, intelligent, and imaginative. Remorseless in the pursuit of an object, and unflinching in the most daring action, she is yet so much a woman as to love passionately—almost tenderly—and when evil follows her policy, haunted in secret by shapes of conscience, which, to her excited and powerful imagination, take tangible forms and beset her path" (180). He seems to imply that Pulcheria goes partly insane. As for the discredited Eudocia, she "defends herself with gentle dignity, but is disgraced and imprisoned" (181); escaping from prison, she comes close to killing her husband, and finally "dies of overwrought grief" (180). Madness is certainly implied here.

The only cheerful variation on this recurrent motif occurs in Anna Cora Mowatt's comedy, *Armand*. Blanche, the heroine, is a secret (although legitimate) daughter of Richelieu; she has been brought up by peasants and she loves Armand, a commoner who rises by pure merit to the rank of Colonel in Louis XV's army, and expresses crypto-republican patriotism:

> a foundling
> By strangers reared, I am the people's child!
> . . . I ask no name save that
> Myself shall win. I bless the generous fate
> That gave no noble blood to swell my veins,
> For had I from the hands of accident
> Nobility received, I could not prove
> My juster title to that high noblesse
> No revolutions level and destroy:
> The true noblesse of genius and of worth. (33)

Mowatt plays with popular convention and audience expectation by keeping the secret of Armand's birth; he does *not* turn out to be the son of a nobleman. In a neat schematizing of women's situation in despotism, Blanche is required to defend her virtue from the lustful king, and assert her independence from her domineering father, who has another marriage in mind for her than union with Armand. "Canst thou thus the name of woman scorn," she reproaches her father, "Her holy mission lightly look upon[?]" "I nor deny her virtues, nor her power / To gild them with her tongue," Richelieu replies (43–44). For once, however, woman's speech is effective. When Louis XV attempts to rape Blanche—"It is thy turn / To sue, and all in vain! thou hast forgot / That I am King, and thou hast no protector!" (55), he says—Blanche stops him with a volley of numbing rhetoric and flounces off:

Thou art my sovereign—I a friendless subject—
I woman, and thou man!—my helplessness
Was of itself a claim to thy protection—
A claim thou hast rejected! Answer, King!
Hast thou done right? Man, was it well to use
Thy strength against my weakness? Thou art dumb!
Thou canst not answer! King of France, I scorn thee! (56)

"Can it be that Virtue's presence awes / Me thus?" the king broods, after her exit. "She speaks, I'm hushed" (56). But once a king, always a king—virtue sways him only temporarily. In the end Blanche needs the combined support of Armand, Richelieu and Blanche's newly discovered grandfather, the Duke D'Antin, to dissuade Louis. He muses, "The warring elements of good and ill / With fearful strife are battling in my soul; / But Policy with Virtue sides, and makes / The victory hers" (58).

The most articulate of the ineffective speaking women in these plays is Cornelia, mother of the Gracchi, whom Louisa McCord represents as Roman virtue incarnate in *Caius Gracchus* (1851). Cornelia delivers many long, closely reasoned, rhetorically complex, and philosophically informed political speeches designed to instruct and guide her son. The ultimate republican mother, she fails. Caius disregards her monitions, to his cost. "Noble mother!" he says, "Forgive me that I have so often spurned / Your wiser councils. Now the ghosts of them, / While your reproach is mute, look mournful back / To show me all my folly, and my sin" (112).

Because Cornelia is a mother, the gender dynamics in *Caius Gracchus* are necessarily different from those of the other European history plays. This play has no titillating seduction plot, nor does it define female virtue as spiritual purity and a feelingful heart. Instead, Cornelia stands for the sternest kind of Roman rationality and self-discipline. Caius is buffeted by contending forces in a political allegory devised according to the once-prevalent (although by 1851 moribund) republican perspective: corruption and luxury are represented by the Senate; demagoguery and rabble by the Revolutionaries and the populace; virtue by Cornelia. Caius, though properly dismayed by the senate's profligacy and admirably devoted to the people, is oblivious to the pitfalls of a historical moment when the people are insufficiently developed, politically, to use their power virtuously. Nor does he realize how much his reformist goals are driven by personal ambition.

Cornelia tries to teach him all this. She argues that democracy will not work unless the people undergo an interim period of tutelage:

> The time's unripe, and you would force it on,
> Not by a gentle teaching to the truth,
> But gag it to your own ideas of right,
> And force mankind to gulp your system down. (90)

She questions his patriotism:

> Call you this,
> This rampant hate, and angry violence,
> Which drives a thoughtless people to the verge
> Of lawless anarchy, which grasps at fraud
> To work its selfish ways, and makes success,
> Not right, its rule of action,—call you this,
> Because you link it with some real wrong
> Inflicted on a thoughtless populace,—
> Call you this patriotism? (89)

For all its abstract political sophistication, the play sets up a problem that it does not, indeed cannot, solve—how the ruler himself is to be controlled during this interim. Cornelia has no power to force him. The suggested solution, that he submit to the control of her benign mentorship, requires an act of voluntary submission that he cannot perform. Therefore, the play shows that this mother, because she is endowed only with the power of the word, has no real power at all. If her son the ruler is already virtuous, he will of course heed her; but if he is already virtuous, he doesn't need her advice. So although Cornelia enunciates principles that are undeniably admirable and abstractly right, there is a complete break between them and the play's political reality. The question how to negotiate the transition from autocracy to workable democracy remains unanswered and unanswerable.

One of the problems here is that Cornelia's behavior and her ideology are firmly bound by severe rules of female decorum. She advises her son at length what to say to the people, but she never dreams of addressing them herself. She counsels her daughter-in-law to "stay within doors" and greet her husband with "quiet comeliness. . . . 'Tis meek endurance, quiet fortitude, / That make [woman's] life and beauty," she advises; woman's "task" is to hide her passions "Till in their faintly-beating pulse, herself / Will scarcely know her blood the same which bounds / Through manlier veins unchecked" (20–21). The same blood is virtually unrecognizable after gender has done its work on women.

Many of the women who believed in gender differentiation interpreted it as politically useful: keeping a distance from the hurly-burly of everyday politics would give women a more elevated, general kind of political influence. Perhaps this is what McCord also means to show in using Cornelia as a mouthpiece for abstract principle. But the plotting, which deprives Cornelia of any influence at all, does not fulfill such a design. McCord's presentation would seem, then, to be implying a women's rights position, in the sense that Cornelia needs a different kind of power from what she has. But outside the boundaries of the play, the author went the other way. A southerner increasingly dedicated to her region's separatist politics—McCord published several essays on political economy from a southern nationalist perspective in the *Southern Quarterly Review, DeBow's*, and the *Southern Literary Messenger* in the early 1850s—she espoused an extreme version of patriarchal politics that undercuts any possibility for women's voices to be more than decorative or represent any political reality except the lost cause that in fact Cornelia stands for.

It seems fairly obvious that the dramatic model animating all these plays of European history, whether they are set in the fourth century B.C. (in *A Tyrant's Victims*) or the immediate past (in *The Enthusiast*), would not be appropriate for plays about American history. This perhaps explains the relatively small number of American subjects in historical plays published by women in this period. In fact, and despite the recorded obsessive patriotism of the American theater in the antebellum era, historical plays by women and men alike on American topics are few in number. Hixon and Hennessee's (admittedly incomplete) finding list of published and unpublished American plays indexes only eleven historical dramas in all between 1800 and 1860 under the rubrics "America—History" and "United States—History." This makes an interesting contrast with fiction, and the explanation would seem to lie in the overriding power of genre conventions. Scott was a good model for historical fiction about the United States; Shakespeare was not a good model for historical drama about the same country.

When women wrote historical plays about American subjects, they tended to focus on what might be called peripheral topics in the archive and tried to shape them by the European model. This means that the omnipresent novelistic trope of the republican daughter is largely absent from drama. Charlotte Barnes Connor's *The Forest Princess; or, Two Centuries Ago* (1848), for example, tells the story of Pocahontas as an encounter between English and Amerindian kingdoms, ending in a marriage that merges two royal lineages. 'Toward the end of the play Pocahontas has a prophetic vision of concord between England and its offspring, the future United States; the family metaphor expresses the play's political theme.

Souls of the prophet-fathers of my race,
Light from the Land of Spirits have ye sent,
To paint the future on my mental sight,
Like the Great River of far Western wilds,
Improvement's course, *unebbing*, shall flow on.
From that beloved soil where I drew breath
Shall noble chiefs arise. But one o'er all,
By heaven named to set a nation free,
I hear the universal world declare,
In shouts whose echo centuries prolong,
"The Father of his Country!" O'er the path
Of Ages, I behold Time leading Peace.
By ties of love and language bound, I see
The Island-Mother and her Giant Child,
Their arms extend across the narrowing seas,
The grasp of lasting friendship to exchange! (263–264)

Connor emphasizes this motif of Anglo-American consanguinity in her preface, where she reminds readers that "the various historians and colonists concur in the assertion that but for the benefactions of Pocahontas, Virginia would have been lost to England." She continues:

The Dutch and the Spaniards were then aiming at a settlement, and would have established themselves there during the delay which must have inevitably occurred, had the British colonists starved to death or abandoned the spot,—a result which Pocahontas alone prevented. How far the aspect of civilization, of national character and government, of literature and science, in America, would have been affected, had other lands given customs, laws, and language to so extensive and central a portion of our continent, is a question well worthy of consideration, and in justice to Pocahontas, should ever be associated with her name. (148)

The main plot of this play concerns just this struggle of various European ethnicities to gain a foothold on the American continent. Because the "Switzer" (i.e., Dutch) villain, Volday, opposes the Anglo hero Smith and betrays the Indians, the interests of the English and the Indians are collapsed into one cause. Although Connor allots Powhatan the conventional gloomy speech about Indian disappearance, her main interest is in showing that the Indians and English are allies and even, thanks to Pocahontas's marriage to John Rolfe, one people. *The Forest Princess* concludes with John Smith assuring the dying Pocahontas that "thy country's sons will task / The sculptor's and the limner's art to pay / Hereafter homage to thy memory," that England too will remember her, and that "Thy name will live for ever!" (265). Notwithstanding this filiopietism, Pocahontas emerges as another striking example of the inefficacy of the woman's voice in history. Not her talk, but her deeds, have historical significance. She has to throw her body in the way of Powhatan's axe to save John Smith; pleading with her father has no effect. Later in the play, when Rolfe is arrested on suspicion of treachery in England, she pleads unavailingly with Prince Charles for her husband's life. Evidence provided by Smith and others saves him. Pocahontas's most significant historical act is, of course, the most conventional type of female behavior; she cements an alliance between kingdoms by marrying the conqueror.

The subject of Harriette Fanning Read's *The New World* (1848)—the Native American encounter with the Spanish—allows the author to demonize the Spanish so as to exonerate the English by contrast. We have already met this familiar motif in American historical narration. As Eliza Robbins expressed it in Volume 3 of her *Tales from American History,*

The arrival of the Spaniard in Southern America was the signal of extermination to a happy and almost innocent race of beings, solely because justice and true religion never entered into the policy of the conquerors. . . . Bad faith, false religion, and the absence of all pure generosity in the Spaniards, not only degraded and extirpated the savage, but depraved the character of the settlers, so that to this day their descendants have neither the political liberty nor the social and personal virtues of men whose ancestors are distinguished by equity, mercy, and the true love of God. (96–97)

Attacks like this encourage readers to reflect with pride on the contrasting record of the northern European settlers; more narrowly, plots about the Spanish in America allow the author to make the Indians sympathetic without having to make the English antagonistic. Read's central character is Alana, daughter of Anacoana, the historical Haitian queen whose murder by the Spanish government established by Columbus (but for whose deeds, according to nineteenth-century hagiographers, Columbus was not responsible) was frequently advanced as a sentimental example of Spanish brutality.

The New World depends on this formula. The plot centers on the lustful desire of Francisco Roldan, "chief Judge of the Island of Haiti," for Alana, who loves Hernando de Guevara, a Castilian nobleman

(Roldan's commoner status introduces an antidemocratic class bias into the play), loves Alana virtuously and hopes to marry her and take her back to Spain. Alana's pleading (of which there is a good deal) comes to nothing: "Thou art my slave," Roldan says to her after fatally stabbing Guevera, "Now kneel and sue for mercy!" (295). But at Alana's request the dying Guevera stabs her: "See, Roldan" (she says), "The slave escapes thee!" (296). At this point Anacoana runs onto the stage "with a shriek" and asks the Spanish to kill her along with her daughter. Although the queen's political activities are overridden by her personal tragedy, the play relies on the belief that political tyranny and sexual aggression are part of the same constellation of male behavior.

Elizabeth Oakes Smith's *Old New York: or, Democracy in 1689* (1853) also follows this formula. The play is about the so-called Leisler's revolt of 1689, when New Yorkers led by Jacob Leisler (1640–1691) briefly resisted the government of William and Mary. Leisler, accused of treason and hanged, was sometimes interpreted as a demagogue, sometimes as an anti-British patriot ahead of his time. The second approach, which Smith takes in *Old New York*, suited New York chauvinists and supported their efforts to take some of the glory of the Revolution away from New England.

The drama pits Leisler, "elected Governor by the people" as the *dramatis personae* describes him, against William Sloughter, "Governor by the Crown." The domestic plot features Leisler's second wife Elizabeth and his daughter Margaret by his first wife, and develops the extraordinary melodramatic twist that Elizabeth was already married to none other than Sloughter, from whom she ran away because she so deeply hated him. Since Sloughter's arrival means that her bigamous history will be exposed, Elizabeth goes so far as to kill her "bastard" child by Leisler, a deed for which the besotted Leisler forgives her. Leisler gets rational, patriotic, political lines like these:

> . . . ye have learned to know a people's worth,
> Have learned how good a thing it is to stand
> In your own strength, unchecked by priest or king.
> Ye are the prophets of the time—the thought
> Of but a handful now, shall be the faith
> Of every common man in time to come.
> From this new soil shall rise that nobler race,
> Where every man shall stand a priest, a king
> In his own right—lord of himself, unbought,
> Unsold; armed in the manhood of a man. (32)

Elizabeth, in contrast, gets a madwoman's lines—like these:

The Tyrants' Victims

Ye bolted flames that down the sailor's mast,
Quench your red arrows in the yeasty wave,
Behold a fitter mark! Ye plague-spots, come;
Ye noisome monsters of the fenny brake,
Enfold a monster unto you akin.
Is there no deadly thing to pity take?
Am I too loathsome for thy arms, O death? (18)

Predictably, Elizabeth's pleadings with Sloughter have no effect on him:
"Thy lips are powerless to my will," he says (57). Or rather, the effect
they have is to renew his lust for her, a lust exacerbated by motives of
revenge. Indeed, Sloughter hates Leisler not only on political grounds, but
also because he "loved and was beloved where I was spurned" (62). As
the capacity of a woman to move men to virtue by rational eloquence is
rejected, the destructive power (for herself and others) of her physical allure is affirmed, condemning her to life in one or another man's cage: "Nay,
my pretty bird," Sloughter tells her when she attempts to leave, "thou art
caged" (57).

Surprisingly, since by 1853 Smith was active on behalf of women's rights,
Elizabeth does not so much resist the autocratic concept of being caged as
aspire to choose her own cage. "Am I not all?" she says to Leisler early
on, "thy friend, thy wife, thy slave?" (10).

there's not a thought
But circles under thine; nor whim, nor will,
That does not own thee master. I am thine
So all, that I have lost my single self. (10–11)

Again, the most likely explanation for this refusal to present the American woman as an incipiently republican figure is generic convention. Even
Sarah Hale, who would never have allotted a woman character such furious rhetoric, seems to have been defeated by the form. Her republican play,
Ormond Grosvenor, published in the *Lady's Book* in 1838, is full of admirable political sentiments but virtually devoid of female speech.

The play is set in South Carolina during the Revolution and concerns
Grosvenor's decision to renounce his English title and join the patriots together with his friend Sullivan from New England. He breaks with England because of the treacherous execution of the patriot Isaac Hayne by
a British officer who has promised to pardon him. The southern setting
enables Hale to develop her favorite theme of transregional union. But the
realities of the war limit the mobility and influence of women. In war, according to one woman, women can only "sit here, / Listening to the sounds
of fearful desolation, / Perchance the groans of friends, of dying friends";

207

but who can say that this is easier than rushing "wildly on midst the strife"? "We'll pray," she winds up, "we'll pray" (16:152). The role of the women characters in wartime is to love, suffer, and support the patriots, while making it clear to the British side that they will always take a republican man over an aristocrat. And this, according to the English themselves, is behavior with world-shaking implications:

Mary Carr's comedy of 1815, *The Fair Americans*, about the War of 1812, similarly divides male and female speech between women support- ing and encouraging their menfolk—"Oh never be the name of Harley or Fairfield, branded by the epithet of cowardice; nor ever be female influ- ence exerted to the dishonour of their friends, family, or country" (9)— and men voicing political theory and commentary:

> *Stanley:* That lady bears a heart of lofty mood,
> Undaunted as a queen.
> *Rauden.* So do they all,
> And this self-arrogance we must repress,
> Or lords will soon be only common men;
> Let such a spirit gain ascendant here,
> And Europe's millions will be roused, and swine
> Will rend and trample all our jewels down.
> These rebels must be crushed. (16:38)

> *Harley:* We are a united people; our rulers are chosen by the majority,
> and the minority submit of course.
> *Major Clifford:* Such have ever been the sentiments of every republic,
> till increase of wealth introduced luxuries, banished simplicity, and un-
> dermined true patriotism. While Rome was poor in wealth, her citizens
> were rich in integrity; but no sooner was its wealth become boundless,
> than she fell.
> *Captain Belford:* America is in one particular an exception from all re-
> publics history record [sic]. . . . She is grateful to her departed heroes.
> *Harley:* You are correct, sir, for the name of Washington still causes our
> hearts to glow with rapture; and an enthusiastic desire to emulate his
> virtues. (39–40)

Perhaps the most interesting of these plays about American history is Delia Bacon's *The Bride of Fort Edward*, which she started writing in 1837 as a stage play and published anonymously, as a closet work, in 1839. The work is about Jane McCrea, and consists of six so-called dialogues deeply marked by Shakespeare. This was Bacon's second approach to the McCrea material; it expanded a prize story on the topic she published in the Philadelphia *Saturday Courier* early in 1832. In 1831 she had brought out *Tales of the Puritans*, containing three long New England stories centered on extraordinary heroines who performed feats at once valorous and exceedingly feminine in their nature. Her challenge here was to make the unlikely Jane McCrea—hapless victim of random slaughter and engaged to a Tory to boot—a heroine of this kind.

History came to her aid. It will be recalled that McCrea's fate, according to Burgoyne's memoirs, had been circulated as extremely successful patriot propaganda; and this ironic twist of fate becomes Bacon's passkey to a Providential reading of McCrea's historical mission. The McCrea figure, called Helen Grey, comes from a patriot family and is a patriot herself, having broken off her engagement to Maitland, her fiancé, when he defected to the English. Now, after two years of pining, Helen has chosen to follow love's dictates and rejoin him. But even as she prepares to do so, she prays for the patriot side: "Let the high cause of right and freedom, whose sad banner, now, on yonder hill, floats in this summer air; whose music on this soft night-breeze is borne—let it prevail—though I, with all this sensitive, warm, shrinking life; with all this new-found wealth of love and hope, lie on its iron way" (68).

Afraid of an attack from the Indian allies of the English, the Grey family is abandoning its home, where Helen stays on alone to meet her lover. "Will you go over to the British side, Helen?" asks her mother (105). "Mother," she replies, "this dark coil hath Heaven wound, not we. The tie which makes his path the way of God to me, was linked ere this war was,—and war cannot undo it now. It is a bitter fate, I know,—a bitter and a fearful one" (106). Rather than coming himself, Maitland sends an Indian escort for Helen. Instinctively terrified of Indians, Helen departs with them knowing in advance what horrible thing is going to happen to her. What she does not know, but the drama exhibits, is how her death furthers the cause for whose success she had prayed. Says Burgoyne: "A young and innocent girl, seeking the protection of our camp, is inhumanly murdered by Indians in our pay. A single tale like this is enough to undo at a blow all that we have accomplished here" (164–165).

Leslie: A martyr's garland she hath won indeed; true Love's young Martyr there she lies.
Elliston: Yet was that love but the wreathed and glittering weapon of a higher doom. In that holy cause, whose martyrs strew a thousand fields, truth's, freedom's, God's, darkly, by *Power Invisible* hath this young life been offered here. (169)

At the end of the drama, the army of common soldiers, who had been "melting away like a snow-wreath" (21), aroused by the bloody story, reject

Burgoyne's offer of amnesty and storm off: "To the death! Freedom for ever!" (174). Soldiers are important in this play, for its politics is about how ordinary people come to recognize the imperatives of the republican and democratic movement of history—not through accepting generalities, but through being moved by concrete instances. And these soldiers stand in for the audience for whom, in Bacon's theorizing, drama was fundamentally designed; when working on *The Bride*, she wrote to her brother that "the object of it is to display a grand and awful truth not in the abstract but in a form better fitted to strike the common mind—the living breathing reality" (Hopkins 59). Her sense that drama had the august mission of instructing the people in democratic principles via concrete examples, gives *The Bride of Fort Edward* particular intensity.

The signs of this mission, too, were what Bacon admired in Shakespeare's plays—except that, over time, she decided that the particular Elizabethan man identified by that name could not have had such lofty aims, and concluded that he was not the author of the plays attributed to him. Gradually Bacon become certain that "Shakespeare's" plays had been plurally authored by members of a secret society founded by Walter Raleigh and headed by Francis Bacon, with Shakespeare merely a front. Pursuing this idea to the verge of madness, she wrote *The Philosophy of Shakespeare's Plays Unfolded* (1857), a book that not only contested literary history, but challenged history itself, since there was not even a shred of evidence in the record that such a society ever existed.

This intellectual audacity, and the ambitions of *The Bride* to instruct the populace in republican virtues and values, are countered by the play's representation of a woman forced into history by being murdered and given significance by men exploiting her mute, lifeless body. Bacon shows men— in particular, high-status men—as the people whose understanding of history enables them to play a role in it. Helen's voice expresses desires that are both fully "womanly" in their commitment to "love" and run counter to history's stern imperatives—she is no daughter of the republic incapable of loving any man who is not a patriot. Admirable in her romantic steadfastness, Helen nevertheless stands for a transcendent ideal of love that cannot be realized in a world still controlled by wars and nations. In this historical present, she has to be thwarted and killed to be made useful. There is no more far-reaching expression of female futility in all these plays.

Sacred dramas, or plays based on Bible history, were not written for commercial staging. Rather, they were pedagogical devices to teach sacred history; if performed at all, they were put on in schools. I have found three published full-scale sacred dramas: Amira Carpenter Thompson's "Esther: A Sacred Drama," in her miscellany *The Lyre of Tioga* (1829); Eliza Cushing's "Esther: A Sacred Drama," serialized in the *Lady's Book* in 1837 and republished in book form in 1840; and Louisa Hall's *Hannah, the*

Mother of Samuel (1839). In striking contrast to the plays examined to this point, but of course in complete consistency with the culture's approach to women in the Old Testament, all three of these plays give women both the power of the word and constructive historical agency.

Hall's *Hannah* is a series of songs and prayers situated narratively at different points in the story of the childless woman who promises that if she bears a child she will give him up to God's service. Since the Bible has little to say about her, the author allows herself to enlarge on the text's implications. She authorizes her work through an apparatus of scholarly notes demonstrating the convergence of her treatment with biblical texts and historical knowledge. The narrative focus is the conflict between mother-love and sacrifice, since Hannah must give up the very child she has longed for. The general historical situation invoked here is that of the mother on the sidelines required to give up her children to history; in this sense Hannah is no different from Cornelia. But in the scholarly notes accompanying the drama, Hall specifically presents Hannah as a type of the Virgin Mary, whose maternal sacrifice is also universal and highly specific: "In this hymn to her babe, the prophetess is supposed to employ such language as is capable of a double application, the one to her babe, the other through her babe to the future Messiah, whose Advent occupies her thoughts continually, and whose kingdom she loved. Such a double applicability of language is not uncommon in the prophetical scriptures" (92–93).

What is to be stressed in terms of female agency and voice are Hannah's awareness of history and her willingness to cooperate with it. The child is not taken from her, she gives it; and, moreover, "she was endowed with a prophetic inspiration; and she was worthy of it, as also of the dignity to which she was appointed in being the parent of Samuel. By her faith he was raised up, in a wonderful Providence, to be a Prophet and a Judge in Israel, and to prepare for the advent of the messiah of mankind" (xi). Here is the familiar theme of the patriotic mother, whose unique nation—the Hebrew state—is ruled by God himself.

The character of Esther receives special treatment in women's writing, because it brings into sharp relief so many questions about the meaning of womanliness and how active a role women might play in history without compromising their sexual identity. Esther's case indeed highlights exactly a woman's use of her visible sexual identity—her beautiful body—to accomplish her patriotic purpose in a world ruled by men, and called out a range of interpretations. In 1820, the poet Maria Gowen Brooks invested Esther's efficacy entirely in the careful staging of her body:

Take ye, my maids, this mournful garb away,
Bring of my glowing gems and garments fair,

A nation's fate impending hangs today,
But on my beauty and your duteous care.

Prompt to obey, her ivory form they lave;
Some comb and braid her hair of wavy gold,
Some softly wipe away the limpid wave
That o'er her dimly limbs in drops of fragrance rolled.

Refreshed and faultless from their hands she came,
Like form celestial clad in raiment bright,
O'er all her garb rich India's treasures frame,
In mingling beams of rain-bow colored light.

(*Judith, Esther, and Other Poems*, 26)

But in 1853, Sarah Hale, while admitting that Esther's "great beauty raised her to the throne of Persia, whereby she saved her countrymen from total extermination" (*Woman's Record*, 37), insisted that her beauty alone was not the cause. She had been carefully educated in piety and patriotism by her Uncle Mordecai; and she had a mind. "This pious and beautiful woman, trusting in heaven and earnestly employing her own influence, succeeded in defeating the malice of [Haman].... Had she not possessed, and exercised too, the highest powers of woman's mind—faith in God, and love, self-sacrificing love for her people—the Jews must have perished" (38).

The two sacred dramas about Esther fall between these interpretations. She is neither so invested in her own beauty as Brooks's heroine, nor so strong-minded as Hale's. In both plays, Mordecai plans the action and Esther obeys him. Thompson's is the more vigorous and independent Esther: given Mordecai's instructions, she says: "The project's fraught with danger. But I will go; perhaps the God I serve will so incline the heart of king Ahasuerus, that he will hear my suit.... I and my maids will fast three days and nights. Then will I go before the king, uncalled, and if I perish, I can but perish once" (*Lyre of Tioga*, 22). Approaching Ahasuerus, she almost faints with terror; but this show of "seeming bashfulness" works in her favor. For once, the pleading woman will succeed:

Esther (*weeps.*).—Forgive, O king, my seeming bashfulness. Bred in the peaceful stillness of my home, I am unus'd to bear the piercing gaze of kings and conquerors; and when the thought glanc'd o'er me that I was come unbidden to thy presence, my timid heart misgave me, and I fear'd to lay my suit before thee.

King.—Fear not, my gentle love, but speak in confidence; and be assur'd what thou requirest shall be granted. (23)

Cushing's Esther is much more domestic and timid. Urging her to present herself as a candidate for Queen, Mordecai says:

> My people are oppressed . . .
> And thou alone canst free them. Thou, the chosen
> The appointed one, the ordained of heaven,
> And raised to greatness for this work alone!

She responds:

> The task thou nam'st is all too vast and high
> It asks a mighty hand, a lofty soul,
> Stern and experienced, wise in council,
> Armed at all points with courage and resolve,
> A fitting instrument for heaven's high will. . . .
> I am a timid maid, powerless and weak,
> That like the cowering dove, shrink in my flight
> From the fierce glancing of the eagle's eye. (26–27)

This debate continues after she becomes queen; Esther is deeply reluctant to approach the king. Cushing seems to be weakening the character to make her ultimate success a product of her faith rather than her willed actions. At the end of the drama, Mordecai emphasizes this point by giving all the glory to God: "Thou hast proved, all feeble as thou wert, / A rod of power in God's directing hand / . . . Oh, ever thus o'er Israel has He watched" (102). Once again, the special historical status of Old Testament women is clear. In these earlier periods it is they alone among women who are not fighting with history, and they alone who are not defeated by it. Especially in drama, the historical woman outside the Bible's dispensation testifies, at the top of her lungs, to her sex's victimization.

Women's Place
in History

ACCORDING TO THE DIVINE NARRATIVE shaping the discourse of these multiform historical writings, the progress of history meant an extension of the spiritual power introduced by Christ into the world until finally the empires of brute force would be entirely transformed into peaceable kingdoms. This script had, of course, enormous gender significance. Because men were endowed with greater physical strength than women, they had dominated the past; as the dominion of physical force contracted, so would the reign of men, and women—the weaker sex—would increasingly enter history decisively and directly.

If brute force no longer held sway, what was to succeed it? Women who worked under the banner of Enlightenment rationalism assumed that it was reason, and saw the world becoming an ever better place for their own sex as their claims to possess minds equal to men's were recognized. These claims recognized, women would no longer be confined to obscure lives of physical drudgery (odd confinement, considering that they were physically weaker than men!), but would be invited to develop their minds and contribute their developed mental powers to the conduct of world affairs. The world would benefit from their talents, and there would be more rapid progress toward the brighter coming day. It was under the light of this optimistic idealism that American women set themselves to learn and write history after the Revolution.

This initial rationalist impulse, which never entirely disappeared, became greatly attenuated over time, as cultural life changed radically between the 1790s and the 1850s. For many reasons, even intellectual women became less and less content with the idea that their contribution to world history was to be nothing more than the gift of a trait they shared equally with men. As other forces in the culture insisted more and more blatantly that women were organized according to different physical and spiritual principles from men—that they were almost not members of the same species, as they were assuredly not members of the same sex—women began

214

searching for something special about themselves, something mystical and magical that the subsidence of brute power would allow to emerge. They reasoned: since the world was increasingly to be dominated by spiritual power, and since women were increasingly to dominate the world, it could only be that women, more than men, were endowed with spirituality. Rather than interpreting the fact of relative physical weakness as a regrettable negative that could be neutralized by rational values, they read it positively to symbolize the same spiritual force that would rule the world when the millennium arrived.

Evidently, then, women who were to be prominent in history henceforth would not be paler versions of the familiar historical type of the great man. As brute force gave way to spiritual power, the great man himself would be obsolescent. George Washington, for example, was no great man of the old pattern; indeed he steadfastly resisted every temptation to behave like an outmoded despot. Even more, then, if women were to figure in history, would they be entirely unlike prominent men of the past. Indeed, they would also be entirely different from prominent women of the past—but of course there *were* no prominent women of the past! How could there have been, if brute force had always held sway?

This dilemma was never far from the minds of the women who wrote history, and who were thinking about women all the time. In many ways, the subject of their work was always women, no matter what they wrote about. The very act of writing history was itself, self-reflexively, the act of inserting a woman into history, as record keeper and referee if not as major player. When it came to women in the past, women's historical writings showed redundantly how misplaced they had been, depicting women as captives and victims of the male despots who had hitherto controlled history.

From this perspective, a virtual absence of prominent women in the historical record was not only to be expected, it was positively to be hoped for. "The life of woman, almost in proportion as it is true to the loftiest impulses and purest principles by which she can be actuated, represents comparatively few incidents claiming circumstantial record or remembrance," wrote Margaret Conkling in the introduction to her biographies of Mary and Martha Washington (xiii). "The Hero, like a majestic river, that bears the wealth of cities on its ample waters, and diffuses benefits to thousands, speeds onward in his high career, his steps resounding in the ears of listening nations; while the mother, from whom, perchance, he derived the intellectual power that impels and sustains this lofty course, still . . . lingers ever in the shade" (Conkling, xiv). To a writer like this—and there were many writers like this—truly powerful women in the record (always excepting the record of the Old Testament) presented a grave historiographical problem. We may describe this problem as the double, perhaps triple, bind of True Womanhood. Any woman who had been effective in a bad time could only have been a bad woman; but if women were innately superior spiritual beings, there were no bad women. The existence of bad men did not pose problems for the writing of history or for the ideology of manhood; not so the existence of bad women. Far from seeking out historical foremothers, then, antebellum women who wrote history preferred to circulate a narrative in which there were no prominent women at all. The absence of women from their accounts was not an antiwoman gesture, nor was it the result of ignorance or negligence. It was a deliberate choice. For, as this further extract from Conkling's memoir of the Washington women makes clear, they knew perfectly well how many prominent women had existed throughout history:

At the feet of the proud daughter of the Ptolemies, the conquerors of the world laid down their crowns, yet Clio, faithful to the truth, withholds the mead of honor from the coward soul that could not brave adversity. The history of Christina, the royal Swedish wanderer, scarce serves, at best, to "point a moral," and awakens no more exalted sentiment than one of pitying regret. Maria Theresa, despite her many and exalted excellences, sacrificed some of woman's first, best duties on the altar of ambition. And who will demand either love or veneration for the memory of England's greatest Queen, renowned as much for her most unfeminine faults, as for her boasted masculine virtues. . . . But when shall the daughters of Columbia be weary of imbibing the benign and hallowed influences inseparably associated with the pure and sacred name of Mary Washington? (70–72)

Conkling's double erasure here denies prominent historical women both their virtue and their historical agency. To her, these women are like the painted idols worshiped by pagans whose materialist minds could not recognize the hidden God who was the real historical actor. Like these idols, the prominent women only appear to be powerful; only the historically unaware would mistake them for the real agent. In contrast, the good woman, in her very invisibility, very much resembles the Protestant God who had hidden himself precisely to make people understand what was meant by the concept of the spirit.

But even as she makes her religious argument in favor of a female obscurity that is identical to spirituality, Conkling clearly shows that there were powerful women in the record, and that readers probably knew about them. She names Christina, Maria Theresa, and Elizabeth I casually, and seems to be sure that "the daughter of the Ptolemies" is enough of a reference to identify Cleopatra.

As we have seen in Chapter 7, American women tourists in the Old

World especially sought out memorials of the historical women they had long thought about. Margaret Fuller, reporting on her visit to the Tower of London, assumes that Mary Queen of Scots is known to all:

As this unhappy, lovely woman stands for a type in history, death, time, and distance do not destroy her attractive power; like Cleopatra, she has still her adorers. . . . Educated under that Medici and Guise influence, engaged in the meshes of secret intrigue to favor the Roman Catholic faith, her tacit acquiescence, at least, in the murder of Darnley, after all his injurious conduct toward her, was just what was to be expected. From a poor, beautiful young woman, longing to enjoy life, exposed both by her position and her natural fascinations to the utmost bewilderment of flattery whether prompted by interest or passion, her other acts of folly are most natural. (*Sad but Glorious*, 70–71)

In fact, and in complete contradiction to assertions that women had played no role in history, antebellum women writers constantly allude to famous historical women. References to (among others) Agrippina, Aspasia, Britomart, Boadicia, Catherine de Medici, Cleopatra, Cornelia, Esther, Isabella, Jezebel, Lucrezia Borgia, Maria Theresa, Marie Antoinette, Semiramus, Zenobia, and a raft of English queens including Elizabeth—to them the greatest and most important monarch, man or woman, of all time—circulate familiarly in their work. And, along with this vast network of casual references, a small number—a very small number—of historical works produced after 1790 began to catalog the presence of women in history for various purposes. The authors of these catalogs include Judith Sargent Murray, Susanna Rowson, Hannah Mather Crocker, Sarah Grimké, Angelina Grimké, Lydia Maria Child, Margaret Fuller, Sarah Hale, Elizabeth Ellet, and Caroline Dall. Except for Elizabeth Ellet, they were not original researchers; they worked by canvassing the major historians or popularizations of their work and extracting the women named there. This strategy of compilation was exactly right for an exercise intended to remind readers of what was already known rather than present new information.

Among the issues to which these catalogues were directed were women's education, abolitionism, women's activism, and, of course, women's rights. When one recalls that the first formal women's rights convention met in 1848, it seems safe to interpret Conkling's 1850 biography of Mary and Martha Washington as a covert attack on the movement. Sarah Hale's compendious *Woman's Record* and Elizabeth Ellet's pioneering research on women of the American Revolution were also designed to oppose women's rights. In fact, where contemporary issues were concerned, histories of women were produced more by conservatives than progressives. And if belief in a woman's essential nature is a conservative belief, then where women's issues are concerned, histories of women were also produced more by conservatives than progressives.

At first glance it seems a reasonable hypothesis that conservative women would interpret historical women unfavorably, to show that women had never done any good when they had public power; while progressive women would describe them approvingly, to build a case for female participation in the political world via precedent. But it also makes sense to imagine that conservative women would interpret historical women favorably, to show that women already had all the power they needed, while progressives would insist that women of the past were too constrained by bad religion and government to be effective in their own right. It seems likely that women who opposed the franchise, more than women who favored it, would attempt to trivialize the public reach of historical women, and to feminize them in the worst sense. As discussed in Chapter 6, Ann Stephens made Bloody Mary persecute Protestants out of sexual jealousy; her Anne Boleyn has no idea that marrying Henry VIII would bring the Reformation to England; her Theroigne de Mericourt destroys the Old Regime in France to gain revenge on the aristocrat who seduced her. Representations like this might be expected from a conservative woman. Still, it could be argued equally from a progressive stance that earlier women had not been able to act to some purpose in history because the time had not been ready for the appearance of Woman as she was meant to be.

In brief, no correlation between a woman writer's views of women's issues and her treatment of women in history can be assumed in advance. The discourse is always specific to the individual writer. In her dispatch from the Tower of London already cited, for example, the supposedly radical Margaret Fuller describes Elizabeth Tudor as an unsexed monster in the most conservative terms. She uses a portrait of Elizabeth to make her assessment: "the face is like a mask—so frightful is the expression of cold craft, irritated vanity and the malice of a lonely breast in contrast with the attitude and elaborate frippery of the dress.... Such can win the world which better hearts (and such Mary's was, even if it had a large black speck in it) are most like to lose" (Sad but Glorious, 71). In contrast to this harsh, hackneyed view of Elizabeth, in Woman's Record the conservative Sarah Hale credits the monarch with extraordinary intelligence and achievement, as well as fully public and political motives: "Her first object, after her accession, was to restore the Protestant religion; to this she was led by interest as well as principle. For the pope treated her in such a manner, that she clearly perceived, if she professed Popery, she must allow her father's divorce from Catharine of Aragon to be void, and consequently herself illegitimate; and this would have annulled her pretensions to the crown" (299). Hale sums up Elizabeth's character at once more judiciously and favorably than Fuller:

That she did not conform her own spirit to the Gospel requirements, but allowed pride, vanity, a violent temper, and selfishness, frequently to obscure her many great qualities, is to be regretted; but compared with the kings her successors, she rises so high above their standard of character, that we almost forget to record her faults. To quote the remarks of a learned historian,—"The page of history has seldom to record a reign more honourable to the intellect and capacity of the person presiding over it, than that of Elizabeth of England." (302)

The only generalization about women's history that seems to me to work dependably across the range of women's historical writings between 1790 and the Civil War is the one I have already offered: there is an ideological mutation from Enlightenment to Victorian values. In the earlier years of the period, women's history was dominated by the Enlightenment idea that mind (unlike body) had no sex; the work was done to demonstrate women's mental equality with men. Later on, women's history was actuated by the idea of women's essential spirituality; the point was to demonstrate a difference between the sexes that made women superior. In the career of especially long-lived women like Emma Willard and Sarah Hale one can trace this change within the work of the single individual. But whether Enlightenment, or Victorian, or some complicated mix of the two, all these writers struggled with the problem of women who figured notably in a historical record from which they were supposed to be absent—the problem, that is, of facts that falsified the theory. Given the difficulties involved, it is not surprising after all that so little work of this kind was undertaken.

Judith Sargent Murray's work makes a particularly interesting place to begin a survey of this material, not only because she was the first historian of woman, but also because she oscillates between sentimental and rationalist interpretations of women in history. I have already mentioned in Chapter 3 that Volume 2 of *The Gleaner* has a sequence of twelve historical letters supposedly written by a mother to her daughter showing how history should be deployed in women's education. Four of the twelve (nos. 47–50) are about Mary Queen of Scots; the mother offers an extended account of Mary as a sentimental, erotic, and pathetically feminized subject for her daughter's sympathetic contemplation:

But alas! how momentary was the bliss!—the evanescent vision soon fled, and the youthful queen was arrayed in the melancholy garb of widowhood! From this moment she seems marked the daughter of sorrow. The death of her mother rendered her return to Scotland indispensable; and, with an aching heart, she prepared to obey the dictates of duty.... Gladly would we remove her from the toils and tumults of a turbulent administration, and shelter her amidst those social haunts which she would dignify and adorn. Yet, conscious of integrity, and with a heart glowing with the benevolent purpose of appeasing conflicting passions, destroying animosities, and healing every breach, she prepared for her voyage to her hereditary dominions. (388–389)

We follow the queen to her imprisonment; we behold, with glowing resentment, the fresh insults to which she is subjected; we mingle our tears with the sympathetic multitude, who lament the degraded majesty of their sovereign! we listen to her sorrows; our attachment to the beauteous mourner is augmented, and we are ardently solicitous to snatch her from impending danger! (401)

Murray's characterization of Elizabeth works through the familiar defeminizing contrast that disqualifies her claim to greatness: "Humanity, my dear girl, must lament Elizabeth's depraved politics.... Whatever question involved the interests of Mary, seemed to possess the power of rousing to action the most nefarious propensities—of narrowing her views, and of yielding her up to the dominion of envy, jealousy, and every ignoble passion!" (405).

"The conduct of Elizabeth was unsexual, unjust, and infinitely cruel," she continues (406); "Thus did Elizabeth sacrifice true glory to her passions. Had the Queen of Scots been less beautiful, less accomplished, and less meritorious, she had not become the victim of hatred and perfidy" (409). Although Murray calls Elizabeth's behavior unsexual, she actually interprets it in profoundly sexual terms, as the expression of jealousy over Mary's femininity. It is impossible that such a motive would have been alleged of a king. Mary and Elizabeth are thus dichotomized in gendered terms as the fair and dark women of a sentimental melodrama (a construction displaying, by the way, that these oppositions were abroad in the culture long before the Jacksonian era in which they are commonly supposed to have developed).

In Volume 3 of *The Gleaner*, Murray embarks on a different kind of project and interprets Elizabeth differently. Four historical letters (nos. 88–91) contend for the equality of the female mind with the male; history is mined for examples of women equally as capable of enduring hardships as men, equally ingenious, resourceful, heroic, brave, patriotic, influential, energetic, eloquent, faithful and persevering in their attachments, capable of governing, and capable of "literary acquirement." And here is Elizabeth in the light of this search: "Elizabeth of England was endowed with energetic talents; her reign was glorious for the people over which she presided; she was undoubtedly a great politician, and governed with uniform vigour; she is characterized as possessing much penetration, and an understanding fruitful of resources; her mind was opened and polished by all the aids of an extensive education, and adversity was among her preceptors" (721).

Murray names two dozen (nonliterary) historical women out of what she says is a catalog of many hundreds to support her claim "that the minds of women are *naturally* as susceptible of every improvement, as those of men" and to argue that "if the triumphs and attainments of the sex, under the various oppressions with which they have struggled, have been thus splendid, how would they have been augmented, had not ignorant or interested men, after clipping their wings, contrived to erect around them almost insurmountable barriers" (710). The whole argument is motivated by her patriotic certainty that, "in this younger world, 'the Rights of Women' begin to be understood" and that, in particular, opportunities for female education "of a more elevated and elevating nature" than needlework are everywhere arising in the United States (703). Murray's brief for an intellectual education of women brings out what looks like a radical sexual egalitarianism favoring female heroes; but the content of that education as exemplified in her history of Mary Queen of Scots would seem to indoctrinate women in an ideology of radical sexual difference, in which it is better to be Mary than Elizabeth, better to be dead than an unsexed woman. But Mary Stuart, notably, is not one of the two dozen women used to demonstrate female equality with men. *The Gleaner* thus juxtaposes incompatible versions of women's history without making any attempt to reconcile them.

In both versions, however, Murray scrutinizes the record of individual women for general truths about women. The writer does not escape—no antebellum writer of women's history escapes—the conviction that every woman must represent Woman in general. And since this sense is lacking from the historical treatment of men, even the most apparently egalitarian woman's history undermines itself. Men in history are, of course, used as examples of general truths, usually about virtue and vice or political theory or even human nature—but not about Man as Eternal Male. The habit of extracting women from history to support one or another argument about essential female nature, no matter what the specific argument might be, has the result, if not of making all women seem more or less the same, of suggesting that all women ought to be more or less the same, and of course of disqualifying numerous nominal women from membership in the sex.

An essay in Susanna Rowson's 1811 *Present for Young Ladies* is internally disjointed like Murray's, although along a somewhat different fault line. Titled "Sketches of Female Character," it has a catalog like Murray's, offered like hers to show that women possess virtues usually associated with men: learning, courage, fortitude. But in introducing the sketch, Rowson writes:

> History with a pen dipped in the blood of millions, wet with the widow's and orphan's tears, records the struggle of contending powers . . . relates the rise and fall of empires, tracing the steps of those . . . striding over heaps of their slaughtered fellow creatures. . . . Let us from scenes like these, of death and horror, turn to the fair page that registers individual merit. Biography is equally authentic, equally instructive, and in general, more interesting than history. (83)

This passage associates women with biography, men with history, in order to exempt women from historical culpability. Women, that is, are objects to be contemplated rather than subjects of activity. (And, indeed, there is far more female biography in antebellum America than there is history of women—but since there is much less female biography than male biography, it is hard to know what to make of this fact.) Yet Rowson also wants to insist on women's historical agency—"innumerable instances may be presented of female courage, fortitude, and talent of every description" (84). Again, one sees that if history is bad, and women are good, then women in history must also somehow be innocent of history. Only a woman-specific historiography involved this particular inner contradiction.

As the tourists' obsession with murdered queens will already have suggested (Chapter 7), the women historians of women tended to picture their ideal in situations of pious resignation to ultimate defeat. For Rowson, as for many others, Lady Jane Grey was a particularly touching instance of feminine heroism—a genteel lover of learning, devoted to her husband, reluctantly accepting the English crown to please conspiratorial male relatives and executed almost at once by a vengeful Mary Tudor. Lady Jane matters to this kind of history not as monarch but martyr: Protestant martyr to a Catholic fanatic, and female martyr to men who make her serve their lust for power. The dynamic is only partly explainable as symptomatic of a general Protestant affection for martyrs. Historical men are praised for their triumphs or, at least, for heroic resistance to greater force; graceful submission does not make a hero. In contrast, a woman expresses her womanhood when she loses, and sacrifices her womanhood when she wins. This sexual asymmetry makes Mary Queen of Scots more valued in these histories than Elizabeth I; the negative judgment of Elizabeth for being *unwomanly* exemplifies the problem of writing women's history through-out the entire period I am surveying—and perhaps haunts it still.

Hannah Mather Crocker's *Observations on the Real Rights of Women* (1818) begins from the Enlightenment position that "Although there must be allowed some moral and physical distinction of the sexes agreeably to the order of nature, and the organization of the human frame, still the sentiment must predominate, that the powers of mind are equal in the sexes." She proposes to "produce examples, both from sacred and profane history, of the great abilities of many females, when called into account, either on political or religious account" (5–6). Stressing women's mental powers—physical inferiority, after all, requires them to work "by reason and persuasion" not force (15)—Crocker catalogs women in history from the Old Testament to the present. The partial coincidence of her list with Rowson's and Murray's suggests that early on a canon of prominent women was emerging that, like all canons, left room for marginal additions and variations. Among names on her list are Zenobia, Jane of Flanders, Queen Elizabeth, Lady Jane Grey, Cornelia; and also Queen Anne, Xantippe, and Mary Shurman, a "painter, musician, engraver, sculptor, philosopher, geometrician," who "understood nine different languages" (36).

The reformist writings of the Grimké sisters—Angelina for abolition and against colonization, Sarah on women's rights—regularly refer to women in history to legitimate their call for female activism. Angelina addressed herself to a female audience, arguing that abolition was right and that it was more than right, it was absolutely mandatory, for women to take part in the movement. Leaning heavily on Old Testament women—Grimké used biblical language and examples throughout her writings—she developed a long catalog of historical women who had acted in public when the cause was just. *An Appeal to the Christian Women of the South* (1836) assures her countrywomen that they can endure (even glory in) the persecution likely to result from their espousing an unpopular cause by citing the Old Testament examples of Miriam, Deborah, Jael, Huldah, and Esther; the New Testament examples of Elizabeth wife of Zacharias, Anna, and Mary Magdalene; and with generalizations about the martyrdom of numerous Roman, Huguenot, Albigensian, and American Quaker women, among others.

Her 1837 *Appeal to the Women of the Nominally Free States* argues with historical examples that women have "wisely and laudably exercised political responsibilities" (10), working as before from the Old Testament (Miriam again) through Rome (the wife and mother of Coriolanus) on through Joan of Arc to Lydia Darrah, who conveyed crucial intelligence to George Washington. "We do not, then, and cannot concede the position, that because this is *a political* subject women ought to fold their hands to idleness, and close their eyes and ears" (13–14). Moreover, she continues, since it was a woman monarch—Elizabeth—who first legalized the African slave trade, "through whose instrumentality so many thousands of victims of oppression have been brought to our land, then *women* are bound to do all they can to exterminate the evil which *woman* exerted her power and authority to bring upon our country and the world" (20). This attack on Elizabeth, at least, allows that she had political motives.

Several of Sarah Grimké's *Letters on the Equality of the Sexes, and the Condition of Women* (1838) name women of achievement in history. Letter 9, on "heroism of women—women in authority" scours the record in no particular order for Philippa, wife of Edward III; Jane, Countess of Montfort; Joan of Arc, whose history is "too familiar to need repetition" (56); Hersilia; Portia; Hortensia; Lady Packington; Lacy Broughton; Anne, Countess of Pembroke; the queens Elizabeth, Maria Theresa, Catherine, and Isabella. "The page of history proves incontestably, not only that they are as well qualified to [sway the sceptre of royalty] as men, but that there has been a comparatively greater proportion of good queens, than of good kings; women who have purchased their celebrity by individual strength of character" (59).

Letter 10 considers the female intellect and adduces such examples as Cornelia, Hypatia, Victoria Colonna, and Isabella of Rosera; "in England the names of many women, from Lady Jane Grey down to Harriet Martineau, are familiar to every reader of history" (64). Behind these visible women, Sarah argues, legions of unknowns authorize such general phrases as "the women of Rome," or "the women of the Revolution." The historical women serve as precedents in these arguments; they show contemporary women that what is asked of them now is just what admirable women have done throughout recorded time.

In 1835 Lydia Maria Child—in process of becoming an abolitionist, but never to be an advocate for women's rights—completed her five volumes of compilation, which she called "The Lady's Family Library," cutting and pasting a mass of different textual materials into a wide-ranging but on the whole deeply conservative representation of women in history. Volume 1 of this "library" contained the memoirs of Madame Guyon and Lady Russell, the first (as Sarah Hale writes in *Woman's Record*) "memorable for her sufferings in defence of her religion" (337), the second for noble fortitude in the face of her husband's execution. Volume 2 has the memoirs of Madame Roland, executed during the Terror, to whom her influential husband (to quote Hale again) "owed his courage, and the power of his talents" (491); and Madame de Staël. Child construes three of these intellectual women as martyrs, and the fourth—in the teeth of these publicity about Staël's sexually free behavior—as a wifely paragon. Volume 3 of the series makes Child's point in its title: *Good Wives*. It assembles biographies of forty-two women from Panthea to Madame Lafayette to argue that women's claim to historical fame must rest in their character as wives, which she translates as selfless suffering; in other words, women's claim to historical fame must be the total absence of fame. This is counter-history indeed. The preface to *Good Wives* lays out this project:

It was my original intention to have entitled this volume, the Wives of Distinguished Men. But great men have sometimes have had bad wives; and it seemed undesirable to perpetuate the memory of such. . . . If this book convince one doubting individual that there really is such a thing as constant, disinterested love, which misfortune cannot in-timidate, or time diminish; . . . If it reveal to one thoughtless wife some portion of the celestial beauty there is in a perfect union of duty and inclination;—if it prevent one young heart from becoming selfish and world-worn;—if it make one of the frivolous, or the profligate, be-lieve in a holy affection, that purifies those who indulge it, blesses them on earth, and fits them to be angels in heaven—then it has not been written in vain. . . . Our mothers were help-mates indeed; and so are many of their daughters; but it is well to be on our guard, lest the household virtues become neglected and obsolete. (9, 12, 13)

The concern for the nation's future, and the attack on worldliness and selfishness, express the familiar ideology of republican womanhood; but Child submerges each woman in her husband and her wifely role with par-ticular intensity (as she would do in *Philothea* as well). Even the promis-ingly titled two-volume set that completes the library—a *History of the Condition of Women, in Various Ages and Nations*—is obsessed with the monogamous couple. The worldwide approach—the first volume is about Asia and Africa, the second about Europe, America, and the South Sea Islands—promises multicultural tolerance; but in practice Child finds the condition of women in all non-Christian societies deplorable because there is no ideology of monogamous marriage. She believes that male respect for women makes women respectable, that only respectable women can be true helpmeets to men, and that this interactive ideal of the couple is unique to Protestant Christianity.

Child is, indeed, unusually fixated on sexual purity, even for an ante-bellum woman. "As moral or intellectual beings, it would be better for [Persian women] to be among the dead than the living" (1:77); "In no part of the world does the condition of women appear more dreary than in Hindostan" (1:117); "A more uncouth and unpleasant sight" than a veiled Mohammedan woman riding on a bullock "cannot well be imag-ined, unless it might be a shrouded corpse thus mounted" (1:123). Child appreciates the ancient Egyptians, crediting them for teaching "the knowl-edge of one God, and of the immortality of the soul" (her point that the Egyptians "with the exception of the lips" do not look like stereotypical Africans disqualifies her, however, as a foremother of the theory of the

Black Athena); but present-day Egypt is "degenerate" (1:223, 225). Her treatment of Africa is permeated equally with a generous indignation against the slave trade and a racist interpretation of black Africans, who,

as distinguished from the Arabs or Moors, are faithful, affectionate, sensitive in their feelings, and liable to almost instantaneous changes from gloom to gayety, according to the circumstances in which they are placed. When in the greatest misery, a kind look or word will animate them, as it does the heart of a little child; but when their cup of suffering is full, the "drop too much" which tyranny seeks to add to the bitter measure, often arouses them to fierce and desperate fury. In a state of freedom they are almost universally gentle, inquisitive, credulous, and fond of flattery. (1:273)

"Low as the Hottentots are on the scale of humanity," she writes a few pages later, "they are by no means destitute of good and agreeable qualities" (1:292). This, from a leading American women abolitionist, speaks volumes about the abolitionist mind. And if it seems that women have been lost in these transgendered descriptions, this is Child's own iterated point: in any nation, she insists, the condition of women depends entirely on men. The two cannot be separated. "Panegyrists cannot raise women above their level, or satirists force them below it. Their character and condition is always in correspondence with that of men; and both sexes have always furnished about an equal number of exceptions to the general character of the age in which they lived" (2:142).

When she turns her attention to Europe, Child, like so many who believed that without Christianity there is no history, becomes historical for the first time. But she does not chronicle the deeds of exceptional individuals. She is, rather, a historian of cultural ideals, looking for a culture with an appropriately spiritual ideal of woman:

The ardor with which chivalry was embraced by all the principal nations of Europe, and the powerful hold it still retains on the imagination, notwithstanding the detestable pride and tyranny of those gallant nobles, is to be attributed to the sacred principles on which the institution was originally founded; viz. the chaste union of the sexes, and the forgetfulness of self in the effort to do good to others. . . . It raised woman to a moral rank in society, unknown to the most refined nations of antiquity—a rank she can never entirely lose, and from which her present comparative freedom is derived. (2:118–119)

Women's comparative freedom, one cannot but note, depends on the extent to which they are chaste and self-sacrificing. Her particular concern with female sexual purity leads Child constantly to assess the condition of women according to the prevalence of what she calls depravity. Exculpation (woman become depraved in societies where they cannot freely choose their mates) and condemnation (depraved women are a threat to national security) mingle in her prose without resolution: "Licentiousness abounds in all cities; it is not confined to a class of women avowedly depraved but sometimes lurks beneath the garb of decency, and even of elegance. In villages there is a better state of things, because the influences of rural life are more pure, and young people generally form marriages of inclination" (2:205).

Turning to the United States, Child reveals more clearly than ever her purpose of indoctrinating readers in the ideology of sexual difference as exemplified in Protestant Christian marriage:

At those periods when reason has run wild, and men have maintained that there was no such thing as unchangeable truth . . . there has always been a tendency to have men and women change places, that the latter might command armies and harangue senates, while men attended to domestic concerns. These doctrines were maintained by infidels of the French revolution, and by their modern disciple, Fanny Wright.

Many silly things have been written, and are now written, concerning the equality of the sexes; but that true and perfect companionship, which gives both man and woman complete freedom *in* their places, without a restless desire to go out of them, is as yet imperfectly understood. The time will come, when it will be seen that the moral and intellectual condition of woman must be, and ought to be, in exact correspondence with that of man, not only in its general aspect but in its individual manifestations. (2:210–211)

The United States, the most virtuous country on earth, is in real danger: "the substantial body of the people have still a religious cast of character; but infidelity has taken strong hold in cities. The connection between religion and marriage is not obvious, but it is real. All infidels, whether they be found in France, England, or America, have a decided tendency to regard the institution of marriage as tyrannical" (2:261). Child's *History of the Condition of Women*, then, is written from a divine perspective in which progress toward the millennium is measured by the progress of women toward their ideal "condition"—that of "chaste union" in monogamous marriage.

Child's history of women makes a interesting contrast here to Hale's *Woman's Record* (1853, 1855), which, although rooted in the same ideology and compiled by a more conservative woman (according to late twentieth-century standards, that is), is much more relaxed about female impropriety throughout the ages, and measures female attainments differently. Here is Cleopatra, for example:

> Her ambition was as unbounded as her love of pleasure.... Her temper was imperious, and she was boundlessly profuse in her expenditures; nor did she ever hesitate to sacrifice, when it suited her own interest, all the decorum of her rank and sex. But we must remember, also, that she lived in an age of crime. She was better than the men her subtle spirit subdued,—for she was true to her country. Never was Egypt so rich in wealth, power and civilization, as under her reign. (32)

Woman's Record solves the problem of biography versus history for women better than any other work of the period by making the two genres work together. It divides its two thousand biographies of celebrated women into four historical periods to illustrate female progress through the ages. In global terms, Hale meant it to be her masterwork, a history of women that was itself an event in history. In immediate terms, she meant it to combat women's righters and abolitionist women.

Each chronological section of Woman's Record corresponds to a higher stage in the development and expression of the female character. In each section there are progressively more biographies; the increase corresponds to the widening impact that women have on public life, as evinced in the ever larger number of celebrated women. Hale outlines the scheme in her preface. The first era runs from the Creation to the birth of Christ, when women "had only their natural gifts of a lovelier organization of form, and a purer moral sense, to aid them in the struggle with sin which had taken possession of the brute strength, and human understanding of men" (xl). From A.D. 1 to A.D. 1500, woman had "the aid of the blessed Gospel, which seems given purposely to develop her powers and sanction her influence" (xli). Around 1500 the invention of print gave a freedom to woman's mind that matched the earlier emancipation of her soul, so that men who are philosophers, philanthropists, patriots, and Christians now "find in educated women, as the Bible represents her mission, and this Record shows her influence and her works, their best earthly helper, counsellor, encourager, and exemplar" (xli). In the fourth era, the United States enters history: "A new element of improvement, now in course of rapid development, is destined to have a wonderful effect on the female mind and character. This element is individual liberty, secured by constitutional laws" (xli).

Margaret Fuller's brief for woman's rights, Woman in the Nineteenth

Century, is multiply historicized and historical. First, it envisions a familiar millennial allegory of history, in which nations in time exemplify the unfolding of ideas, and in which the mental emancipation of women, the increasing recognition that they are human beings and individual souls, signifies a world progress identified particularly with the United States, where the doctrine that "all men are created equal," though implemented only fitfully, has nevertheless been enunciated and therefore "cannot fail sooner or later to be acted out" (in Steele, 254). Second, it catalogs historical women as evidence of what women have always been capable of. Third—and this is an innovation—it compiles images of women in literature, on the grounds that a culture's images of women index its respect for them.

This approach reflects Fuller's literary orientation as well as her convictions that a nation's literature is a facet of its history and that ideas are the causes of practice. At the same time, her preference for literature over "life" may reveal a Utopian ambivalence about how deeply one should become mired in the past, when the world's real work involved the future. Caroline Dall reports that during one of Fuller's formal conversations on Greek mythology (in 1841), "Sophia Ripley asked if the mythology had been a prophecy of the Greek mind to itself, or if the nation had experienced life in any wide or deep sense. Margaret seemed a little out of patience, and no wonder! She said it did not matter which. The question was, what could *we find* in the myth, and what did the Greeks mean we should find there" (*Margaret and Her Friends*, 51). When Dall, according to her account, herself said that "it made a good deal of difference to me whether the Orphic Mythology came before or after that of Homer," Fuller responded that "she did not like a mind always looking back" (52).

Fuller's lists of historical women occur at different places in the explication; they include Semiramis, Elizabeth of England, Catherine of Russia. "What an intellectual triumph was that of the lonely Aspasia, and how heartily acknowledged! . . . Roman women—Sappho! Eloisa! . . . Across the ages, forms lean, trying to touch the hem of their retreating robes" (266–267). She refers to the women of Sparta, Athens, and Rome, to Eve and the Virgin Mary, Isabella of Castile, Madame Roland, Mary Wollestonecraft, Lady Jane Grey, Iphegenia, Persica, Victoria Colonna, Abigail Adams and Lady Russell, Boadicia, Godiva, Queen Emma, Anne Hutchinson. All of this material leads up to an address to the "women of my country," women "of English, old English nobleness." "If you have a power," Fuller exhorts, demonstrating just how fully a woman of the nineteenth century she was herself, "it is a moral power" (341).

The woman most fully discussed in *Woman in the Nineteenth Century* is Queen Elizabeth. Since Fuller is so keen in this book to insist on female self-reliance, one might have expected Elizabeth to receive strongly favorable treatment, but this does not happen. Through two contrasts—between Isabella and Elizabeth, and between Mary Stuart and Elizabeth—Fuller characterizes the English monarch as an only partly developed woman. Isabella and Elizabeth assimilate royal power to their womanly essence in opposite ways; the former shows that it "did not unfit a woman for the duties of a wife and a mother," Elizabeth that "it could enable her to live and die alone, a wide energetic life, a courageous death." Mary Stuart and Elizabeth "seem types, moulded by the spirit of the time, and placed upon an elevated platform" to exemplify two kinds of women for ages to come. Mary is "woman such as the conduct and wishes of man in general is likely to make her, lovely even to allurement, quick in apprehension and weak in judgment, with grace and dignity of sentiment, but no principle," without "steadfast wisdom, or self-restraining virtue." Elizabeth, however, is woman "half-emancipated and jealous of her freedom,"

mannish, not equally manly, strong and prudent more than great or wise; able to control vanity, and the wish to rule through coquetry and passion, but not to resign these dear deceits, from the very foundation, as unworthy a being capable of truth and nobleness. . . . The time and her position called on her to act the wise sovereign, and she was proud that she could do so, but her tastes and inclinations would have led her to act the weak woman. She was without magnanimity of any kind. (277–278)

On the whole, then, Fuller concludes, she is glad that it was Isabella rather than Elizabeth "who furnished Columbus with the means of coming hither" (278), even though she has attributed nothing to Isabella beyond her talent for domesticity.

The association of Isabella with the discovery of America was conventional American history. In *The Female Student* (1833), for example, Almira Hart Phelps said:

We may, my dear pupils, justly feel a pride in the thought, that a *woman was the first to comprehend the sublime conceptions of Columbus*; and providential indeed does it appear that this woman was a sovereign, able as well as willing to aid the genius which her mind appreciated. Isabella—let the daughters of Columbia ever hold thy name in reverence! let them remember that, without thy aid, their own dear country might even now have been a wilderness, shared by the savage heathen, and the scarcely more savage beast of the forest! (167–168)

But Fuller was not supposed to be a conventional woman. The conquest of Granada, the expulsion of the Jews, the institution of the Inquisition—there was plenty of material to make Isabella a political, powerful, bigoted, and unscrupulous monarch, had Fuller chosen to. Especially given Fuller's extreme Protestantism, one might have expected her to make this choice. But: Isabella was married, and Elizabeth was not. To depict the independent Elizabeth between Isabella the housewife and Mary the belle, is to read these regal women according to the domestic gender allegories and sentimental fictions of the mid-nineteenth century, which shows how little Fuller could imagine the equal or individual or transcendentalist female soul she was insisting that every woman possessed. And if an emancipated spirit like Fuller could not escape her moment, it is hardly surprising that others could not either.

If, then, one had some hope that histories of women would express a late-twentieth-century sense of things, these examples show how nonhistorical such a hope must be. The instances of Caroline Dall and Elizabeth Ellet—the one feminist and the other antifeminist, both sharing ideas of women that make them seem as much alike as different—will complete *my* catalog. Dall, corresponding editor of the *Una* (a radical woman's journal published in Providence by Paulina Wright Davis), contributed many historical essays about women to the magazine. Some of these appeared in her *Historical Pictures Retouched* in 1860. Among other projects, she rescues Aspasia from Hale's critical discussion of her in *Woman's Record*, rescues Hypatia from the alleged misrepresentations in Kingsley's novel, and surveys "The Women of Bologna" along with "The Contributions of Women to Medical Science." In her essay on the "Duties and Influence of Women," Dall the feminist writes like any cultist of an invigorated version of true womanhood:

A well-educated, highly principled negro is the best argument for African freedom: so an intelligent woman, feeling an interest in the well-being of her nation and the world, and capable at once of orderly house-keeping, a delicate toilet, acute argument, or vigorous *work* (and no person is educated who has not a vocation), makes the strongest appeal for the whole freedom of her sex. . . . The greatest mistake which a woman can commit is to suppose that she has no *influence*. In addition to that which she possesses as a human being, she has a peculiar share as a woman. It is her duty to make it of the highest kind. (172, 174)

The essay develops a list of historical women who misused their influence: Lucretia Borgia, for example, and "the atrocious Lady Hamilton. . . . That this woman invented the shawl dance is reason enough why every modest girl should shrink from it" (185). In an essay on Madame de Staël, insisting

231

counterfactually that "during her long life, the breath of scandal never touched her," that "gifted as she was, longing to love and be beloved with all the intensity of a passionate nature, she yet remained irreproachable" (212–213), Dall launches a furious attack on the corrupt ways in which women throughout history have usually exercised political power.

Women, uneducated to perceive the higher relations of party questions, throw all their weight and wealth . . . on the side of a temporary success, for lover, child, or friend. [In France] the vile mistress of a prince . . . became so active as an agent of political cliques, that a government vessel was not long ago deputed to bring her to our own shores. [In Washington] women sell the votes that their own baseness brings within their power, and feminine maneuvering and dishonor accomplish that for which all the strength of manly life has been found insufficient. (207–208)

Dall is agitating for women on behalf of an ideal and deploys the historical record to show how far women are from it. Like Child's, Dall's conservatism partly reflects an obsession with sexual purity. While advancing all kinds of testimony to learned expertise—as, for example, she discards a faulty representation of Aspasia's character: "the publication of Thirlwall and Grote, of excellent translations of Plato, Aristophanes, and Xenephon, leaves us no excuse for such ignorance as is displayed in the volume alluded to" (5)—her spirited defenses of Aspasia, of Staël, and of other historical women always and only concern their sexual behavior. Undoubtedly historical women had been discredited through attacks on their sexual conduct, and certainly contemporary women striving for public voice had to contend with rumor and innuendo about their private lives also. Still, Dall's remarks about the power of corrupt women suggest both that women were surviving such attacks and also that Dall herself would more likely be an attacker than a defender if a woman's sexual life was not altogether beyond reproach. From this perspective, depraved women should simply not be written about at all.

In none of these writings about women in history does one encounter the idea that there might have been numerous women who "deserved" to be in the record but had somehow been omitted from it by the prejudices of historians. If anything, as we have seen, the record might at times seem too full of women whose presence required explaining, or explaining away. The only kind of scholarship that these women historians did was comparative; they chose among representations of women in different historical sources and attempted to reconcile competing interpretations. The mother in Murray's *The Gleaner* asks her daughter whether she prefers Stuart's to Robinson's interpretations of Mary Queen of Scots, and approves her choice of Stuart: "Doctor Stuart proposes himself as the *historian*, and not as the *panegyrist* of Mary; and *as his means of information were probably as direct and infallible as those of any other writer*, I yield him my *cheerful and grateful* credence" (388).

The lone producer of an original women's archive was Elizabeth Ellet, who published five books between 1848 and 1852 about the participation of American women in the Revolution. These include three biographical volumes called *Women of the American Revolution* (two in 1848, one in 1850); a history of the Revolution from the civilian point of view titled *A Domestic History of the American Revolution* (1850); and, finally, a book about the settlement of the post-Revolutionary frontiers, *Pioneer Women of the West* (1852). The first two volumes of *Women of the American Revolution* take the familiar shape of a compilation of goodwife biographies. Although Ellet mainly used published sources in putting them together, she tried to flesh out the record by consulting surviving kin. Her preface acknowledges that requests for archival materials had not been answered as fully as she had hoped, and complains in familiar ways about the "inherent difficulty in delineating female character,"

which impresses itself on the memory of those who have known the individual by delicate traits, that may be felt but not described. The actions of men stand out in prominent relief, and are a safe guide in forming a judgment of them; a woman's sphere, on the other hand, is secluded, and in very few instances does her personal history, even though she may fill a conspicuous position, afford sufficient incident to throw a strong light on her character. This want of salient points for descriptions must be felt by all who have attempted a faithful portraiture of some beloved female relative. (1:xi)

Although this approach to women's lives would seem to preclude writing history about them, Ellet does want to argue that these eventless existences profoundly influenced the outcome of the Revolution, which means she needs to start thinking about what constitutes an event in history. Here I must quote at some length:

Patriotic mothers nursed the infancy of freedom. Their counsels and their prayers mingled with the deliberations that resulted in a nation's assertion of its independence. They animated the courage, and confirmed the self-devotion of those who ventured all in the common cause. They frowned upon instances of coldness or backwardness; and in the period of deepest gloom, cheered and urged onward the desponding. They willingly shared inevitable dangers and privations, relinquished without regret prospects of advantage to themselves, and parted with those they loved better than life, not knowing when they were to meet again. It is almost impossible now to appreciate the vast influence of woman's patriotism upon the destinies of the infant republic. We have no means of showing the important part she bore in maintaining the struggle, and in laying the foundations on which so mighty and majestic a structure has arisen. History can do it no justice; for history deals with the workings of the head, rather than the heart. . . . We can only dwell upon individual instances of magnanimity, fortitude, self-sacrifice, and heroism, bearing the impress of the feeling of Revolutionary days, indicative of the spirit which animated all, and to which, in its various and multiform exhibitions, we are not less indebted for national freedom, than to the swords of the patriots who poured out their blood. (1:14–15)

These sentences gesture toward a kind of history that had never yet been written, a history of the ordinary rather than the exceptional. This, combined with her archival recovery work, makes Ellet significantly different from the historians of women who worked entirely with exceptional cases, and different again from Child, who did not allot any specific agency to women even in the construction of their own condition. Ellet seems almost to be anticipating social history in a twentieth-century sense (and some present-day historians have interpreted her in this light).

Nevertheless, in antebellum context Ellet may be clearly seen as trying to write history consistent with a republican millennialist ideology that takes history's motive force away from exceptional men and woman involved in monarchies and despotisms, and invests it in the people. The approach does not imply that history should always have been written from this point of view, only that the historical change represented by the Revolution demands a new kind of history. That the Revolution both caused and signified a paradigm shift in the historical process is, of course, fundamental to the republican millennial paradigm to which just about all Americans writing history seem to have subscribed before the Civil War. Ellet's innovation is to highlight the contribution of women. The innovation brings women to a new kind of prominence by subsuming them within a historical scheme whose conventional meaning is not contested, indeed is passionately accepted.

The exemplary women celebrated in the first two volumes of *Women of the American Revolution* are clear examples of old-fashioned virtue. In these volumes, despite an expressed desire to represent the whole population, Ellet quite naturally depends heavily on the more accessible and often already published records of elite women. (In fact, some reviewers criticized her for claiming more originality than she delivered.) Still more importantly, Ellet deliberately looks for "matrons" whose names "deserve to live in remembrance" (1:22), which is to say, for goodwives. Her choice produces a monitory vision of republican woman working to sustain, support, and cheer the men who do history's real labor:

And throughout this scene of varied perplexity, when the heart of the statesman was oppressed by trouble without—disappointment, ingratitude—all that makes a politician's life so wretched, he was sure to find his home happy, his wife smiling and contented, with no visible sorrow to impair her welcome, and no murmur to break the melody of domestic joy. It sustained him to the end. This was humble, homely heroism, but it did its good work in cheering and sustaining a spirit that might otherwise have broken. (1:52)

Obviously Ellet means this image to play a part in contemporary debates over women's sphere. She stands for the old-style republicanism in which civic virtue must always override personal desire, and by contrasting the hardy, virtuous yet genteel dames of the Revolution with the super-sensitively refined, falsely genteel, malingering, luxury-loving, idle, dependent, and self-seeking modern woman, she shows how far short the contemporary woman falls of the standard. Both women's rights and its opposite, the extreme cult of true womanhood in which female spirituality equates to passive submissiveness, are her targets: "Let our indolent fine ladies blush for themselves when they learn that a woman of mind and intelligence, whose rare powers of conversation charmed the social circle, actually carded, spun, wove, cut and made all the clothes worn by an officer of the army in active service during the southern campaign . . . and that the material of her own dress was manufactured by her own hands!" (1:326).

The third volume of *Women of the American Revolution* takes a new tack. Here, Ellet insists, all the material comes from unpublished sources. The proportion of obscure women described is much larger, although the purposes for which they are described remains the same. In addition, Ellet points out, she has

occasionally added to the sketches of the women, notices of brave men nearly related to them, whose services deserved mention, with anecdotes illustrative of the war or the state of the country. This has been done only where no account of the individual or of the incident is given in any published work. Many among the actors in that momentous drama, whose deeds should have been recorded, are scarcely mentioned by name in historical books, and no full history has ever been written of some parts of the Confederacy. (3:iii)

Recovering women's stories is now part of a much larger effort to bring the Revolution back to modern memory in all its force. "Official" history, she is maintaining, has tended to remove the war from the people who actually fought it. The war was not a series of exploits by a coterie of brilliant military leaders and inspired statesmen. It was, rather, the joint effort of all the people from the seaboard to the frontiers and beyond, north and south. In this book, Ellet attempts to plant the Revolution on every square foot of American soil.

Ordering her biographical sketches narratively according to the received view of the war's progress through the states, Ellet moves south from New England and inland from the coast and increasingly centers her account on the terrains made vulnerable to attack by the departure of men to the front. This focus allows her to discover the Tories, and to present the war in its aspect as a Civil War as much as an uprising against a foreign power. Insisting nevertheless that the war was a united effort by all the people, she deploys patriotism as a means of distinguishing the true people from the false. Given the 1850 publication date of this third volume, Ellet probably had the future stability of the Union in mind as she wrote it; the contemporary applications of her work go beyond attacks on women's rights and female self-pampering.

Moreover, as the narrative works outward to the frontiers, Ellet also discovers or rediscovers the Indian allies of the Tories and British troops. Her focus on heroic female preservation of hearth and home while men are at the front leads her to a systematic and thorough demonizing of Native Americans. It is as though, with the men off fighting conventional battles at the front, the future of the continent is played out as a rearguard combat between women and Indians, with the former standing for progressive Christian republican values and the latter representing the powers of darkness. Working through a series of accounts of Indian atrocities on the borders during the Revolution, Ellet links American Revolutionary female heroism to the long panorama of Indian wars that marked the history of the United States from the start: "In the midst of those trials and sufferings were enacted deeds of heroism and chivalry which might well challenge a comparison with those of the Pequod War and King Philip" (3:310); "From the landing of these pilgrims at Nashville, they were regarded by the various tribes of Indians around them as intruders, and a war of extermination was waged upon them" (3:313). Another contribution or intervention in contemporary political debate—this time on the question of territorial expansion—is evident here.

As for what they convey about women: Volume 1 recounts the greatest number of female exploits, while Volumes 2 and 3 focus more on female endurance and suffering—connected in Volume 2 to pillaging and looting, and in Volume 3 to Indian brutality. Since the action in the latter two vol-

NoYes

umes is much more intense and violent than in 1, the overall impression is still that "history" evades women, that they are far more effective on the sidelines as witness and testimony than in the fray. As though recognizing this fact (or perhaps more mundanely to recirculate her researches), Ellet ran much of the material in *Women of the American Revolution* through a new format and published it as *A Domestic History of the American Revolution* in 1850. Linda Kerber has written of this book that it tries "to place gender at the narrative center of the Revolutionary experience" and to "tell the history of the American Revolution from the perspective of both men and women," and comments that it is the only history of the war she has read "that devotes as much space to women as to men." But she adds that it is not women's history; "it seeks to be holistic" ("History Can Do It No Justice," 5–6). Indeed the word "domestic" in Ellet's title does not invoke a separate female sphere; Ellet uses it to make the republican point that men and women alike live in a domestic world which the Revolution was fought to preserve.

In pursuit of its object, *A Domestic History* de-emphasizes the biographical aspect of the material it reuses, frequently omitting the women's names, for example, and always leaving out the apparatus of chronology, genealogy, and physical appearance that had been part of the sketches in her earlier book. The result is at once more ideologically democratic and more narratively historical than the earlier sequence, but, as Kerber notes, it is no longer women's history. It is an experiment in connecting women's stories to a Revolutionary narrative still made up of military events.

If Ellet's practice had changed, her claims for women's—or rather, woman's—influence in the Revolution had not. Indeed she repeated them in the same words: "It is almost impossible now to appreciate the vast influence of woman's patriotism upon the destinies of the infant republic. We have no means of showing the important part she bore in maintaining the struggle," and so on, right through "the swords of the patriots who poured out their blood" (42). The demonization of the English, the Loyalists, and the Indians is even more extreme in this book than in the earlier volumes. The implicit concern with sectional issues in those books becomes explicit here, as in her conclusion, which strives to enlist all Americans and especially women in the project of saving the Union:

The men and women of America during the Revolution, acted with one heart and one mind. In their entire devotion to the cause—whether at the East, in the Middle States, or at the South—one spirit is seen to govern them. They thought not of sectional distinctions; they felt and acted like brethren. . . . Let all Americans who love their country ponder on the lesson conveyed. Let them cherish the UNION of these States, as they honor the memory of those noble men who did and suffered so much to cement it. Let them never part with that precious legacy bought with their fathers' blood and transmitted to them to be kept inviolate for their own children. For the security of this inestimable possession, let them sacredly preserve the spirit of disinterestedness, of patriotism, of RELIGION—the seed of all that is good and elevated in the social life of the Republic. (307–308)

The unspoken and underrepresented presence in Ellet's books, especially obvious given this finale, is the African American. Astonishingly, as she works her way through the southern states, Ellet has almost nothing to say about slavery; the African Americans presented are always personally loyal to their patriot mistresses and masters and equally devoted to the Union. The appeal to Americans to preserve the Union, then, if not proslavery, is at least antiabolitionist; and this along with the expansionist sentiments of Volume 3 of *Women of the American Revolution* points again to Ellet's interventionist purposes in these volumes. So too with the last of these American history books, *Pioneer Women of the West* (1852). Like *A Domestic History*, it is structured as a series of biographical sketches or memoirs organized in a narrative of progressive white settlement on the contemporary frontier. Working from south to north, it begins with Tennessee as a refuge for impoverished revolutionary veterans—thus making settlement a direct result of the Revolution and in some senses a continuation of it—and ends with Michigan.

The book's repeated event is Indian warfare; Native Americans are portrayed from a strikingly hostile perspective almost without exception; the only Native Americans to whose killing Ellet objects are the Moravian Christianized Indians of Pennsylvania. This is no saga of voluntary vanishing, or melancholy displacement; Ellet is as close to a genocidal writer as one is likely to find. Eradicating the Native American population is for her just the most heroic of many challenges faced by the post-Revolutionary population filling up the continent.

Ellet describes this book as "an appropriate supplement" to her work on the Revolution. "So obvious a consequence of the Revolution was the diffusion of the spirit of emigration, that the one work naturally calls for the other, the domestic history of the period being incomplete without it" (v). The expansionist narrative says that the Revolution produced pioneers because the government was too poor to indemnify the patriots for wartime losses. Thus arose the "necessity of making a home among the savages of a great wilderness, and reducing that wilderness to a state of law, order, and refinement" (223). The settlers, then, were the patriots themselves, removed to a new field of endeavor. On the frontier, they retained some of the heroic qualities that enabled them to wage a successful Revolution; and these were exactly the qualities needed for settling a wild territory.

tory. The hand of God is visible, as the locus of national identity moves from the seaboard to the frontiers. The hardships of settlement keep alive a heroism that is otherwise disappearing from American life, but which is as necessary now for the tasks of nation-building as it was when the pilgrims landed on Plymouth Rock.

The role of women in all this is just what it has always been in these historical narratives. The matrons who "nursed the infancy of the Republic," she writes, "were formed by early training in habits of energetic industry, and familiarity with privation and danger, to take their part in subduing the wilderness for the advance of civilization" (13–14).

No, these are probably not the women one would have created if it were really possible to shape the world to one's desire. But if the past is worth knowing at all, it is worth knowing as accurately as possible. These were Christian republican woman, proud of themselves, and jubilantly on the march. Their writings are not like ours, and they themselves, insofar as their writings define them, are not like us. They are also far from conforming to any paradigm of sequestered, submissive, passive domesticity that we might patronizingly attempt to impose on them according to some misguided millennial narrative of our own. From first to last, belief and pride in their extraordinary mission animated and captivated these women who wrote history in every form, and authorized them to enter the public sphere of print in diverse, highly visible, ways. They saw themselves at work for women, for the nation, for God. To write and publish history, from their point of view, put them in the historical vanguard. It was after all they, and not the women they wrote about, who were the truly important women in history. Whether they were right or wrong in these imaginings, there is little question that through this work they did participate directly and extensively in the print discourses of the national public life.

Biographical Notes on American Women Writers of History

COMPILED BY ERIC GARDNER

ADAMS, HANNAH

Born on 2 Oct. 1755 to Thomas and Elizabeth (Clark) Adams in Medfield, Mass.; never married; died on 15 Dec. 1831, in Brookline, Mass.; buried in Mt. Auburn Cemetery, Cambridge, Mass. Occupations: weaving bobbin lace (early life); writer; tutor.
Sources: NAW, 1:9–11; AWW, 1:12–13 (says mother's name is Eleanor).

BACON, DELIA SALTER

Born on 2 Feb. 1811 to the Rev. David and Alice (Parks) Bacon in (now) Tallmadge, Ohio; never married; died on 2 Sept. 1859, in Hartford, Conn.; buried in Grove St. Cemetery, New Haven. Occupations: teacher; "conversation" holder; lecturer.
Sources: NAW, 1:79–81; AWW, 1:85–87.

BEECHER, CATHARINE ESTHER

Born on 6 Sept. 1800 to the Rev. Lyman and Roxana (Foote) Beecher in E. Hampton, N.Y.; never married; died on 12 May 1878, in Elmira, N.Y.; buried in Woodlawn Cemetery, Elmira. Occupations: teacher; girls' school founder and principal; writer of educational and domestic treatises; lecturer.
Sources: NAW, 1:121–124; AWW, 1:131–133.

BERARD, AUGUSTA BLANCHE

Born on 29 Oct. 1824 to Claudius and Mary (Nichols) Berard in West Point, N.Y.; probably never married; died in either 1901 or 1906. Occupations: teacher; textbook writer.
Sources: Adams, 26; Wilson and Fiske, 1:243 (under Claudius); Wallace, 40.

BISHOP, HARRIET E.

Born on 1 Jan. 1817 to Putnam and Miranda (Wright) Bishop in Panton, Vt.; married on 12 Sept. 1858 to John McConkey (widowed harnessmaker); marriage dissolved 13 Mar. 1867, resumed maiden name; died on 8 Aug. 1883 in St. Paul, Minn,; buried in Oakland Cemetery. Occupations: teacher; introduced schools and Sunday schools to Minn. (Baptist); woman's suffrage.
Source: NAW, 1:151–152.

BLEECKER, ANN ELIZA SCHUYLER

Born in Oct. 1752 to Brandt and Margaret (Van Wyck) Schuyler in New York, N.Y.; married on 29 Mar. 1769 to John James Bleecker in New York, N.Y.; died on 23 Nov. 1783 in Tomhanick, N.Y.; buried in Reformed Dutch Burial Ground, Albany, N.Y. Occupations: none.
Sources: NAW 1:177–178; AWW 1:176–178.

BLUNT, ELLEN KEY

Born in 1821; resided in Md.; died in 1884. No additional biographical data available.
Source: NUC.

BOOTH, MARY LOUISE

Born on 19 Apr. 1831 to William Chatfield and Nancy (Monsell) Booth in Millvill (Yaphank), N.Y.; never married; lived with Mrs. Anne W. Wright for many years; died on 5 Mar. 1889 in New York, N.Y.; buried in Cypress Hills Cemetery, Brooklyn. Occupations: vest maker; amanuensis; writer; piece-rate reporter for *NY Times*; ed. *Harper's Bazar* (1867–1889); translator; literary hostess.
Sources: NAW, 1:207–208; AWW, 1:192–194.

BOTTA, ANNE CHARLOTTE LYNCH

Born on 11 Nov. 1815 to Patrick and Charlotte (Gray) Lynch in Bennington, Vt.; married in 1855 to Vincenzo Botta (prof. Italian at NYU) in New York, N.Y.; died on 23 Mar. 1891 in New York, N.Y. Occupations: teacher; writer; tutor; literary hostess.
Sources: NAW, 1:212–214; AWW, 1:196–198.

BRIDGMAN, ELIZA JANE GILLETT

Born on 6 May 1805 to Canfield and Hannah (_____) Gillett in Derby, Conn.; married on 28 June 1845 to Elijah Coleman Bridgman (missionary, 1801–1861) in Hong Kong; died on 10 Nov. 1871 in Shanghai; buried in Shanghai. Occupations: teacher; girls' school principal; missionary.
Source: NAW, 1:239–240.

BROOKS, MARIA GOWEN

Born c. 1794 to William and Eleanor (Cutter) Gowen in Medford, Mass.; married on 26 Aug. 1810 to John Brooks (d. 1823) in Boston, Mass.; died on 11 Nov. 1845 in Matanzas, Cuba. Occupation: writer.
Sources: NAW, 1:244–246; AWW, 1:243–245.

BULLARD, ANNE TUTTLE JONES

Born on 31 Jan. 1808 to Samuel and Anna (Turtle) Jones in Acton, Mass.; married on 2 June 1829 to the Rev. Artemus Bullard (d. 1855) in Mass.; died after 1878. Occupation: writer (used pseudonym Mrs. Caustic).
Sources: Marshall 9; *Vital . . . Acton*, 71; Barton, 14–15.

CARR, MARY

Lived in Philadelphia. Occupations: writer; publisher; ed. *The Intellectual Regale* (1814–1815). No other biographical data available.

CAULKINS, FRANCES MANWARING

Born on 26 Apr. 1795 to Joshua and Fanny (Manwaring) Caulkins in New London, Conn.; never married; died on 3 Feb. 1869 in New London; buried in Cedar Grove Cemetery, New London. Occupations: teacher; writer; religious activist; first woman in Mass. Historical Society.
Sources: NAW, 1:313–314; AWW, 1:325–327.

CAZNEAU, JANE MARIA ELIZA MCMANUS

Born on 6 Apr. 1807 to William Telemachus and Catharina (Coons) McManus near Troy, N.Y.; married in 1825 to Allen B. (or William F.) Storms; divorced 1831; second marriage c. 1848 to William Leslie Cazneau (d. 1876); died on 12 Dec. 1878 at sea on way from Jamaica to N.Y. (off Cape Hatteras). Occupations: writer, *NY Sun*; interpreter for Polk (Spanish); polemicist for Mexican, Cuban annexation; supporter of Walker in Nicaragua; ed. *La Verdad*.
Sources: NAW, 1:315–317; AWW, 1:328–329.

CHANDLER, ELIZABETH MARGARET

Born on 24 Dec. 1807 to Thomas and Margaret (Evans) Chandler in Centre (N. Wilmington), Del.; never married; died on 2 Nov. 1834 near Adrian (AWW says Tecumseh), Mich.; buried in Sec. 21, Raisin Twp., Lenawee Co., Mich. Occupations: abolitionist activist; ed. staff *The Genius of Emancipation* (1826–1834); ed. *Ladies Repository of Genius* (1829).
Sources: NAW, 1:319–320; AWW, 1:329–331.

CHENEY, HARRIET VAUGHAN FOSTER

Born on 9 Sept. 1796 to John and Hannah (Webster) Foster in Brighton, Mass.; married in 1830 to Edward Cheney (d. 1845) in Montreal, Canada; died on 14 May 1889. Occupations: writer; ed., *Snow Drop* (first Canadian child's magazine).
Sources: Adams, 59; New, 71–72; Blain, 200–201.

CHESEB[O]RO[UGH], CAROLINE

Born on 30 Mar. 1825 to Nicholas Goddard and Betsey (Kimball) Cheseborough in Canandaigua, N.Y.; never married; died on 16 Feb. 1873 in Piedmont, N.Y. Occupations: fiction writer; teacher, Packer Institute, Brooklyn (1865–1873); magazinist.
Sources: AWW, 1:346–348; Adams, 60; Wilson and Fiske, 1:599; Blain, 201; Hart, 512–516.

CHILD, LYDIA MARIA FRANCIS

Born on 11 Feb. 1802 to David Convers and Susannah (Rand) Francis in Medford, Mass.; married on 19 Oct. 1828 to David Lee Child (1794–1874) in Boston, Mass.; died on 20 Oct. 1880 in Wayland, Mass.; buried Wayland Cemetery. Occupations: teacher; writer; ed. *Juvenile Miscellany* (1826–1834), *Anti-Slavery Standard* (1841–1843); abolitionist.

Sources: NAW, 1:330–333; AWW, 1:354–355.

CLOUGH, MARTHA ANN

No biographical data available.

COMFIELD, AMELIA STRATTON

No biographical data available.

CONANT, HANNAH O'BRIEN CHAPLIN

Born on 5 Sept. 1809 to the Rev. Jeremiah and Marcia S. (O'Brien) Chaplin in Danvers, Mass.; married on 12 July 1830 to Thomas Jefferson Conant (prof. Waterville [Colby] College); died on 18 Feb. 1865 in Brooklyn, N.Y. Occupations: writer; ed. *Mother's Monthly Journal*, Utica, N.Y. (1838–1839); translator.
Sources: NAW, 1:370–371; AWW, 1:391–393.

CONKLING, MARGARET COCKBURN

Born on 27 Jan. 1814 to Alfred and ——— Cockburn or Conkling in N.Y. [?]; marital status uncertain; died on 28 July 1890 in Jersey City, N.J. Occupations: writer; translator (wrote as "Mrs. Steele").
Sources: Wilson and Fiske, 1:707; Wallace, 95.

CONNOR, CHARLOTTE MARY SANFORD BARNES

Born in 1818 to John and Mary (Greenhill) Barnes; married in 1846 to Edmond S. Connor (popular actor, manager Arch Street Theater, Philadelphia); died on 14 Apr. 1863 in New York, N.Y. Occupations: actress, writer.
Sources: AWW, 1:104–105 (under Barnes); Blain, 64 (under Barnes); Robinson, 159–161.

COOPER, SUSAN AUGUSTA FENIMORE

Born on 17 Apr. 1813 to novelist James Fenimore and Susan Augusta (De Lancey) Cooper at Heathcote Hill, Mamaroneck, N.Y.; (AWW says Scarsdale, N.Y.); never married; died on 31 Dec. 1894 in Cooperstown, N.Y.; buried in Christ Church Cemetery, Cooperstown, N.Y. Occupations: writer; biographer of JFC; philanthropist.
Sources: NAW, 1:382–383; AWW, 1:404–405.

CROCKER, HANNAH MATHER

Born on 27 June 1752 to the Rev. Samuel (son of Cotton) and Hannah (Hutchinson) Mather in Boston, Mass.; married on 13 Apr. 1779 to the Rev. Joseph Crocker (d. 1797) in Boston, Mass.; died on 11 July 1829 in Roxbury, Mass.; buried in Mather Tomb, Copps Hill, Boston, Mass. Occupations: writer (in later life).
Sources: NAW, 1:406–407; AWW, 1:420–421 (says mother's name Mehitable [Cove] Mather).

CUMMINS, MARIA SUSANNA

Born on 9 Apr. 1827 to David and Maria Franklin (Kittredge) Cummins in Salem,

Mass.; never married; died on 1 Oct. 1866 in Dorchester, Mass. Occupation: novelist.
Sources: NAW, 1:415–416; AWW, 1:436–437.

CUSHING, CAROLINE ELIZABETH WILDE

Born on 26 Apr. 1802 to Samuel Sumner and _____ Wilde in Hallowell, Maine; married 23 Nov. 1824 to Caleb Cushing in Newburyport, Mass.; died on 28 Aug. 1832 in Newburyport, Mass.; buried in New Hill Cemetery, Newburyport, Mass. Occupation: none.
Sources: Fuess, 1:58, 129–130, *passim*.

CUSHING, ELIZA LANESFORD FOSTER

Born on 19 Oct. 1794 to John and Hannah (Webster) Foster in Brighton, Mass.; married in 1833 to Frederick Cushing (d. 1846) in Mass.; died on 4 May 1886. Occupations: writer; ed. *Snow Drop* (with sister Harriet Cheney), *Literary Garland*.
Sources: Allibone, 1:463; Pilon, 321–322; New, 85–86.

DALL, CAROLINE WELLS HEALEY

Born on 22 June 1822 to Mark and Caroline (Foster) Healey in Boston, Mass.; married on 24 Sept. 1844 to Charles Henry Appleton Dall (1816–1886) in Mass.; (separated 1855); died on 17 Dec. 1912 in Washington, D.C. Occupations: teacher; writer; Sunday school teacher; social and women's suffrage activist.
Sources: NAW, 1:428–429; AWW, 1:448–450.

DANIELS, EUNICE K. TRUE

Born on 14 Nov. 1806 in Plainfield, N.H.; married in Aug. 1830 to William Daniels in Plainfield, N.H.; died on 16 June 1841 in Plainfield, N.H.; buried in N.H. Occupation: none.
Source: Daniels, intro, *passim*.

DAVIDSON, LUCRETIA MARIA

Born on 27 Sept. 1808 to Oliver and Margaret (Miller) Davidson in Plattsburgh, N.Y.; never married; died on 27 Aug. 1825 in Plattsburgh, N.Y. Occupation: none.
Sources: NAW, 1:436–438; AWW, 1:465–466.

DAVIDSON, MARGARET MILLER

Born on 27 June 1787; married to Oliver Davidson; died on 27 June 1844. Occupation: pushed for posthumous publication of daughters' works.
Sources: Allibone, 1:480; Burke, 180; Wilson and Fiske, 2:88 (under daughter Lucretia); Griswold, 152–156 (under daughters).

DAVIDSON, MARGARET MILLER

Born on 26 Mar. 1823 to Oliver and Margaret (Miller) Davidson in Plattsburgh, N.Y.; never married; died on 25 Nov. 1838 in Saratoga, N.Y. Occupation: none.
Sources: NAW, 1:436–438; AWW, 1:467–468.

DAVIS, MARY ELIZABETH MORAGNE

Born in 1816 to Isaac and Margaret Blanton (Caine) Moragne near Charleston, S.C.; married in 1842 to William Hervey Davis (1808–1892) in S.C.; died in 1903 in Talladega, Ala. Occupation: teacher.

Sources: Kirk, 461; Hart, 453–457 (under Moragne); Craven, intro, *passim.*

DORSEY, ANNA HANSON MCKENNEY

Born on 12 Dec. 1815 to William and Chloe Ann (Lanigan) McKenney in Washington, D.C.; married in 1837 to Lorenzo Dorsey; died on 26 Dec. 1896 in Washington, D.C. Occupations: writer; Roman Catholic polemicist.

Sources: AWW, 1:531–532; Adams, 62–63; Wilson and Fiske, 2:206; Delaney, 342.

DUPUY, ELIZA ANN

Born in 1814 to Jesse and M.A. [probably Mary Anne Thompson Sturdivant] Dupuy in Petersburg, Va.; never married; died on 29 Dec. 1880 in New Orleans, La. Occupations: fiction writer; governess.

Sources: NAW, 1:533–535; AWW, 1:551–552.

EASTMAN, MARY HENDERSON

Born in 1818 to Thomas and Anna Maria (Truxton) Henderson in Warrenton, Va.; married in June 1835 to Seth Eastman (military; artist; 1833–1875) in West Point, N.Y.; died on 24 Feb. 1887 in Washington, D.C.; buried in Oak Hill Cemetery, D.C. Occupation: writer.

Sources: NAW, 1:545–546; AWW, 1:568–569.

ELLET, ELIZABETH FRIES LUMMIS

Born in Oct. 1812 (?) to Dr. William Nixon and Sarah (Maxwell) Lummis in Sodus Point, N.Y.; married c. 1835 to William Henry Ellet (1806–1859); died on 3 June 1877 in St. Vincent's Hospital, New York, N.Y.; buried in Greenwood Cemetery, Brooklyn, N.Y. Occupation: writer.

Sources: NAW, 1:569–570; AWW, 1:581–583.

EMBURY, EMMA CATHARINE MANLY

Born in 1806 to James and Elizabeth (Post) Manley in New York, N.Y.; married in May 1828 to Daniel Embury in Brooklyn, N.Y.; died on 10 Feb. 1863 in Brooklyn, N.Y. Occupations: writer; ed. staff *Godey's Lady's Book, Graham's Magazine, Ladies Companion.*

Sources: AWW, 1:594–596; Adams, 119; Wilson and Fiske, 2:341; May, 218–235; Hart, 139–152.

EVANS, SARAH ANN

Married on 18 Nov. 1833 to Louis Ferdinand Lehmanowski in Washington, D.C. No other biographical data available.

Sources: AWW, 1:600–601; American Antiq., 2:1225; Walker, 5:426

FARNHAM, ELIZA WOOD BURHANS

Born on 17 Nov. 1815 to Cornelius and Mary (Wood) Burhans in Rensselaerville,

N.Y.; married on 12 July 1836 to Thomas Jefferson Farnham (1804–1848), probably in Ill.; second marriage 23 Mar. 1852 to William Fitzpatrick; divorced June 1856; died on 15 Dec. 1864 in New York, N.Y.; buried in Friends Cemetery, Milton-on-Hudson, N.Y. Occupations: teacher; writer; lecturer; matron at Sing Sing Women's Prison 1844–1848; matron at Stockton Female Insane Asylum 1861; Civil War nurse; social activist.
Sources: NAW, 1:598–600; AWW, 2:11–12.

FARRAR, ELIZA WARE ROTCH

Born on 21 July 1791 to Benjamin and Elizabeth (Barker) Rotch in Dunkirk, France; married on 10 Oct. 1828 to John Farrar (prof. math at Harvard, d. 1853); died on 22 Apr. 1870 in Springfield, Mass. buried in Mt. Auburn Cemetery, Cambridge, Mass. Occupations: writer; literary hostess.
Sources: NAW, 1:601–602; AWW, 2:14–16.

FAUGERES, MARGARETTA BLEECKER

Born on 11 Oct. 1771 to John James and Ann Eliza Schuyler Bleecker in (prob.) New York, N.Y. (AWW says Tomanick, N.Y.); married on 14 July 1792 to Peter Faugeres (French physician); died on 14 Jan. 1801 in Brooklyn, N.Y. Occupation: teacher.
Sources: NAW, 1:602, cross ref'd to mother 1:177–178; AWW, 2:16–18.

FOLLEN, ELIZA LEE CABOT

Born on 15 Aug. 1787 to Samuel and Sally (Barrett) Cabot in Boston, Mass.; married on 15 Sept. 1828 to Charles Theodore Christian Follen (German refugee, German teacher, minister; 1796–1840); died on 26 Jan. 1860 in Brookline, Mass.; buried in Mt. Auburn Cemetery, Cambridge, Mass. Occupations: teacher; Sunday school teacher; tutor; writer; ed. *Christian Teacher's Manual* (1828–1830), *Child's Friend* (1843–1850); abolitionist.
Sources: NAW, 1:638–639; AWW, 2:58–60.

FORD, SALLIE ROCHESTER

Born on 1 Oct. 1828 to James Henry and Demaretta (Pitts) Rochester in Rochester Springs, Ky; married in 1855 to Samuel Howard Ford (1819–?); died in 1910. Occupations: writer; co-ed. *Children's Repository*; Baptist and missionary activist.
Sources: AWW, 2:67–69; Adams, 134; Wilson and Fiske, 2:501 (under Samuel).

FOSTER, HANNAH WEBSTER

Born on 10 Sept. 1758 to Grant and Hannah (Wainwright) Webster in Salisbury, Mass.; married on 7 Apr. 1785 to the Rev. John Foster probably in Boston, Mass.; died on 17 Apr. 1840 in Montreal, Canada. Occupation: writer.
Sources: NAW, 1:650–651; AWW, 2:72–73.

FULLER (OSSOLI), MARGARET

Born on 23 May 1810 to Timothy and Margaret (Crane) Fuller in Cambridgeport, Mass.; married in summer 1849 to Giovanni Angelo (Marchese d' Ossoli) in Italy; died on 19 July 1850 at sea off coast of Fire Island. Occupations: teacher; "conversation" holder; writer; ed. *The Dial* (1840–1842); critic and columnist for *New York Tribune* (1844–1849).

Sources: NAW, 1:678–82; AWW, 3:314–318 (under Ossoli).

GERTRUDE, MARY

No biographical data available. Possibly a pen name.

GILMAN, CAROLINE HOWARD

Born on 8 Oct. 1794 to Samuel and Anna (Lillie) Howard in Boston, Mass.; married on 14 Dec. 1819 to the Rev. Samuel Gilman (d. 1858) probably in Boston, Mass.; died on 15 Sept. 1888 in Washington, D.C.; buried in Charleston, S.C. Occupations: writer; ed. *Rose Bud* (later *Southern Rose,* 1832–1839).

Sources: NAW, 2:37–39; AWW, 2:128–130.

GOULD, HANNAH FLAGG

Born on 3 Sept. 1789 to Benjamin and Griselda Apthorp (Flagg) Gould in Lancaster, Mass.; never married; died on 5 Sept. 1865 in Newburyport, Mass. Occupation: writer.

Sources: AWW, 2:161–163; Adams, 153; Wilson and Fiske, 2:693 (under Benjamin).

GRIMKÉ (WELD), ANGELINA EMILY

Born on 20 February 1805 to John Faucheraud and Mary (Smith) Grimké in Charleston, S.C.; married on 14 May 1838 to Theodore Weld (abolitionist) in Philadelphia, Pa.; died on 26 Oct. 1879 in Hyde Park, Mass.; buried in Mt. Hope Cemetery, Boston, Mass. Occupations: teacher; writer; abolitionist activist.

Sources: NAW, 2:97–99; AWW, 2:185–187.

GRIMKÉ, SARAH MOORE

Born on 26 Nov. 1792 to John Faucheraud and Mary (Smith) Grimké in Charleston, S.C.; never married (lived with sister); died on 23 Dec. 1873 in Hyde Park, Mass.; buried in Mt. Hope Cemetery, Boston, Mass. Occupations: writer; abolitionist and women's rights activist; teacher.

Sources: NAW, 2:97–99; AWW, 2:187–189.

HAIGHT, SARAH ROGERS

Born in New York, N.Y.; married to Richard K. Haight; Occupations: none. No other biographical data available.

Sources: Marshall, 25; Hale, 828–829; Allibone.

HALE, SARAH JOSEPHA BUELL

Born on 24 Oct. 1788 to Gordon and Martha (Whittlesey) Buell in Newport, N.H.; married on 23 Oct. 1813 to David Hale (?–1822) in Newport (?); died on 30 Apr. 1879 in Philadelphia, Pa.; buried in W. Laurel Hill Cemetery, Philadelphia, Pa. Occupations: teacher (1806–1813); writer; ed. *Ladies Magazine* (1828–1834), *Juvenile Miscellany* (1834–1836), *Godey's Lady's Book* (1834–1877).

Sources: NAW, 2:110–114; AWW, 2:211–216.

Biographical Notes

HALL, FANNY W.

Born c. 1796 to Rev. William and ____ Hall in Grafton, Vt.; never married; died after 1870. No other biographical data available.
Sources: Wallace, 190; Gilman, 112.

HALL, LOUISA JANE PARK

Born on 2 Feb. 1802 to John and ____ Park in Newburyport, Mass.; married in 1840 to Edward B. Hall; died on 8 Sept. 1892 in Cambridge, Mass.; buried in Mass. Occupation: writer.
Sources: AWW, 2:222–223; Adams, 166; Wilson and Fiske, 3:42 (says father's name James); Blain, 476; May, 171–180.

HALL, SARAH EWING

Born on 30 Oct. 1761 to John and Hannah (Sargent) Ewing in Philadelphia, Pa.; married in 1782 to John Hall; died on 8 Apr. 1830 in Philadelphia, Pa.; buried in Pa. Occupations: writer; informal ed. asst. *The Port Folio.*
Sources: AWW, 2:224–225; Adams, 166; Marshall, 25; Todd, 147; Blain, 477; Wilson and Fiske, 3:44.

HANNA, SARAH R. FOSTER

Born in 1802 in Washington Co., N.Y.; married in Sept. 1848 to the Rev. Thomas Hanna (d.1864) in Pa.; died in 1886. Occupations: teacher; principal (mainly Washington Female Seminary in Pa.).
Sources: Kirk, 2:759; Branton, 221–231.

HASTINGS, SALLY (SARAH) ANDERSON

1773–1812. No other biographical data available.
Source: Wallace, 200.

HASTINGS, SUSANNA WILLARD JOHNSON

Born on 13 July 1730 to Josiah and Hannah (____) Willard in Harvard, Mass.; married in 1747 to James Johnson; second marriage, n.d., to Mr. Hastings; died in 1810 in Charleston, N.H. Occupations: none.
Sources: AWW, 2:262–264; Todd, 153–154.

HATTON, ANNIE JULIA KEMBLE

Born in 1764 to Roger and Sarah (Ward) Kemble in Worcester, England; married in 1783 to Mr. Curtis (bigamist) in England; second marriage, 1792 to William Hatton (d. 1806); died in 1838 in Wales. Occupations: writer; playwright.
Sources: Marshall, 26; Blain, 499; Perkins, 425–426; Bordman, 656; Stephens, 250.

HAWTHORNE, ELIZABETH MANNING

Born on 7 Mar. 1802 to Nathaniel and Elizabeth Clark (Manning) Hawthorne in Salem, Mass.; never married; died on 1 Jan. 1883 in Beverly, Mass.; buried in Mass. Occupations: none.
Source: AWW, 2:267–269.

HENING, MRS. E.

No biographical data available.

HENTZ, CAROLINE LEE WHITING

Born on 1 June 1800 to John and Orpah (Danforth) Whiting in Lancaster, Mass.; married on 30 Sept. 1824 to Nicholas Marcellus Hentz (1797–1856) probably in Lancaster, Mass.; died on 11 Feb. 1856 in Marianna, Fla.; buried in Marianna Episcopal Cemetery. Occupations: teacher; writer.
Sources: NAW, 2:184–186; AWW, 2:285–286.

HEWITT (STEBBINS), MARY ELIZABETH MOORE

Born on 23 Dec. 1807 to Joseph and Betsey (___) Moore in Malden, Mass.; married c. 1827 to James L. Hewitt; second marriage after 1851 to Mr. R. Stebbins; died after 1856. Occupation: writer. No other biographical data available.
Sources: AWW, 2:288–290; Adams, 183, 358; Wilson and Fiske, 3:192–193; May, 342–349; Hart, 354–362; Corey, 56.

HOLLEY, MARY PHELPS AUSTIN

Born on 30 Aug. 1784 to Elijah and Esther (Phelps) Austin in New Haven, Conn.; married on 1 Jan. 1805 to Horace Holley (d. 1827) Conn.; died on 2 Aug. 1846 in New Orleans, La.; buried in St. Louis Cemetery, New Orleans, La. Occupations: teacher; writer; governess.
Source: NAW, 2:204–205.

HOWE, SARAH M.

No biographical data available.

HUNTER, MARTHA FENTON

No biographical data available.

JACOBS, SARAH SPRAGUE

Born on 17 Mar. 1813 to the Rev. Bela and Sarah (Sprague) Jacobs in Cranston (N. Pawtucket), R.I.; never married; died after 1870. Occupation: teacher. No other biographical data available.
Sources: AWW, 2:386–387; Adams, 206; Wilson and Fiske, 3:395; Baldwin, 1:391.

JOHNSON, ANNA CUMMINGS [MINNIE MYRTLE]

1818–1892 (?). Biographical data limited and contradictory.
Sources: Allibone, 1:969; Wallace; Marshall.

JONES, ELECTA FIDELIA

Born c. 1806; never married; died before 1854. No other biographical data available.
Source: Jones.

JUDSON, ANN HASSELTINE

Born on 22 Dec. 1789 to John and Rebecca (Burton) Hasseltine in Bradford, Mass.;

Biographical Notes

married on 5 Feb. 1812 to Adoniram Judson (missionary, d. 1850) probably in Mass.; died on 24 Oct. 1826 in Amherst near Rangoon, Burma; buried on island of St. Helena. Occupations: teacher; missionary.
Source: NAW, 2:295–297.

JUDSON, EMILY CHUBBOCK [FANNY FORESTER]

Born on 22 Aug. 1817 to Charles and Lavinia (Richards) Chubbock in Eaton, N.Y.; married on 2 June 1846 to Adoniram Judson (missionary, d. 1850) in Hamilton, N.Y.; died on 1 June 1854 in Hamilton, N.Y. Occupations: teacher; writer; missionary.
Sources: NAW, 2:297–298; AWW, 2:428–430.

KETELTAS, CAROLINE

No biographical data available.

KILBOURN, DIANA TREAT

No biographical data available.

KINZIE, JULIETTE AUGUSTA MAGILL

Born on 11 Sept. 1806 to Arthur William and Frances (Wolcott) Magill in Middletown, Conn.; married on 9 Aug. 1830 to John Harris Kinzie in New Hartford, N.Y.; died on 15 Sept. 1870 in Amagansett, N.Y. (summering); buried in Graceland Cemetery, Chicago, Ill. Occupations: writer; Chicago social leader; philanthropist.
Sources: NAW, 2:336–337; AWW, 2:465–466.

KIRKLAND, CAROLINE MATILDA STANSBURY

Born on 11 Jan. 1801 to Samuel and Eliza (Alexander) Stansbury in New York, N.Y.; married on 10 Jan. 1828 to William Kirkland (d. 1846) in N.Y.; died on 6 Apr. 1864 in New York, N.Y.; buried in Greenwood Cemetery, Brooklyn, N.Y. Occupations: teacher; director, girls schools; writer; ed. several periodicals and annuals; social activist.
Sources: NAW, 2:337–339; AWW, 2:471–473.

LEE, ELIZA BUCKMINSTER

Born in either 1788 (AWW) or 1794 (Wilson) to Joseph and Sarah (Stevens) Buckminster in Portsmouth, N.H.; married in 1827 to Thomas Lee; died on 22 June 1864 in Boston, Mass.; Occupation: writer.
Sources: AWW, 2:536–537; Adams, 227; Wilson and Fiske, 3:662; Blain, 641; Perkins, 597.

LEE, HANNAH FARNHAM SAWYER

Born in 1780 (bap. 12 Nov.) to Micajah and Sibyll (Farnham) Sawyer in Newburyport, Mass.; married on 20 Jan. 1807 to George Gardner Lee in Newburyport, Mass.; died on 17 Dec. 1865 in Boston, Mass. Occupation: writer.
Sources: AWW, 2:538–540; Adams, 227; Wilson and Fiske, 3:662; Blain, 642; Hart, 521–524; *Vitals . . . Newburyport*, 1:344 and 2:424.

LEE, MARY ELIZA (BETH)

Born on 23 Mar. 1813 to William and Eliza (_____) Lee in Charleston, S.C.; never married; died on 23 Sept. 1849 in Charleston, S.C. Occupation: writer.
Sources: AWW, 2:541–543; Adams, 227; Wilson and Fiske, 3:675 (under uncle Thomas Lee); May, 466–470; Hart, 458–462.

LE VERT, OCTAVIA CELESTE WALTON

Born on 11 Aug. 1811 to George and Sally Minge (Walker) Walton near Augusta, Ga.; married on 6 Feb. 1836 to Henry Strachey Le Vert in Mobile, Ala.; died on 12 Mar. 1877 near Augusta, Ga.; buried in Walker Family Cemetery, US Arsenal, Augusta, Ga. Occupations: none.
Sources: NAW, 2:394–395; AWW, 2:565–567 (says birthdate 18 Aug. 1810).

LEWIS, SARAH ANNA BLANCHE ROBINSON
(WROTE UNDER ESTELLE/STELLA)

Born on Apr. 1824 to John N. and _____ Robinson in Baltimore, Md.; married in 1841 to Sylvanus D. Lewis; divorced 1858; died on 24 Nov. 1880 in London, England. Occupation: writer.
Sources: AWW, 2:571–573; Allibone, 1:1096; Hale, 727–728; Marshall, 35; Hart, 507–511; Allibone (says born 24 Apr. to Dr. John Robinson); Griswold, 263–266; Perkins.

LIPPINCOTT, SARAH JANE CLARKE [GRACE GREENWOOD]

Born on 23 Sept. 1823 to Thaddeus and Deborah (Baker) Clarke in Pompey, N.Y.; married on 17 Oct. 1853 to Leander K. Lippincott, probably in Philadelphia, Pa.; died on 20 Apr. 1904 in New Rochelle, N.Y.; buried in New Brighton, Pa. Occupations: writer; ed. Little Pilgrim (1853–1875); newspaper and magazine correspondent; lecturer.
Sources: NAW, 2:407–409; AWW, 3:13–15.

LOCKE, JANE ERMINA STARKWEATHER

Born on 25 Apr. 1805 to Charles and Deborah (Brown) Starkweather in Worthington, Mass.; married in 1829 to John Goodwin Locke in Mass.; died on 8 Mar. 1859 in Ashburnham, Mass.; buried in Mass.; Occupations: writer; newspaper correspondent for Boston Journal and Daily Atlas (1850–1854); writer of prefaces for James Monroe Publishing Co.
Sources: AWW, 3:24–26; Adams, 232; Wilson and Fiske, 3:751.

LOGAN, DEBORAH NORRIS

Born on 19 Oct. 1761 to Charles and Mary (Parker) Norris in Philadelphia, Pa.; married on 6 Sept. 1781 to George Logan (d. 1821) in Philadelphia, Pa.; died on 2 Feb. 1839 north of Philadelphia, Pa.; buried in north of Philadelphia, Pa. Occupations: ed. William Penn and James Logan's correspondence.
Sources: NAW, 2:418–419; AWW, 3:26–28.

MCCORD, LOUISA SUSANNAH CHEVES

Born on 3 Dec. 1810 to Langdon and Mary Elizabeth (Dulles) Cheves in Charles-

ton, S.C.; married on 2 May 1840 to David James McCord; died on 23 Nov. 1879 in Charleston, S.C.; buried in Magnolia Cemetery, Charleston, S.C. Occupations: writer; Southern polemicist; translator.
Sources: NAW, 2:450–452; AWW, 3:71–73.

MARSH, CAROLINE CONSTANCE CRANE

Born on 1 Dec. 1816 in Berkeley, Mass.; married in 1838 to George Perkins Marsh (1801–1882) in Mass.; died in 1891. Occupations: none.
Sources: Adams, 247; Wilson and Fiske, 4: 217 (under father-in-law).

MEDINA, LOUISA HONOR DE

Born c. 1813 in England; married c. 1837 to Thomas S. Hamblin (d. 1853, manager of Bowery Theater, New York, N.Y.); died on 12 Nov. 1838 in New York, N.Y. Occupation: house playwright for Bowery Theater.
Sources: Bordman, 507; Banham, 653–654; Robinson, 626–628.

MORTON, SARAH WENTWORTH APTHORP

Born in Aug. 1759 (bap. 29 Aug.) to James and Sarah (Wentworth) Apthorp in Boston, Mass.; married on 24 Feb. 1781 to Perez Morton (d. 1837) in Mass.; died on 14 May 1846 in Quincy, Mass.; buried in Apthorp Tomb, King's Chapel, Boston, Mass.; Occupations: none.
Sources: NAW, 2:586–587; AWW, 3:230–232.

MOS[E]BY, MARY WEBSTER

Born in Apr. 1791 in Henrico Co., Va. (adopted by grandfather Robert Pleasants—Quaker); married in Feb. 1810 to John Garland Mosby in Va.; died on 19 Nov. 1844 in Richmond, Va. Occupations: none.
Sources: AWW, listed as Webster, Mary Moseby Pleasants but no entry; Allibone, 2:1377; Hale, 883; Knight, 314; Mosby, 124.

MOWATT, ANNA CORA OGDEN

Born on 5 Mar. 1819 to Samuel Gouverneur and Eliza (Lewis) Ogden in Bordeaux, France; married on 6 Oct. 1834 to James Mowatt (d. 1851) in New York, N.Y.; second marriage 6 June 1854 to William Foushee Ritchie (separated 1861); died on 21 July 1870 in Twickenham, England; buried in Kensington Green Cemetery, London, England. Occupations: writer; actress; public reader; magazinist.
Sources: NAW, 2:596–598; AWW, 3:481–483 (under Ritchie).

MURRAY, JUDITH SARGENT

Born on 1 May 1751 to Winthrop and Judith (Saunders) Sargent in Gloucester, Mass.; married on 3 Oct. 1769 to John Stevens (d. 1786) in Gloucester, Mass.; second marriage Oct. 1788 to the Rev. John Murray (d. 1815) in Gloucester, Mass.; died on 6 July 1820 in Natchez, Miss.; buried in Bingamon Cemetery, St. Catherines Creek, Miss. Occupation: writer.
Sources: NAW, 2:603–605; AWW, 3:240–241.

NOWELL, SARAH ALLEN

Born c. 1811 in Mass.; married c. 1838 (husband deceased before 1849); living in Boston in 1850. No other biographical data available.
Sources: Nowell; 1850 Census of Suffolk County, Mass. (Chelsea), 422.

ORNE, CAROLINE CHAPLIN

Died in 1882. Occupation: writer (over 250 magazine stories). No other biographical data available.
Sources: Adams, 277; Hart, 436–440.

PAINE, CAROLINE

No biographical data available.

PEABODY, ELIZABETH PALMER

Born on 25 Feb. 1778 to Joseph and Elizabeth (Hunt) Palmer in Boston, Mass.; married on 2 Nov. 1802 to Nathaniel Peabody in Andover, Mass.; died on 11 Jan. 1853 in West Newton, Mass. Occupation: teacher.
Sources: Wallace, 348; Endicott, 43 (under Nathaniel); Tharp *passim*.

PEABODY, ELIZABETH PALMER

Born on 16 May 1804 to Nathaniel and Elizabeth (Palmer) Peabody in Billerica, Mass.; never married; died on 3 Jan. 1894 in Jamaica Plain, Boston; buried in Sleepy Hollow Cemetery, Concord, Mass. Occupations: writer; teacher; bookshop owner; publisher; ed. of collections (e.g., *Aesthetic Papers*), *Kindergarten Messenger*; lecturer.
Sources: NAW, 3:31–34; AWW, 3:355–357.

PEIRSON, LYDIA JANE WHEELER

Born in 1802 in Middleton, Conn.; married in 1844 to Oliver Peirson; died in 1862 in Adrian, Mich. Occupations: none.
Sources: Adams, 291; Wilson and Fiske, 4:703; May, 303–312; 1850 Census of Tioga County, Pa. (Liberty), 268.

PHELPS, ALMIRA HART LINCOLN

Born on 15 July 1793 to Samuel and Lydia (Hinsdale) Hart in Berlin, Conn.; married on 4 Oct. 1817 to James Hart Lincoln (d. 1823); second marriage 17 Aug. 1831 to John Phelps (d. 1849); died on 15 July 1884 in Baltimore, Md.; buried in Greenmount Cemetery, Baltimore. Md. Occupations: teacher; principal of girls' schools; author of science textbooks; second woman in American Assoc. for the Advancement of Science (1859).
Sources: NAW, 3:58–60; AWW, 3:379–381 (says first husband Samuel Lincoln, second marriage in 1832).

PIERCE, SARAH

Born on 26 June 1767 to John and Mary (Paterson) Pierce in Litchfield, Conn.; never married; died on 19 Jan. 1852 in Litchfield, Conn.; buried in Litchfield, Conn. Occupations: teacher; founder and principal of Litchfield Female Seminary.
Sources: NAW, 3:67–68.

PIKE, MARY HAYDEN GREEN

Born on 30 Nov. 1824 to Elijah Dix and Hannah Claflin (Hayden) Green in Eastport, Maine; married on 28 Sept. 1845 to Frederick Augustus Pike (US congressman, d. 1886); died on 15 June 1908 in Baltimore, Md.; buried in Calais, Maine. Occupations: teacher; writer; abolitionist; landscape painter.
Sources: NAW, 3:68–69; AWW, 3:391–393.

PINCKNEY, MARIA HENRIETTA

Born ? to Charles Cotesworth and ___ (Middleton) Pinckney in S.C.; never married; died before 1852 in S.C. Occupations: writer; Southern polemicist. No other biographical data available.
Sources: Allibone, 1:1597; Hale, 469–470; Knight, 345.

PLATO, ANN

Born ca. 1820 in Hartford, Conn. Occupation: teacher. No other biographical data available.
Sources: Schockley, 26–28.

POGSON (SMITH), SARAH

Born to John and Ann (Wood) Pogson in Woodside House, Essex, England; married to Judge Peter Smith (of Peterboro, N.Y.); died in Charleston, S.C. No other biographical data available.
Sources: AWW, 4: 118–120 (under Smith); Marshall, 57; May, 46–47.

PORTER, SARAH MARTYN

Married in Oct. 1767 to John Porter (d. 1813) in Boxford, Mass.; died on 1831 in Williamstown, Vt. No other biographical data available.
Sources: AWW, 3:408–410; Todd, 259–260; *Vitals . . . Boxford* 190 (marriage intent lists her as Mrs. Sarah Martyn).

PRATT, FRANCES HAMMOND

No biographical data available.

PRINCE, NANCY GARDNER

Born 15 Sept. 1799 in Newburyport, Mass. to Thomas and ___ Gardner; married on 15 Feb. 1824 to Mr. Prince probably in Gloucester, Mass. No other biographical data available.
Sources: Shockley, 48–51.

PUTNAM, ELLEN TRYPHOSA HARRINGTON

No biographical data available.

PUTNAM, MARY TRAIL SPENCE LOWELL

Born on 3 Dec. 1810 to Charles and Harriet Brackett (Spence) Lowell in Boston, Mass.; married on 25 Apr. 1832 to Samuel R. Putnam (1797–1861) in Boston, Mass.; died on 1 June 1898 in Boston, Mass.; buried in Mt. Auburn Cemetery, Boston, Mass. Occupations: writer; translator.

Sources: AWW, 3:429–431; Adams, 306; Wilson and Fiske, 5:143 (under Samuel's father Samuel); Blain, 880; Lowell, 120.

READ, HARRIETTE FANNING

Born in Jamaica Plain, Mass. Occupations: actress; writer. No other biographical data available.

Sources: AWW, 3:447–449; Allibone 2:1751; Wallace, 373; Blain, 889; May, 429–435.

RICHARDS, MARIA TOLMAN

Born on 8 Oct. 1821 in Dorchester, Mass.; married on 9 June 1842 to the Rev. Samuel Richards in Dorchester, Mass. Occupations: teacher; lecturer; mission society.

Sources: Adams, 314; Wilson and Fiske, 5:239; *Vitals . . . Dorchester,* 181.

ROBBINS, ELIZA

Born on 26 Aug. 1786 to Edward H. and ⸺ Robbins in Boston, Mass.; probably never married; died in 1853. Occupations: teacher; textbook writer.

Sources: Adams, 317; Wilson, 7:229.

ROBINSON, MRS. JOHN HOVEY

Married to John Hovey (Maine physician and dime novelist 1825–1890). No other biographical data available.

Sources: Burke, 623.

ROBINSON, SARA TAPPAN DOOLITTLE LAWRENCE

Born on 12 July 1827 to Myron A. and ⸺ Lawrence in Belchertown, Mass.; married on 30 Oct. 1851 to Charles Robinson (1818–1894, Free-Soil gov. Kans.); died on 16 Nov. 1911 in Kans. Occupations: none.

Sources: Adams, 319; Wilson and Fiske, 5:285 (under husband); Sobel, 459–460; Wilson, *Governor passim.*

ROBINSON, THERESE ALBERTINE LUISE VON JAKOB [TALVI]

Born on 26 Jan. 1797 to J.H. and ⸺ von Jakob in Halle, Germany; married in 1828 to E. Robinson (prof. of theology); died on 13 Apr. 1869/70 in Hamburg, Germany; buried in New York, N.Y. Occupations: writer; translator; philologist; folklorist.

Sources: Adams, 319; Wallace, 386; Marshall, 51; Ward, 241; Hale, 775; Hart, 224–228.

ROE, ELIZABETH ANN LYON

Born on 11 June 1805 to Matthew and Beaula (⸺) Lyon in Lyon Co., Ky.; married on 11 Nov. 1821 to the Rev. John Roe (1800–1871) in Eddyville, Ky.; died after 1885 in Ill. No other biographical data available.

Sources: Roe *passim.*

ROWSON, SUSANNA HASWELL

Born c. 1762 to William and Susanna (Musgrave) Haswell in Portsmouth, England;

married in 1787 to William Rowson in England; died on 2 Mar. 1824 in Boston, Mass.; buried in St. Matthew's Church, South Boston, Mass.; moved to Mt. Hope Cemetery, Dorchester, Mass., in 1866. Occupations: teacher; principal of girls' schools; governess; actress; writer. *Sources:* NAW, 3:202–204.

ROYALL, ANNE NEWPORT

Born on 11 June 1769 to William and Mary (___) Newport near Baltimore, Md.; married in 1797 to Capt. William Royall (d.1813) in Va.; died on 1 Oct. 1854 in Washington, D.C.; buried in Congress Cemetery. Occupations: writer; ed. newspapers: *Paul Pry* (3 Dec. 1831 to 19 Nov. 1836), *The Huntress* (2 Dec. 1836 to 2 July 1854). *Sources:* NAW, 3:204–205; AWW, 3:509–510.

SANSAY, LEONORA HASSALL

Born to William (?) and ___ Hassall in Philadelphia, Pa.; married in 1800 to Louis Sansay in Philadelphia, Pa.; died after 1823. No other biographical data available. Occupation: writer. *Sources:* Lapsansky, 29–37.

SCHNEIDER, ELIZA CHENEY ABBOTT

1809–1856. No other biographical data available. *Sources:* Allibone, 2:1950.

SCHOOLCRAFT, MARY HOWARD

Born in Aug. 1812 in Beaufort Co., S.C.; married on 13 Jan. 1847 to Henry Rowe Schoolcraft (1793–1864) in Washington, D.C.; died after 1865. No other biographical data available. *Sources:* AWW, 4:36–37; Adams, 331; Allibone, 2:1953; Osborn.

SCOTT, ANNA M. STEELE

Occupation: missionary. No other biographical data available. *Sources:* Allibone, 2:1956; Wallace, 403.

SEDGWICK, CATHARINE MARIA

Born on 28 Dec. 1789 to Theodore and Pamela (Dwight) Sedgwick in Stockbridge, Mass.; never married; died on 31 July 1867 in West Roxbury, Mass.; buried in Stockbridge, Mass. Occupations: writer; philanthropist. *Sources:* NAW, 3:256–258; AWW, 4:46–48.

SEDGWICK, SUSAN LIVINGSTON RIDLEY

Born c. 1789 to Matthew and Catherine (Livingstone) Ridley; married in 1808 to Theodore Sedgwick (1780–1839, brother of Catharine); died on 20 June 1867 in Stockbridge, Mass. Occupation: children's writer. *Sources:* AWW, 4:48–49; Adams, 335; Wilson and Fiske, 5:451 (under family entry); Perkins, 959.

SHARP, ISABELLA OLIVER

Born in 1771 (AWW says 1777) to James and Mary (Buchanan) Oliver in Cumberland Co., Pa.; married to James (?) Sharp; died in 1843. No other biographical data available.

Sources: AWW, 4:68–69; Blain, 741.

SHINDLER, MARY STANLEY BUNCE PALMER DANA

Born on 10 Feb. 1810 (AWW says 15 Feb.) to Benjamin M. and Mary S. Palmer in Charleston, S.C.; married in June 1835 (AWW says 1830) to Charles E. Dana; second marriage May 1848 to Rev. Robert D. Shindler (1814–1874); died on 3 Feb. 1883 in Nacogdoches, Tex.; buried in Nacogdoches, Tex. Occupations: none.

Sources: AWW, 4:77–78; Adams, 342; Hart, 153–161; Erickson, 2:65.

SHUCK, HENRIETTA HALL

Born on 28 Oct. 1817 to Addison and ____ Hall in Kilmarnock, Va.; married on 8 Sept. 1835 to Jehu Lewis Schuck (1812–1863 missionary in China); died on 27 Nov. 1844 in Hong Kong. Occupations: missionary.

Sources: Adams, 343; *Encyclopedia,* 2:1201.

SIGOURNEY, LYDIA HOWARD HUNTLEY

Born on 1 Sept. 1791 to Ezekiel and Zerviah (Wentworth) Huntley in Norwich, Conn.; married on 16 June 1819 to Charles Sigourney (d. 1854) in Hartford, Conn.; died on 10 June 1865 in Hartford, Conn.; buried in Spring Grove Cemetery, Hartford, Conn. Occupations: teacher; writer; philanthropist; ed. staff *Godey's Lady's Book, Graham's Magazine;* ed. gift books.

Sources: NAW, 3:288–290; AWW, 4:78–81.

SMITH, ELIZABETH OAKES PRINCE

Born on 12 Aug. 1806 to David and Sophia (Blanchard) Prince in N. Yarmouth, Maine; married on 6 Mar. 1823 to Seba Smith in Maine; died on 15 Nov. 1893 in Hollywood, N.C.; buried in Patchogue, N.Y. Occupations: writer; correspondent *NY Tribune;* temperance and women's rights activist; lecturer; pastor.

Sources: NAW, 3:309–310; AWW, 4:109–111.

SMITH, LUCY MACK

Born on 8 July 1776 to Solomon and ____ Mack in Gilsum, N.H.; married on 24 Jan. 1796 to Joseph Smith (d. 1840) in Tunbridge, Vt.; died on 8 May 1855 in Nauvoo, Ill.; buried in Nauvoo, Ill. Occupations: farmer; boarding-house keeper; piecework and odd jobs.

Sources: Phillips, 11–17; Smith, *passim.*

SMITH, MARGARET BAYARD

Born on 20 Feb. 1778 to Col. John Bubenheim and Margaret (Hodge) Bayard near Schuylkill River (AWW says near Philadelphia), Pa.; married on 29 Sept. 1800 to Samuel Harrison Smith (journalist) probably in Philadelphia, Pa.; died on 7 June 1844 in Washington, D.C.; buried in Rock Creek Cemetery, D.C. Occupations: writer; hostess; philanthropist.

Sources: NAW, 3:317–318; AWW, 4:116–118.

SNELLING, ANNA L. PUTNAM

Died c. 1859 in New York, N.Y. No other biographical data available.
Sources: Allibone, 2:2171; Wallace, 426.

SOUTHWORTH, EMMA DOROTHY ELIZA NEVITTE

Born on 26 Dec. 1819 to Charles LeCompte and Susannah (Wailes) Nevitte in Washington, D.C.; married on 23 Jan. 1840 to Frederick Hamilton Southworth; separated 1844; died on 30 June 1899 in Georgetown, D.C.; buried in Oak Hill Cemetery, D.C. Occupations: teacher; writer.
Sources: NAW, 3:327–328; AWW, 4:131–133.

STEPHENS, ANN SOPHIA WINTERBOTHAM

Born on 30 Mar. 1810 to John and Ann (Wrigley) Winterbotham in Humphreysville (Seymour), Conn.; married in 1831 to Edward Stephens (d. 1862); died on 20 Aug. 1886 in Newport, R.I.; buried in Greenwood Cemetery, Brooklyn, N.Y. Occupations: writer, ed. or ed. staff, *Portland Magazine, Ladies Companion, Graham's Magazine, Petersons Magazine, Mrs. Stephens Illustrated New Monthly.*
Sources: NAW, 3:360–362; AWW, 4:163–164.

STOWE, HARRIET BEECHER

Born on 14 June 1811 to Lyman and Roxana (Foote) Beecher in Litchfield, Conn.; married on 6 Jan. 1836 to Calvin Ellis Stowe (1802–1886) in Cincinnati, Ohio; died on 1 July 1896 in Hartford, Conn.; buried Andover Theological Seminary Chapel. Occupations: teacher; writer; abolitionist.
Sources: NAW, 3:393–402; AWW, 4:175–178.

SWAYZE, MRS. J. C.

No biographical data available.

THOMPSON, AMIRA CARPENTER

No biographical data available.

TRUESDELL, MARY

No biographical data available.

TUTHILL, LOUISA CAROLINE HUGGINS

Born on 6 July 1799 to Ebenezer and Mary (Dickerman) Huggins in New Haven, Conn.; married on 6 Aug. 1817 to Cornelius Tuthill (d. 1825) in New Haven, Conn.; died on 1 June 1879 in Princeton, N.J. Occupation: writer.
Sources: NAW, 3:487–488; AWW, 4:271–272.

WALLIS, MARY DAVIS COOK

Born c. 1804 in Salem, Mass. Occupations: missionary activist. No other biographical data available.
Source: Wallis.

WARD, MARIA

No biographical data available. Possibly a pen name.

WARE, KATHARINE AUGUSTA RHODES

Born in 1797 in Quincy, Mass.; married in 1819 to Charles Ware (US Naval officer); died in 1843 in Paris, France. No other biographical data available.
Sources: AWW listed, but no entry; Adams, 406; Wilson and Fiske, 6:358.

WARNER, ANNA BARTLETT

Born on 31 Aug. 1827 (AWW says 1824) to Henry Whiting and Anna (Bartlett) Warner in New York, N.Y.; never married; died on 15 Jan. 1915 in Highland Falls, N.Y. Occupations: writer; bible classes for West Point cadets.
Sources: NAW, 3:543–545; AWW, 4:332–333.

WARNER, SUSAN BOGART

Born on 11 July 1819 to Henry Whiting and Anna (Bartlett) Warner in New York, N.Y.; never married; died on 17 Mar. 1885 in Highland Falls, N.Y. Occupations: writer; bible classes for West Point cadets.
Sources: NAW, 3:545–546; AWW, 4:334–336.

WARREN, MERCY OTIS

Born on 14 Sept. 1728 (oldstyle date; AWW says 25 Sept.) to James and Mary (Allyne) Otis in Barnstable, Mass.; married on 14 Nov. 1754 to James Warren (d. 1808) in Mass.; died on 19 Oct. 1814 in Plymouth, Mass.; buried in Burial Hill, Plymouth, Mass. Occupations: writer; political polemicist.
Sources: NAW, 3:545–546; AWW, 4:338–340.

WHITMAN, SARAH HELEN POWER

Born on 19 Jan. 1803 to Nicholas and Anna (Marsh) Power in Providence, R.I.; married on 10 July 1828 to John Winslow Whitman (d. 1833) in Jamaica, N.Y.; died on 27 June 1878 in Providence, R.I.; buried in Old North Burial Ground, Providence, R.I. Occupations: writer; women's suffrage and spiritualism activist.
Sources: NAW, 3:597–598; AWW, 4:404–406.

WILLARD, EMMA HART

Born on 23 Feb. 1787 to Samuel and Lydia (Hinsdale) Hart in Berlin, Conn.; married on 10 Aug. 1809 to Dr. John Willard (d. 1825); second marriage 17 Sept. 1838 to Dr. Christopher Yates; divorced 1843; died on 15 Apr. 1870 in Troy, N.Y.; buried in Oakwood Cemetery, Troy, N.Y. Occupations: teacher; principal and founder Troy Female Seminary; textbook writer; eductional theorist.
Sources: NAW, 3:610–613; AWW, 4:423–426.

WILLIAMS, CATHARINE READ ARNOLD

Born on 31 Dec. 1787 to Alfred and Amey (Read) Arnold in Providence, R.I.; married in 1824 to Horatio N. Williams; divorced 1826; died on 11 Oct. 1872 in Providence, R.I. Occupations: teacher; writer.
Sources: AWW, 4:429–431; Adams, 425; Wilson and Fiske, 6:520.

WILLSON, ARABELLA M. STUART

No biographical data available.

Biographical Notes

WILSON, AUGUSTA JANE EVANS

Born on 8 May 1835 to Matt Ryan and Sarah Skrine (Howard) Evans in Wynnton, Ga.; married on 2 Dec. 1868 to Col. Lorenzo Madison Wilson (d. 1891); died on 9 May 1909 in Mobile, Ala.; buried in Magnolia Cemetery, Mobile, Ala. Occupation: writer.

Sources: NAW, 3:625–626; AWW listed, but no entry.

WINDLE, MARY JANE

Born in 1825 in Wilmington, Del. No other biographical data available.
Sources: AWW, 4:439–440; Allibone, 3:2790; Burke, 814–815; Wallace, 512; Hart, 463–469.

WOOD, SARAH (SALLY) SAYWARD BARRELL KEATING

Born on 1 Oct. 1759 to Nathaniel and Sally (Sayward) Barrell in York, Maine; married on 23 Nov. 1778 to Richard Keating (d. 1783) in York, Maine; second marriage 28 Oct. 1804 to Gen. Abiel Wood (d. 1811); died on 6 Jan. 1855 in Kennebunk, Maine. Occupation: writer.
Sources: NAW, 3:649–650; AWW, 4:452–454.

WRIGHT, FRANCES

Born on 6 Sept. 1795 to James and Camilla (Campbell) Wright in Dundee, Scotland; married on 22 July 1831 to Guillaume Sylvan Casimir Phiquepal D'Arusmont in Paris, France; divorced 1850; died on 13 Dec. 1852 in Cincinnati, Ohio; buried in Spring Grove Cemetery, Cincinnati, Ohio. Occupations: writer; women's rights lecturer; social reformer; journalist *New Harmony Gazette, Free Enquirer*.
Sources: NAW, 3:675–680; AWW, 1:458–460 (under D'Arusmont; says husband William D'Arusmont).

Main Sources

(NAW) James, Edward T., ed. *Notable American Women, 1607–1950: A Biographical Dictionary*. 3 vols. Cambridge, Mass.: The Belknap Press of Harvard University, 1971.

(AWW) Mainiero, Lisa, ed. *American Women Writers: A Critical Reference Guide from Colonial Times to the Present*. 4 vols. New York: Frederick Ungar Publishing Co., 1979–1982.

Other Sources

Adams, Oscar Fay. *A Dictionary of American Authors*. 5th ed., revised and enlarged. New York: Houghton Mifflin Co., 1904.

Allibone, S. Austin. *A Critical Dictionary of English Literature and British and American Authors Living and Deceased from the Earliest Accounts to the Latter Half of the Nineteenth Century*. 3 vols. Philadelphia: J. B. Lippincott & Co., 1858–1871.

American Antiquarian Society (comp.) *Index of Marriages in the Massachusetts Central and the Columbian Centinal, 1784 to 1840*. Boston: G. K. Hall, 1961.

Baldwin, Thomas W. *Vital Records of Cambridge, Massachusetts to the year 1850.* 2 vols. Boston: New England Historical Genealogy Society, 1914.

Banham, Martin, ed. *The Cambridge Guide to World Theatre.* Cambridge: Cambridge University Press, 1988.

Barton, William Sumner. *A Genealogical Sketch of Dr. Artemus Bullard of Sutton and His Descendants.* Worcester: Lucius Goddard, 1878.

Blain, Virginia, Patricia Clements, and Isobel Grundy. *The Feminist Companion to Literature in English: Women Writers from the Middle Ages to the Present.* New Haven: Yale University Press, 1990.

Bordman, Gerald. *The Oxford Companion to American Theater.* 2d ed. New York: Oxford University Press, 1992.

Branton, Harriet K. "Sarah Forster Hanna and the Washington Female Seminary." *Western Pennsylvania Historical Magazine* 61.3 (July 1978): 221–231.

Burke, W.J., and Will D. Howe. *American Authors and Books, 1640 to the Present Day.* 3d revised ed., revisions by Irving Weiss. New York: Crown Publishers, Inc., 1962.

Corey, D., compiler. *Births, Marriages and Deaths in the Town of Malden 1649–1850.* Cambridge, Mass.: City of Malden, 1903.

Craven, Delle Mullen, ed. *The Neglected Thread: A Journal from the Calhoun Community 1836–1842, by Mary E. Moragne.* Columbia, S.C.: University of South Carolina Press, 1951.

Daniels, Eunice K. True. *Poems.* New York: John F. Trow, 1843.

Delaney, John J., and James Edward Tobin. *Dictionary of Catholic Biography.* Garden City, N.Y.: Doubleday & Co., 1961.

Encyclopedia of Southern Baptists. 2 vols. and supplement. Nashville: Broadman Press, 1958, 1971.

Endicott, C. M., compiler. *A Genealogy of the Peabody Family;* Revised by William S. Peabody. Boston: David Clapp & Son, 1867.

Erickson, Carolyn Reeves, compiler. *Nacogdoches County Cemetery Records.* 5 vols. Nacogdoches, Tex.: King Printing Co., 1975.

Fuess, Claude M. *The Life of Caleb Cushing.* 2 vols. New York: Harcourt, Brace & Co., 1923. Cited from the reprint, Hamden, Conn.: Anchor Books, 1964.

Gilman, Marcus D. *The Bibliography of Vermont; or, A List of Books and Pamphlets Relating in Any Way to the State.* Burlington, Vt.: Free Press Association, 1897.

Griswold, Rufus. *The Female Poets of America.* 2d ed. Philadelphia: Carey & Hart, 1854.

Hale, Sarah Josepha. *Woman's Record.* 2d ed. New York: Harpers, 1855.

Hart, John Seely. *Female Prose Writers of America.* Philadelphia: E. H. Butler & Co., 1855.

Jones, Electa F[idelia]. *Stockbridge, Past and Present.* Springfield, Mass.: Samuel Bowles & Co., 1854.

Kirk, John Foster. *A Supplement to Allibone's Critical Dictionary of English Literature and British and American Authors.* 2 vols. Philadelphia: J. B. Lippincott & Co., 1891.

Knight, Lucien Lamar, compiler. *Biographical Dictionary of Southern Authors.*

Biographical Notes

(Vol. 15 of the Library of Southern Literature) Atlanta: Martin & Hoyt Co., 1929. Reprinted Detroit: Gale Research, 1978.

Lapsansky, Phillip S. "Afro-Americana: Rediscovering Leonora Sansay." In *The Annual Report of the Library Company of Philadelphia for the Year 1992.* Philadelphia: Library Co. of Philadelphia, 1993.

Lowell, Delmar, compiler. *The History and Genealogy of the Lowells of America.* Published by the Author, 1899.

Marshall, Alice Kahler. *Pen Names of Women Writers: From 1600 to the Present.* Camp Hill, Pa: Alice Kahler Marshall, 1985.

May, Caroline. *The American Female Poets.* Philadelphia: Lindsay & Blakiston, 1848.

Morris, Celia. *Fanny Wright: Rebel in America.* Urbana: University of Illinois Press, 1992 (orig. edition 1984).

Mosby, James H. *Our Noble Heritage.* Privately printed, 1975.

New, W. H., ed. *Dictionary of Literary Biography Volume 99: Canadian Writers before 1890.* Detroit: Gale Research, 1990.

Nowell, Sarah Allen. *Poems.* Boston: A. Tompkins, 1850.

Osborn, Chase S. and Stellanova. *Schoolcraft—Longfellow—Hiawatha.* Lancaster, Pa.: Jacques Cattell Press, 1942.

Perkins, George, Barbara Perkins, and Phillip Leininger. *Benet's Reader's Encyclopedia of American Literature.* New York: HarperCollins, 1991.

Phillips, Emma M. *33 Women of the Restoration.* Independence, Mo.: Herald House, 1960.

Pilon, Henri, ed. *Dictionary of Canadian Biography. Vol. XI: 1881–1890.* Toronto: University of Toronto Press, 1982.

Robinson, Alice M., Vera Mowery Roberts, and Milly S. Barranger, eds. *Notable Women in the American Theater: A Biographical Dictionary.* New York: Greenwood Press, 1989.

Roe, Elizabeth Ann. *Recollections of a Frontier Life.* Rockford, Ill.: Gazette Publishing House, 1885.

Schockley, Ann Allen. *Afro-American Women Writers, 1746–1933: An Anthology and Critical Guide.* Boston: G. K. Hall, 1988.

Smith, Lucy Mack. *Biographical Sketches of Joseph Smith . . .* Liverpool: For Orson Pratt, 1853.

Sobel, Robert, and John Raimo, eds. *Biographical Dictionary of the Governors of the United States, 1789–1978.* Westport, Conn.: Microform Review, Inc., Meckler Books, 1978.

Stephens, Meic, ed. *The Oxford Companion to the Literature of Wales.* New York: Oxford University Press, 1986.

Tharp, Louise Hall. *The Peabody Sisters of Salem.* Boston: Little, Brown, 1950.

Todd, Janet, ed. *A Dictionary of British and American Women Writers, 1660–1800.* Totowa, N.J.: Rowman & Allanheld, 1985.

Toye, William, ed. *The Oxford Companion to Canadian Literature.* Toronto: Oxford University Press, 1983.

Vital Records of Acton, Massachusetts to the Year 1850. Boston: New England Historical Genealogy Society, 1923.

Vital Records of Boxford, Massachusetts to the End of the Year 1849. Topsfield, Mass.: Topsfield Historical Society, 1905.

Vital Records of the town of Dorchester, Massachusetts from 1826–1849. Boston: Municipal Printing Office, 1905.

Vital Records of Newburyport, Massachusetts to the End of the Year 1849. 2 vols. Salem: Essex Institute, 1911.

Walker, Homer A., compiler. *Historical Court Records of Washington, District of Columbia*. 15 vols. Privately published for Lucinda Walker, n.d.

Wallace, W. Stewart, compiler. *A Dictionary of North American Authors Deceased before 1950*. Toronto: Ryerson Press, 1951.

Wallis, Mary Davis Cook. *Life in Feejee*. Boston: William Heath, 1851. Reprinted Gregg Press, 1987.

Ward, Robert E. *A Bio-Bibliography of German-American Writers, 1670–1970*. White Plains, N.Y.: Kraus International Publications, 1985.

Wilson, Don W. *Governor Charles Robinson of Kansas*. Lawrence: University of Kansas Press, 1975.

Wilson, James Grant, ed. *Appleton's Cyclopaedia of American Biography*. Vol. 7. New York: D. Appleton & Co., 1901. Reprinted Detroit: Gale Research, 1968.

Wilson, James Grant, and John Fiske, eds. *Appleton's Cyclopaedia of American Biography*. 6 vols. New York: D. Appleton & Co., 1888–1889. Reprinted Detroit: Gale Research, 1968.

1850 Federal Census of Tioga County, Pennsylvania (Liberty Township) and Suffolk County, Massachusetts (Chelsea).

Historical Works
by American Women

Adams, Hannah. *A View of Religions.* Boston: Manning & Loring, 1791, 1798, 1801.

———. *A Summary History of New England.* Dedham: H. Mann & J. H. Adams, 1799.

———. *An Abridgement of the History of New-England, for the Use of Young Persons.* Boston: Belcher & Armstrong, 1807.

———. *History of the Jews.* 2 vols. Boston: John Eliot, Jun., 1812.

———. *A Dictionary of All Religions and Religious Denominations.* [4th ed, rev., of *A View of Religions.*] New York: James Eastburn; Boston: Cummings & Hilliard, 1817.

———. *A Memoir of Miss Hannah Adams, Written by Herself. With Additional Notices, by a Friend* [Hannah F. S. Lee]. Boston: Gray & Bowen, 1832.

Bacon, Delia Salter. *Tales of the Puritans.* New Haven: A. H. Maltby, 1831.

———. *The Bride of Fort Edward, Founded on an Incident of the Revolution.* New York: S. Colman, 1839.

———. "Historical Lessons." *New York Herald,* Dec. 1, 8, 10, 17, & 21, 1852; Jan. 4, 1853.

———. "William Shakespeare and His Plays: An Inquiry Concerning Them." *Putnam's* 7 (1856):1–19. (Reprinted in Theodore Bacon, *Delia Bacon, a Biographical Sketch* [Boston: Houghton, Mifflin & Co. 1888], 98–155.)

———. *The Philosophy of the Plays of Shakespeare Unfolded.* London: Groombridge & Sons; Boston: Ticknor & Fields, 1857.

Beecher, Catharine Esther. "American Women: Will You Save Your Country?" [1845]. In *Educational Reminiscences and Suggestions,* 209–237. New York: J. B. Ford & Co., 1874.

Berard, Augusta. *School History of the United States.* Philadelphia: H. Cowperthwait & Co., 1855.

———. *School History of England.* New York: A. S. Barnes & Burr, 1861.

Bishop, Harriet E. *Floral Home; or, First Years of Minnesota.* New York: Sheldon, Blakeman & Co., 1857.

———. *Dakota War-Whoop.* St. Paul: D. D. Merrill, 1863. (Published under her married name, McConkey.) (Cited from the reissue, Minneapolis: Ross & Haines, 1970.)

Bleecker, Ann Eliza. "The History of Maria Kittle." In *Posthumous Works, in Prose and Verse*. New York: T. & J. Swords, 1793. (Published separately, Hartford: Elisha Babcock, 1797.)

Blunt, Ellen Key. *Bread to My Children*. Philadelphia: J. B. Lippincott, 1856.

Booth, Mary Louise. *History of the City of New York, From Its Earliest Settlement to the Present Time*. New York: W.R.C. Clark & Meeker, 1859.

Botta, Anne Charlotte. See Lynch, Anne Charlotte.

Bridgman, Eliza J. Gillett. *Daughters of China; or, Sketches of Domestic Life in the Celestial Empire*. New York: Robert Carter & Bros., 1853.

Brooks, Maria Gowen. *Judith, Esther, and Other Poems*. Boston: Cummings & Hilliard, 1820.

———. *Zophiel; A Poem*. Boston: Richardson & Lord, 1825 (First canto published separately).

———. *Zophiel; A Poem*. Boston: Carter & Hendee, 1833.

Bullard, Anne Tuttle. *The Stanwood Family; or The History of the American Tract Society*. Boston: Printed by T. B. Marvin, for the Massachusetts Sabbath School Union, 1830.

———. *The Reformation; A True Tale of the Sixteenth Century*. Boston: Massachusetts Sabbath School Society, 1832.

———. *Sights and Scenes in Europe; A Series of Letters from England, France, Germany, Switzerland and Italy, in 1850*. St. Louis: Chambers & Knapp, 1852. (Letters originally written for the Missouri Republican, dedicated "to the ladies of the first presbyterian church, St. Louis, Mo.")

Carr, Mary. *The Fair Americans*. Philadelphia: By Mrs. Carr, 1815.

Caulkins, Frances Manwaring. *History of Norwich, Connecticut, from Its Settlement in 1660, to January 1845*. Norwich: Thomas Robinson, 1845.

———. *History of New London, Connecticut, from the First Survey of the Coast in 1612, to 1852*. New London: By the author, 1852. ("In 1860, some of the volumes of this history being still in sheets, twenty pages were added and bound up with the original book, thus giving eight years additional records." In 1895, the 1860 version was reprinted with a memoir, New London: H. D. Utley.)

———. *History of Norwich, Connecticut, from Its Possession by the Indians, to the Year 1866*. Hartford: By the Author, 1866.

Cazneau, Jane. *Texas and Her Presidents. With a Glance at Her Climate and Agricultural Capabilities*. New York: E. Winchester, 1845.

———. *Eagle Pass; or, Life on the Border*. New York: Putnam, 1852. (Cited from the reissue, Austin: Pemberton Press, 1966.)

Chandler, Elizabeth Margaret. *The Poetical Works of Elizabeth Margaret Chandler: With a Memoir of Her Life and Character, by Benjamin Lundy; and Philanthropic and Moral Essays*. Philadelphia: Lemuel Howell, 1836.

Cheney, Harriet Vaughan. *The Rivals of Acadia; An Old Story of the New World*. Boston: Wells & Lilly, 1827.

———. *A Peep at the Pilgrims in Sixteen Hundred Thirty-six; A Tale of Olden Times*. Boston: Wells & Lilly, 1824.

———. *Confessions of an Early Martyr*. Boston: Benjamin H. Greene, 1846.

Chesebro', Caroline. *Victoria; or, The World Overcome.* New York: Derby & Jackson, 1856.

Child, Lydia Maria. *Hobomok, A Tale of Early Times.* Boston: Cummings, Hilliard & Co., 1824. (Cited from the reissue, New Brunswick: Rutgers University Press, 1986.)

———. *Evenings in New England, Intended for Juvenile Amusement and Instruction; By an American Lady.* Boston: Cummings, Hilliard, & Co., 1824.

———. *The Rebels; or, Boston before the Revolution.* Boston: Cummings, Hilliard, & Co., 1825.

———. *The First Settlers of New-England; or, Conquest of the Pequods, Narragansets and Pokanokets: as Related by a Mother to Her Children, and Designed for the Instruction of Youth.* Boston: Munroe & Francis, 1828.

———. *The Mother's Book.* Boston: Carter, Hendee & Babcock, 1831.

———. *The Coronal: A Collection of Miscellaneous Pieces.* Boston: Carter & Hendee, 1831, 1832.

———. *Good Wives.* Boston: Carter, Hendee & Co., 1833. (Cited from the 1846 edition, New York: C. S. Francis & Co.)

———. *The History of the Condition of Women, in Various Ages and Nations.* 2 Vols. Boston: John Allen & Co., 1835.

———. *An Appeal, in Favor of That Class of Americans Called Africans.* New York: John S. Taylor, 1836.

———. *Philothea; A Romance.* Boston: Otis, Broaders, & Co., 1836.

———. *Fact and Fiction; A Collection of Stories.* New York: C. S. Francis & Co., 1846.

———. *The Progress of Religious Ideas, Through Successive Ages.* 3 Vols. New York: C. S. Francis & Co., 1855.

———. *Autumnal Leaves.* New York: C. S. Francis & Co., 1857.

Clough, Martha Ann. *Zuleika; or, The Castilian Captive.* Boston: F. Gleason, 1849.

Comfield, Amelia [Stratton]. *Alida; or, Miscellaneous Sketches of Occurrences During the Late American War.* New York: For the Author, 1841.

Conant, Hannah O'Brien. *Popular History of the Translation of the Holy Scriptures, into the English Tongue.* New York: I. K. Funk, 1859.

Conkling, Margaret Cockburn. *Florian's History of the Moors of Spain.* New York: Harper & Bros., 1840. (Translation.)

———. *Memoir of the Mother and Wife of Washington.* Auburn: Derby, Miller & Co., 1850.

Connor, Charlotte Barnes. *Plays, Prose and Poetry.* Philadelphia: E. H. Butler & Co., 1848.

Cooper, Susan Fenimore. *Mount Vernon: A Letter to the Children of America.* New York: D. Appleton & Co., 1859.

Crocker, Hannah Mather. *A Series of Letters on Free Masonry.* Boston: John Eliot, 1815.

———. *Observations on the Real Rights of Women.* Boston: For the Author, 1818.

Cummins, Maria Susanna. *Haunted Hearts.* Boston: J. E. Tilton, 1864.

Cushing, Caroline W. *Letters, Descriptive of Public Monuments, Scenery, and Manners in France and Spain.* 2 vols. Newburyport: E. W. Allen & Co., 1832.

Cushing, Eliza Lanesford. *Saratoga: A Tale of the Revolution*. Boston: Cummings, Hilliard & Co., 1824.

———. *Yorktown: An Historical Romance*. Boston: Wells & Lilly, 1826.

———. *Esther: A Sacred Drama*. Boston: Joseph Dowe, 1840.

Dall, Caroline Healey. *See* Fuller, Margaret: *Margaret and Her Friends*.

———. *Historical Pictures Retouched*. Boston: Walker, Wise & Co., 1860.

Daniels, Eunice K. True. *Poems*. New York: John F. Trow, 1843.

Davidson, Lucretia. *Amir Khan, and Other Poems: The Remains of Lucretia Maria Davidson*. New York: G. & C. & H. Carvill, 1829.

Davidson, Margaret [Miller]. *Selections from the Writings of Mrs. Margaret M. Davidson*. Philadelphia: Lea & Blanchard, 1843.

Davidson, Margaret Miller. *Biography & Poetical Remains*. Philadelphia: Lea & Blanchard, 1842.

Davis, Mary Elizabeth. *See* Moragne, Mary Elizabeth.

Dorsey, Anna Hanson (McKenney). *Tears on the Diadem; or, the Crown and the Cloister; A Tale of the White and Red Roses*. New York: Edward Dunigan, 1846.

———. *Flowers of Love and Memory*. Baltimore: John Murphy, 1849.

Dupuy, Eliza Ann. *The Conspirator*. New York: D. Appleton & Co., 1850.

———. *Ashleigh: A Tale of the Olden Time*. Cincinnati: H. B. Pearson, 1854.

———. *The Huguenot Exiles; or, The Times of Louis XIV. A Historical Novel*. New York: Harper & Bros., 1856.

Eastman, Mary Henderson. *Dahcotah; or, Life and Legends of the Sioux around Fort Snelling*. New York: John Wiley, 1849.

———. *The American Aboriginal Portfolio*. Philadelphia: Lippincott, Grambo & Co., 1853.

———. *The Romance of Indian Life*. Philadelphia: Lippincott, Grambo & Co., 1853.

———. *Chicora, and Other Regions of the Conquerors and the Conquered*. Philadelphia: Lippincott, Grambo & Co., 1854.

Ellet, Elizabeth. Teresa Contarini. In *Poems, Translated and Original*. Philadelphia: Key & Biddle, 1835.

———. *Scenes in the Life of Joanna of Sicily*. Boston: Marsh, Capen, Lyon, & Webb, 1840.

———. *The Women of the American Revolution*. 3 vols. New York: Baker & Scribner (Vols. 1 & 2, 1848; Vol. 3, 1850).

———. *A Domestic History of the American Revolution*. New York: Baker & Scribner, 1850.

———. *Pioneer Women of the West*. New York: Charles Scribner, 1852.

———. *Women Artists in All Ages and Countries*. New York: Harper, 1859.

Embury, Emma Catherine. *Guido, a Tale; Sketches from History; and Other Poems, By Ianthe*. New York: G. & C. Carvill, 1828.

Evans, Augusta Jane. *Inez; A Tale of the Alamo*. New York: Harper & Bros., 1855.

———. *Beulah*. New York: Derby & Jackson, 1859.

———. *Macaria*. New York: John Bradburn, 1864.

Evans, Sarah Ann. *Resignation: An American Novel*. Boston: For the Author, by John B. Russell, 1825.

Farnham, Eliza Wood. *California, In-Doors and Out; or, How We Farm, Mine and Live Generally in the Golden State.* New York: Dix, Edwards, 1856.

Farrar, Eliza Ware. *The Young Lady's Friend.* Boston: American Stationers' Co., 1836.

Faugeres, Margaretta V. [Bleecker]. *Essays in Prose and Verse.* In *Posthumous Works in Prose and Verse,* by Ann Eliza Bleecker. New York: T. & J. Swords, 1793.

———. *Belisarius.* New York: T. & J. Swords, 1795.

Follen, Eliza Lee Cabot. *Poems.* Boston: William Crosby, 1839.

Ford, Sallie Rochester. *Mary Bunyan, The Dreamer's Blind Daughter. A Tale of Religious Persecution.* New York: Sheldon & Co., 1860.

Foster, Hannah. *The Coquette.* Boston: Samuel Etheridge, 1797. (Cited from the reissue, New York: Oxford University Press, 1984.)

———. *The Boarding School.* Boston: I. Thomas & E. T. Andrews, 1798.

Fuller, Margaret. *Margaret and Her Friends, or Ten Conversations with Margaret Fuller upon the Mythology of the Greeks and Its Expression in Art, Beginning March 1, 1841, Reported by Caroline W. Healey [Dall].* Boston: Roberts Bros., 1895.

———. *Woman in the Nineteenth Century.* New York: Greeley & McElrath, 1845. Reprinted in *The Essential Margaret Fuller,* ed. Jeffrey Steele. New Brunswick: Rutgers University Press, 1992.

———. *These Sad but Glorious Days: Dispatches from Europe to The New York Herald, 1846–1850.* Ed. Larry J. Reynolds & Susan Belasco Smith. New Haven: Yale University Press, 1991.

———. "Autobiographical Romance." In *The Essential Margaret Fuller,* ed. Jeffrey Steele. New Brunswick: Rutgers University Press, 1992. (Steele dates this 1840–1841; orig. pub. in *Memoirs.* Boston: Phillips, Sampson, & Co., 1852.)

Gertrude, Mary. *Philip Randolph: A Tale of Virginia.* New York: D. Appleton, 1845.

Gilman, Caroline. *Letters of Eliza Wilkinson, during the Invasion and Possession of Charlestown, S.C. by the British in the Revolutionary War.* New York: Samuel Colman, 1839.

———. *Verses of a Life Time.* Boston & Cambridge: James Munroe & Co., 1839.

Gould, Hannah Flagg. *Poems.* Boston: Hilliard, Gray & Co., 1839.

———. *New Poems.* Boston: William J. Reynolds & Co., 1850.

Greenwood, Grace. *Poems.* Boston: Ticknor, Reed & Fields, 1850.

———. *Greenwood Leaves.* Boston: Ticknor, Reed & Fields, 1850.

———. *Greenwood Leaves; Second Series.* Boston: Ticknor & Fields, 1854 [copyright 1852].

———. *Haps and Mishaps of a Tour in Europe.* Boston: Ticknor, Reed & Fields.

———. *Merrie England; Travels, Descriptions, Tales and Historical Sketches.* Boston: Ticknor & Fields, 1855.

———. *A Forest Tragedy and Other Tales.* Boston: Ticknor & Fields, 1856.

———. *Bonnie Scotland; Tales of Her History, Heroes, and Poets.* Boston: Ticknor & Fields, 1861.

Grimké, Angelina Emily. *An Appeal to the Christian Women of the South.* New York: American Anti-Slavery Society, 1836.

———. *An Appeal to the Women of the Nominally Free States.* New York: W. S. Dorr, 1837. (Cited from the reissue, Boston: Isaac Knapp, 1838.)

Grimké, Sarah. *Letters on the Equality of the Sexes, and the Condition of Women.* Boston: Isaac Knapp, 1838.

Haight, Sarah Rogers. *Letters from the Old World; by a Lady of New-York.* New York: Harper & Bros., 1840.

Hale, Sarah J. *Northwood; A Tale of New England.* Boston: Bowles & Dearborn, 1827.

———. *Sketches of American Character.* Boston: Putnam & Hunt, 1829.

———. *Northwood; or, Life North and South, Showing the True Character of Both.* New York: H. Long & Bro., 1852.

———. *Liberia; or, Mr. Peyton's Experiments.* New York: Harper & Bros., 1853.

———. *Woman's Record; or, Sketches of All Distinguished Women from "the Beginning" till A.D. 1850.* New York: Harper & Bros., 1853. (Cited from the 2nd ed., 1855.)

———. "A Course of Reading for Young Ladies." *Godey's Lady's Book* 34, 35 (Mar.–Nov. 1847).

———. "Ormond Grosvenor." *Godey's Lady's Book* 16 (1838): 33–40, 49–53, 145–152.

Hall, Fanny W. *Rambles in Europe; or, a Tour through France, Italy, Switzerland, Great Britain, and Ireland, in 1836.* New York: E. French, 1838. (Cited from the 1839 ed.)

Hall, Louisa J. *Joanna of Naples.* Boston: Hilliard, Gray & Co., 1838.

———. *Hannah, the Mother of Samuel.* Boston: James Munroe, 1839.

———. *Miriam, & Joanna of Naples, with other pieces in Verse and Prose.* Boston: W. Crosby & H. P. Nichols, 1850.

Hall, Sarah Ewing. *Conversations on the Bible.* 4th ed. Philadelphia: Harrison Hall, 1827 (orig. pub. 1818).

———. *Selections from the Writings.* Philadelphia: H. Hall, 1833.

Hanna, Sarah R. *Bible History: A Text-Book for Seminaries, Schools, and Families.* New York: A. S. Barnes & Burr, 1860.

Hastings, Sally. *Poems on Different Subjects.* Lancaster: Printed and Sold by William Dickson, For the Benefit of the Authoress, 1808.

Hastings, Susanna Willard Johnson. *Narrative of the Captivity of Mrs. Johnson.* Walpole, N.H.: David Carlisle, Jun., 1796.

Hatton, Annie Kemble. *Tammany,* 1794. [Lost play.]

Hathorne, Elizabeth. *Peter Parley's Universal History.* Boston: S. G. Goodrich, 1838. [Collaborated with her brother Nathaniel Hawthorne on volume he produced; her precise contribution is unknown.]

Hening, [Mrs.] E. F. *History of the African Mission of the Protestant Episcopal Church.* New York: Stanford & Swords, 1850.

Hentz, Caroline Lee. *De Lara; or, The Moorish Bride.* Tuscaloosa: Woodruff & Olcott, 1843.

———. *Constance of Werdenberg; or, The Heroes of Switzerland.* Macon, Ga.: *Georgia Citizen,* Apr.–May 1853. (Play originally performed in 1832.)

——— . *Lovell's Folly.* Cincinnati: Hubbard & Edmonds, 1833.

——— . *Human and Divine Philosophy.* Tuscaloosa: Journal and Flag Office, 1844.

Hewitt, Mary Elizabeth. *Poems, Sacred, Passionate and Legendary.* New York: Lamport, Blakeman & Law, 1854. (A reissue of *Songs of Our Land.* Boston: W. D. Ticknor, 1846.)

Holley, Mary Austin. *Texas; Observations, Historical, Geographical, and Descriptive.* Baltimore: Armstrong & Plaskitt, 1833. (Cited from the reprint, New York: Arno Press, 1973.)

——— . *Texas.* Lexington: J. Clarke & Co., 1836. (Cited from the reprint, Austin: Texas Historical Society, 1985.)

Howe, Sarah M. *Eustatia; or, The Sybil's Prophecy. A Tale of England, France and Spain.* Boston: F. Gleason, 1852.

——— . *The Soldier's Daughter; or, The Conspirators of La Vendee. A Romance of Napoleon's Times.* New York: Garrett & Co., copyright 1853.

Hunter, Martha Fenton. *The Clifford Family; or, A Tale of the Old Dominion; By One of Her Daughters.* New York: Harper & Bros., 1852.

Jacobs, Sarah Sprague. *The White Oak, and Its Neighbors.* Boston: Sabbath School Union, 1853.

Johnson, Anna Cummings. *The Iroquois; or, The Bright Side of Indian Character.* New York: D. Appleton, 1855.

——— . *Peasant Life in Germany.* New York: Charles Scribner, 1858.

——— . *The Cottages of the Alps; or, Life and Manners in Switzerland.* New York: Charles Scribner, 1860.

Jones, Electa F. *Stockbridge, Past and Present; or, Records of an Old Mission Station.* Springfield: Samuel Bowles & Co., 1854.

Judson, Ann Hasseltine. *A Particular Relation of the American Baptist Mission to the Burman Empire, in a Series of Letters Addressed to Joseph Butterworth, Esq., M.P., London.* Washington City: J. S. Meehan, 1823.

——— . *Life of Mrs. Ann H. Judson* [by James D. Knowles]. Boston: Lincoln & Edmonds, 1830.

Judson, Emily Chubbuck. *Memoir of Sarah B. Judson, Member of the American Mission to Burmah, by "Fanny Forester".* New York: L. Colby, 1848.

——— . *An Olio of Domestic Verses.* New York: Lewis Colby, 1852.

——— . *The Kathayan Slave, and Other Papers Connected with Missionary Life.* Boston: Ticknor, Reed, & Fields, 1853.

Keteltas, Caroline M. *The Last of the Plantaganets.* New York: R. Craighead, 1844.

Kilbourn, Diana Treat. *The Lone Dove: A Legend of Revolutionary Times.* Philadelphia: G. S. Appleton, 1850.

Kinzie, Juliette. *Narrative of the Massacre at Chicago, Aug. 15, 1812, and of Some Preceding Events.* Chicago: Ellis & Fergus, 1844.

——— . *Wau-bun; the "Early Day" in the North-West.* New York: Derby & Jackson, 1856.

Kirkland, Caroline. *Holidays Abroad; or Europe from the West.* 2 Vols. New York: Baker & Scribner, 1849.

——— . *Memoirs of Washington.* New York: D. Appleton & Co., 1857.

A Lady of New York. *Over the Ocean, or Glimpses of Travel in Many Lands.*

New York: Paine & Burgess, 1846. [Sometimes incorrectly attributed to Sarah Haight.]

Le Vert, Octavia Walton. *Souvenirs of Travel.* Mobile & New York: S. H. Goetzel, 1857.

Lee, Eliza Buckminster. *Sketches of a New England Village, in the Last Century.* Boston: James Munroe & Co., 1838.

———. *Delusion; or, The Witch of New England.* Boston: Hilliard, Gray & Co., 1840.

———. *Naomi; or, Boston Two Hundred Years Ago.* Boston: W. Crosby & H. P. Nichols, 1848.

———. *Memoirs of Reverend Joseph Buckminster, D. D.* Boston: W. Crosby & H. P. Nichols, 1849.

———. *Parthenia; or, The Last Days of Paganism.* Boston: Ticknor & Fields, 1858.

Lee, Hannah Farnham Sawyer. *Grace Seymour.* 2 vols. New York: Elam Bliss, 1830.

———. *Historical Sketches of the Old Painters.* Boston: Hilliard, Gray & Co., 1838.

———. *The Life and Times of Martin Luther.* Boston: Hilliard, Gray & Co., 1839.

———. *The Life and Times of Thomas Cranmer.* Boston: Hilliard, Gray & Co., 1841.

———. *The Huguenots in France and America.* Cambridge, Mass.: J. Owen, 1843.

———. *Familiar Sketches of Sculpture and Sculptors.* Boston: Crosby, Nichols, & Co., 1854.

Lewis, Sarah Anna. *Records of the Heart.* New York: D. Appleton & Co.; Philadelphia: G. S. Appleton, 1844.

Lippincott, Sara Jane Clarke. *See* Greenwood, Grace.

Locke, Jane Ermina. *Miscellaneous Poems.* Boston: Otis, Broaders, & Co., 1842.

———. *The Recalled; in Voices of the Past, and Poems of the Ideal.* Boston & Cambridge: James Munroe & Co., 1854.

Logan, Deborah Norris. *Correspondence between William Penn and James Logan.* 2 vols. Philadelphia: For the Historical Society of Pennsylvania by J. B. Lippincott, 1870, 1872. [Vols. 9 and 10 of the Pennsylvania Historical Society Memoirs. Transcripts delivered to the society in 1820.]

———. *Memoir of Dr. George Logan of Stenton.* Philadelphia: The Historical Society of Pennsylvania, 1899. [Written 1821.]

Lynch, Anne Charlotte. *Poems.* 2d ed. New York: G. P. Putnam, 1853. (1st ed. 1849.)

———. *Hand-Book of Universal Literature.* New York: Derby & Jackson, 1860.

McCord, Louisa S. *Caius Gracchus.* New York: H. Kernot, 1851.

Marsh, Caroline Crane. *Wolfe of the Knoll, and Other Poems.* New York: Charles Scribner, 1860.

Medina, Louisa. *Last Days of Pompeii.* New York: Samuel French, 1844.

Moragne, Mary Elizabeth. *The British Partizan; A Tale of the Times of Old.* Augusta, Ga.: William T. Thompson, 1839.

Morton, Sarah Wentworth. *Beacon Hill; A Local Poem, Historic and Descriptive, Book I.* Boston: Manning & Loring, For the Author, 1797.

Historical Works

——. *The Virtues of Society; A Tale Founded on Fact.* Boston: Manning & Loring, For the Author, 1799.

——. *My Mind and Its Thoughts, in Sketches, Fragments, and Essays.* Boston: Wells & Lilly, 1823.

Mosby, Mary Webster. *Pocahontas.* Philadelphia: Herman Hooker, 1840.

Mowatt, Anna Cora. *Pelayo; or, The Cavern of Covadonga.* New York: Harper & Bros., 1836.

——. *Plays.* Boston: Ticknor & Fields, 1855.

Murray, Judith Sargent. *The Gleaner.* 3 vols. Boston: I. Thomas & E. T. Andrews, 1798. (Cited from the reissue, Schenectady: Union College Press, 1992.)

Nowell, Sarah Allen. *Poems.* Boston: A. Tompkins, 1850.

——. *The Shadow on the Pillow, and Other Stories.* Boston: A. Tompkins, 1860.

Orne, Caroline Chaplin. *Lionel Ainsworth; or, The Young Partisan's Doom.* New York: Samuel French, n.d. [1850s]

Paine, Caroline. *Tent and Harem; Notes of an Oriental Trip.* New York: D. Appleton & Co., 1859.

Peabody, Elizabeth. *Sabbath Lessons; or, An Abstract of Sacred History; To Which Is Annexed, a Geographical Sketch of the Principal Places Mentioned in Sacred History.* Salem: Joshua Cushing, 1813. (1st ed. 1810.)

Peabody, Elizabeth Palmer. *First Steps to the Study of History; Being Part First of a Key to History. Questions Adapted to Irving's Life and Voyages of Columbus; and Robertson's History of America.* Boston: Hilliard, Gray & Co., 1832.

——. *Key to History, Part II; The Hebrews.* Boston: Marsh, Capen & Lyon, 1833.

——. *Key to History, Part III; The Greeks.* Boston: Marsh, Capen & Lyon, 1833.

——. "The Spirit of the Hebrew Scriptures." *Christian Examiner* 16 (May & July 1834): 174–202, 305–320.

——. *The Polish-American System of Chronology; Reproduced, with Some Modifications, from General Bem's Franco-Polish Method.* Boston: Putnam, 1851. (1st ed. Boston: G. P. Putnam, 1850.)

——. *Crimes of the House of Austria Against Mankind.* New York: G. P. Putnam, 1852.

——. *Chronological History of the United States, Arranged with Plates on Bem's Principle.* New York: Sheldon, Blakeman, 1856.

——. *Universal History, Arranged to Illustrate Bem's Charts of Chronology.* New York: For the Author by Sheldon & Co., 1859.

——. "My Experience as a Teacher: Principles and Methods of Education." *American Journal of Education* 32 (1882):721–742.

——. "The Dorian Measure" [1848]. In *Last Evening with Allston; and Other Papers,* 73–135. Boston: D. Lothrop & Co., 1886.

Peirson, Lydia Jane. *The Forest Minstrel.* Philadelphia: J. W. Moore, 1846.

Phelps, Almira Hart Lincoln. *The Female Student; or, Lectures to Young Ladies, Comprising Outlines and Applications of the Different Branches of Female Education, for the Use of Female Schools, and Private Libraries.* 2d ed. New York: Leavitt, Lord & Co., 1836. (1st ed. 1833.)

Pierce, Sarah. *Sketches of Universal History, Compiled from Several Authors; For the Use of Schools.* Vol. 1, New Haven: Joseph Barber, 1811; Vol. 2, New

Haven: Joseph Barber, 1816; Vol. 3, New Haven: T. G. Woodworth, 1817; Vol. 4, New Haven: T. G. Woodworth, 1818.

Pike, Mary Hayden Green. *Agnes.* Boston: Phillips, Sampson & Co., 1858.

Pinckney, Maria Henrietta. *Essays, Religious, Moral, Dramatic and Poetical; Addressed to Youth; and Published for a Benevolent Purpose. By a Lady.* Charleston: Archibald E. Miller, 1818.

Plato, Ann. *Essays; Including Biographies and Miscellaneous Pieces, in Prose and Poetry.* Hartford: For the Author, 1841. (Reprinted New York: Oxford University Press, 1988.)

Pogson, Sarah. *The Female Enthusiast; A Tragedy in Five Acts.* Charleston: For the Author, by J. Hoff, 1807.

Porter, Sarah. *The Royal Penitent; in Three Parts, to Which is Added, David's Lamentation over Saul and Jonathan.* Concord: George Hough, 1791.

Pratt, Frances Hammond. *La Belle Zoa; or, The Insurrection of Hayti.* Albany: Weed, Parsons & Co., 1854.

Prince, Nancy. *Narrative of the Life and Travels of Mrs. Nancy Prince.* Boston: N. Prince, 1850. (Reprinted New York: Marcus Wiener, 1990.)

Putnam, Ellen Tryphosa Harrington. *Captain Molly; The Story of a Brave Woman.* New York: Derby & Jackson, 1857.

Putnam, Mary Lowell. "History of the Constitution of Hungary and its Relations with Austria." *Christian Examiner* 48 (May 1850): 444–498; 49 (Nov. 1850): 417–481; 50 (Mar. 1851): 279–352.

Read, Harriette Fanning. *Dramatic Poems.* Boston: W. Crosby & H. P. Nichols, 1848.

Richards, Maria Tolman. *Life in Judea; or, Glimpses of the First Christian Age.* Philadelphia: American Baptist Publication Society, 1854.

———. *Life in Israel; or, Portraits of Hebrew Character.* New York: Sheldon, Blakeman & Co., 1857.

———. *The Year of the Jubilee; or, Familiar Phases of Hebrew Life.* New York: Sheldon, Blakeman & Co., 1857.

Robbins, Eliza. *Tales from American History.* New York: W. Burgess, 1829.

———. *Tales from American History, 2nd series* [later Vol. 2]. New York: J. & J. Harper, 1832.

———. *Grecian History; Adapted to the Use of Schools, and Young Persons.* New York: Roe Lockwood, 1833.

———. *English History; Adapted to the Use of Schools, and Young Persons.* New York: Roe Lockwood, 1834.

———. *Tales from American History, Vol. 3.* New York: Harper & Bros, 1840.

Robinson, Mrs. John Hovey. *Evelyn; The Child of the Revolution.* Boston: Hotchkiss, 1850.

Robinson, Sara Tappan Lawrence. *Kansas; Its Interior and Exterior Life.* Boston: Crosby, 1855.

Robinson, Therese Albertine. *See* Talvi.

Roe, Elizabeth A. *Aunt Leanna; or, Early Scenes in Kentucky.* Chicago: For the Author, 1855.

Rowson, Susanna. *Rebecca; or, The Fille de Chambre.* London: William Lane, 1792; 1st American ed. Philadelphia: H & P. Rice, 1794.

———. *Reuben and Rachel; or, Tales of Old Times*. 2 vols. Boston: Manning & Loring for D. West, 1798.

———. *An Abridgment of Universal Geography, Together with Sketches of History*. Boston: John West, 1806.

———. *A Present for Young Ladies*. Boston: John West, 1811.

———. *Biblical Dialogues between a Father and His Family; Comprising Sacred History from the Creation to the Death of Our Savior Christ*. Boston: Richardson & Lord, 1822.

———. *Exercises in History, Chronology, and Biography*. Boston: Richardson & Lord, 1822.

Royall, Anne. *Sketches of History, Life, and Manners, in the United States*. New Haven: For the Author, 1826.

———. *The Tennessean*. New Haven: For the Author, 1827.

———. *Letters from Alabama on Various Subjects*. Washington, 1830. (Cited from the reissue, *Letters from Alabama 1817–1822*, ed. Lucille Griffith. University, Al.: University of Alabama Press, 1969.)

Sansay, Leonora. *Secret History; or, The Horrors of St. Domingo*. Philadelphia: Carr, for Bradford & Inskeep, 1808.

Schneider, Eliza Cheney. *Letters from Broosa, Asia Minor*. Chambersburg, Pa.: German Reformed Church, 1846.

Schoolcraft, Mary Howard. *The Black Gauntlet: A Tale of Plantation Life in South Carolina*. Philadelphia: J. B. Lippincott & Co., 1860. (Reprinted Westport, Conn.: Greenwood for Negro Universities Press, 1969.)

Scott, Anna M. *Day Dawn in Africa; or, Progress of the Protestant Episcopal Mission at Cape Palmas, West Africa*. New York: Protestant Episcopal Society, 1858.

Sedgwick, Catharine Maria. *Hope Leslie; or, Early Times in the Massachusetts*. New York: White, Gallaher & White, 1827. (Cited from the reissue, New Brunswick: Rutgers University Press, 1987.)

———. *Tales and Sketches*. Philadelphia: Carey, Lea & Blanchard, 1835.

———. *The Linwoods; or, "Sixty Years Since" in America*. New York: Harper & Bros., 1835.

———. *Letters from Abroad, to Kindred at Home*. 2 vols. New York: Harper & Bros., 1841.

———. *Tales and Sketches, 2d Series*. New York: Harper & Bros., 1844.

Sedgwick, Susan Anne Livingston. *The Young Emigrants; A Tale Designed for Young Persons*. Boston: Carter & Hendee, 1830.

———. *Allen Prescott; or, The Fortunes of a New-England Boy*. New York: Harper & Bros., 1834.

———. *Walter Thornley; or, A Peep at the Past*. New York: Harper, 1859.

Sharp, Isabella Oliver. *Poems on Various Subjects*. Carlisle: A. London, 1805.

Shindler, Mary Stanley. *Charles Morton; or, The Young Patriot*. New York: Dayton & Newman, 1843.

Shuck, Henrietta. *Scenes in China; or, Sketches of the Country, Religion, and Customs of the Chinese, by the late Mrs. Henrietta Shuck, Missionary of China*. Philadelphia: American Baptist Publication Society, 1852.

Sigourney, Lydia Huntley. *Traits of the Aborigines of America: A Poem*. Cambridge: From the University Press, 1822.

———. *Sketch of Connecticut, Forty Years Since*. Hartford: Oliver D. Cooke & Sons, 1824.

———. *Evening Readings in History: Comprising Portions of the History of Assyria, Egypt, Tyre, Syria, Persia, and the Sacred Scriptures; With Questions, Arranged for the Use of the Young, and of Family Circles*. Springfield: G. & C. Merriam, 1833.

———. *Sketches*. Philadelphia: Key & Biddle, 1834.

———. *Zinzendorff; and Other Poems*. New York: Leavitt, Lord & Co., 1835.

———. *History of Marcus Aurelius*. Hartford: Belknap & Hamersley, 1836.

———. *Pocahontas; and Other Poems*. New York: Harper & Bros., 1841.

———. *Pleasant Memories of Pleasant Lands*. Boston: James Munroe & Co., 1842.

———. *Myrtis; with other Etchings and Sketchings*. New York: Harper & Bros., 1846.

———. *The Western Home; and Other Poems*. Philadelphia: Parry & McMillan, 1854.

———. *Lucy Howard's Journal*. New York: Harper & Bros., 1858.

———. *The Man of Uz; and Other Poems*. Hartford: Williams, Wiley & Waterman, 1862.

———. *Letters of Life*. New York: D. Appleton, 1866.

Smith, Elizabeth Oakes. *The Western Captive; or, The Times of Tecumseh*. New York: *The New World*, ed. Park Benjamin, nos. 27 & 28 (Oct. 1842). (Book, New York: J. Winchester, 1842.)

———. "The Christian Sisters." In *The New World*, ed. Park Benjamin, no. 28 (Oct. 1842).

———. "The Sagamore of Saco." *Graham's* 33 (Jul. 1848): 47–52. (Expanded into a dime novel in 1868.)

———. *The Roman Tribute; or, Attila the Hun*. [Lost play.]

———. *Old New York; or, Democracy in 1689*. New York: Stringer & Townsend, 1853.

Smith, Lucy Mack. *Biographical Sketches of Joseph Smith, the Prophet, and His Progenitors for Many Generations*. Liverpool: For Orson Pratt by S. W. Richards, 1853.

Smith, Margaret Bayard. *A Winter in Washington*. 3 vols. New York: E. White & E. Bliss, 1824.

Snelling, Anna L. *Kabaosa; or, The Warriors of the West. A Tale of the Last War*. New York: D. Adee, 1842.

Southworth, E.D.E.N. *Love's Labor Won*. Philadelphia: T. B. Peterson & Bros., 1862. Serialized in *Peterson's* in 1857.

Stephens, Ann Sophia. *Alice Copley; A Tale of Queen Mary's Time*. Boston: "Yankee" office, 1844.

———. *Clara*. Serialized in *Peterson's* 6 (1844): 65–69, 96–103, 133–138, 169–176, 202–210.

———. *Sir Henry's Ward; A Tale of the Revolution*. Serialized in *Graham's* 29 (1846): 45–50, 67–83, 109–113, 194–199, 252–259, 265–276.

Historical Works

———. "The King's Legacy." *Graham's* 28 (1846):133–139, 145–150.

———. *The Tradesman's Boast.* Boston: Gleason, 1846. Serialized in *Peterson's* 9 (1846):25–30, 62–68, 99–105, 137–142, 167–175, 200–210.

———. *Anne Boleyn.* Serialized in *Peterson's* 10 (1846):37–41, 101–107, 135–141, 171–177, 198–209.

———. *The Lady Mary.* New York: F. M. Lupton, 188-. Serialized in *Peterson's* 11 (1847):41–47, 81–88, 115–121, 153–158, 189–195, 213–226.

———. *Lost and Found.* Serialized in *Peterson's* 13 & 14 (1848): 7–10, 55–61, 112–117, 156–160, 191–196, 222–237; 31–36, 65–71, 96–102, 138–142, 173–179, 203–211.

———. *The Belle of Liege.* Serialized in *Peterson's* 31 & 32 (1857): 233–239, 376– 381, 445–451; 57–61, 139–145, 270–276, 338–344, 419–423.

———. *The Royal Sisters.* Serialized in *Mrs. Stephens' New Monthly Illustrated Magazine* 3 (1857):1–13, 55–60, 103–109, 166–172, 232–238, 284–290.

———. *Mary Derwent.* Philadelphia: T. B. Peterson & Bros., 1858.

———. *Barbara Stafford* and *King Philip's Daughter.* Twelve-part serial divided between two journals and differently titled in each: *Mrs. Stephens' Monthly New Illustrated Magazine* 4 (1858):7–13, 110–117, 177–184, 231–238, 303– 309, 370–375; *Peterson's* 34 (1858):56–64, 127–135, 199–206, 270–274, 348–356, 417–429. Published in novel form as *Silent Struggles; or, Barbara Stafford* (Philadelphia: T. B. Peterson, 1865).

———. *The Ruling Passion.* Serialized in *Peterson's* 37 & 38 (1860):56–63, 145– 154, 231–240, 308–317, 388–397, 465–474; 57–66, 136–145, 210–219, 291– 299, 380–389, 447–457. Published in book form as *The Rejected Wife* (Philadelphia: T. B. Peterson & Bros., 1863).

Stowe, Harriet Beecher. *Sunny Memories of Pleasant Lands.* 2 vols. Boston: Phillips, Sampson & Co., 1854.

———. *The Minister's Wooing.* New York: Derby & Jackson, 1859.

———. *Agnes of Sorrento.* Boston: Ticknor & Fields, 1862. (Cited from the Riverside Edition [Boston: Houghton, Mifflin, 1890].)

Swayze, [Mrs.] J. C. Ossawattomie Brown; or, the Insurrection at Harper's Ferry. New York: Samuel French, 1859.

Talvi. *History of the Colonization of America.* Originally in German & published in Germany, 1847; English translation, Talvi's History of the Colonization of America, ed. William Hazlitt, esq. London: T. C. Newby, 1851.

———. *Historical View of the Languages and Literature of the Slavic Nations.* New York: George P. Putnam, 1850.

———. *Heloise; or, The Unrevealed Secret.* New York: D. Appleton & Co., 1850.

———. *Life's Discipline: A Tale of the Annals of Hungary.* New York: D. Appleton & Co., 1851.

Thompson, Amira [Carpenter]. *The Lyre of Tioga.* Geneva, N.Y.: For the Author by J. Rogert, 1829.

Truesdell, Mary [Von Hogel]. *Tippecanoe: A Legend of the Border.* N.p., 1840.

Tuthill, Louisa Caroline. *History of Architecture from the Earliest Times; Its Present Condition in Europe and the United States.* Philadelphia: Lindsay & Blakiston, 1848. (Reprinted Detroit: Garland, 1988.)

———. *The Young Lady's Home.* Philadelphia: Lindsay & Blakiston, 1848.

Wallis, Mary Davis [Cook], *Life in Feejee*. Boston: William Heath, 1851. (Cited from the reprint, Ridgewood, N.J.: Gregg Press, 1967.)

Ward, Maria. *Female Life Among the Mormons: A Narrative of Many Years' Personal Experience*. New York: J. C. Derby, 1855.

Ware, Katharine Augusta. *Power of the Passions; and Other Poems*. London: William Pickering, 1842.

Warner, Anna Bartlett. *My Brother's Keeper*. New York: D. Appleton, 1855.

Warner, Susan. *The Wide, Wide World*. New York: George P. Putnam, 1851. Reprinted New York: Feminist Press, 1987.

Warren, Mercy Otis. *Poems, Dramatic and Miscellaneous*. Boston: I. Thomas and E. T. Andrews, 1790. (Reprinted Delmar, N.Y.: Scholars' Facsimile & Reprints, 1980.)

Whitman, Sarah Helen. *Hours of Life, and Other Poems*. Providence: George H. Whitney, 1853.

Willard, Emma. *A Plan for Improving Female Education*. Middlebury: J. W. Copeland, 1819.

———. *Ancient Geography, As Connected with Chronology, and Preparatory to the Study of Ancient History*. Hartford: Oliver D. Cooke, 1822.

———. *History of the Rise, Progress and Termination of American Revolution*. 3 vols. Boston: Manning & Loring, 1805. (Cited from the two-volume reissue, Indianapolis: Liberty Press, 1988.)

———. *History of the United States, or Republic of America; Exhibited in Connection with Its Chronology and Progressive Geography, by Means of a Series of Maps . . . Designed for Schools and Private Libraries*. New York: White, Gallaher & White, 1828; New York, White, Gallaher & White, 1831.

———. *Abridgement of the History of the United States; or, Republic of America*. New York: N. & J. White, 1832; New York: A. S. Barnes & Co., 1852; A. S. Barnes & Co., 1868.

———. *Journal and Letters, from France and Great-Britain*. Troy: N. Tuttle, 1833.

———. *A System of Universal History, in Perspective*. Hartford: F. J. Huntington, 1835; New York, A. S. Barnes & Co., 1850.

———. *Last Leaves of American History; Comprising Histories of the Mexican War and California*. New York: G. P. Putnam, 1849.

———. *Guide to the Temple of Time; and Universal History, for Schools* (Willard's *Historic Guide*). New York: A. S. Barnes; Cincinnati: H. W. Derby & Co., 1849.

Williams, Catharine Read. *Tales; National and Revolutionary*. Providence: H. H. Brown, 1830.

———. *Aristocracy; or, The Holbey Family*. Providence: J. Knowles, 1832.

———. *Tales: National and Revolutionary*, Vol. II. Providence: H. H. Brown, 1835.

———. *Biography of Revolutionary Heroes: Containing the Life of Brigadier Gen. William Barton, and also, of Captain Stephen Olney*. Providence: By the Author, 1839.

———. *The Neutral French; or, The Exiles of Nova Scotia*. 2 vols. Providence: By the Author, 1841.

Willson, Arabella M. *The Lives of Mrs. Ann H. Judson, Mrs. Sarah B. Judson and Mrs. Emily C. Judson, *Missionaries to Burmah*. New York and Auburn: Miller, Orton & Mulligan, 1855.

Wilson, Augusta Jane. *See* Evans, Augusta Jane.

Windle, Mary Jane. *Truth and Fancy; Tales, Legendary, Historic, and Descriptive*. Philadelphia: C. Sherman, 1850.

Wood, Sarah Sayward Barrell Keating. *Julia and the Illuminated Baron*. Portsmouth, N.H.: Charles Peirce, 1800.

———. *Ferdinand & Elmira: A Russian Story*. Baltimore: Samuel Butler, 1804.

Wright, Frances. *Altorf*. Philadelphia: M. Carey & Son, 1819.

Notes on Sources

Chapter 1

There are no comprehensive histories of American women writers or American women's writings. The strategies and struggles of some professional American women writers are described from very different viewpoints in Susan Phinney Conrad, *Perish the Thought: Intellectual Women in Romantic America 1830–1860* (New York: Oxford University Press, 1976); Susan Coultrap-McQuin, *Doing Literary Business: American Women Writers in the Nineteenth Century* (Chapel Hill: University of North Carolina Press, 1990); and Mary Kelley, *Private Woman, Public Stage: Literary Domesticity in Nineteenth-Century America* (New York: Oxford University Press, 1984). Neither general nor specialized histories of American women before 1900 make women's professional or nonprofessional work as writers part of their subject, although they do consider literacy, education, and writing specifically focused on abolitionism or women's rights. See, e.g., Paula Baker, "The Domestication of Politics: Women and American Political Society, 1780–1920," *American Historical Review* 89 (1984):620–647; Anne M. Boylan, *Sunday School: The Formation of an American Institution, 1790–1880* (New Haven: Yale University Press, 1988); Ann Braude, *Radical Spirits: Spiritualism and Women's Rights in Nineteenth-Century America* (Boston: Beacon, 1989); Nancy Cott, *The Bonds of Womanhood: "Woman's Sphere" in New England, 1780–1835* (New Haven: Yale University Press, 1977); Elaine F. Crane, "Dependence in the Era of Independence: The Role of Women in a Republican Society," in Jack P. Greene, ed., *The American Revolution: Its Character and Limits* (New York: New York University Press, 1987), 253–272; Carl N. Degler, *At Odds: Women and the Family in America from the Revolution to the Present* (New York: Oxford University Press, 1980); Ellen Carol DuBois, *Feminism and Suffrage: The Emergence of an Independent Women's Movement in America, 1848–1860* (Ithaca: Cornell University Press, 1978); Barbara Leslie Epstein, *The Politics of Domesticity: Women, Evangelism, and Temperance in Nineteenth-Century American Thought* (Middletown, Conn.: Wesleyan University Press, 1981); Sara M. Evans, *Born for Liberty: A History of Women in America* (New York: Free Press, 1989); Eleanor Flexner, *Century of Struggle: The Woman's Rights Movement in the United States* (New York: Atheneum, 1971); Lori D. Ginzberg, *Women and the Work of Benevolence: Morality, Politics and*

Class in the Nineteenth-Century United States (New Haven: Yale University Press, 1990); Janet Wilson James, ed., *Women in American Religion* (Philadelphia: University of Pennsylvania Press, 1980); Polly Welts Kaufman, *Women Teachers on the Frontier* (New Haven: Yale University Press, 1984); Michael McGerr, "Political Style and Women's Power, 1830–1945," *Journal of American History* 77 (1990):864–885; Mary Beth Norton, *Liberty's Daughters: The Revolutionary Experience of American Women, 1750–1800* (Boston: Little, Brown, 1980); Norton, "The Evolution of White Women's Experience in Early America," *American Historical Review* 89 (1984):593–619; William L. O'Neill, *Feminism in America: A History* (New Brunswick: Transaction, 1989 [originally published 1969]); Mary P. Ryan, *Womanhood in America From Colonial Times to the Present* (New York: New Viewpoints, 1975); Ryan, *Cradle of the Middle Class: The Family in Oneida County, New York 1790–1865* (Cambridge: Cambridge University Press, 1981); Ryan, *Women in Public: Between Banners and Ballots, 1825–1880* (Baltimore: Johns Hopkins University Press, 1990); Jean Fagan Yellin, *Women and Sisters: The Antislavery Feminists in American Culture* (New Haven: Yale University Press, 1990).

American literary histories focused on the public print sphere, in contrast, typically present writing as a scene from which women are already excluded. Jürgen Habermas's influential *The Structural Transformation of the Public Sphere* (Cambridge, Mass.: MIT Press, 1989 [originally published 1961]) has nothing to say about women; its public sphere is a nondomestic space from which they are presumably excluded. For feminist criticism of Habermas, see Jean Bethke Elshtain, *Public Man, Private Woman: Women in Social and Political Thought* (Princeton: Princeton University Press, 1981); Nancy Fraser, *Unruly Practices: Power, Discourse and Gender in Contemporary Social Theory* (Minneapolis: University of Minnesota Press, 1989); Susan Moller Okin, *Women in Western Political Thought* (Princeton: Princeton University Press, 1979); and Carole Pateman, *The Sexual Contract* (Stanford: Stanford University Press, 1988). Two empirical studies of women in the public sphere are Madelyn Gutwirth, *The Twilight of the Goddesses: Women and Representation in the French Revolutionary Era* (New Brunswick: Rutgers University Press, 1992) and Joan B. Landes, *Women and the Public Sphere in the Age of the French Revolution* (Ithaca: Cornell University Press, 1988); both show that French Revolutionary politicians debarred women from the public sphere rather than encouraged their entrance into it. But findings about France (more specifically, about Paris) have no necessary implications for the United States; see Patrice Higonnet, *Sister Republics: The Origins of French and American Republicanism* (Cambridge, Mass.: Harvard University Press, 1988).

Other works mentioned in this chapter are: Barbara Bardes and Suzanne Gossett, *Declarations of Independence: Women and Political Power in Nineteenth-Century American Fiction* (New Brunswick: Rutgers University Press, 1990); Nina Baym, *Woman's Fiction: A Guide to Novels by and about Women in America, 1820–1870* (Ithaca: Cornell University Press, 1978 [2d ed. Urbana: University of Illinois Press, 1993]); Baym, *Feminism and American Literary History: Essays* (New Brunswick: Rutgers University Press, 1992); Michael Davitt Bell, *Hawthorne and the Historical Romance of New England* (Princeton: Princeton University Press, 1971); Lawrence Buell, *New England Literary Culture: From Revolution Through*

Renaissance (New York: Cambridge University Press, 1986); Linda Kerber, "Separate Spheres, Female World, Woman's Place: The Rhetoric of Women's History," *Journal of American History* 75 (1989):9–39; Jane Tompkins, *Sensational Designs: The Cultural Work of American Fiction, 1800–1860* (New York: Oxford University Press, 1985); Nancy Walker, *A Very Serious Thing: Women's Humor and American Culture* (Minneapolis: University of Minnesota Press, 1988); Joyce Warren, *Fanny Fern: An Independent Woman* (New Brunswick: Rutgers University Press, 1992); Emily Stipes Watts, *The Poetry of American Women from 1632 to 1945* (Austin: University of Texas Press, 1977); Sandra Zagarell, "Expanding 'America': Lydia Sigourney's *Sketch of Connecticut*, Catharine Sedgwick's *Hope Leslie*," *Tulsa Studies in Women's Literature* 6 (1987):225–245; Zagarell, "'America' as Community in Three Antebellum Village Sketches," in Joyce Warren, ed., *The (Other) American Traditions: Nineteenth-Century Women Writers* (New Brunswick: Rutgers University Press, 1993), pp. 143–163. For works about Margaret Fuller, see the note to Chapter 6.

Chapters 2 and 3

For discussions of the republican ideology of women inspired by the American Revolution, see: Ruth H. Bloch, "The Gendered Meanings of Virtue in Revolutionary America," *Signs* 13 (1987):37–58; Joan R. Gunderson, "Independence, Citizenship, and the American Revolution," *Signs* 13 (1987):59–77; Mary Kelley, "'Vindicating the Equality of Female Intellect': Women and Authority in the Early Republic," *Prospects: An Annual Journal of American Cultural Studies* 17 (1992):1–27; Linda K. Kerber, *Women of the Republic: Intellect and Ideology in Revolutionary America* (Chapel Hill: University of North Carolina Press, 1980); Kerber, "The Republican Mother: Women and the Enlightenment—An American Perspective," *American Quarterly* 28 (1976):187–205; Kerber, "The Republican Ideology of the Revolutionary Generation," *American Quarterly* 37 (1985):474–495; Jan Lewis, "The Republican Wife: Virtue and Seduction in the Early Republic," *William & Mary Quarterly* 44 (1987):689–721; Rosemarie Zagarri, "Morals, Manners, and the Republican Mother," *American Quarterly* 44 (1992):192–215.

For women's education and reading practices, see: Nina Baym, "At Home with History: History Books and Women's Sphere Before the Civil War," *Proceedings of the American Antiquarian Society* 101 (1991):275–295; Baym, *Novels, Readers and Reviewers: Responses to Fiction in Antebellum America* (Ithaca: Cornell University Press, 1984); Catharine Beecher, *Educational Reminiscences and Suggestions* (New York: J. B. Ford & Co., 1874); Henry Barnard, ed., *Educational Biography: Memoirs of Teachers and Educators* (New York: F. C. Brownell, 1861); Ruth H. Bloch, "American Feminine Ideals in Transition: The Rise of the Moral Mother, 1785–1815," *Feminist Studies* 4 (1978):100–126; Richard D. Brown, *Knowledge Is Power: The Diffusion of Information in Early America, 1700–1865* (New York: Oxford University Press, 1989); Lawrence A. Cremin, *American Education: The National Experience, 1783–1876* (New York: Harper & Row, 1980); Cathy N. Davidson, *Revolution and the Word: The Rise of the Novel in America* (New York: Oxford University Press, 1986); Isabelle Webb Entrikin, *Sarah Josepha Hale and Godey's Lady's Book* (Philadelphia: Lancaster, 1946); Vena Bernadette Field, *Constantia: A Study of the Life and Works of Judith Sargent Murray, 1751–*

1820 (Orono: University of Maine Studies, 1931 [2d series, no. 17]); Ruth E. Finley, *The Lady of Godey's: Sarah Josepha Hale* (Philadelphia: J.B. Lippincott, 1931); Blythe Forcey, "Charlotte Temple and the End of Epistolarity," *American Literature* 63 (1991):225–241 [on maternal narrators]; William J. Gilmore, *Reading Becomes a Necessity of Life: Material and Cultural Life in Rural New England, 1780–1835* (Knoxville: University of Tennessee Press, 1989); Kelley, "Vindicating"; Kerber, *Women of the Republic*; Kerber, "Daughters of Columbia: Educating Women for the Republic, 1787–1805," in Stanley Elkins & Eric McKitrick, eds., *The Hofstadter Aegis: A Memorial* (New York: Alfred A. Knopf, 1974), 46–59; Anne L. Kuhn, *The Mother's Role in Childhood Education: New England Concepts 1830–1860* (New Haven: Yale University Press, 1947); John Lord, *The Life of Emma Willard* (New York: D. Appleton & Co., 1873).

Also, Mary Peabody Mann, "Reminiscences of School Life and Teaching," *American Journal of Education* 32 (1882):743–752; Patricia Jewell McAlexander, "The Creation of the American Eve: The Cultural Dialogue on the Nature and Role of Women in Late Eighteenth-Century America," *Early American Literature* 9 (1975):252–266; Mary Beth Norton, *Liberty's Daughters: The Revolutionary Experience of American Women, 1750–1800* (Boston: Little, Brown, 1980); Elizabeth Palmer Peabody, "My Experience as a Teacher: Principles and Methods of Education," *American Journal of Education* 32 (1882):721–742; Peabody, *Lectures in the Training Schools for Kindergartners* (Boston: D. C. Heath & Company, copyright 1886, pub. 1893); Jo Anne Preston, "Domestic Ideology, School Reformers, and Female Teachers: Schoolteaching Becomes Women's Work in Nineteenth-Century New England," *New England Quarterly* 66 (1993):531–551; Frederick Rudolph, ed., *Essays on Education in the Early Republic* (Cambridge, Mass.: Harvard University Press, 1965); Benjamin Rush, "Plan for the Establishment of Public Schools" (1786), in Rudolph, ed., pp. 10–26; Rush, "Thoughts Upon Female Education, Accommodated to the Present State of Society, Manners, and Government in the United States of America" (1787), in Rudolph, ed., pp. 27–44; Kathryn Kish Sklar, *Catharine Beecher: A Study in American Domesticity* (New Haven: Yale University Press, 1973); Emily Vanderpoel, comp., *Chronicles of a Pioneer School from 1792 to 1833, Being the History of Miss Sarah Pierce and Her Litchfield School* (Cambridge [Mass.]: [Harvard] University Press 1903); Vanderpoel, *More Chronicles of a Pioneer School from 1792 to 1833* (New York: Cadmus, 1927); Albert J. Von Frank, "Sarah Pierce and the Poetic Origins of Utopian Feminism in America," *Prospects: An Annual Journal of American Cultural Studies* 14 (1989):45–63; Emma Willard, *A Plan for Improving Female Education* (Middlebury, Vt.: J. W. Copeland, 1819); Willard, *Letter, Addressed as a Circular to the Members of the Willard Association, for the Mutual Improvement of Female Teachers; Formed at the Troy Female Seminary, July, 1837* (Troy, N.Y.: Elias Gates, 1838]; Thomas Woody, *A History of Women's Education in the United States, Vol. I.* (New York and Lancaster, Pa.: The Science Press, 1929); Ronald J. Zboray, *A Fictive People: Antebellum Economic Development and the American Reading Public* (New York: Oxford University Press, 1993).

For the rising middle class and its literary values, see: Stuart M. Blumin, *The Emergence of the Middle Class: Social Experience in the American City, 1760–1900* (Cambridge: Cambridge University Press, 1989); Richard H. Brodhead, *The*

School of Hawthorne (New York: Oxford University Press, 1986); Richard L. Bushman, *The Refinement of America: Persons, Houses, Cities* (New York: Knopf, 1992); Ann Douglas, *The Feminization of American Culture* (New York: Knopf, 1977); Karen Halttunen, *Confidence Men and Painted Women: A Study of Middle-Class Culture in America, 1830–1870* (New Haven: Yale University Press, 1982).

Other works referred to in these two chapters are William Hill Brown, *The Power of Sympathy* (Albany: New College and University Press, 1970 [orig. pub. 1789]); Harriet Wilson, *Our Nig*, ed. Henry Louis Gates, Jr. (New York: Random House, 1983 [orig. pub. 1859]); Elizabeth Stoddard, *The Morgesons*, ed. Lawrence Buell and Sandra A. Zagarell (Philadelphia: University of Pennsylvania Press, 1984 [orig. pub. 1862]). For Sarah Hall's contributions to the *Port Folio*, see Randolph C. Randall, "Authors of the *Port Folio* Revealed by the Hall Files," *American Literature* 11 (1940):379–416.

Chapter 4

Some of the important sources for the women's historical writing are named in Chapter 3 and elsewhere in this study. The chief sources for writing the American Revolution were David Ramsay's 1789 *History of the American Revolution* and John Marshall's *Life of Washington* (1804–1807); for New England history, writers consulted the various separate sources or, after Hannah Adams published her synthesis, cribbed from her. Writers also used textbooks and popularizations of these major sources, with the result that an unauthored, impersonal discourse circulated and recirculated through these historical productions as the voice of Truth, or History, itself.

On historiography, and the connection between producing national histories and nation-building, see: Peter Alter, *Nationalism* (London: Edward Arnold, 1989); Benedict Anderson, *Imagined Communities: Reflections on the Origin and Spread of Nationalism* (London: Verso, 1983); Homi K. Bhabha, ed., *Nation and Narration* (London: Routledge, 1990); George H. Callcott, *History in the United States, 1800–1860; Its Practice and Purpose* (Baltimore: Johns Hopkins University Press, 1970); Linda Colley, *Britons: Forging the Nation, 1707–1837* (New Haven: Yale University Press, 1992); R. G. Collingwood, *The Idea of History* (Oxford: Oxford University Press, 1949); Arthur Danto, *Analytical Philosophy of History* (Cambridge, Mass.: Cambridge University Press, 1965); Ernest Gellner, *Nations and Nationalism* (Oxford: Basil Blackwell, 1983); Eric J. Hobsbawm and Terence Ranger, eds., *The Invention of Tradition* (Cambridge, Mass.: Cambridge University Press, 1983); Hobsbawm, *Nations and Nationalism since 1780: Programme, Myth, Reality* (Cambridge, Mass.: Cambridge University Press, 1990); Greg Kucich, "Romanticism and Feminist Historiography," *The Wordsworth Circle* 24 (1993):133–140; John T. Marcus, *Heaven, Hell, and History: A Survey of Man's Faith in History from Antiquity to the Present* (New York: Macmillan, 1967); Louis Mink, "Narrative Form as a Cognitive Instrument," in Robert Canacy and Henry Kozinki, eds., *The Writing of History: Literary Form and Historical Understanding* (Madison: University of Wisconsin Press, 1978), pp. 129–158; George L. Mosse, *Nationalism and Sexuality: Respectability and Abnormal Sexuality in Modern Europe* (New York: Howard Fertig, 1985); George H. Nadel, "Philosophy of History Before Historicism," *History and Theory* 3 (1964):291–315; Andrew Parker, et al., eds., *Nationalisms and Sexualities* (New York: Routledge, 1992); Joan Wallach Scott, *Gender and the Politics of History* (New York: Columbia University Press, 1988); David D. Van Tassel, *Recording America's Past: An Interpretation of the Development of Historical Studies in America, 1607–1884* (Chicago: University of Chicago Press, 1960); Eugen Weber, *Peasants into Frenchmen: The Modernization of Rural France, 1870–1914* (Stanford: Stanford University Press, 1976); Hayden White, *Metahistory: The Historical Imagination in Nineteenth-Century Europe* (Baltimore: Johns Hopkins University Press, 1974); White, *The Content of the Form: Narrative Discourse and Historical Representation* (Baltimore: Johns Hopkins University Press, 1987). Typically, women are not a topic in these works; in more recent theories they enter nation-building as marginalized, excluded, or stigmatized beings.

For Puritan and Revolutionary historiography, United States republican and millennial ideologies, and American school texts, see: Joyce Appleby, "Republicanism in Old and New Contexts," *William and Mary Quarterly* 43 (1986):20–34; Bernard Bailyn, *The Ideological Origins of the American Revolution* (Cambridge, Mass.: Harvard University Press, 1967); Lance Banning, "Jeffersonian Ideology Revisited: Liberal and Classical Ideas in the New American Republic," *William and Mary Quarterly* 43 (1986):3–34; John F. Berens, *Providence and Patriotism in Early America, 1640–1815* (Charlottesville: University Press of Virginia, 1978); Ray Allen Billington, *The Protestant Crusade, 1800–1860: A Study of the Origins of American Nativism* (New York: Macmillan, 1938); Ruth H. Bloch, *Visionary Republic: Millennial Themes in American Thought, 1756–1800* (Cambridge: Cambridge University Press, 1985); Theodore Dwight Bozeman, *To Live Ancient Lives: The Primitivist Dimension in Puritanism* (Chapel Hill: University of North Carolina Press, 1988); Lawrence Buell, *New England Literary Culture: From Revolution Through Renaissance* (New York: Cambridge University Press, 1986); Callcott, *History in the United States, 1800–1860*; Charles Carpenter, *History of American Schoolbooks* (Philadelphia: University of Pennsylvania Press, 1963); Conrad Cherry, ed., *God's New Israel: Religious Interpretations of American Destiny* (Englewood Cliffs: Prentice-Hall, 1971); Kenneth Cmiel, *Democratic Eloquence: The Fight Over Popular Speech in Nineteenth-Century America* (New York: William Morrow, 1990).

Also, Lester H. Cohen, *The Revolutionary Historians: Contemporary Narratives of the American Revolution* (Ithaca: Cornell University Press, 1980); James West Davidson, *The Logic of Millennial Thought: Eighteenth-Century New England* (New Haven: Yale University Press, 1977); Ruth Miller Elson, *Guardians of Tradition: American Schoolbooks of the Nineteenth Century* (Lincoln: University of Nebraska Press, 1964); Sister Marie Leonore Fell, *The Foundations of Nativism in American Textbooks, 1783–1860* (Washington, D.C.: Catholic University of America Press, 1941); Lawrence J. Friedman, *Inventors of the Promised Land* (New York: Knopf, 1975); Peter Dobkin Hall, *The Organization of American Culture, 1700–1900: Private Institutions, Elites and the Origins of American Nationality* (New York: New York University Press, 1982); Robert T. Handy, *A Christian America: Protestant Hopes and Historical Realities, Second Edition* (New York: Oxford University Press, 1984); Nathan O. Hatch, *Sacred Cause of Liberty: Republican Thought and the Millenium in Revolutionary New England* (New Haven: Yale University Press, 1977); Daniel Walker Howe, *The Political Culture of the American Whigs* (Chicago: University of Chicago Press, 1979); Linda K. Kerber, "The Republican Ideology of the Revolutionary Generation," *American Quarterly* 37 (1985):474–495; Kerber, "Separate Spheres, Female World, Women's Place: The Rhetoric of Women's History," *Journal of American History* 75 (1988):9–39; Michael Krause and David B. Joyce, *The Writing of American History* (Norman: University of Oklahoma Press, 1985); David Levin, *History as Romantic Art: Bancroft, Prescott, Motley, and Parkman* (Stanford: Stanford University Press, 1959); Laura McCall, "'The Reign of Brute Force Is Now Over': A Content Analysis of *Godey's Lady's Book*, 1830–1860," *Journal of the Early Republic* 9 (1989):217–236; Jean V. Matthews, "Whig History': The New England Whigs and a Usable Past," *New England Quarterly* 51 (1978):193–208; Henry F. May, *The Enlightenment in America* (New York: Oxford University Press, 1976).

Also, John A. Nietz, *Old Textbooks* (Pittsburgh: University of Pittsburgh Press, 1961); Nietz, *The Evolution of American Secondary School Textbooks* (Rutland, Vt.: Charles E. Tuttle, 1966); Bessie Louise Pierce, *Public Opinion in the Teaching of History* (New York: A. A. Knopf, 1926); J.G.A. Pocock, *The Machiavellian Moment: Florentine Political Thought and the Atlantic Republican Tradition* (Princeton: Princeton University Press, 1975); Daniel T. Rodgers, "Republicanism: The Career of a Concept," *Journal of American History* 79 (1992):11–38; Agnew O. Roorbach, *Development of the Social Studies in American Secondary Education Before 1861* (Philadelphia: University of Pennsylvania Press, 1937); Lewis O. Saum, *The Popular Mood of Pre–Civil War America* (Westport, Conn.: Greenwood Press, 1980); Arthur H. Shaffer, *The Politics of History: Writing the History of the American Revolution 1783–1815* (Chicago: Precedent, 1975); Robert E. Shalhope, "Republicanism, Liberalism, and Democracy: Political Culture in the Early Republic," *Proceedings of the American Antiquarian Society* 102 (1992):99–152; Kenneth Silverman, *A Cultural History of the American Revolution* (New York: Thomas Y. Crowell, 1976); William Raymond Smith, *History as Argument: Three Patriot Historians of the American Revolution* (The Hague: Mouton, 1966); Edward Stone, "Kossuth's Hat: Foreign Militants and the American Muse," *ESQ* 23 (1977):36–40; Ernest Lee Tuveson, *Millennium and Utopia: A Study in the Background of the Idea of Progress* (Berkeley: University of California Press, 1949); Tuveson, *Redeemer Nation: The Idea of America's Millenial Role* (Chicago: University of Chicago Press, 1968); Michael Warner, *The Letters of the Republic: Publication and the Public Sphere in Eighteenth-Century America* (Cambridge, Mass.: Harvard University Press, 1990); Rush Welter, *The Mind of America, 1820–1860* (New York: Columbia University Press, 1975); Garry Wills, *Under God: Religion and American Politics* (New York: Simon & Schuster, 1990); Gordon A. Wood, *The Creation of the American Republic, 1776–1787* (Chapel Hill: University of North Carolina Press, 1969); Wood, *The Radicalism of the American Revolution* (New York: Knopf, 1992).

For Native American issues in the United States before the Civil War, see: James Axtell, *The Invasion Within: The Contest of Cultures in Colonial North America* (New York: Oxford University Press, 1985); Robert F. Berkhofer, Jr., *Salvation and the Savage: An Analysis of Protestant Missions and American Indian Response, 1787–1862* (Lexington: University of Kentucky Press, 1965); Berkhofer, *The White*

Man's Indian: The History of an Idea from Columbus to the Present (New York: Knopf, 1978); Brian W. Dippie, *The Vanishing American: White Attitudes and U.S. Indian Policy* (Middletown, Conn: Wesleyan University Press, 1982); Richard Drinnon, *Facing West: The Metaphysics of Indian-Hating and Empire-Building* (Minneapolis: University of Minnesota Press, 1980); Reginald Horsman, *Race and Manifest Destiny: The Origins of American Racial Anglo-Saxonism* (Cambridge, Mass.: Harvard University Press, 1981); Robert W. Mardock, *The Reformers and the American Indian* (Columbia: University of Missouri Press, 1971); Francis Paul Prucha, *American Indian Policy in the Formative Years: The Indian Trade and Intercourse Acts, 1790–1834* (Cambridge, Mass.: Harvard University Press, 1962); Wilcomb E. Washburn, *Red Man's Land / White Man's Law: A Study of the Past and Present Status of the American Indian* (New York: Scribners, 1971).

For biographical and analytical studies of the better-known women whose work is considered in this chapter, see: Katherine Susan Anthony, *First Lady of the Revolution: The Life of Mercy Otis Warren* (Garden City: Doubleday, 1958); Helen G. Baer, *The Heart Is like Heaven: The Life of Lydia Maria Child* (Philadelphia: University of Pennsylvania Press, 1964); Henry Barnard, ed., *Educational Biography: Memoirs of Teachers and Educators* (New York: F. C. Brownell, 1861); Ruth M. Baylor, *Elizabeth Palmer Peabody: Kindergarten Pioneer* (Philadelphia: University of Pennsylvania Press, 1965); Nina Baym, "From Enlightenment to Victorian: Toward a Narrative of American Women Writers Writing History," in *Feminism and American Literary History: Essays* (New Brunswick: Rutgers University Press, 1992), pp. 105–120; Baym, "Women and the Republic: Emma Willard's Rhetoric of History," in *Feminism and American Literary History*, pp. 121–135; Baym, "The Ann Sisters: Elizabeth Peabody's Gendered Millennialism," in *Feminism and American Literary History*, pp. 136–150; Baym, "Mercy Otis Warren's Gendered Melodrama of Revolution," *South Atlantic Quarterly* 90 (1991):531–554; Emma Lydia Bolzau, *Almira Hart Lincoln Phelps: Her Life and Work* (Philadelphia: University of Pennsylvania Press, 1936); Alice Brown, *Mercy Warren* (New York: Scribners, 1903); Deborah Pickman Clifford, *Crusader for Freedom: A Life of Lydia Maria Child* (Boston: Beacon, 1992); Lester H. Cohen, "Mercy Otis Warren: The Politics of Language and the Aesthetics of Self," *American Quarterly* 35 (1983):481–498; Cohen, "Explaining the Revolution: Ideology and Ethics in Mercy Otis Warren's Historical Theory," *William & Mary Quarterly* 37 (1980):200–218; Lawrence J. Friedman and Arthur H. Shaffer, "Mercy Otis Warren and the Politics of Historical Nationalism," *New England Quarterly* 48 (1975):194–215.

Also, Philip F. Gura, "Elizabeth Palmer Peabody and the Philosophy of Language," *ESQ* 23 (1977):154–163; Joan Hoff Wilson and Sharon L. Billinger, "Mercy Otis Warren: Playwright, Poet, and Historian of the American Revolution," in J. R. Brink, ed., *Female Scholars: A Tradition of Learned Women before 1800* (Montreal: Eden Press, 1980), pp. 161–182; Maud Macdonald Hutcheson, "Mercy Warren, 1728–1814," *William & Mary Quarterly* 10 (1953):378–402; John Lord, *The Life of Emma Willard* (New York: D. Appleton & Co., 1873); Alma Lutz, *Emma Willard: Daughter of Democracy* (Boston: Houghton, Mifflin, 1929); Milton Meltzer, *Tongue of Flame: The Life of Lydia Maria Child* (New York: Thomas Y. Crowell, 1965); Margaret Neussendorfer, "Elizabeth Palmer Peabody," in Joel Myerson, ed., *The Transcendentalists: A Review of Research and Criticism* (New

Notes on Sources

York: Modern Language Association of America, 1984), pp. 233–241; Cheryl Z. Oreovicz, "Mercy Warren and 'Freedom's Genius'" *University of Mississippi Studies in English* 5 (1987):215–230; William S. Osborne, *Lydia Maria Child* (Boston: G. K. Hall, 1980); Patricia L. Parker, *Susanna Haswell Rowson* (Boston: Twayne, 1986); James Parton, et al., *Eminent Women of the Age; Being Narratives of the Lives and Deeds of the Most Prominent Women of the Present Generation* (Hartford, Conn.: S. M. Betts & Co., 1869); Elizabeth P. Peabody, *Letters of Elizabeth P. Peabody; American Renaissance Woman*, ed. Bruce A. Ronda (Middletown, Conn.: Wesleyan University Press, 1984); Clyde N. Wilson, *Dictionary of Literary Biography, Vol. 30: American Historians, 1607–1865* (Detroit: Gale, 1984); Sarah Butler Wister and Agnes Irwin, eds., *Worthy Women of Our First Century* (Philadelphia: Lippincott, 1877); R. W. G. Vail, "Susanna Haswell Rowson, the Author of Charlotte Temple: A Bibliographical Study," *Proceedings of the American Antiquarian Society* 42 (1932):47–160; John B. Wilson, "A Transcendental Minority Report," *New England Quarterly* 29 (1956):147–158; Wilson, "Elizabeth Peabody and Other Transcendentalists on History and Historians," *Historian* 30 (1967):72–86.

Chapter 5

The most important anthologies of women's poetry at the mid-nineteenth century were Rufus Wilmot Griswold, *The Female Poets of America* (Philadelphia: Carey & Hart, 1849; 2d ed. Philadelphia: Parry & McMillan, 1856); Caroline May, *The American Female Poets* (Philadelphia: Lindsay & Blakiston, 1848); Thomas Buchanan Read, *The Female Poets of America* (Philadelphia: E. H. Butler, 1849). A recent collection is Cheryl Walker's *American Women Poets of the Nineteenth Century: An Anthology* (New Brunswick: Rutgers University Press, 1992).

Few general studies of American poetry before 1900 consider women poets besides Anne Bradstreet and Emily Dickinson; specialized studies of women's poetry of the period typically focus on domestic, funerary, and emotive lyrics. For work with some bearing on the material discussed in this chapter, see: Aaron Kramer, *The Prophetic Tradition in American Poetry* (Rutherford, N.J.: Farleigh Dickinson University Press, 1968); Cheryl Walker, *The Nightingale's Burden: Women Poets and American Culture before 1900* (Bloomington: Indiana University Press, 1982); Emily Stipes Watts, *The Poetry of American Women from 1632 to 1945* (Austin: University of Texas Press, 1977). On Bible women (but mainly in illustrations), see Mary De Jong, "Dark-Eyed Daughters: Nineteenth-Century Popular Portrayals of Biblical Women," *Women's Studies* 19 (1991):283–308. More specialized studies include: Nina Baym, "Reinventing Lydia Sigourney," in *Feminism and American Literary History: Essays* (New Brunswick: Rutgers University Press, 1992), pp. 151–166; Julie Ellison, "Race and Sensibility in the Early Republic: Ann Eliza Bleecker and Sarah Wentworth Morton," *American Literature* 65 (1993):445–474; Annie Finch, "The Sentimental Poetess in the World: Metaphor and Subjectivity in Lydia Sigourney's Nature Poetry," *Legacy: A Journal of Nineteenth-Century American Women Writers* 5 (1988):3–18; Gordon Haight, *Mrs. Sigourney: The Sweet Singer of Hartford* (New Haven: Yale University Press, 1930); Emily Pendleton and Harold Milton Ellis, *Philenia: The Life and Works of Sarah Wentworth Morton, 1759–1846* (Orono: University of Maine Studies, 1931 [2d series, no. 20]); Lydia Huntley

Sigourney, *Letters of Life* (New York: D. Appleton & Co., 1866); Ann Douglas Wood, "Mrs. Sigourney and the Sensibility of the Inner Space," *New England Quarterly* 45 (1972):163–181.

Chapter 6

There are scattered secondary materials on some of the women whose works are considered in this chapter. For studies of Mercy Otis Warren, see the note to Chapter 4. See also: Hannah Adams, *A Memoir of Miss Hannah Adams, Written by Herself, with Additional Notices, by a Friend* (Boston: Gray & Bowen, 1832); Fawn M. Brodie, *No Man Knows My History: The Life of Joseph Smith, the Mormon Prophet,* 2d ed. (New York: Knopf, 1971 [Lucy Mack Smith]); Joan Jacobs Brumberg, *Mission for Life: The Judson Family and American Evangelical Culture* (New York: New York University Press, 1984); Lawrence Buell, *New England Literary Culture: From Revolution Through Renaissance* (Cambridge & New York: Cambridge University Press, 1986 [Eliza Buckminster Lee]); Buell, "Joseph Stevens Buckminster: The Making of a New England Saint," *Canadian Review of American Studies* 10 (1979):1–29 [Eliza Buckminster Lee]; Charles Capper, *Margaret Fuller, an American Romantic Life: The Private Years* (New York: Oxford University Press, 1992); Bell Gale Chevigny, "To the Edges of Ideology: Margaret Fuller's Centrifugal Evolution," *American Quarterly* 38 (1986):173–201; Frances Smith Foster, *Written by Herself: Literary Production by African American Women, 1746–1892* (Bloomington: Indiana University Press, 1993 [Nancy Prince]); Polly Welts Kaufman, *Women Teachers on the Frontier* (New Haven: Yale University Press, 1984 [Harriet Bishop]); Rebecca Smith Lee, *Mary Austin Holley* (Austin: University of Texas Press, 1962); Zylpha S. Morton "Harriet Bishop: Frontier Teacher," *Minnesota History* 28 (1947):132–141; Linda King Newell and Valeen Tippetts Avery, *Mormon Enigma: Emma Hale Smith* (New York: Doubleday, 1984 [Lucy Mack Smith]); Jan Shipps, *Mormonism: The Story of a New Religious Tradition* (Urbana: University of Illinois Press, 1985 [Lucy Mack Smith]); Homer Socolofsky, *Kansas Governors* (Lawrence: University Press of Kansas, 1990 [Sara Tappan Robinson]); Eli Thayer, *A History of the Kansas Crusade, Its Friends and Foes* (New York: Harper & Bros., 1889 [Sara Tappan Robinson]); Sandra Zagarell, "Expanding 'America': Lydia Sigourney's *Sketch of Connecticut,* Catharine Sedgwick's *Hope Leslie,*" *Tulsa Studies in Women's Literature* 6 (1987):225–245; Zagarell, "'America' as Community in Three Antebellum Village Sketches," in Joyce Warren, ed., *The (Other) American Traditions: Nineteenth-Century Women Writers* (New Brunswick: Rutgers University Press, 1992), pp. 143–163. See also the bibliography following the Biographical Notes.

Chapter 7

By excluding women in advance, the recent outpouring of theoretical and analytical work on travel and touring has created an all-male discourse to which women are returned, by some feminist scholars, as uncomfortable and disruptive participants. See, e.g., Mary A. Favret, *Romantic Correspondence: Women, Politics and the Fiction of Letters* (Cambridge, Mass.: Cambridge University Press, 1993); and Sarah Mills, *Discourses of Difference: An Analysis of Women's Travel Writing and Colonialism* (London: Routledge, 1991).

For theories of traveling and tourism dominated by the colonizing approach, see Laurence Goldstein, *Ruins and Empire: The Evolution of a Theme in Augustan and Romantic Literature* (Pittsburgh: University of Pittsburgh Press, 1977); Mary Louise Pratt, *Imperial Eyes: Travel Writing and Transculturation* (New York: Routledge, 1992); and Valerie Smith, ed., *Hosts and Guests: The Anthropology of Tourism* (Philadelphia: University of Pennsylvania Press, 1977). For studies that praise travelers at the expense of tourists, see James Buzard, *The Beaten Track: European Tourism, Literature, and the Ways to "Culture," 1800–1918* (New York: Oxford University Press, 1993); Donald Horne, *The Great Museum: The Re-presentation of History* (London: Pluto, 1984); and Dean MacCannell, *The Tourist: A New Theory of the Leisure Class* (New York: Schocken, 1976). For a discussion of the construction of Europe and especially Italy as an esthetic site, see Lawrence S. Rainey, *Ezra Pound and the Monument of Culture: Text, History, and the Malatesta Cantos* (Chicago: University of Chicago Press, 1991). More appreciative accounts of tourism are found in Rose Macauley, *Pleasure of Ruins* (London: Weidenfeld & Nicolson, 1953); and Christopher Mulvey, *Anglo-American Landscapes: A Study of Nineteenth-Century Anglo-American Travel Literature* (New York: Cambridge University Press, 1983).

Mulvey is also useful as a study of Americans abroad. Other works on this topic are Paul R. Baker, *The Fortunate Pilgrims: Americans in Italy 1800–1860* (Cambridge, Mass.: Harvard University Press, 1964); Foster Rhea Dulles, *Americans Abroad: Two Centuries of European Travel* (Ann Arbor: University of Michigan Press, 1964); Paul Giles, *American Catholic Arts and Fictions: Culture, Ideology, Aesthetics* (New York: Cambridge University Press, 1992 [Stowe's *Agnes of Sorrento*]); Harold F. Smith, *American Travellers Abroad: A Bibliography of Accounts Published Before 1900* (Carbondale: Southern Illinois University, 1969); William L. Vance, *America's Rome*, 2 vols. (New Haven: Yale University Press, 1989); Nathalia Wright, *American Novelists in Italy: The Discoverers, Allston to James* (Philadelphia: University of Pennsylvania Press, 1965 [Stowe's *Agnes of Sorrento*]).

For readings of Madame de Staël's *Corinne*, as well as the novel's impact on women writers and the literature of tourism, see Paula Blanchard, "*Corinne* and the 'Yankee Corinna': Madame de Staël and Margaret Fuller," in Avriel H. Goldberger, ed., *Woman as Mediatrix: Essays on Nineteenth-Century Women Writers* (Westport, Conn.: Greenwood Press, 1987), 39–46; Madelyn Gutwirth, *Madame de Staël, Novelist: The Emergence of the Arist as Woman* (Urbana: University of Illinois Press, 1978); Ellen Moers, *Literary Women* (Garden City: Doubleday, 1976).

For Anne Royall, see George Stuyvesant Jackson, *Uncommon Scold: The Story of Anne Royall* (Boston: B. Humphries, 1937).

Chapter 8

For theories of historical fiction, see George Lukacs, *The Historical Novel* (Atlantic Highlands, N.J.: Humanities Press, 1978 [orig. pub. in English 1962, written winter 1936/7]); Harry E. Shaw, *The Forms of Historical Fiction: Sir Walter Scott and His Successors* (Ithaca: Cornell University Press, 1983).

For an interpretation of American fiction in terms of a "family conflict" between England and America, see Kenneth Silverman, *A Cultural History of the American Revolution* (New York: T. Y. Crowell, 1976); for an interpretation of American fiction in terms of intergenerational political conflict see Jay Fliegelman, *Prodigals and Pilgrims: The American Revolution against Patriarchal Authority* (New York: Cambridge University Press, 1982); neither of these studies focuses on gender. Studies addressed wholly or in part to American historical fiction include: Louise K. Barnet, *The Ignoble Savage: American Literary Racism, 1790–1890* (Westport, Ct: Greenwood Press, 1975); Nina Baym, *Novels, Readers and Reviewers: Responses to Fiction in Antebellum America* (Ithaca: Cornell University Press, 1984); Michael Davitt Bell, *Hawthorne and the Historical Romance of New England* (Princeton: Princeton University Press, 1971); Lawrence Buell, *New England Literary Culture: From Revolution Through Renaissance* (New York: Cambridge University Press, 1986); George Dekker, *The American Historical Romance* (New York: Cambridge University Press, 1987); Ernest E. Leisy, *The American Historical Novel* (Norman: University of Oklahoma Press, 1950); Lillie Deming Loshe, *The Early American Novel* (New York: Columbia University Press, 1907); Lucy Maddox, *Removals: Nineteenth-Century American Literature and the Politics of Indian Affairs* (New York: Oxford University Press, 1991); Leland S. Person, Jr., "The American Eve: Miscegenation and A Feminist Frontier Fiction," *American Quarterly* 37 (1985):668–685; David S. Reynolds, *Faith in Fiction: The Emergence of Religious Literature in America* (Cambridge, Mass.: Harvard University Press, 1981); Sherry Sullivan, "Indians in American Fiction: 1820–1850: An Ethnohistorical Perspective," *CLIO* 15 (1986):239–257.

Relevant work on individual novels or authors discussed in this chapter includes: Kenneth Walter Cameron, *Philothea: A Novel of the Transcendental Movement in New England* (Hartford: Transcendental Books, 1975); Christopher Castiglia, "In Praise of Extra-vagant Women: *Hope Leslie* and the Captivity Romance," *Legacy* 6 (1989):3–16; Delle Mullen Craven, ed., *The Neglected Thread: A Journal from the Calhoun Community, 1836–1842* (Columbia: University of South Carolina Press, 1951 [Mary Elizabeth Moragne Davis]); Julie Ellison, "Race and Sensibility in the Early Republic: Ann Eliza Bleecker and Sarah Wentworth Morton," *American Literature* 65 (1993):445–474 [The History of Maria Kittle]; Barbara Ann Bardes and Suzanne Gossett, *Declarations of Independence: Women and Political Power in Nineteenth-Century American Fiction* (New Brunswick: Rutgers University Press, 1990); Bardes and Gossett, "Women and Political Power in the Republic: Two Early American Novels," *Legacy* 2 (1985):13–30 [*Northwood* and *Hope Leslie*]; Susan K. Harris "The Female Imaginary in Harriet Beecher Stowe's *The Minister's Wooing*," *New England Quarterly* 66 (1993):179–198; Joan D. Hedrick, *Harriet Beecher Stowe: A Life* (Oxford & New York: Oxford University Press, 1994); Mary Kelley, "Negotiating a Self: The Autobiography and Journals of Catharine Maria Sedgwick," *New England Quarterly* 66 (1993):366–398; Dana D. Nelson, *The Word in Black and White: Reading "Race" in American Literature, 1638–1867* (New York: Oxford University Press, 1992 [Hope Leslie]); Carroll Smith-Rosenberg, "Subject Female: Authorizing American Identity," *American Literary History* 5 (1993):481–511 [*Reuben and Rachel*]; William R. Taylor, *Cavalier and Yankee: The Old South and American National Character* (New York: George Braziller, 1961 [*Northwood*]); Sandra Zagarell, "Expanding 'America': Lydia

Notes on Sources

Sigourney's *Sketch of Connecticut*, Catharine Sedgwick's *Hope Leslie*," *Tulsa Studies in Women's Literature* 6 (1987):225–245; Zagarell, "America' as Community in Three Antebellum Village Sketches," in Joyce Warren, ed., *The (Other) American Traditions: Nineteenth-Century Women Writers* (New Brunswick: Rutgers University Press, 1993), 143–163. Carolyn Karcher's introduction to Lydia Maria Child's *Hobomok* (New Brunswick: Rutgers University Press, 1986) and Mary Kelley's introduction to Catharine Maria Sedgwick's *Hope Leslie* (New Brunswick: Rutgers University Press, 1987) should also be consulted.

Chapter 9

For general surveys of American drama, see David Grimsted, *Melodrama Unveiled: American Theater and Culture, 1800–1850* (Chicago: University of Chicago Press, 1968); Walter J. Meserve, *An Emerging Entertainment: The Drama of the American People to 1828* (Bloomington: Indiana University Press, 1977); Meserve, *Heralds of Promise: The Drama of the American People During the Age of Jackson, 1828–1849* (Westport, Conn.: Greenwood Press, 1986); Arthur Hobson Quinn, *A History of the American Drama from the Beginnings to the Civil War*, 2d ed. (New York: Appleton-Century-Crofts, 1951).

For individual studies, see Theodore Bacon, *Delia Bacon: A Biographical Sketch* (Boston: Houghton, Mifflin, 1888); Eric Wollencott Barnes, *The Lady of Fashion* (New York: Charles Scribner's Sons, 1954 [Mowatt]); Caroline Healey Dall, *What We Really Know about Shakespeare* (Boston: Roberts Bros., 1886 [Bacon]); Helen R. Deese, "A New England Women's Network: Elizabeth Palmer Peabody, Caroline Healey Dall, and Delia S. Bacon," *Legacy* 8 (1992):77–91; Elizabeth Fox-Genovese, *Within the Plantation Household: Black and White Women of the Old South* (Chapel Hill: University of North Carolina Press, 1988 [McCord]); Vivian C. Hopkins, *Prodigal Puritan: A Life of Delia Bacon* (Cambridge, Mass.: Harvard University Press, 1959); Kathleen L. Nichols, "Earlier American Women Dramatists: From National to Sexual Politics," *Theatre History Studies* 11 (1991):129–150; George C. Rable, *Civil Wars: Women and the Crisis of Southern Nationalism* (Urbana: University of Illinois Press, 1991 [McCord]); Samuel Schoenbaum, *Shakespeare's Lives* (New York: Oxford University Press, 1970 [Bacon]); Mary Alice Wyman, *Two American Pioneers: Seba Smith and Elizabeth Oakes Smith* (New York: Columbia University Press, 1927). For studies of Mercy Otis Warren, see the note to Chapter 4.

Chapter 10

The search for early writers of women's history, like the search for women historians more broadly, has been shaped by a contemporary, professional idea of what constitutes history writing. Therefore, the findings are scant. Relevant material to this chapter includes Nina Baym, "Onward Christian Women: Sarah J. Hale's History of the World," *New England Quarterly* 68 (1990):249–270; Scott E. Casper, "An Uneasy Marriage of Sentiment and Scholarship: Elizabeth F. Ellet and the Domestic Origins of American Women's History," *Journal of Women's History* 4 (1992):10–35; Caroline Healey Dall's account of one of Margaret Fuller's conversation series, *Margaret and her Friends* (Boston: Roberts Bros, 1895); Mary De Jong, "Dark-Eyed Daughters: Nineteenth-Century Popular Portrayals of Biblical

Women," *Women's Studies* 19 (1991):263–308; Vena Bernadette Field, *Constantia: A Study of the Life and Works of Judith Sargent Murray, 1751–1820* (Orono: University of Maine Studies, 1931 [2d series, no. 17]); Linda K. Kerber, "History Can Do It No Justice: Women and the Reinterpretation of the American Revolution," in Ronald Hoffman and Peter J. Albert, eds., *Women in the Age of the American Revolution* (Charlottesville: University Press of Virginia, 1989), pp. 3–42 [Ellet]); Joel Myerson, "Caroline Dall's Reminiscences of Margaret Fuller," *Harvard Library Bulletin* 22 (1974):414–428; Myerson, "Mrs. Dall Edits Miss Fuller: The Story of *Margaret and Her Friends*," *Papers of the Bibliographical Society of America* 72 (1978):187–200.

Index

Index

About the Author

Nina Baym is Professor of English and Jubilee Professor of Liberal Arts and Sciences at the University of Illinois at Urbana-Champaign. She is the author of *The Shape of Hawthorne's Career; Woman's Fiction: A Guide to Novels by and about Women in America, 1820–1870;* and *Novels, Readers, and Reviewers: Responses to Fiction in Antebellum America.* A selection of her most important essays has been published in *Feminism and American Literary History.*